Maoism in India

The rise of Maoism as one of the organized political movements in India is the outcome of a historical situation. Both colonialism and the failure of the Indian state to implement land reforms more stringently in the aftermath of independence resulted in terrible sufferings of the marginalized, land-dependent sections of society.

Through historical analysis, this book assesses the ideological articulation of the contemporary ultra-left movement in India, including Maoism which is gradually expanding in India. The authors provide answers to the following issues: Is Maoism reflective of the growing disenchantment of the people in the affected areas with the state? Is it a comment on 'the distorted development planning' pursued by the Indian state? Is this an outcome of the processes of the 'deepening of democracy' in India? Using Orissa as a case study, the book raises questions on India's development strategy. The authors argue that Maoism provides critical inputs for an alternative paradigm of development, relevant for 'transitional societies' and that it is still a powerful ideology for the poorer parts of the world, although its ideological appeal has declined internationally.

Bidyut Chakrabarty is Professor in Political Science at the University of Delhi, India.

Rajat Kumar Kujur is Lecturer in Political Science at G.M. College, Sambalpur, Orissa, India.

T0347390

Routledge Contemporary South Asia Series

Maoism in India

Reincarnation of ultra-left wing extremism
in the twenty-first century

**Bidyut Chakrabarty and
Rajat Kumar Kujur**

LONDON AND NEW YORK

First published 2010
by Routledge
2 Park Square, Milton Park, Abingdon, Oxon OX14 4RN

Simultaneously published in the USA and Canada
by Routledge
711 Third Ave, New York, NY 10017

Routledge is an imprint of the Taylor & Francis Group, an informa business

First issued in paperback 2012

© 2010 Bidyut Chakrabarty and Rajat Kumar Kujur

Typeset in Times New Roman by Pindar NZ, Auckland, New Zealand

British Library Cataloguing in Publication Data
A catalogue record for this book is available from the British Library

Library of Congress Cataloging-in-Publication Data
Chakrabarty, Bidyut, 1958–
Maoism in India: reincarnation of ultra-left wing extremism in the 21st
century / Bidyut Chakrabarty and Rajat Kumar Kujur.
   p. cm. — (Routledge contemporary South Asia series; 22)
   Includes bibliographical references and index.
   1. Left-wing extremists—India—Case studies. 2. Communism—
India—Case studies. 3. Left-wing extremists—India—Orissa. 4.
Communism—India—Orissa. 5. Orissa (India)—Social conditions—21st
century. 6. Orissa (India)—Politics and government—21st century, I. Kujur,
Rajat Kumar. II. Title.
HN690.Z9R317 2009
335.43'450954—dc22   2009018171

ISBN13: 978-0-415-54486-3 (hbk)
ISBN13: 978-0-203-86648-1 (ebk)
ISBN13: 978-0-415-53352-2 (pbk)

Dedicated to those who though abhor 'violence of the strong and meek alike', believe in 'sacrifice', 'justice' and 'compassion'

Contents

Tables

Preface and acknowledgments

Maoism in India is our dream project. We have been working on this subject for quite some time. Our interest was sustained by many colleagues and also several academic institutions in India and abroad. It was Professor J. Mohan Rao, the former director of the Institute of South Asian Studies (ISAS), Singapore (and now professor in the department of Economics, University of Massachusetts, Amherst, USA), who not only mooted the idea of writing a book, but also supported our research at the outset. We are thankful to him for his keen interest in the project at a time when meta-narratives were not usually encouraged. After Professor Rao left, it was Hernaikh at the ISAS who sustained our interest in the project by his regular emails underlining the importance of the project not only for the academia, but also for those seeking to change the world in adverse circumstances. Without his constant reminder, the project would have been shelved. The findings that were first presented in a round-table discussion in 2007 at the ISAS, gave us impetus to further explore this rather neglected area of social enquiry. We also appreciate the support of our respective academic institutions for having brought out the best from us by putting us in no-win situations. We put on record our appreciation of the government officials for being frank with us when we solicited their views and opinions on the Maoist movement. We are grateful to those activists who might not have always agreed with us for having shared their idea of a social upheaval in a semi-colonial and semi-feudal society like India. We fondly remember the contribution of our teachers who ignited our restlessness for research in areas of human concerns that are always difficult to pursue. Our publishers are always supportive. We gratefully acknowledge the contribution of our publishers for having helped us develop some of the new dimensions of left-wing extremism in India that we simply referred to in our past publications. Rajendra contributed significantly to our project. Sunil always remains helpful. We are thankful to them. Dipakda continues to remain our pathfinder. We gratefully acknowledge his constant support to our academic venture. I am grateful to Professor Ashok Prasad and Mr Amit Jamwal for their support in completing the project.

The book would not have been same without the extensive comments of the reviewers. We were drawn to new dimensions of such a human discontent as the Maoist movement that we would have missed had the reviewers not identified the gaps in our argument. We express our heartfelt gratitude to them and also

Routledge academic editor Dorothea for the trouble she took during the preparation of the manuscript.

Our families always stood by us. Without the care that we always receive from our respective families, especially our parents, it would not have been possible for us to concentrate on academic pursuits. Our children are creative distractions while our wives' appreciation of our 'not-always-so-rewarding' ventures creates our appetite for research on subjects which are not easy to pursue. Maoism is a difficult terrain, both intellectually and otherwise, and yet it was possible to complete a full-length monograph on this largely due to the confidence of our well-wishers in our intellectual capability. Finally, the book will have served its goal and we will have fulfilled our mission if the readers find its content socially meaningful and intellectually provocative.

Bidyut Chakrabarty and
Rajat Kumar Kujur, Delhi 2009

Introduction[1]

I

Maoism is a continuity of ultra-left wing radicalism that was ideologically articulated in the form of the Naxalbari movement in the late 1960s in India. Drawn on classical Marxism and Leninism, the Maoists spearheaded a politically meaningful campaign in the subcontinent that has undoubtedly put forward a new discourse of development by challenging both the state and market-led development paradigm. Unlike the Naxalbari movement of the past, the Maoist movement is not only geographically well spread out, it has given a powerful voice to the peripheral sections of Indian society. In view of the ideological uprising of Spring Thunder, which became famous in the Naxalbari movement, Maoism can be said to have articulated Marxism in the changed socio-economic and political environment of a globalizing world. The expressions, Naxalites and Maoists, are therefore used interchangeably to denote the same ultra-left wing radical movement, especially in the official records and contemporary visual and print media. It is true that differences between the two movements in two completely different historical phases are merely cosmetic given the clear ideological compatibility between these two movements representing serious endeavours in pursuing an ideological purpose based on 'the reinvention' of Marxism in the non-industrialized world. In the industrially developed countries, Marxism articulated its ideological responses keeping in the mind the adverse impact of 'mechanical industrialization' subjecting 'the producers of services and goods' to alienation. Maoism is a Marxist formulation to address the basic contradiction in an agricultural society where feudal land relations are still well-entrenched. Maoism is not 'a revisionist' doctrine, but an extension of Marxism that is being interpreted and also reinterpreted to make the doctrine contextually relevant. This is a creative exercise because given the growing complexities of Indian society due to an equally complex unfolding of her development trajectory since independence in 1947, it is difficult, if not impossible, to comprehend India's socio-economic reality in a straitjacketed formula. Furthermore, because of colonialism and its obvious devastating role for more than two centuries, India's growth was skewed and was naturally tuned to the consolidation of British power in India. So the political authority was neither responsible for a uniform development of the country nor was accountable to the governed. In independent India, political authority was transferred. But the euphoria over this shift was short-lived since the planned economic development programme that the independent India pursued did not appear to be appropriate to fulfil the aspired goal of 'socialistic pattern of society'. Instead, by creating severe economic imbalances across the country, the Nehruvian development planning completely lost its viability especially when the market-compliant development programme was introduced following the adoption of the 1991 New Economic Programme by India's political elite. The phase that began by officially accepting economic liberalization is different from its past on a variety of counts. Besides projecting the obvious adversities of market-drawn development plans, this phase also witnessed the mass mobilization over numerous 'new macro issues', particularly environment and displacement of people due to indiscriminate industrialization. The indigenous population seems to be hard-hit and it is therefore not surprising that Maoism has struck an emotional chord with the tribal population in areas where the forest land is being taken away at the cost of the habitat for industrial purposes. By challenging the land-grabbing by the industrial houses and also the government, the Maoists in these areas have become 'the true saviour' of the tribal population. In fact, this is a major factor explaining the growing consolidation of Maoism in a large number of constituent Indian states. Besides attacking feudal forces, Maoism has thus raised those issues which do not belong to its ideological fold in the classical Marxist sense. Broadly speaking, Maoism is politico-ideological platform seeking to articulate 'the neglected voice' of the peripheral sections of Indian society that have become critical to India's contemporary development trajectory. One has to be careful in assessing its future because the story of Maoism is also one of factional feuds, personal rivalry and corrupt practices that perhaps account for its slow success in building a united platform for espousing the cause of 'the wretched of the earth'.

II

Maoism is an outcome of the steady democratization of the political processes with the participation of the masses not only during elections, but also in the interim period. In other words, sustained participation of the people in the democratic processes has unleashed a process that has gone beyond mere voting by empowering people in a manner that radically changed the contour of Indian politics. The process is getting translated as rage and revolt making India 'a country of a million little mutinies'.[2] But these mutinies created tangible space for the democratic aspiration to flourish. And also, they make the state available for those who hitherto remain peripheral for any political transactions. The process is significant for another related reason, namely, democratic empowerment of the lower strata of society and formerly excluded groups led to an articulation of voices that always remained 'feeble' in the past. Since these groups interpreted 'their disadvantage and dignity in caste terms, social antagonism and competition for state benefits expressed themselves increasingly in the form of intense caste rivalries'.[3] So the growing importance of caste in contemporary Indian politics is essentially a modern phenomenon and not a mere continuity of the past. This is theoretically puzzling since caste action in India, articulated in modern political vocabulary, cannot be comprehended within the available liberal democratic parameters unless one is drawn to the empirical context that radically differs from the typical liberal society in the west. In the changed socio-economic context, caste has gained salience because of its '"encashability in politics" [which] is now dominated by the numerically stronger lower and middle castes [and] the upper castes are now facing a very real reverse discrimination'.[4] So democratization seems to have set in motion a process whereby peripheral sections of society who remained peripheral because of well-entrenched caste prejudices become politically significant due to their demographic preponderance. This may sound paradoxical since democratization, as an empowering process, has made the numerically stronger sections aware of their importance in contemporary politics without undermining [sic] their caste identity that brings people together irrespective of class differences. In this sense, democratization seems to have legitimized caste by re-affirming its role in cementing a bond among various social groups who, despite being differently placed in class terms, are drawn to each other because of their caste affiliation.

Politicization and democratization seem to be dialectically interlinked. As a result, the outcome of this intermingling may not be predictable. In a typical western liberal context, deepening of democracy invariably leads to consolidation of 'liberal values'. In the Indian context, democratization is translated in greater involvement of people not as 'individuals', which is a staple to liberal discourse, but as communities or groups. Individuals are getting involved in the public sphere not as 'atomized' individuals but as 'members of primordial communities' drawn on religious, caste or *jati* (sect within a caste) identity. Similarly, a large section of women is being drawn to the political processes not as 'women' or individuals, but as members of a community holding a sectoral identity. Community identity seems to the governing force. It is not therefore surprising that the so-called peripheral groups continue to maintain their identities with reference to the social groups (caste, religion or sect) to which they belong while getting involved in the political processes despite the fact that their political goals remain more or less identical. Nonetheless, the processes of steady democratization have contributed to the articulation of a political voice, hitherto unheard of, which is reflective of radical changes in the texture of the political. By helping to articulate the political voice of the marginalized, democracy in India has led to 'a loosing of social strictures' and empowered the peripherals to be confident of their ability to improve the socio-economic conditions in which they are placed.[5] This is a significant political process resulting in what is euphemistically characterized as 'a silent revolution' through a meaningful transfer of power from the upper caste elites to various subaltern groups within the democratic framework of public governance. Rajni Kothari captures this change by saying that 'a new democratic process' seems to have begun 'at a time when the old democracy is failing to deliver the goods [leading to] a new revolution representing new social churnings that are already under way … in the electoral and party processes, as also within the deeper arenas of the non-party political processes'.[6] It is true that democracy in India has given voice to the peripherals. What is however ironical is its failure to create an adequate space in which 'a sense of public purpose can be articulated'. Hence, citizens are 'left with a profound sense of disenchantment'. A pattern seems to have developed where 'individuals and groups expend inordinate energy to colonize or capture government institutions in seeking to promote their interests over others. [T]here is much activity in politics, but little of it is directed to public purposes that all can share'.[7] In theoretical terms, the process can be said to have led to what Anne Philips calls 'the politics of presence',[8] which is articulated as responses of the 'dispossessed or disinherited' to social exclusion, nurtured by the age-old socio-economic imbalances. What is critical here is 'the presence of a voice', powerful indeed on occasions, testifying the resentment of 'the marginalized' seeking to redress their genuine grievances within the democratic space available. In this sense, the politics of presence can metaphorically be described as 'nurseries' of 'the politics of violence' if the former is found to be inadequate in addressing meaningfully 'the well-entrenched social exclusion' on ethnic, racial, religious or gender considerations.[9] The basic arguments that come out of this discussion are two-fold: (a) democracy is undoubtedly an empowering device that brought the 'neglected sections' to the centre stage of Indian politics not only during elections, but also otherwise; (b) democracy may have contributed to a voice that does not seem to be critical to the extent it is expected due presumably to the appropriation of government institutions by the vested socio-economic interests. This is a major paradox in Indian democracy that certainly gave voice to the masses, but failed to make the *vox populi* or the voice of the people meaningful in governance. It is thus being increasingly realized that 'representative democracy ... has [not only] failed and has [also] become more oppressive and serves the interest of the market and acts as a collaborator of global market-capitalists'.[10] Nonetheless, the state no longer remains 'an external entity' to the people presumably as 'a result of the deepening reach of the developmental state under conditions of electoral democracy'.[11] The increasing democratization (whether through electoral politics or otherwise) resulting in the participation of the socio-economically peripheral sections in the political processes therefore seems to have articulated alternative discourses by challenging the state-sponsored market-centric neoliberal policies.

The steady growth of ultra-left wing extremism in the so-called 'red corridor' is also illustrative of a tension between 'the over powering state' and the people who are suffering despite 'the ever flowing FDI (Foreign Direct Investment) and the rising Sensex (the index of India's Stock Exchange) in the era of liberalization and globalization'. The Maoist expansion in the past few years has been phenomenal – from 55 districts in nine states in 2003 to 170 districts in 15 states in 2006. Explanations may vary. But what is critical is the failure of governance over the years and gradual roll-back of the state from key social sectors (primary health, elementary education, among others) that adversely affected the poor in both urban and rural India. The failure of the state to reach out to the poor and also its mal-governance (due to inefficiency, corruption, exploitation and state-engendered violence) leading to 'retreat of governance' have resulted in creating 'a power vacuum' as well as a space for the Maoist to strike roots and gain legitimacy among 'the impoverished'. It is therefore not surprising that the US National Intelligence

Council has warned that 'India is likely to experience heightened violence and instability in several parts of the country because of the growing reach of the Maoist-Naxalite movement'.[12]

The Maoist experiment is an example of a situation where the state is unable to comprehend the articulation of the political in a way that is, for obvious reasons, not appreciated by the state. But the movement has raised significant questions on development. And also a paradox simply because while the state is keen to extend preferential policies to the Other Backward Classes (OBCs) to effectively address the age-old social imbalances it has no design whatsoever to challenge the vested interests in the red corridor (the area where Maoism is a strong competing ideology) presumably because of the consolidation of radically different textures of the political that will not serve the vote bank politics. Like the red corridor that poses difficult questions for Indian democracy, 'the insurgency-prone' north-east India also identifies the policy failure of the political leadership in critically engaging with the issues of democratic fervour. Instead of addressing the genuine difficulties of the people in this region that could have been resolved within the democratic framework, the politics of 'containment' and 'concealment' has led to 'garrison mentality' that invariably avoids 'dialogue' and draws on 'brute force' to set things right. What is probably most appropriate is to understand the regional articulation of the political as reflective of popular democratic zeal that would involve 'reinventing the current dynamics of legislatures, judiciaries and elected governments in the north-east. [It would also mean] ironing out the amorphous norms of citizenship that pass off either as protective discrimination or political appeasement of ethno-nationalist political aspirations'.[13] Like the Maoists, insurgency in the north-east also suggests a clear failure of governance in this region because the issues that inform 'the militants' are all linked with the demands for amenities for basic human existence. The difficult issues need to be tackled within the democratic framework and neither 'granting of special economic packages' (as every Indian prime minister does once they assume power in New Delhi) nor increasing the army personnel will defuse the crisis. No one seems to recognize that unless governance and politics in the region moves away from its militaristic mindset and is tempered with the notions of transparency and justices, violence would remain a ubiquitous presence in the transformation of the north-east India.

III

With the onset of macroeconomic reforms in the 1990s, the state-led developmental plans seem to have lost their significance in a situation where the non-state actors became critical in redefining the state agenda. India has adopted reforms in perhaps a very guarded manner. One probably cannot simply wish away the theoretical justification of state intervention in a transitional economy. Reasons are plenty. Socialist principles may have been forgotten, but the importance of the state in the social sector cannot be minimized unless a meaningful alternative is mooted.

Economic liberalization in India ushered in reforms 'by stealth'[14] as it was more or less accepted as a fait accompli to avoid the massive balance of payment crisis in 1991. Apart from the domestic compulsion, two major international events undermined 'the basic premises of the earlier social consensus regarding the development strategy'.[15] First, was the collapse of the former Soviet Union and its East European satellite states that moved towards 'a market-oriented economic system' eschewing altogether the model of planned economic development. Second, the spectacular success of 'the socialist market economy' of China with the opening of the economy since 1978 and its concomitant favourable economic fallouts cast serious doubts on India's development strategy, based on economic nationalism.

Nonetheless, the importance of the prevalent 'politico-institutional context' cannot be undermined while conceptualizing the impact of economic reform in India. In a significant way, the institutional legacy of 'a well-entrenched state' affected the post-reform possibilities in India. As a commentator argues, 'India's bureaucratized regime – the license-quota-permit raj – has had major, unintended consequences on post-transition patterns: all [state] governments and central regimes continue to rely on state-led strategies of reform; there is no "Washington Consensus" or "neo-liberal" route to reforms in India'.[16] There is no doubt that economic reforms brought about radical changes in India's political economy. Yet, the old regulatory regime of the bygone era remained critical in the path and processes of liberalization in a very decisive way. What thus proliferates across India is 'state-guided routes to liberalization rather than market fundamentalism'. This is reflected in the obvious distortions in India's economy. There are two economies – one affluent and the other predominantly agricultural – are emerging … and this division can be seen across the social and regional landscape of India. The technology-based export-oriented city-centred economy is flourishing in the new economic environment while the agricultural economy remains backward and those associated with this 'have little expectation of a better future [and] remain preoccupied with the daily struggle to secure a livelihood'.[17]

Seeking to articulate the typical Indian response to liberalization, the 1991 Industrial Policy thus suggested several steps to 'unshackle the Indian industrial economy from the cobwebs of unnecessary bureaucratic control' though within the overall control of the state. Four specific steps were recommended: first, the government decided to abolish 'industrial licensing policy' except for a shortlist of industries related to security and strategic concerns, social reasons, hazardous chemicals and overriding environmental reasons. Second, the government also endorsed 'direct foreign investment up to 51 per cent foreign equity in high priority industries'. To avoid bottlenecks, an amendment to the 1973 Foreign Exchange Regulation Act was suggested. Third, it was also decided to withdraw protection of 'the sick public sector units' and there would be 'a greater thrust on performance improvement' to ensure accountability of those involved in these state-sponsored enterprises. Finally, the 1991 Policy sought to remove 'the threshold limits of assets in respect of those companies functioning under the MRTP (Monopolies and Restrictive Trade Practices) Act'. By seeking to amend this act, the 1991 Policy suggested elimination of 'the requirement of prior approval of the Union Government for establishment of new undertakings, expansion of undertakings, merger, amalgamation and take over and appointments of Directors under certain circumstances'. The Indian response to economic liberalization is most creative, if judged contextually. The Nehruvian socialist pattern of society cannot be so easily dispensed with for historical reasons and globalization may not be an appropriate strategy for economic development in a poor country like India because in its present form, argues Joseph Stiglitz, it seems like 'a pact with the devil'. A few people may have become wealthier, but for most of the people, closer integration into the global economy, 'has brought greater volatility and insecurity, and more inequality'.[18] Economic liberalization is thus a double-edged device, which, while improving the lives of some Indians, has also left millions more untouched. Hence, it has been rightly pointed out that the essence of economic liberalization in India can be captured by a Buddhist proverb suggesting that 'the key to the gate of heaven is also the key that could open the gate to hell'. Indeed, the danger and opportunity are so intricately intermingled in economic reforms that 'the journey to the promised land of [economic prosperity] could easily turn into a hellish nightmare of poverty and widening inequality for the majority'.[19]

IV

Environmental issues seem to have played a critical role in the consolidation of Maoism in areas where forests are being depleted for rapid industrialization. Environmentalism in India is articulated in two ways: (a) showing concern for continuous degradation of natural resources and the need to protect them and (b) insisting on the rights of the communities over natural resources and their equitable distribution and sustainable use.[20] While propagating the Maoist ideology, the Naxal activists invariably refer to 'the brutal exploitation' of forest resources by underlining that 'the imperialist forces have … looted their forests and destroyed their way of life'.[21] In such a scenario, the politics of environmental degradation becomes the medium of clash of interest between the indigenous population and those supporting industrialization. At the micro level, the environmental issues have also become the bone of contention between the state and the citizens owing to the moves on the part of the state to exploit nature in various forms for the economic development of the country. Thus, the felling of the trees for the sake of economic development of the region through the medium of commercial forestry evoked sharp reaction from the natives of the hill areas getting consolidated in the famous 'Chipko Movement' in Uttaranchal during the 1970s. In this and other such environmental movements in the country the core issues, therefore, happen to be the obvious conflict between the monopolizing rights of the state over the environmental resources to foster the economic development in the way deemed fit by it, and the increasing urge among the people to assert their rights over the access to and use of natural resources, in addition to keeping the natural ecosystem immune from any irreparable loss owing to the commercial activities.

Historically, the roots of the environmental conflicts in India lie in the adoption of a particular model of development in the country after independence. Between the two available somewhat, if not complete, indigenous models of development, namely the Gandhian and the Nehruvian models, the political leadership of the country unhesitatingly went for the latter in utter disregard for the former. Conceptually, the Gandhian model of economic development was very much eco-friendly owing to its emphasis on small-scale industries, village and cottage industries, local production and consumption of the things utilizing the locally available resources and decentralized economy and polity, with complete rejection of the idea of heavy industrialization and commercial exploitation of resources for the sake of profit and amassing of wealth by few people. In contrast, the Nehruvian model of development, drawing its ideological inspiration and practical implementation from the system prevailing in the Soviet Union, was rooted in the mode of centrally planned economic development of the economy with stress on heavy industrialization in the state sector, adoption of capital- intensive technologies in place of labour-intensive technologies of development and creation of mega-developmental projects in various parts of the country irrespective of the environmental and human costs involved in the execution of such projects. Hence, in the early decades of India's independence, the construction of the modern temples of independent India went unopposed presumably due to the ignorance of the people regarding the environmental cost involved in such projects, and the lack of concerted and formidable movements to fight for the cause of environmental issues in the country.

The Nehruvian model of development led to the lopsided growth of the economy causing, among others, severe damage to the environment largely due the excessive commercial exploitation of the natural resources to the detriment of the fragile ecosystem. Given the obvious importance of the environment in human existence, the environmental movements turned out to be the new pedestals of waging people's struggle against the oppressive and anti-people policies of the governments. There are three types of environmental movements that gained pre-eminence since the 1970s. First, the inception of the environmental movements in India may be reckoned to be the agitation of the people to assert their rights over the access to and use of forest products as against the state-sponsored move of allowing the commercial exploitation of forests by private interests. Championed by the illiterate and politically novice female-dominant sections of the population, the high point in such movements happen to be the Chipko movement of the Uttaranchal during the first half of 1970s. Taking clues and inspiration from the Chipko movement, a number of other forest movements were also started in various parts of the country, such as the Appiko movement in Karnataka and Bharat Jana Andolan in Bastar, which succeeded in highlighting the centrality of the forest resources in the life of the native peoples and inculcated the spirit of struggle in the people to fight for their cherished possessions. Second, the conflicts over the marine and hydraulic resources have also gained momentum during the 1980s and 1990s on the issue of over-exploitation of marine resources for commercial purposes. Chilka Bachao Andolan of Orissa is the classic example when the people of the region consisting mainly of the local fishermen struggled against the proposed harmful and commercial ventures such as mechanized fishing, deep-sea fishing and marine farming. Later on, such struggles extended to the protection of riverbeds from encroachment by government agencies in the name of various types of developmental activities, a fine example of which happens to be the ongoing 'Save Yamuna Campaign' to protest against the construction of the games village for the 2010 Commonwealth Games in Delhi on the riverbeds of the Yamuna. Third, the environmental movements have also taken up the cudgels against the big dams and the large multi-purpose river valley projects in recent times. Starting with the Silent River Valley Project of Kerala during the 1970s, the struggles against the big dams gained currency during the construction of the Tehri Dam in Uttaranchal and the Narmada Valley Project in Gujarat in present times.

What brought people together are those environment-related issues that are critical in human existence. In this sense, environmental issues seem to be universal in character. Furthermore, reflective of alternative paradigms for development keeping in tact the ecological balance, these movements were driven by the rural masses for whom 'the access to the gift of nature was linked to their very survival'. Environmentalism in India is therefore a uniquely constructed ideology upholding the rights of the communities over natural resources and their equitable distribution and sustainable use. Not only have these movements sensitized the political authority in India, they have also made people aware of the critical importance of ecology in development. Besides challenging the top-down and hegemonic power relations and decision-making processes, these people-centric movements are serious endeavours at articulating decentralization in its true meaning by being sensitive to what is euphemistically defined as 'grassroots issues'.

V

What then, is Maoism? The simple answer is that it is a brand of radical ideology drawing on the political ideas of Mao besides the classical Marxism. At a rather complex level, it is an ideological response to India's journey as an independent nation that followed a specific path of development. Hence, Maoism is also an ideological package seeking to articulate an alternative with roots in both orthodox Marxism and also the Chinese variety. That Maoism goes beyond 'the arm chair revolutionaries' to inspire 'the have-nots' under most adverse circumstances to fight for their cause also reveals its meaningful role in galvanizing those at the grass roots. As an ideology, Maoism addresses the genuine socio-economic grievances of the people in the affected areas by mapping out an exploitation-free social order that remains the primary goal of the movement. The aim may remain unfulfilled though there is no doubt that Naxalites are inspired to believe that the Maoist objective of an equitable society will surely be attained.

Maoism in India has thrived on the objective conditions of poverty that has various ramifications. Undoubtedly, high economic and income disparity and exploitation of the impoverished, especially 'the wretched of the earth', contribute to conditions, conducive to revolutionary and radical politics. India's development strategy since independence was hardly adequate to eradicate the sources of discontent. The situation seems to have become worse with the onset of globalization that has created 'islands of deprivation' all over the country. As the state is being dragged into the new development packages which are neither adequate nor appropriate for the 'peripherals', Maoism seems to have provided a powerful alternative. The argument, drawn on poverty, is strengthened by linking the past deficits with the disadvantages inherent and perceived in the present initiatives for globalization. The Orissa case (and also Chhattisgarh) is an eye-opener because Maoism has gained enormously due to 'the displacement' of the indigenous population in areas where both the state-sponsored industrial magnates and other international business tycoons have taken over land for agro-industries. Here is a difference between the present Maoism and the Naxalbari movement. In case of the latter, it was an organized peasant attack against peculiar 'feudal' land relations, particularly in West Bengal whereas the Maoists in Orissa and Chhattisgarh draw on 'displacement' of the local people due to zealous support of the state for quick development through 'forced' industrialization.

The steady expansion of Maoist influence is therefore attributed to its success in persuading 'the exploited masses' to take part in the movement as possibly the only way out of their sub-human existence. The grass-roots situation is so appalling that there is hardly a difference of opinion between the Naxalites espousing a violent path to create a new social order and the government officials involved in combating 'the red menace'. Justifying the armed revolution to overturn the prevalent exploitative system, Ajit Buxla, a Maoist responsible for mobilizing the tribals in Malkangiri, a district in Orissa, did not find it incongruent to resort to violence. In his words, 'when you see death taking tolls on your near and dear ones and you know their life could have been saved had they been given proper and timely medication, you are forced to believe that the existence of state has nothing to do with the life of poor and marginalized'.[22] Corroborating the feeling, Bidhu Bhusan Mishra, the Inspector General of Police, Government of Orissa, was more categorical in explaining the increasing influence of Maoism in rural Orissa, by saying that 'the lack of development, grievances of the tribals and poor, and the absence of administration have been conducive to the spread of left wing extremism in Orissa'.[23] Two important points come out of these two statements, made by individuals with completely different aims: first, in view of the terrible plight of those in the periphery due to stark poverty, Maoism seems to have gained enormously by ideologically articulating an alternative to the prevalent inequitable world; and second, the failure of the state in reaching out to the marginalized continues to baffle the administrators and also the governed. As an official confirms, 'Naxalites operate in a vacuum created by inadequacy of administrative and political institutions, espouse local demands and take advantage of the prevalent disaffection and injustice among the exploited segments of the population and seek to offer an alternative system of governance which promises emancipation of these segments'.[24] It is not therefore surprising that the prime minister of India in his address to the 2007 chief ministers' conference suggested that without meaningfully addressing 'development needs of the affected people', the Naxalism cannot be effectively combated. As he argued:

> development and internal security are two sides of the same coin. Each is critically dependent on the other. Often, the lack of development and the lack

of any prospects for improving one's lot provide a fertile ground for extremist ideologies to flourish ... At the same time, development cannot take place in the absence of a secure and stable environment ... I have said in the past that the Left Wing Extremism is probably single biggest security challenge to the Indian state. It continues to be so and we cannot rest in peace until we have eliminated this virus.[25]

The basic thrust of the argument, made by the prime minister, relates to the realization that the conventional coercive method does not seem to be adequate unless the genuine socio-economic grievance of those sustaining the Naxal campaign are meaningfully addressed. This is endorsed by the reports submitted by the Expert Committee of the Planning Commission and the Second Administrative Reforms Commission. By making a comparative survey of 20 severely Naxal-affected districts in five states – Andhra Pradesh, Bihar, Chhatisgarh, Jharkhand and Orissa – with 20 non-affected districts in the same states, the Committee found a direct correspondence between the rise and consolidation of left-wing extremism and lack of development. One of the major factors that account for the consolidation of Naxalism is undoubtedly the lack of faith of the rural masses in the government machinery that is invariably geared to protect those relatively better placed in socio-economic terms. There are areas where government functionaries are hardly visible and the funds, earmarked for welfare schemes, are mostly appropriated by those in complicity with government officials. In commenting on the role of the paramilitary and police forces, the Committee found that these combative forces needed to be sensitized to the human needs to effectively challenge 'the red menace'. The second Administrative Commission that submitted its report entitled 'Combating Terrorism' in June 2008 puts the Naxals on par with *jihadis* clinging on to 'religious fundamentalism'. Like the Expert Committee, the Commission also agreed that the roots of Naxalism were to be located in the development trajectory of these Indian states where large sections of population continued to suffer due to distorted economic growth. The Commission thus recommended a multi-pronged strategy based on political consensus, good governance and socio-economic development and respect for the rule of law. What is remarkable is the fact that the government of India, while articulating its response, took into account the major recommendations possibly to re-orient its policies vis-à-vis Maoism and those areas where it has evolved as an organic movement.

To review and monitor different mechanisms of the Naxal problem the government of India constituted an Empowered Group of Ministers (EGoM), a Standing Committee of Chief Ministers of Concerned States, a coordination centre, a task force under the Special Secretary (Internal Security) and an Inter Ministerial Group (IMG) headed by the Additional Secretary (Naxal Management). By evolving a two-prong strategy, the government seeks to address 'the Naxal menace' at two levels: although it is necessary to conduct proactive and sustained operations against the extremists and put in place all measures required for this, it is also necessary to simultaneously give focused attention to development and governance issues, particularly at the cutting-edge level. The Ministry of Home Affairs in its annual reports lists several schemes – such as the Backward Districts Initiatives, the Backward Regions Grant Fund, the National Rural Employment Guarantee Scheme, the Prime Minister's Gram Sadak Yojna (rural roadways), the National Rural Health Mission Scheme and Sarva Siksha Abhiyan (universal education) – to meaningfully articulate the role of the government in eradicating poverty at the grass roots. In fact, it was agreed upon by those involved in the anti-Naxal cell of the government of India that so long as the masses were reeled in poverty Maoism was likely to flourish because of its success in (a) projecting an exploitation-free world after the revolution and in (b) dismissing the role of the government in ameliorating the conditions of the poverty-stricken people given their historical failure since independence. Maoism is therefore not merely a law and order problem; it is also an ideological battle underlining serious lacuna in India's development strategy since independence. With various welfare schemes in place, government initiatives are likely to yield results in due course, which will perhaps be serious threat to Maoism drawing on 'lack of development' as perhaps the most effective agenda in the Maoist campaign.

It is true that Maoists have drawn on the genuine socio-economic grievances of the poverty-stricken masses for political mobilization in favour of their ideological campaign. This is one side of the story; the other part dwells on how they seek to fulfil their aim. As true Maoists, Naxalites unhesitatingly resort to violent means to change the inequitable society. An unconfirmed source suggests that the People's Liberation Guerrilla Army that was formed in 2000 has more than 10,000 armed cadres nationwide, a 25,000-strong people's militia and 50,000 members in village-level units.[26] In absolute terms, the military strength may not be so alarming. What is worrisome, as government notes underline, is 'the simultaneous attack at multiple locations by large number of Naxalites in a military type operations ... looting of weapons at Giridih (Jharkhand), detention of a passenger train in Latchar (Orissa) [and] looting of explosives from the NDMC magazine in Chhatisgarh'.[27] There are reasons to believe that the Naxalite Guerrilla Army has so far not only succeeded in sustaining its grip in the so-called liberated zones, but has also brought new areas under its control by following a completely different kind of tactics to overpower government paramilitary forces. On 29 June 2008, the Maoists, for the first time, showcased their ability in the tricks of marine warfare when they chose to attack a motor launch inside the Balimela reservoir in the Malkangiri district of Orissa that left 34 people dead. The official combatant force comprised members from the specially created paramilitary wing, known as the greyhound commandos. The incident took place in the area that is claimed by the Naxals as the liberated zone; the area where Malkangiri district of Orissa shares a border with the Bastar area of Chhattisgarh and Khammam district of Andhra Pradesh. Malkangiri is separated from Andhra by the Sileru river and from Chhattisgarh by the Sabrei river. Besides the Sileru and Sabrei, there is another interstate river, the Mahendrataneya, between Orissa and Andhra. Operationally, this is the area where Naxals have recently raised a boat wing to facilitate faster movement of their cadres and weapons.[28]

Similar to a typical Leninist organization, the entire Maoist activities are governed by a centralized leadership that has so far remained free from factional feud. The killing of Swami Laxmananda Saraswati, a Vishwa Hindu Parishad (VHP) leader, and four of his associates in Kandahmal in Orissa on 23 August 2008, however, led to the rise of a powerful faction condemning the act because of the probable repercussions on inter-communal relations in this small Orissa town with a sizeable section of dalit Christians. The merciless killing of Saraswati and his associates that triggered attacks on Christians in Orissa have split the Communist Party of India (Maoist) on religious lines for the first time, with many Hindu members breaking away to form a rival group. As the media reports confirm, the new group calls itself 'IDGA-Maoist', the acronym for 'Idealist Democratic Guerrilla Army of CPI (Maowadi)'. According to police sources, this group, also known as M2, is made up of Hindu Maoists, who were appalled by the murder of the 84-year-old Saraswati. 'The content of M2 leaflets prove beyond doubt that Saraswati's murder has divided the Maoists which has people from both Christian and Hindu faiths ... M2 criticizes conversions and quotes Lord Krishna's sermons in the *Bhagwad Gita*', the sources said. Although the extremists profess they don't work for a religious ideology and they target all exploiters; but Saraswati's killing appears to have provoked a debate on inter-communal relations, the police further endorses. Whatever be the outcome of the debate, the fact that such an issue gained prominence also reveals that Maoists do not seem to be as free from religious prejudices as they so vociferously claim.[29]

VI

This book provides a synthetic account of the rise and consolidation of Maoism as a politically meaningful and ideologically persuasive movement in India, especially in the last decade. Given the diversity in the articulation of Maoist ideology, it may not be easy to identify a pattern except that the Maoist cadres, regardless of their location, draw on Marxism and its Maoist interpretation. Besides the ideological appeal of 'new democracy' suggesting class collaboration, the Maoists are organized on the basis of issues bringing the exploited masses under one platform. For instance, displacement of the tribals from the forest land is an issue that transcends the geographical boundaries and it is not therefore surprising that the affected tribals, whether in Orissa, Madhya Pradesh, Andhra Pradesh or Chhatisgarh, come together to challenge governmental policies of land encroachment for industrial purposes. While combating the anti-tribal government design, the Indian Maoists, by sharply challenging the well-entrenched feudal interests in rural India, seem to have translated one of the basic tenets of Maoism. That Maoism has converted 'docile masses' into 'rebels' even in adverse circumstance, is a powerful testimony of its ideological appeal to 'the wretched of the earth'. The story of the growth and consolidation of Maoism in India is told in seven analytical chapters.

Chapter 1 is about the nature of the movement in different parts of India and Chapter 2 dwells on the historical trajectory of Maoism. By focusing on the future Maoist roadmap for the country, Chapter 3 underlines the importance of deliberations within the organization to arrive at a decision. This chapter is also an elaboration of the processes of democratic centralism as a major driving force to involve the cadres in matters relating to the execution of the Maoist plans and programmes. Chapters 4 and 5 concentrate on Orissa, one of the constituent states in federal India that remains a citadel of the Maoist organization for reasons connected with its peculiar socio-economic evolution since the British withdrawal from India in 1947. Chapter 6 deals with the organization network supporting the movement by drawing on field data and also the Maoist constitution that proposes a specific organizational structure to articulate and also translate into reality its ideological goal. Maoism no longer remains a mere academic description; instead, it has become an organic movement involving 'the wretched of the earth'. Hence, Chapter 7 undertakes a critical review of the Maoist existential ideology that has gradually expanded its domain by redefining its ideological commitment in accordance with the prevalent socio-economic and political milieu. The chapter is also a long statement on the future of Maoism that has grown steadily despite state-engineered atrocities on those supportive of Marxism-Leninism-Maoism.

This book is about a socio-political movement drawing on an alternative ideological discourse that appears to have lost its credibility to a significant extent with the collapse of the former Soviet Union and its satellite states in Eastern Europe in the late 1980s. Interestingly, the Maoist effort in India continues to remain effective in mobilizing 'the disinherited sections' of Indian society. It is too premature to comment on the future of the movement. Nonetheless, there is no doubt that as an ideology Maoism has certainly galvanized 'the poorest of the poor' in a large number of constituent Indian states. With the enthusiastic acceptance by the Indian state of neoliberal economic policies, the indigenous population seems to have been hard-hit because not only have they been deprived of their 'habitat', they have also lost their means of livelihood as forest lands are taken away by 'the outsiders' for commercial gains. Maoism appears to have evolved its organic roots in such circumstances in which people seem to have lost faith in the state that has reportedly been appropriated by 'the vested interests'. Maoism cannot therefore be reduced to a mere 'law and order' problem; its roots are located in governmental failure to comprehend and meaningfully address the human issues that remain at the heart of the 'disenchantment' of those who historically remain 'marginalized' in the Indian state. This perhaps explains why the Maoist movement – which India's prime minister has acknowledged to be the single most serious threat to the country – has found such fertile ground in India's 'heartland'.

Notes

1 The introduction draws on the following works: (a) Bidyut Chakrabarty, *Indian Politics and Society Since Independence: Events, Processes and Ideology*, Routledge, London and New York, 2008 and (b) Bidyut Chakrabarty and Rajendra Kumar Pandey, *Indian Government and Politics*, New Delhi: Sage, 2008.
2 V.S. Naipaul, *A Million Mutinies*, London: Heinemann, 1991, 106. According to Naipaul, every protest movement strengthens the state 'defining it as the source of law and civility and reasonableness'. The institutionalization of power in the form of democratic state gives 'people a second chance, calling them back from the excesses

with which, in another century, or in other circumstances (as neighbouring countries showed), they might have had to live: the destructive chauvinism of the *Shiv Sena*, the tyranny of many kinds of religious fundamentalism … the film-star corruption and the racial politics of the South, the pious Marxist idleness and nullity of Bengal'.

3 Sudipta Kaviraj, 'Modernity and Politics in India', *Daedalus*, Winter 2000, 156–57.
4 Satish Deshpande, *Contemporary India: A Sociological View*, New Delhi: Penguin, 2003, 103.
5 Javeed Alam, *Who Wants Democracy?*, New Delhi: Orient Longman, 2004, 22. According to Alam, 'democracy in India is an assertion of the urge for more self-respect and the ability to better oneself'.
6 Rajni Kothari, *Memoirs*, New Delhi: Rupa & Co., 2002, 200.
7 Pratap Bhanu Mehta, *The Burden of Democracy*, New Delhi: Penguin, 2003, 129–30.
8 Anne Phillips, *The Politics of Presence*, Oxford: Clarendon Press, 1995.
9 For an analytical treatment of 'the politics of inclusion' as an alter-ego of 'the politics of exclusion', see Zoya Hasan, *Politics of Inclusion: Castes, Minorities and Affirmative Action*, New Delhi: Oxford University Press, 2009.
10 Sanjay Sanghvi, 'The New People's Movement in India', *Economic and Political Weekly*, 15 December 2007, 116.
11 Partha Chatterjee, 'Democracy and Economic Transformation in India', *Economic and Political Weekly*, 19 April 2008, 54.
12 The report of the US National Intelligence Council is quoted in *The Times of India*, New Delhi, 22 November 2008.
13 Sanjay Barbora, 'Rethinking India's Counter-Insurgency Campaign in North-East', *Economic and Political Weekly*, 2 September 2006, 3811.
14 Rob Jenkins, *Democratic Politics and Economic Reform in India*, Cambridge: Cambridge University Press, 1999, 172–207. Since economic reforms were not 'strategy-based' but 'crisis-driven' Indian hardly had a choice and was thus more or less forced to accept 'the conditionalities' imposed by the donor agencies.
15 Suresh D. Tendulkar and T.A. Bhavani, *Understanding Reforms: Post 1991 India*, New Delhi: Oxford University Press, 2007, 85.
16 Aseema Sinha, 'The Changing Political Economy of Federalism in India: A Historical Institutional Approach', *India Review*, vol. 3 (1), Janaury 2004, 51.
17 Francine R. Frankel, *India's Political Economy, 1947–2004*, Oxford University Press, 2005, 625.
18 Joseph Stiglitz, *Making Globalization Work: The Next Steps to Global Justice*, London: Allen Lane, 2006, 292. This argument was forcefully made by Margit Bussmann in 'When Globalization Discontent Turns Violent: Foreign Economic Liberalization and Internal War', *International Studies Quarterly*, vol. 51 (1) March 2007, 79–97.
19 Amit Bhaduri and Deepak Nayyar, *The Intelligent Person's Guide to Liberalization*, New Delhi: Penguin, 1996, 159.
20 Sanjay Sanghvi follows this argument in detail in 'The New People's Movements in India', *Economic and Political Weekly*, 15 December 2007. According to Sanghvi, 'the *pani panchayat* experiment' (movement for rights over water) initiated by Vilasrao Salunkhe during the severe drought in the 1970s in Maharashtra is perhaps one of the glaring examples demonstrating how critical the role of the local people was in asserting the 'first right of the village/group of villages over the water in their stream/river and its equal distribution and sustainable use'.
21 An activist named Roopi was quoted by *The Times of India* reporter that was published in *The Times of India*, 22 February 2008.
22 Interview with Ajit Buxla, conducted in his hideout in the district of Malkangiri, 9 December 2006.
23 Interview with Bidhu Bhusan Mishra, the Inspector General of Police, Government of Orissa, available at http://www.satp.org.

24 Ministry of Home Affairs, *Status Paper on the Naxal Problem*, Internal Security Division, 18 May 2006, 1.
25 *Hindustan Times*, 21 January 2007.
26 Gautam Navlakha, 'Maoists in India', *Economic and Political Weekly*, 3 June 2006, 2187.
27 Minutes of the 20th meeting of the Coordination Centre, Ministry of Home Affairs (IS Division), Government of India, 31 March 2006 – quoted in Nandini Sundar, *Subalterns and Sovereigns: An Anthropological History of Bastar (1854–2006)*, New Delhi: Oxford University Press, 2008, 267.
28 Information drawn on interviews conducted in Malkangiri in December 2008.
29 Information obtained from *The Times of India*, 6 January 2009.

1 Maoism, governance and the red corridor

Maoism in India is a context-driven and ideologically charged political campaign to address critical socio-economic issues. At one level, it is a political movement seeking to redress the genuine socio-economic grievances at the grass roots; at another, perhaps more significant level, Maoism represents a serious search for an alternative development paradigm, drawn on a persuasive critique of the Nehruvian state-directed development plans and programmes. Inspired by reinvented Marxism of Maoist variety, the Indian counterpart is a creative intervention in an ideological domain that seems to have lost its 'appeal' following the disintegration of the former Soviet Union and her satellite East European states. Based on the idea that organic complementaries between agriculture and industry, between town and country are critical to development, Maoism actually reiterates an old dictum that a deep bond between these two sectors of the economy is what holds the nation together.

Maoism is a powerful ideological statement on the processes of development in India. It is not therefore a strange coincidence that 'ultra-left extremism' resurfaced in areas that are economically backward and thus politically most assertive in challenging the projects that seem to be critically linked with the processes of globalization. The India shining campaign appears to be a paradox and perhaps a campaign without substance in view of the growing consolidation of Maoism across the length and breadth of India. Given the fact that 13 out of 28 Indian states have already been affected, one simply cannot wish it away as a ripple that will disappear in no time. Furthermore, the fact that the Indian Home Ministry's open acknowledgement that Maoists are a significant political force in as many as 170 (out of 604) districts in India also indicates the ideological viability of the movement at the grass roots. Drawing on the doctrinal support from Marxism-Leninism and the strategic inspiration from the political ideas of Mao Tse-tung, the ideology that contemporary Maoists seek to articulate is also a response to the failure of India's developmental strategies. In this sense, despite its unique appeal immediately after independence, the Nehruvian scheme of the socialistic pattern of society was hardly an effective strategy for a uniform socio-economic development across the country. So, Maoism is also an outcome of 'disillusionment' with an ideology that was judiciously articulated by independent India's political leadership as perhaps the most appropriate strategy for economic development. In other words, given the socio-economic roots, it can safely be argued that, besides its ideological appeal, Maoism is also a contextual response to 'mal governance' or 'lack of governance' in the affected areas. This chapter therefore seeks to dwell on those factors that provide a plausible explanation for the growing significance of the 'red corridor' or 'red belt' in contemporary India. Since 'compact revolutionary zones' or the red corridor, as characterized by the Home Ministry is an articulation of obvious mass discontent, one cannot dismiss Maoism as 'an infantile disorder'. Instead, it has raised serious questions not only on India's development strategies, but also on the state that seemed to have failed to gauge 'the erosion of state' at the grass roots due to its uncritical faith in the planning-driven economic model. One should not also lose sight of the contemporary context of globalization that, by linking the domestic capital with its global counterpart, theoretically substantiates the major Marxist formulation that the market-driven capitalism is borderless and hence is naturally expansive for its survival.

Three important questions

Maoism is the outcome of a historical situation in which people suffer due to reasons connected with India's past and present. Colonialism had a role to play and the failure of the Indian state to implement land reforms most stringently in the aftermath of independence also resulted in terrible sufferings of the land-dependent marginalized sections of society. Hence, it is perhaps most appropriate to assess Maoism in India keeping in mind the historical perspective that is peculiar to a transitional society like India. The following questions are therefore relevant to understand the ideological articulation of the contemporary ultra-Left movement in India, including Maoism, which is expanding gradually for a variety of reasons:

1   Is Maoism reflective of the growing disenchantment of the people in the affected areas with the state?
2   Is this a comment on 'the distorted development planning', pursued by the Indian state?
3   Is this an outcome of the processes of 'deepening of democracy' in India?

There is no doubt that the rapid growth of Maoism is largely due to the economic neglect of a large section of those in the periphery. One cannot, however, rule out the growing democratization or deepening of democratic processes in which people are organically involved that also contributed significantly to the articulation of the 'people's voice'. In this sense, an intensive discussion of the political economy of development in post-colonial India will be perfectly in order.

With the onset of macroeconomic reforms in the 1990s, the state-led developmental plans seem to have lost their significance in a situation where the non-state actors grew in importance in redefining the state agenda.[1] India has adopted reforms in perhaps a very guarded manner. One probably cannot simply wish away the theoretical justification of state intervention in a transitional economy. Reasons are plenty. Socialist principles may not have been forgotten, but the importance of the state in the social sector cannot be minimized unless a meaningful alternative is mooted. This is reflected in the obvious distortions in India's economy. On the basis of an empirical study of Andhra Pradesh and other supporting data, the author thus argues that 'two economies – one affluent and the other predominantly agricultural economy – are emerging … and this division can be seen across the social and regional landscape of India'.[2] The technology-based export-oriented city-centred economy is flourishing in the new economic environment while the agricultural economy remains backward and those associated with this 'have little expectation of a better future [and] remain preoccupied with the daily struggle to secure a livelihood'.[3]

It is true that economic liberalization is a significant influence and yet, the importance of the prevalent 'politico-institutional context' cannot be undermined while conceptualizing the impact of economic reform in India. In a significant way, the institutional legacy of 'a well-entrenched state' affected the post-reform possibilities in India. As a commentator argues, 'India's bureaucratized regime – the license-quota-permit raj – has had major, unintended consequences on post-transition patterns: all [state] governments and central regimes continue to rely on state-led strategies of reform; there is no "Washington Consensus" or "neo-liberal" route to reforms in India'.[4] There is no doubt that economic reforms brought about radical changes in India's political economy. Yet, the old regulatory regime of the bygone era remained critical in the path and processes of liberalization in a very decisive way. What thus proliferates across India is 'state-guided routes to liberalization rather than market fundamentalism'.[5]

It is now plausible to argue that Maoism has its roots [sic] in a peculiar political economy of development which India preferred to pursue immediately after independence.

Political economy of India as a nation state

India's post-colonial political economy is neither purely capitalist nor feudal but a peculiar mixture of the two. Hence the path of development that India adopted can never be conceptualized in a straightforward manner just like India's evolution as a nation in the aftermath of decolonization in 1947. The preamble to the Constitution of India laid the foundation of the socialistic pattern of society in which the state remained the most critical player. Accordingly, the Directive Principles of State Policy (Part IV of the Constitution) emphasize that the goal of the Indian polity is not unbridled laissez-faire but a welfare state where the state has a positive duty to ensure to its citizens social and economic justice with dignity of individual consistent with the unity and integrity of the nation. By making them fundamental in the governance and making the laws of the country and duty of the state to apply these principles, the founding fathers made it the responsibility of future governments to find a middle way between individual liberty and the public good, between preserving the property and privilege of the few and bestowing benefits on the many in order to liberate the powers of men equally for contributions to the common good.[6] This led to, as a commentator rightly points out, 'paradoxical socialism' in India that approximated to what the Fabian socialists championed as socialism. Fabian socialism, it was further argued, was 'an intellectual tool [that] facilitated, when required, a distancing of oneself from the revolutionary left while still maintaining a claim to socialism; and, possibly more importantly, justifying a socialism brought about by an elite who were great believers in science'.[7] Independence in 1947 provided the founding fathers with a chance to translate their ideological vision into concrete development programmes in which the role of state was hailed as a prime mover. The new institutional matrix that the state-led development programmes provided consisted of 'a regulatory regime' comprising (a) public sector expansion, (b) discretionary controls over markets and private economic activities and (c) stringent foreign exchange and import controls. The first two had their roots in the ideology of socialism while the last one had its roots in economic nationalism. Taken together, they articulated 'activism of the newly established nation state'[8] to guide the economic system 'in a desired direction by means of intentionally planned and rationally coordinated state policies'.[9]

In this model of state-directed development, the most significant instrument was the Planning Commission that came into being in January 1950 despite serious opposition of the Gandhians within the Congress Working Committee. However, the cabinet resolution that finally led to the creation of the Commission underlined three major principles as special terms of reference in the preparation of the plans that largely defused opposition. These principles were: (a) that the citizens, men and women equally, have the right to an adequate means of livelihood; (b) that the ownership and control of the material resources of the country are so distributed as best to subserve the common good; (c) that the operation of the economic system does not result in the concentration of wealth and means of production to the common detriment.[10] Underlining the ideological commitment of the nation, the 1948 Industrial Policy Resolution therefore begins by stating that

> [t]he nation has now set itself to establish a social order where justice and equality of opportunity shall be secured to all the people. For this purpose, careful planning and integrated efforts over the whole field of national activity are necessary; and the Government of India propose to establish a National Planning Commission to formulate programmes of development and to secure its execution (para 1).

Accordingly, the 1948 Industrial Policy Resolution insisted that the state should play a progressively active role in the development of critical industries, such as (a) industries manufacturing arms and ammunition, production and control of atomic energy and the ownership and management of railway transport and (b) basic industries, namely iron, coal and steel, aircraft manufacture, shipbuilding and mineral oils. This resolution was reiterated in the 1955 Avadi session of the Congress by underlining that in view of the declared objective of being a socialist pattern of society, the state shall play a vital role in planning and development. The next landmark event confirming the intention of an activist state was the Industrial Policy Resolution of 1956 that was adopted after parliament had accepted

in December 1954 a socialist pattern of society as the objective of social and economic policy and the Second Five Year Plan (also known as Mahalanobis Plan)
articulated this ideological goal in formal terms. P.C. Mahalanobis, the architect
of the plan, argued for state-controlled economic development for accelerating the
tempo of growth under 'the autarkic industrialization strategy'.[11] Hence, he insisted
that basic and heavy industries should remain in the public sector for two reasons:
(a) the private sector may not be able to raise adequate resourced for these very
capital-intensive industries and even if it managed it would command a monopol-
istic control that was deemed detrimental to social welfare; and (b) by controlling
allocation of output of basic and heavy industries according to social priorities, it
was certain that the government would be able to channel private sector growth to
fulfil its ideological goal. In seeking to achieve the objective of a socialist pattern of
society, the Nehru-led government envisaged an expanded role of the public sector
and the importance of planning in all-round development of the country.

Planning for development: a panacea or failure?

As an operational tool, planning seems formidable to structure the role of the state
in accordance with its ideological underpinning. Therefore, not only is planning an
instrument tuned to economic regeneration, it is inextricably tied to the regime's
political preferences as well. This is, however, not to conceptualize the relationship between planning and the ideological slant of the regime in a deterministic
way, but to underline the complex interdependence which entails, at the same time,
an interplay of various pulls and pressures in a rapidly changing social fabric.
Planning is thus 'an exercise of instrumental rationality ... institutionalized ...
outside the normal processes of representative politics [and executed] through a
developmental administration'.[12] Notwithstanding the critical significance of planning as a developmental aid in India, argues Aseema Sinha, 'was and continues
to be constrained by the pattern of mediation between the centre and regions'.[13]
Furthermore, a centralized planning also led to the expansion of regionalism in
India presumably because of 'haphazard and unequal' development of constituent
provinces. Regional differences and politico-economic conflicts arising out of a
centrally engineered scheme remain critical in post-independent India's political
economy, besides the exogenous influences in the wake of globalization.

Historically, the Congress was persuaded by the arguments supporting planning
for development. Contrary to Gandhi's explicit opposition to 'planned development', the Congress party showed ample interest in socialistic means, including
planning and heavy industrialization as 'essential to make revolutionary changes
in the present economic and social structure of society and to remove gross
inequalities' since 1929. Within two years, the 1931 Karachi Congress adopted
a resolution insisting on state ownership of 'key industries and services, mineral
resources, railways, waterways, shipping and other means of public transport'.
However, in 1934, the Congress Working Committee passed a resolution at
Banaras stressing that 'large and organized industries are in no need of the services
of Congress organizations or of any Congress effort on their behalf'. Critical of

the above, Jawaharlal Nehru rallied support to reformulate the resolution with a view to soliciting Congress backing for industrialization and planning, which, he believed, was the only available means to attain substantial economic development in India.[14] A compromise formula was reached in Bombay at the Congress Working Committee meeting in September 1934. Even though top priority was accorded to small-scale cottage industries, encouraged by partial support of the party, as neither the Congress fund nor its organizational support was available, Nehru in his 1936 Faizpur presidential address argued strongly in favour of heavy industrialization and coordination of human resources through planning.

Planning seems to have provided the Congress stalwarts with a platform to articulate different ideological positions. Drawing on their respective ideological leanings, Nehru hailed industrialism while Gandhi opposed it since he felt that instead of contributing to the general welfare, machine civilization would not only expose Indians to a worse kind of exploitation but also lead to a general degradation of human life. Although Nehru and Gandhi were poles apart on occasions, the former, unlike his militant colleague Subhas Bose, never pursued his differences with the latter to the extent of causing a split within the Congress. Despite the adverse ideological implication of aligning with Gandhi, Nehru as a pragmatist participated wholeheartedly in the Gandhi-led freedom struggle for he knew the attainment of independence was prior to ideology. So, the controversy involving Gandhi and Nehru vis-à-vis planning and industrialization was just a signpost indicating the tension that was most likely in view of the Congress effort to create an anti-British platform incorporating even contradictory ideologies. By making a case for planning and industrialization there is no doubt that Nehru ushered in a new era in the Indian independence struggle.[15]

The above detailed description of the evolution of planning is illustrative of Nehru's uncritical faith in planning though he acknowledged that planning was to be guided by what he characterized as 'integrated planning'. Hence, he observed, '[The] Planning Commission has performed an essential task; without which it could not have progressed ... We are a federal structure and it has served to bring the various states together and have integrated planning. If it had not been there, the central government could not have done its job because immediately difficulties would have arisen that the central government was encroaching the rights of the States'.[16] It was almost natural that planning was to become an important instrument for development once he took over as India's prime minister. Planning was envisaged as 'a pre-condition' and was based on the assumption that 'spontaneous development cannot be expected'.[17] Economic planning in South Asia is, as Myrdal further argues, 'not [therefore] the result of development, but is employed to foster development ... The underdeveloped countries in this region are thus compelled to undertake what in the light of Western history appears as a short-cut'.[18] Despite the euphoria over planning, it left a large number of people below the poverty line. Even those sympathetic to the strategy of planned development believed that, 'If Indian society values growth with equity, as plan document repeatedly emphasize, India has still a long way to go in adapting institutions and aspirations in that direction'.[19] While explaining the failure of planning to accomplish the Nehruvian goal of 'balanced and equitable growth', Sukhamoy Chakravarty, who was otherwise a supporter of the state-led development programme, attributed the failure to the lack of coordination among those involved in the framing of planning and also 'the information failure'. In his words, 'plans did not work because the desired coordination among the different actors was faulty, either because "messages" were faulty, or because they were transmitted with delay, or went contrary to the specific interests of the actors involved and were therefore evaded'.[20] Besides the inherent weaknesses of the planning processes, India's development strategy did not yield the desired results presumably because of the failure in evolving 'a broad political consensus on priorities'.[21] This is true that planning failed to evolve a mechanism for equitable distribution of economic resources and was also detrimental to capitalist development in India. Planning was merely an ideological tool of the state to intrude, rather mechanically, into the economic processes that may not always follow what is planned in advance. As Meghnad Desai argues, 'the Green Revolution, and the context of owner-cultivation in which it made its impact, brought capitalism irreversibly to the country side'.[22] This is a significant structural change in Indian economy which 'came independently of planning'. What it had shown was the gradual but steady decline of planning as an instrument of rapid economic development in India where capitalism had a skewed growth due to a variety of historical reasons. Desai thus concludes that 'planning has lost the driving seat it once had [because] ... the driving force will come from the capitalist social relations in the Indian economy'. Instead of altogether rejecting, what it suggests is the changing role of the Planning Commission based on appreciating the capitalist path of development. In the words of Desai

> Planning [requires to be] interactive and predictive in an econometric way. It will be strategic rather than pervasive. It will start with a given growth rate. The growth rate that will emerge from the interactive predictive quinquennial exercise will set a feasible bound. It will require further iterative and counterfactual work with the available models to explore whether a higher growth path is achievable, and if so, what constraints need to be removed.[23]

This is the quintessence of the argument that Desai puts forward to re-orient the instruments for economic development, including planning for a well-defined scheme drawn on the basic principles of capitalist growth, as explained by classical Marxism. Hence, 'planning designed for an insulated national economy ... is not appropriate'.[24] Instead, it has to take into account the new material conditions involving the growing importance of the global economy, especially the non-state actors, like the IMF, World Bank and other transnational donor agencies. One cannot simply ignore this changed milieu and hence the national economies need to come to terms with them as best as they could. So, the most meaningful step for steady economic growth is 'a rapid integration of the Indian economy into capitalism'.[25] The formula works in a spectacular way in the cases of China, Taiwan and Korea, where capitalism is not discriminatory but pro-people as well. Socialism in India failed in its basic objective. Those at the bottom continued to suffer. The mixed-economy strategy seeking also to pursue the state-led capitalist development thus largely failed because Indian economy 'had grown too slowly to qualify as a capitalist economy ... [and] by its failure to reduce inequalities had forfeited any claims to being socialist'.[26] Such an argument led Desai to believe that 'India's problem is not so much capitalism but that it is stuck with a backward version of capitalism'.[27] So economic growth is, as Desai argues, rooted in a complete overhauling of the economy, supported by a strong political will endorsing, for instance, various anti-poverty programmes and cutting subsidies to the rich. Under these changed circumstances, it is also possible for the state to play a dynamic role in pursuing economic agenda in favour of those at the bottom who always suffered in the name of the much euphoric socialistic planning. While explaining the failure of the state-led development paradigm in India, Atul Kohli thus argues that 'the Achilles heel of Indian political economy is not so much its statist model of development as much as the mismatch between the statist model and the limited capacity of the state to guide social and economic change ... [By] trying to reconcile political preferences of both the left and right in the context of a fragmented state, [the Indian policy makers] failed both at radical redistribution and at ruthless capitalism-led economic growth'.[28] The euphoria over the role of the public sector for a balanced economic growth was short-lived. Except for financial enterprises in banking, insurance and petroleum-producing enterprises, none of the public sector units became viable.[29] This created a paradoxical situation. While 'socialist rhetoric' was useful for building and sustaining 'a stable political base' for the ruling authority, the pro-poor policies were hardly seriously pursed. As a result, not only were the business houses alienated, the poor also felt cheated. This perhaps explains why 'the state-led economic growth or political efforts at redistributions and poverty alleviation' did not succeed to the extent it was possible in Korea where the state pushed (rather ruthlessly) capitalist growth, or in China where the state directed radical poverty alleviation.[30]

With the consolidation of globalization, it is true that there is no alternative to economic reforms. It is also true that without a proper political backing, economic reforms are just mere devices without much substance. In India, the same political leadership that had been the guardian of the old order emerged as the champion of the new. Is this 'a genuine change or [mere] electoral window dressing', Desai asks.[31] Given the present dispensation of power in India, the future of economic reform does not appear to be as bright as in South East Asian countries or China. One of the primary conditions for a sustained reform package is a government which is ideologically compatible with an adequate numerical strength in the legislature. As of now, political system does not appear to be stable due to too frequent elections and is thus not equipped to pursue economic reforms in a sustained manner. 'An unreformed political system is', Desai laments, 'an obstacle to fundamental and irreversible economic reform'.[32]There is no magical way. What is required is a change of attitude because 'it is quite clear that India must liberalize' for sustained economic growth. Indian resistance to liberalization, as Desai argues, comes from the elite interests and not from the poor. At the forefront are the organized sector industrialists who benefited from the policy of protection and are now scared of competition. The state has a crucial role to play in the changed circumstances. What must be junked is 'state ownership [of non-profit and non-viable enterprises] as it has proven to be wasteful and growth-retarding'.[33] Still, 'reform is a contentious issue [and] India, [as of now], is not an enthusiastic reformer'. Yet, there is no doubt that reform is a sure contribution to economic growth, as the examples from South East Asia demonstrate. For India, clinging to liberalization is 'a resumption of history [because] India as a trading and manu-facturing nation [was] able to compete on a world scale [in] cotton textile in the days before independence'.[34]

Changing economic horizon

The introduction of macroeconomic reforms in 1991 was a serious challenge to the state-led developmental plans and programmes. Given the clear failure of the Nehruvian socialistic pattern of society that was espoused so zealously by the political leadership immediately after the 1947 independence of India, the 1991 New Economic Policy did not appear to have raised many eyebrows. Nonetheless, the principles governing the socialistic pattern of society cannot be said to have completely disappeared; instead, the Indian state seems to have adopted a context-specific strategy in which state intervention is appreciated so long as a meaningful alternative remains unavailable. Furthermore, one cannot simply gloss over larger 'political-philosophical issues' involved here. The argument that the march of the market economy has been resisted by Indian elites' infatuation for socialistic principles does not appear persuasive in the light of the visible mass opposition to economic liberalization. As Pranab Bardhan argues, 'our collective passion for group equity, for group rather than individual rights and the deep suspicion of com-petition in which the larger economic interests are given an opportunity to gobble up the small, work against the forces of market and allocational efficiency'.[35] This passion was particularly strengthened by Gandhi who gave 'sensitive and elo-quent expression to this anti-market, anti-big capital, small-is-beautiful populism' while mobilizing masses against the British for freedom. Economic reforms have created conditions in which those persuaded by the Gandhian moral critique of market expansion and competition are even drawn to the Left-radical forces for building active grass-roots movements all over the country for the protection of the environment, of women's rights and of the traditional livelihood of the indigenous people. In such circumstances, development or market seems to be synonymous with 'dispossession of the little people and with despoliation of the environment'. Major strands in the political culture thus, as Bardhan rightly concludes, 'provide a non-too-hospitable climate for market reforms'.[36] This appears to be 'inevitable' given the growing feeling of the majority of the Indian populace that the aim of the market-driven economic reforms is to consolidate the technology-based-expo rt-oriented –city-centric economy at the cost of agriculture which is the mainstay of the Indian economy. People do not judge economic liberalization in terms of what it does for growth or efficiency. The real litmus test is whether it improves their living conditions.

Economic reforms and Special Economic Zones (SEZ)

The introduction of market-driven economic reforms in 1991 in India perhaps due to the fiscal crisis that Indians failed to overcome without financial support from the World Bank and IMF had hardly brought benefits to the marginalized. Instead, the creation of Special Economic Zones (SEZ) out of prime agricultural land in various part of India for industrial purposes renders land-dependent population jobless and homeless. As a Maoist document underlines the adverse human consequence of SEZ by stating

> today the reactionary ruling classes of the country are bent upon transforming vast tracts of fertile agricultural land into neo-colonial enclaves if it means enacting blood-baths all over the country. Thousands of *crores* (ten million) of rupees have already flown from big business and imperialists Multi National Corporations into the coffers of the ruling class in India. It is clear that the battle-lines are drawn for an uncompromising war between the haves and have-nots between those who want to turn our mother land into a heaven for the international capital, the Indian big business and the handful filthy rich on the one hand and the vast majority of the destitute, poverty-stricken masses, particularly the peasantry, on the other. There is no middle ground: either one is with the vast masses or with the filthy rich. Two hundred and thirty seven SEZs have already been approved and lakhs of acres of fertile agricultural land are being forcibly acquired by the various state and central governments. In Orissa, Jharkhand, Chhattisgarh, Andhra Pradesh, Maharashtra, Haryana and several other states, lakhs of the people are rendered homeless due to anti-people projects. The CPI (Maoist) calls upon the oppressed masses, particularly the peasantry, to transform every SEZ into a battle zone, to kick out the real outsiders – the rapacious MNCs, compradror big business houses, their (boot lickers) and the land mafia – who are snatching away their lands and all means of livelihood and colonizing the country.[37]

As a result, the state that zealously pursued the path of reforms seems to have lost its credibility to those involved in 'everyday struggle' for survival.

Historical continuity

Maoism in India is an articulation of 'the ultra left wing ideology' in the context of globalization. This is a movement drawn on the genuine socio-economic grievances of the marginalized sections of Indian society, including the tribals. While the earlier movements were largely confined to specific geographic areas, Maoism is perhaps the one that is expanding gradually to the country as a whole. That this movement is organically linked with the reality is also indicative of socio-economic circumstances in which a majority of India's population lives. Despite various legislations for land reforms, the progress is not worthwhile. There are some states where adoption of land reforms has radically altered the agrarian system and thus ameliorated the conditions of the marginalized. However, the story of land reforms is not uniform. It is not therefore surprising that Maoism is a significant force in those Indian states where measures for land reforms remain half-hearted and are never pursued seriously. That the movement is gradually expanding in new areas also suggests that Maoism is informed by an ideology seeking to enable 'the wretched of the earth' to fulfil 'an espoused dream' of dignified survival as human beings.

The geographic expanse

The red corridor is not an academic expression. This is an empirical reality linking a significant part of the subcontinent. Although the Nepali Maoists have abdicated the path of violent revolution by joining the government, it will not be wrong to suggest that the red corridor represents a vast land mass stretching from Pashupati in Nepal to Tirupati in Tamil Nadu. A perusal at the spread of the movement clearly shows that the red belt runs through a compact geographical zone involving 13 Indian states including Uttar Pradesh, Bihar, West Bengal, Jharkhand, Orissa, Madhya Pradesh, Chhattisgarh, Andhra Pradesh, Maharashtra, Karnataka and Tamil Nadu. Of these states, Andhra Pradesh and West Bengal are perhaps the only two Indian provinces where the ultra-Left extremism had flourished in the 1960s in the name of the Naxalbari movement. The fact that ultra-Left ideologies have now become significant in mass mobilization in states other than West Bengal and Andhra Pradesh clearly suggests the ideological depth of Maoism, which is, besides being inspired by Mao's national democracy, also a contextual articulation of 'the lived experience' of 'the wretched of the earth'. Furthermore, one can also identify a pattern if one is drawn to those locations where the movements appear to be well-entrenched. As evident, Maoism is a strong ideological current in areas bordering two or more provinces in the red belt. For instance, Maoism in Orissa is a significant influence in Koraput,[1]Malkangiri, Gajapati and Ganjam districts on the border of Andhra Pradesh and Mayurbhanj, Sundargarh, Sambalpur, Deogarh and Keonjhar districts on the Jharkhand border.[38] And mostly, these areas have dense forests or difficult hilly terrain where mere survival is most difficult given the appalling poverty in which people live there. These areas traditionally remained beyond the reach of 'any development projects, social welfare schemes and agencies of administration'. The hilly and forest belt, as well as the plains, which are marked by 'extremely distressing socio-economic conditions' seemed to have favoured the Maoists 'with a secure and popular base'.[39] So far, 13 of the Indian states have been adversely affected (see Table 1.1). The Maoist movement is perhaps most intense (and also most organized) in part of Chhattisgarh, Jharkhand, Andhra Pradesh, Orissa, West Bengal, Madhya Pradesh and Maharashtra. One of the basic reasons that caused significant mass discontent is certainly 'unfinished agrarian reforms and lack of basic amenities of human existence'. Maoism seems to have struck an emotional chord with the tribals drawing on forest resources for their survival. Besides this, there are certain specific factors that appear to have brought the tribals and other affected people closer to Maoism as perhaps the only

Table 1.1 Indian states affected by Maoism

States	Numbers of districts affected
Bihar	25
Jharkhand	20
Andhra Pradesh	19
Orissa	14
Chhattisgarh	10
West Bengal	9
Madhya Pradesh	6
Maharashtra	6
Uttar Pradesh	6
Karnataka	5
Kerala	2
Uttarakhand	2
Tamil Nadu	1

Source: *The Times of India,* 22 September 2007.

way to get rid of exploitation. What led to mass discontent were massive transfer of forest and agricultural land for developing industry, machine-dependent mining and infrastructural facility for agribusiness. By resorting to violence, the executive forces, especially police and paramilitary forces, alienated the inhabitants in the forest land and emerged as 'their principal enemy'. As a result, the *sarkar* (government) became 'an exploiter' in the form of 'forest officials' who denied their entry to the forests, the police who demanded bribes and state-sponsored contractors who paid less than the minimum wage.

Ramification of ultra-left wing extremism

Broadly speaking, the political outfits clinging to ultra-left wing extremism seem to be ideologically compatible though they differ from one another in terms of 'the tactical line' or the methodology of revolution. Of these outfits, CPI (Maoist) seems to have gained prominence presumably because of its growing popularity in the red corridor. Formed on 16 September 2004 out of a merger of Andhra Pradesh-based People's War Group (PWG) and the Maoist Communist Centre (MCC) of Bihar, CPI (Maoist) succeeded in releasing their colleagues from jails in Orissa and Bihar in 2006. Besides the two successive jailbreaks, the Maoists drew national attention by launching successful attacks on the government-sponsored resistance campaign – Salwa Judum, which is a paramilitary force seeking to combat violence by violence although it emerged primarily as a peace mission seeking to bring back 'the disillusioned youth' to the mainstream.[40] The revealing account of Salwa Judum and its activities in the affected district of Chhattisgarh is available in a report prepared by a group of prominent civil and human rights activists.[41] The creation of Salwa Judum, rather than containing 'the Red Menace' will further aggravate the situation at the grass roots. A security personnel involved in 'combative exercises' in the affected districts expressed his apprehension by saying that 'Salwa Judum is a double-edged sword [because] instead of gunning for the Naxalites [it] has created another group and making them professional, licensed goondas'.[42]

Ideology and its articulation

Maoists drew sustenance from the prevalent inequities. As a district officer noted, 'this problem of Naxalbari is not just a law and order problem, but also a social and economic problem'. He further added, 'if I look at it from an administrator's perspective then along with law and order we have to bring total development and progress to this region'.[43] Besides the well-entrenched feudal land relations, displacement of the tribals from their natural habitat is also another factor that has hardly received attention from the political authority. In other words, the failure to address genuine socio-economic grievances in the affected areas seems to have created a space for Maoism to strike roots. Given the massive transfer of forest and agricultural land for developing industry, machine-dependent mining and infrastructure facilities for agribusiness, it is but natural for Maoists to emerge as saviours for their commitment to fight against the socio-economic imbalances, artificially created to benefit one class against another. For the *adivasis* (tribals), the *sarkar* (government) thus becomes one of the agents of exploitation in these areas that always colludes with local-vested interests. The failure of the state to provide the bare minimum necessities for survival confirms this image that has played a critical role in tribal-mobilization for the Maoist political goal. Local tribal people who constitute a majority in most of the affected districts appear to have been alienated from the state to a significant extent, as the District Collector submits by saying that 'law and order and police will take care of exactly 50% of the problem … If we use police strength to suppress them, shake them, force them to run, or kill them, we can only solve 50% of the problem. *You cannot solve this problem as long as the public is not with you*' (emphasis added).[44]

There is no doubt that Maoism draws on a version of Marxism-Leninism that Mao Tse-tung evolved while leading China for new democracy. The aim and programme of the Maoist Party is

> to carry on and complete the already ongoing and advancing New Democratic Revolution in India as a part of the world proletarian revolution by overthrowing the semi-colonial, semi-feudal system under the neo-colonial form of indirect rule, exploitation and control. The revolt will be carried out and completed through armed agrarian revolutionary war, protracted people's war with the armed seizure of power remaining as its central principal task, encircling the cities from the countryside and thereby finally capture them. Hence the

countryside as well as the Protracted People's War will remain as 'centre of gravity' of the party's work while urban work will be complementary to it.[45]

Accordingly, Maoism holds that India is a semi-feudal and neocolonial country and its semi-feudal social character serves as a base for imperialism of a virulent variety in the context of a globalizing world facilitating exploitation by a class of big comprador-bureaucrat capitalists acting on behalf of the global capital. The basic task of the revolution is, therefore, to eliminate feudalism, comprador-bureaucratic capitalism and imperialism. The major contradiction in India is between feudalism and the toiling masses. This determines the present stage of national democratic revolution in which the apparently antagonistic classes will form a unit to liquidate feudalism and bureaucratic capitalism. Seeking to build new democracy, Maoism emphasizes 'meaningful land reforms, coupled with large investments in agriculture to regenerate the soil destroyed by the green revolution and also protection of forests'.[46] Although drawn on Marxism-Leninism, Maoism has also sought to adapt itself to the peculiar Indian social reality by seeking to fight against social oppression, especially untouchability, casteism and gender discrimination.

The government responses

For the government, ultra-left wing extremism is reduced to 'a law and order' problem ignoring its socio-economic dimension. As a result, the government resorted to what is known as 'the police approach' to combat a growing movement that gradually became a security threat to the Indian state. The barrel of the gun does not appear to solve the problem. 'Police and other security forces are', argued a police chief, 'just fire fighters. There is fire, throw some water on it. The flames will die down a bit. But tomorrow the fire will burn again'.[47] What is critical, therefore, is to avoid the application of coercion to eradicate 'the Red Menace', but to take care of the developmental needs of the people who are presumably drawn to Maoism as a last resort to survive amidst crisis. Recently, there has been a change in the governmental attitude, as Prime Minister Dr Manmohan Singh has outlined. By making a distinction between the hard-core revolutionary who needs to be dealt with severely and foot-soldier who can be weaned-off from the path of violence through socio-economic packages, Dr Singh has suggested a significant shift in policies dealing with ultra-left wing extremism. Central to his statement is the idea that the so-called red menace is more a socio-economic problem and less a problem of law and order. 'Our strategy, therefore, argued the prime minister, 'has to be to walk on two legs – to have an effective police response while focusing on reducing the sense of deprivation'. Critical of state-sponsored coercion, he felt the need for compassion while devising means 'to combat Naxalism' because 'we are dealing, after all with our own people, even though they may have strayed into the path of violence'.[48] This is a significant statement which led to radical changes in government policies towards Maoism. It is true that the path of violence can never solve the problems of the poor; what is thus needed is 'good governance', which includes effective implementation of development programmes, periodic monitoring and ensuring that there no pilferages of government funds. This was articulated in a document, produced by the Home Ministry by saying that 'there is a consensus that this is not primarily a security problem but has roots in the feeling of oppression and desperation fuelled by poverty and lack of development'. Hence, the government is required to adopt 'a methodology for more focused action for effective implementation of development schemes in states/districts affected by Naxal problem'.[49] This is what led to the constitution of an anti-Naxal cell in the union ministry of Home Affairs and also Inter-ministerial Committee, headed by a senior minister of the union government in Delhi. While the latter will monitor the implementation of the developmental packages meant for the affected areas, the former will be responsible for devising policies and steps to address the issue by means other than violence as well. Following the governmental commitment in May 2006, the Planning Commission of India appointed an expert committee to asses the growing 'Red Menace'.[50]

For the first time in the history of the Naxalite movement a government-appointed committee has put the blame on the state for the growth of the movement. Providing statistics of 125 districts from the Naxal-hit states, the committee has found out that the state bureaucracy has pitiably failed in delivering good governance in these areas. The committee has also severely criticized the states for their double standard in making Pachayats truly the units of local self governance. Recognizing the Naxalite movement as a political movement, the Planning Commission-appointed committee has ascribed its growth to people's discontent and complete failure of the system. Findings of the report recommend rigorous training for the police force not only on humane tactics of controlling rural violence but also on the constitutional obligation of the state for the protection of fundamental rights. Coming down heavily on the civil war instrument of Salwa Judum, the committee asked for its immediate suspension. Making a departure from the usual government position, the Expert Committee concludes that the development paradigm pursued since independence has aggravated the prevailing discontent among marginalized sections of society. Citing democratic principles the report also argues for right to protest and finds that unrest is often the only thing that actually puts pressure on the government to make things work and for the government to live up to its own promises. Nonetheless, there has hardly been a noticeable change in the government response to 'the Red Ultras', as the proceedings of the 2009 chief ministers' conference show. Defending the argument for Salwa Judum, the union government endorsed the idea by underlining that 'there was no harm in the village community taking defensive action against the Naxals in the affected districts'.[51] The idea of 'strong joint operation' against them was also appreciated by the chief ministers. Nevertheless, it was also felt that 'mere coercive operations' did not seem to be adequate with meaningful steps 'to eradicate poverty' in these areas. Hence, it was also agreed that 'the battle against Naxalism must be fought on twin fronts of security as well as development'.[52] Among the priorities was the employment generation for the local youth in the violence-affected districts and construction of roads for regular supply of basic necessities in the remote areas.

The state has therefore devised a two-prong strategy on those pursuing ultra-left wing radicalism: on the one hand, given its genuine socio-economic roots, several programmes have already been adopted to ameliorate the conditions of the poor in the affected states of India; on the other hand, the Indian state has also devoted a great deal of attention to improve its combative capacity by developing 'special forces' on the lines of the greyhounds of Andhra Pradesh. This force will be created in six Maoist-hit states – West Bengal, Chhatisgarh, Jharkhand, Madhya Pradesh, Bihar and Maharashtra, as the latest government report suggests. According to this report, Chhatisgarh has already begun the process of 'raising a 13,000 strong crack commando forces to tackle left wing violence'. The existing Chhatisgarh Armed Forces that was converted into the Chhatisgarh Commando Battalion will, the report furthermore confirms, 'confront Maoist menace in rural and forested areas in the state'.[53] Besides this formal outfit, the state government of Chhatisgarh was reported to have formulated a plan to strengthen the non-official vigilante group Salwa Judum by recruiting 'young and active boys who will be trained by experts imparting training to commandos of National Security Guard and personnel of Border Security Force and Indo-Tibetan Border Police'.[54] This has created a piquant situation especially in the light of the recent supreme court order (2009) that clearly restrained the state from arming the members of the Salwa Judum, which is a civil vigilante agency. In its order, the supreme court, despite having shared the concern of the state, did not find it appropriate 'to arm the common man to fight the Naxalites'. Asking the state to withdraw such a programme as 'arming common men will create a dangerous situation', the apex court further insists that the state should concentrate more on 'economic development' in the area by creating 'employment opportunities in the naxal areas under the National Rural Employment Guarantee Act, besides providing adequate infrastructure and education facilities'.[55] What is revealing in the 2009 supreme court order is the fact that Maoism is not merely a law and order problem, but an outcome of India's development trajectory, pursued under the state-led development programmes. While being critical of the government design of arming Salwa Judum, the supreme court therefore felt that given the stark poverty of the poor at the grass roots what is required are the developmental plans and programmes to address their genuine socio-economic grievances.

Orissa as a case study

Orissa, a state in the eastern part of India, bordering West Bengal, Bihar and Andhra Pradesh, is perhaps one of those states where Maoism seems to have struck an emotional chord with those particularly in forest lands and also inaccessible hilly terrain. The reasons are not difficult to seek. On the basis of a spot survey,[56] it is evident that most of those who are staunch Maoists seem to have been drawn to Maoism as perhaps the only alternative for survival against all odds. In a situation when even a one full meal a day remains a distant goal for most of these tribals, the ideological appeal of Maoism seems to have acted favourably. Maoism seems to have gained acceptability among the tribal youth in Orissa due to severe poverty and also the failure of the government to provide bare minimum necessity to those living 'in inaccessible hilly terrain'. The Planning Commission of India has recently identified Orissa as having the highest poverty ratio of any major Indian state, with around 48 per cent (17 million) of its population living below poverty line as against a national figure of 26 per cent. This state is also one of those areas with high infant mortality rates due to lack of bare minimum medical facilities. The health care is in terrible shape as the state has the rare distinction of having the lowest number of doctors in the world. Even though the state is poverty-stricken, surprisingly less than 5 per cent of the population has access to subsidized food aimed at poverty alleviation.[57]

Concluding observations

The red corridor is a reality and Maoism is critical to its meaningful existence simply because of significant socio-cultural differences among the affected states within an area stretching from Nepal to Tamil Nadu. The red corridor is a sharp comment on the processes of development that has been pursued in these areas by the government and its agents disregarding completely the socio-economic require-ments of 'the peripheral' sections of society. As a result, governance is largely articulated in terms of 'the maintenance of law and order'.

Although Maoism has raised critical socio-economic issues, it is still perhaps in its embryonic state for a variety of reasons. First, Maoism is, in its present form, a politically-contrived approach to genuine socio-economic grievances which is, inter alia, limiting its ideological appeal given the lack of serious attention on the economic agenda. Second, the rise and consolidation of various factions seem to be crippling the movement. Despite waging the 'people's struggle', the dissent-ers raise issues relating to the authoritarian functioning of the organization. Even the role of *Jan Adalat* (people's court) has caused dissension among the ranks for indulging in 'kangaroo justice' meted out to the dissenters from within, suspected police informers and to those refusing to accept their instructions. Finally, Maoists are not free from charges of corruption. There are reports that Maoists regularly receive kickbacks from the contractors involved in projects for infrastructural development in the affected Indian provinces.[58] Other sources of fund-raising include the operation of illegal mines, sale of tendu leaves and the illegal sale of various forest products and narcotics. There are also evidences to suggest that the Maoists control the production of opium in the Malkangiri districts in almost 100 acres of land with the help of local cultivators. The produce (worth 60 million rupees) is supplied to neighbouring states such as Chhattisgarh, Andhra Pradesh, Bihar and Madhya Pradesh every year. Furthermore, as the police source confirms, more than 100 quintals of ganja (marijuana) are produced in Malkangiri. In fact, ganja is cultivated throughout the year in areas controlled by the Maoists. The consignment is smuggled out of the district by 'tribal conduits' to markets across state borders via the jungle routs.[59] As the data show, the source of funding for the movement may not have pleased the dedicated cadres and not only has this alien-ated a significant section of 'genuine workers', it has also caused a serious dent in its support base. Furthermore, the Maoist threat and attack on government officials and contractors has also led to the withdrawal of a large number of developmental projects from these districts. These are primarily tribal-dominated areas and the presence of the armed cadres and the police has created 'a fear psychosis' among the local inhabitants. Government officials also remain withdrawn for fear. The result is that there is 'little signs of governance and whenever governance fails, Maoists step in'.[60]

Nonetheless, Maoism is neither a ripple nor a mere law and order problem; instead, it is a well-thought out diagnosis of India's socio-economic ills that cannot be put under the carpet for obvious reasons. By raising critical developmental issues involving people, Maoism has also provoked a serious debate on the state-led and planning-driven model of development. The red corridor is thus not an academic expression, but is a significant conceptualization of a reality that so far remains 'peripheral' for all practical purposes.

In the context of 'a million mutinies',[61] Maoism is a refreshing theoretical input in two complementary senses: first, by raising doubts on the state-led development paradigm and also state-led globalization in a transitional socio-economic milieu, like India, the Maoists have sought to articulate an alternative [sic], meaningful to the poverty-stricken masses regardless of caste, class and creed; second, the growing popularity of Maoism is also indicative of 'the disenchantment' of those drawn to Maoism within the Indian state, which is constitutionally 'liberal' but functionally partisan for a variety of historical reasons. Maoism is thus reflective of an all-pervasive 'social revolution' through a process of 'deepening of democracy' that India is experiencing in recent times. What distinguishes Maoism from other forms of social revolution, however, is its serious endeavour in mobilizing socio-economically peripheral sections of society ultimately for 'the seizure of political power'.

Notes

1 For details, see Ashutosh Varshney, 'India's Democratic Challenge', *Foreign Affairs*, vol. 86 (2), March/April, 2007, 93–106.
2 Francine R. Frankel, *India's Political Economy, 1947–2004*, Oxford University Press, 2005, 625.
3 Francine R. Frankel, *India's Political Economy, 1947–2004*, Oxford University Press, 2005, 625.
4 Aseema Sinha, 'The Changing Political Economy of Federalism in India: A Historical Institutional Approach', *India Review*, vol. 3 (1), January 2004, 51.
5 Aseema Sinha, 'The Changing Political Economy of Federalism in India: A Historical Institutional Approach', *India Review*, vol. 3 (1), January 2004, 55.
6 Articles 38 and 39 spell out the sentiments. Article 46 underlines the concern for the weaker sections, including scheduled castes and scheduled tribes.
7 Bengamin Zachariah, *Developing India: An Intellectual and Social History*, New Delhi: Oxford University Press, 2005, 235. In making this argument Zachariah draws on Stephen Howe's *Anti-Colonialism in British politics: The Left and the End of Empire, 1918–1954*, Oxford: Clarendon Press, 1993. According to Howe, many of the strands of anti-colonial policies in Britain originated in romantic identification with downtrodden peoples rather than in critiques of imperialism and capitalism.
8 Suresh D. Tendulkar and T.A. Bhavani, *Understanding Reforms: Post 1991 India*, New Delhi: Oxford University Press, 2007, 18–19.

9 Gunnar Myrdal, *Asian Drama: An Inquiry Into the Poverty of Nations*, vol. 2, New York: Pantheon, 1968, 709–10.
10 Francine R. Frankel, *India's Political Economy, 1947–2004*, Oxford University Press, 2005, 85.
11 Suresh D. Tendulkar and T.A. Bhavani, *Understanding Reforms: Post 1991 India*, New Delhi: Oxford University Press, 2007, 24.
12 Partha Chatterjee, 'Development Planning and the Indian state' in Partha Chatterjee (ed.), *State and Politics in India*, New Delhi: Oxford University Press, 1997, 271, 279.
13 Aseema Sinha, *The Regional Roots of Developmental Politics in India: A Divided Leviathan*, Bloomington and Indianapolis: Indiana University Press, 2005, 277.
14 *Hindustan Standard*, 27 September 1934.
15 I have dwelled on this aspect of the freedom struggle in my 'Jawaharlal Nehru and Planning, 1938–41: India at the Crossroads', *Modern Asian Studies*, vol. 26 (2), 1992, 275–87.
16 Jawaharlal Nerhu on planning (a press release), *Hindustan Times*, 17 August 1963.
17 Gunnar Myrdal, *Asian Drama: An Inquiry into the Poverty of Nations*, vol. 2, New York: Pantheon, 1968, 739.
18 Gunnar Myrdal, *Asian Drama: An Inquiry into the Poverty of Nations*, vol. 2, New York: Pantheon, 1968, 739.
19 Sukhamoy Chakravarty, *Development Planning: The Indian Experience*, Oxford: Clarendon Press, 1987, 89.
20 Sukhamoy Chakravarty, *Development Planning: The Indian Experience*, Oxford: Clarendon Press, 1987, 39–40.
21 According to Sukhamoy Chakravarty, India's development prospects 'cannot be ensured merely by technocratically inclined civil servants. While technocrats can obviously suggest more efficient means for pre-designed goals, the problem of goal-setting is inherently a socio-historical process. Societies which have grown fast during the recent period have done so not because the sum total of problem solving effort has been vastly greater in any measurable sense, but because they could succeed in evolving a broad consensus on priorities'. Sukhamoy Chakravarty, *Development Planning: The Indian Experience*, Oxford: Clarendon Press, 1987, 89.
22 Meghnad Desai, *Development and Nationhood: Essays in the Political Economy of South Asia*, New Delhi: Oxford University Press, 2005, 121.
23 Ibid., 139.
24 Ibid., 137.
25 Ibid., 157.
26 Jagdish N. Bhagwati, 'Indian Economic Policy and Performance: A Framework for a Progressive Society' in his *Essays in Development Economics*, Cambridge: MIT Press, 1985, quoted in Ramchandra Guha, *India after Gandhi: The History of the World's Largest Democracy*, London: Picador, 2007, 469.
27 Meghnad Desai, *Development and Nationhood: Essays in the Political Economy of South Asia*, New Delhi: Oxford University Press, 2005, 158.
28 Atul Kohli, *State-Directed Development: Global Power and Industrialization in the Global Periphery*, Cambridge: Cambridge University Press, 2005, 258.
29 Pranab Bardhan provides a graphic illustration of the performance of the public sector in the first three decades of India's independence in *The Political Economy of Development*, New Delhi: Oxford University Press, 2008 (reprint), 63–64.
30 Atul Kohli, *State-Directed Development: Global Power and Industrialization in the Global Periphery*, Cambridge: Cambridge University Press, 2005, 279.
31 Meghnad Desai, *Development and Nationhood: Essays in the Political Economy of South Asia*, New Delhi: Oxford University Press, 2005, 161
32 Ibid., 175.
33 Ibid., 189.
34 Ibid., 196.

35 Pranab Bardhan, *The Political Economy of Development in India*, New Delhi: Oxford University Press, 2008, 136.
36 Ibid., 137.
37 Rob Jenkins, *Democratic Politics and Economic Reform in India*, Cambridge: Cambridge University Press, 1999, 172–207. Since economic reforms were not 'strategy-based' but 'crisis-driven' India hardly had a choice and was thus more or less forced to accept 'the conditionalities' imposed by the donor agencies.
38 Suresh D. Tendulkar and T.A. Bhavani, *Understanding Reforms: Post 1991 India*, New Delhi: Oxford University Press, 2007, 85.
39 Aseema Sinha, 'The Changing Political Economy of Federalism in India: A Historical Institutional Approach', *India Review*, vol. 3 (1), January 2004, 51.
40 Ibid., 55.
41 Francine R. Frankel, *India's Political Economy, 1947–2004*, Oxford University Press, 2005, 625.
42 Ibid.
43 Mihir Shah, 'Governance Reform Key to NREGA (National Rural Employment Guarnatee Act) Success', *The Hindu*, 14 March 2008.
44 Joseph Stiglitz, *Making Globalization Work: The Next steps to Global Justice*, London: Allen Lane, 2006, 292. This argument was forcefully made by Margit Bussmann in 'When Globalization Discontent Turns Violent: Foreign Economic Liberalization and Internal War', *International Studies Quarterly*, vol. 51 (1), March 2007, 79–97.
45 Amit Bhaduri and Deepak Nayyar, *The Intelligent Person's Guide to Liberalization*, New Delhi: Penguin, 1996, 159.
46 Statement of the Communist Party of India (Maoist), Central Committee, 16 March 2007 (available from a participant in Orissa).
47 This appears to be a pattern. The two districts in West Bengal – Purulia and Midnapur – where Maoism holds considerable influence are also those districts that are on the border of Jharkhand.
48 Sumanta Banerjee, 'Beyond Naxalbari', *Economic and Political Weekly*, 22 July 2006.
49 Since Salwa Judum was a peace mission, villagers asking for a gun or a licence for firearms for self-protection against Maoist attack were denied because (a) if licenced guns are provided these can be looted by Naxalites or the licencee could be killed to get his gun and (b) an armed person can later join the Naxalites organization, which will enhance the strength of the Naxalites. Sudeep Chakravarti, *Red Sun: Travels in Naxalite Country*, New Delhi: Penguin, 2008, 49.
50 'Fact-Finding report on the Salwa Judum, Dantewara District', All-India team, People's Union for Civil Liberties (PUCL), Chhattisgarh and PUCL, Jharkhand, People's Union for Democratic Rights (PUDR), Delhi, Association for Democratic Rights (APDR), West Bengal and Indian Association for the Protection of Democratic Rights (IAPL), November 2005. The report was released to the press on 2 December 2005, http://www.pucl.org/Topics/Human-rights/2005/salwa-judum-report.htm.
51 Quoted in Sudeep Chakravarti, *Red Sun: Travels in Naxalite Country*, New Delhi: Penguin, 2008, 173.
52 K.R. Pisda, the district collector of Dantewada (Chhattisgarh) was quoted in Sudeep Chakravarti, *Red Sun: Travels in Naxalite Country*, New Delhi: Penguin, 2008, 42.
53 Ibid., 43.
54 Locally available proscribed documents outlining the programme and ideological aims of Maoists.
55 Azad, 'Maoists in India: A rejoinder', *Economic and Political Weekly*, 14 October 2006, 4380.
56 Quoted in Sudeep Chakravarti, *Red Sun: Travels in Naxalite Country*, New Delhi: Penguin, 2008, 174.

57 The prime minister's statement quoted in Sudeep Chakravarti, *Red Sun: Travels in Naxalite Country*, New Delhi: Penguin, 2008, 173.
58 Quoted from 'Road to End Naxal Menace?', *The Times of India*, 22 September 2007. Even the government admits that the Naxal problem has now affected 125 districts (over 20% of total 604) of 13 states expanding from just 55 five years ago. As Table 1.1 demonstrates (see p. 28).
59 Headed by D. Bandopadhyay, a retired IAS officer who played a key role in dealing with Naxalites in West Bengal in the 1970s. The other members of the expert committee are Prakash Singh, former UP DGP and an expert on Naxal issues; Ajit Doval, former director of Intelligence Bureau; B.D. Sharma, retired bureaucrat and activist; Sukhdeo Thorat, University Grants Commission chairman and K. Balagopal, human rights lawyer. The committee was specifically asked to study development issues to deal with the causes of discontent, unrest and extremism. The committee submitted its report in June 2008, which is now available on the Planning Commission's website.
60 Home Minister's statement in *The Times of India*, 9 January 2009.
61 Proceedings of the meeting, as reported in *The Hindu*, 8 January 2009.
62 The government report, quoted in *The Times of India*, 7 February 2009.
63 Ibid.
64 The order of the Supreme Court of India, quoted in *The Hindu*, 6 February 2009.
65 Dr Kujur made an in-depth study of Maoism in Orissa on the basis of his field data, which is difficult to get otherwise.
66 Drawn on Rajat Kujur, 'Underdevelopment and Naxal Movement', *Economic and Political Weekly*, 18 February 2006.
67 As a contractor admits on anonymity, 'the Maoists do not allow to construct a bridge in Malkangiuri district to avoid police raids. They also charged 10% of the total project. The Maoists also sometimes ask the contractors to pay by kind'. Local interview, 18 December 2006.
68 Interview with local police officials on conditions of anonymity, 20 December 2006.
69 Interview with the police in Malkangiri on conditions of anonymity, 20 December 2006.
70 V.S. Naipaul, *India: A Million Mutinies Now*, New York: Penguin, 1992.

2   Genesis of Maoism in India

From a rebellion for land rights to a socio-political movement critiquing India's state-led development paradigm and finally to a serious threat for country's internal security, the Maoist movement has indeed come a long way. This Maoist journey has been the most unusual one as it travelled from an unknown village of Naxalbari in West Bengal to reach 509 police stations comprising 7,000 villages in 11 states, namely Andhra Pradesh, Chhattisgarh, Bihar, Jharkhand, Orissa, Maharashtra, Uttar Pradesh, Madhya Pradesh, West Bengal, Tamilnadu, Karnataka and Kerala.[1] The level of violence is significant in the affected districts of Andhra Pradesh, Chhattisgarh, Jharkhand, Bihar, Maharashtra and Orissa. There are reports that the Naxals are fast targeting some regions in Uttaranchal and Haryana. As per the 2006 data, today 40 per cent of the country's geographical area and 35 per cent of the country's total population is affected by the problem of Naxal violence. This is no simple mathematics, as it implies that the problem of Naxalism is more acute than the problems in Kashmir and the north-east.[2] During January and February 2007 the CPI (Maoist) conducted its Ninth Congress, signalling yet another phase in the cycle of Maoist insurgencies in India. For the Naxal leadership this came as a grand success since the Maoists were holding a unity congress after a gap of 36 years – their Eighth Congress was held in 1970. The Maoists claim that the Congress resolved the disputed political issues in the party through debates and discussions in which both the leaders and the led participated with mutual respect to one another.[3] This claim is politically significant in two ways: not only does this formally recognize the prevalence of inter/intra-organizational feuds among the ultra-radical outfits, it is also a persuasive testimony of the Maoist efforts to sort out differences through meaningful dialogues among themselves.

The data in Table 2.1 from the Union Home Ministry is not just a statement but an astounding revelation of a grave danger, the shadow of which looms over the whole system of India's democratic governance. It is not only the number of deaths but also the loss of country's physical territory that is something more worrisome. It leaves no room for romanticism. In no unclear terms it reveals that the Naxal threat is real.

What are the reasons that have kept this movement alive for a period of about four decades? Despite all the tall claims made by successive governments, people in the Naxal-affected regions continue to lead miserable lives. The metamorphic

Table 2.1 Fatalities from Naxal/Maoist violence, 2002–2007

	2002	*2003*	*2004*	*2005*	*2006*	*2007*
Number of incidents	1465	1597	1533	1608	1509	1565
Civilians killed	382	410	466	524	521	460
Policemen killed	100	105	100	153	157	236
Naxalites killed	141	216	87	225	272	141

Source: *Annual Report 2007–2008*, Ministry of Home Affairs, Government of India.

growth of violence and the inability of the State to come out with a well-thought out strategy have entirely paralyzed the rural administration in the Naxal-infested regions. The ill-represented national government, non-responsive state governments, failed institutions of local self-government and the establishment of *Naxal Janata Sarkar*[4] particularly in the Naxal-dominant regions have led to the formation of a vicious nexus between bureaucrats, politicians, contractors and Naxals, not to assist the downtrodden but to make Naxalism a lucrative business. On the other hand, throughout all these decades the Naxal movement has never been able to prepare a development formula for the people for whom it claims to have waged a war against the State. Also there is little hope if the Naxal rank and file would ever come closer to the level where policies are made, or programmes are implemented. The aim of this chapter is to acquaint the readers with the organizational evolution of Maoism in its contemporary articulation in India. Drawn on Marxism-Leninism and Mao's political ideas, Maoism is undoubtedly a continuity of the erstwhile Naxalbari movement. In fact, the similarity is obvious given the compatible ideological roots. This is probably the reason why Maoism is also identified as Naxalism in contemporary political discourses that also include the official characterization of the movement. Despite semantic differences in the nomenclature, Maoism and Naxalism seem to be ideologically identical. In contemporary literature, both these expressions are therefore interchangeably used to mean the ultra-left wing extremism in India that appears to be pervasive in the so-called 'red corridor'.

Roots of Maoism

In order to understand the current phase of Maoism we need to understand different aspects of organizational transformation that occurred within the Naxalite movement during the last decade or so because the movement is a reflection of continuity and change. That the nature of the movement differs from one district to another is suggestive of the extent to which the local socio-economic circumstances remain critical in its articulation. For instance, in the tribal districts of Orissa, Maoism consolidates its support by concentrating on tribal rights over forest products. In non-tribal districts, the movement draws on by challenging the feudal land relations. In other words, Maoism is adapted to the prevalent socio-economic issues while setting its agenda for 'the downtrodden'.

Despite having drawn ideological impetus from the same source, Maoists are highly fragmented and are prone to factional squabbles to settle personal scores among themselves. The fragmented character of the movement gave rise to all possible trends and groupings and thereby paving the way for new avenues of organizational conflict. Due to its fragmented character the movement witnessed many past leaders and cadres making a comeback as though from oblivion. This aspect of Naxal organizational politics is very important to understand as it also enabled the re-emergence of a whole range of questions that were supposed to have been already resolved once and for all.

A prelude to the growth of the Naxalite movement in India

To understand the genesis of the Naxalite movement one needs to locate it within the framework of the Communist movement in India. To be more specific, any study on the Naxalite movement cannot overlook the importance of the rise and fall of Telangana movement (1946–1951). For Indian Communists, peasant movement in Telangana would always remain the glorious chapter in the history of peasant struggles. It was 'a simple peasant movement against feudal oppression and Nizam's autocracy that had grown into a partisan struggle for liberation'.[5] In that sense, the Telangana movement was the first serious effort by sections of the Communist party leadership to learn from the experiences of the Chinese revolution and to develop a comprehensive line for India's democratic revolution. Despite the role of the committed activists, the movement remained confined to the districts of Warangal and Nalgonda where the communist leadership implemented the ideological programme. This limited success seemed to have 'convinced the CPI leadership that Telangana was soon going to be the pattern all over the Nizam's state and then for the rest of the country'.[6] That these signals were too deceptive to be taken seriously was evident when the movement was finally withdrawn in 1951, just two years after it began, for parliamentary politics in which CPI enthusiastically participated. Nonetheless, the Telangana experiment facilitated the growth of three distinct lines in the Indian Communist movement. First, the line promoted by Ranadive and his followers rejected the significance of the Chinese revolution, and advocated the simultaneous accomplishment of the democratic and the socialist revolutions based on city-based working class insurrections. The group drew inspiration from Stalin and fiercely attacked Mao as another Tito.

Second, the line mainly professed and propagated by the Andhra Secretariat which drew heavily from the Chinese experiences and the teachings of Mao in building up the struggle of Telangana. The Andhra leadership, successfully spearheaded the movement against the Nizam, however, it failed to tackle the complex question of meeting the challenge of the Government of India. The Nehru government embarked on the road to parliamentary democracy, conditioning it with reforms like the 'abolition of Zamindari system'. All these objective conditions facilitated the dominance of a centrist line put forward by Ajay Ghosh and Dange.

This line characteristically pointed out the differences between Chinese and Indian conditions and pushed the party along the parliamentary road, which articulated the third line in the Indian Communist movement. The third ideological line was translated in 1957 when the Communists succeeded in forming a government in Kerala, which, however, was soon overthrown and following the India-China war, the party split into two in 1964, namely the Communist Party of India and the Communist Party of India (Marxist). While the CPI preached the theory of 'peaceful road to non-capitalist development', the CPI (M) went ahead with the centrist line. Though there were serious differences in ideological and tactical lines both the parties went ahead with their parliamentary exercises and formed the United Front government in West Bengal.

Assessment of past movements

One can draw two conclusions on the basis of careful reading of the socio-political processes in which two left-radical movements of the past – Tebhaga (1946-1947) and Telangana (1946–1951) – were organized.[7] First, these movements were organized by political parties drawn on Marxism-Leninism and Maoism. It is true that these movements failed to attain the goal of radical agrarian reforms for a variety of reasons. Yet, by raising a powerful voice against feudal exploitation, they seemed to have begun a process of social churning that became critical for the future movements. Second, these movements had also articulated an alternative to the state-led development paradigm, which was hardly adequate to get rid of the well-entrenched feudalism. These movements were therefore watersheds in independent India's political history and also powerful statements on the failure of the state to redress peasant grievances due to reasons connected with the ideological priority of the ruling authority that replaced the colonial power following the 1947 transfer of power. Despite their failure, these movements had undoubtedly sensitized Indian society to the desperate efforts made by the rural poor to escape the intolerable conditions of economic oppression and social humiliation. There is also no doubt that the Naxalbari movement served as a catalyst in West Bengal, where it made its first appearance during the introduction of 'land reforms' when the state of West Bengal was under the rule of the left-led United Front government.

In the backdrop of political uncertainty of far-reaching consequences, one particular incident that took place in an unknown location involving some unknown people, hugely transformed the history of left-wing extremism in India. In a remote village called Naxalbari in West Bengal one tribal youth named Bimal Kissan, having obtained a judicial order, went to plough his land on 2 March 1967. The local landlords attacked him through their goons. Tribal people of the area retaliated and started forcefully capturing back their lands. What followed was a rebellion, which left one police sub-inspector and nine tribals dead. This particular incident acquired a larger appeal in about two months on the basis of the open support it garnered from cross sections of Communist revolutionaries belonging to the state units of the CPI (M) in West Bengal, Bihar, Orissa, Andhra Pradesh, Tamil Nadu, Kerala, Uttar Pradesh and Jammu and Kashmir. Though the United Front government of West Bengal, steered by the CPI and the CPI (M), with all repressive measures, was able to contain the rebellion within 72 days, these ultra-radical units finally regrouped in May 1968 and formed All India Coordination Committee of Communist Revolutionaries (AICCCR). 'Allegiance to the armed struggle and non-participation in the elections' were the two cardinal principles that the AICCR adopted for its operations. However, differences cropped up over how armed struggle should be advanced and this led to the exclusion of a section of activists from Andhra Pradesh and West Bengal, led respectively by T. Nagi Reddy and Kanai Chatterjee.

On the issue of annihilation of class enemy the Kanai Chatterjee group had serious objections as they were of the view that the annihilation of the class enemy should only be taken up after building up mass agitations. However majority in the AICCCR rejected this and went ahead with the formation of the Communist Party of India (Marxist-Leninist) in May 1969. This led Chatterjee to join the Maoist Communist Centre (MCC). The CPI (M-L) held its first congress in 1970 in Kolkata and Charu Mazumdar was formally elected its general secretary.

The Naxalbari movement (1969–1972): a review

The Naxalbari movement was a short-lived 'spring thunder' that helped reconceptualize political discourses in India. This was primarily an agrarian struggle against brutal feudal exploitation that led to a massive anti-state confrontation. Hailing the Naxalbari movement, the *People's Daily*, the mouthpiece of the Chinese Communist party, thus commented that 'a peal of spring thunder has crashed over the land of India. Revolutionary peasants in the Darjeeling area [in West Bengal] have risen in rebellion. Under the leadership of a revolutionary group of the Indian Communist Party, a red area of rural revolutionary armed struggle has been established in India. This is a development of tremendous significance for the Indian people's revolutionary struggle'.[8] Challenging the status-quoist state, the movement inspired a large section of Indian youth to undertake even 'armed struggle' for seizure of political power. When it was launched, the centre of gravity of the movement was rural West Bengal that later shifted to urban areas in various Indian states. In terms of its geographical expanse, the movement was not as widespread as its contemporary incarnation, namely Maoism. Nonetheless, there is no doubt that the Naxalbari movement provided the ideological impetus to Maoism that is a contemporary response to the prevalent socio-economic imbalances in the globalized India.

The Naxalbari movement was not 'suddenly created in 1967, nor did it fall from heaven by the grace of God, not was it a spontaneous outburst'.[9] It was the culmination of long drawn anti-feudal struggles in the Indian state of West Bengal that began with movements against 'illegal extortion' of *jotedars* (landlords). It was therefore argued in the *People's Daily* that the Naxalbari movement was 'an inevitability ... because the reactionary rule has left [the people] with no alternative'.[10] At the outset, this was an agrarian struggle that 'combined both institutional and non-institutional means of exercising power as the participants developed some kind of a disciplined peasant militia, comprised mainly by tribal Santal, Oraon and Munda communities, with traditional arms like bows and arrows'.[11] In course of time, the movement that was considered to be 'a prairie fire' lost its momentum for a variety of reasons: primary among them was the failure of the leadership to sustain 'the revolutionary enthusiasm' of the masses, as Kanu Sanyal, one of the top Naxal leaders, admitted by saying that

> [a]fter we went underground during 1967–68 and later during 1969–72, most of us lost touch with the reality of the situation on the ground; unfortunately we learnt much later that what was being dished out by our top leaders and others including the party organs were either distorted or highly exaggerated accounts which suited 'the high command's dictates' and in the process the revolutionary potential suffered incalculable damage.[12]

There are two important reasons for the gradual decline of the Naxalbari movement, as Sanyal underlines. First, what caused the breakdown of the movement was a tactical failure to build an ideology-driven organization of the exploited classes. Unable to form 'a revolutionary front of all revolutionary classes' comprising 'poor and landless peasants and also the workers', the CPI (M-L) leadership insisted on guerilla war for 'the seizure of power'. Emphasizing guerilla warfare waged by the peasantry 'as the only form of struggle in the present stage of revolution', the party ignored 'the need for mass organizations or for an agrarian programme as a concomitant of peasant struggle'. Holding Charu Majumdar, the main ideologue of the party, responsible for such a futile tactical line, Sanyal further argues that not only did Majumdar reject 'the ideas of a mass organization', he also advocated 'the building of a secret organization through which the poor and landless peasants can establish their leadership of the peasant movement'.[13] Despite strong opposition by his colleagues, Majumdar was hardly persuaded because in his opinion revolution was possible only 'by organizing guerilla war by poor and landless peasants ... Guerilla war is the only tactic of the peasants' revolutionary struggle [that] cannot be achieved by any mass organization through open struggle'.[14] The second tactical line that caused irreparable damage to the movement was 'the battle of annihilation' as Majumdar characterized. Appreciating the battle of annihilation as 'both a higher form of class struggle and the starting point of guerilla war', Majumdar supported the annihilation campaign even to the extent of alienating his colleagues by arguing that

> [o]nly by waging class struggle – the battle of annihilation – the new man will be created, the new man who will defy death and will be free from all thought of self-interests. And with this death-defying spirit he will go close to the enemy, snatch his rifle, avenge the martyrs and the people's army will emerge. To go close to the enemy, it is necessary to conquer all thought of self. And this can be achieved only by the blood of martyrs. That inspires and creates new men out of the fighters, fills them with class hatred and makes them close to the enemy [to] snatch his rifle with bare hands.[15]

The annihilation line caused consternation among the leaders and also the rank and file of the movement. Characterizing the annihilation line as 'a terrorism of a very low kind', Ashim Chatterjee critiqued Majumdar by saying that 'this was nothing more than secret assassination by small armed groups. Such actions do not, in any way', he further argued

> raise the class consciousness of workers and peasants or enthuse them to organize on a class basis. Rather they inhibit their natural feelings of class hatred within the bounds of individual revenge and retribution ... All communists recognize that by ... annihilating individual capitalists or individual landlords, the capital or the system of feudal exploitation will not be eliminated, nor will a proletarian dictatorship or the rule of workers and peasants be created. It is natural for those at a low level of political consciousness to go for the apparently simple solution of annihilating the individual capitalist or the individual landlord.[16]

Not only was the annihilation line criticized by Chatterjee, it was also condemned by the Naxal activists at the grass roots. In his appraisal of the Naxalbari movement, Prabhat Jana, an activist in Orissa, found the annihilation totally incompatible with Marxism-Leninism. As he argued

> individual terror – secret assassination of individuals – does tremendous harm to the cause of revolution instead of helping it in two significant ways: first, it diverts the Party from the path of class struggle, from the path of people's war. It is petty-bourgeois subjectivism [dreaming] to create mass upsurge through individual terror by a handful of militants'.

Second, annihilation line was suicidal because 'a handful of militants isolated from the people can easily be suppressed by the enemy'. [So] "it belittles the enemies" strength from the tactical point of view'.[17] The annihilation campaign, instead of contributing to the cause of the movement, damaged its future to a significant extent. While a large section of the people were 'antagonized, thousands of cadres tortured, maimed and imprisoned and several hundreds – both leaders and cadres – died'.[18]

Besides clear tactical failures, the movement was also handicapped due to lack of proper ideological guidance. For instance, in order to do away with the bourgeois cultural traditions, the party instructed the cadres to burn the portraits and deface and destroy the statutes of 'the heroes' of the Bengal renaissance in Calcutta and elsewhere. This step, instead of fulfilling the ideological aim of the movement, alienated the urban middle class to a significant extent. Supporters were bewildered because instead of ideologically combating the influence of the bourgeois cultural traditions, the party resorted to easy means that shocked 'the middle class that was brought up to revere the pro-imperialist and cultural leaders'.[19]

Besides the ideological bankruptcy, the Naxalbari movement received a serious jolt when its ideological mentor, the Chinese Communist party, threatened to withdraw support and came out strongly against the Naxal leadership for having deviated from Marxism-Leninism. Communist China viewed that particular stage of revolution in India as 'people's democratic revolution' in which the principal task was to overthrow feudalism and the domination of imperialism and to distribute land among the peasants, the Chinese leadership, particularly Chou Enlai, insisted that the Indian revolutionaries should, as a strategy, build a united front of the exploiting classes, including the capitalists. It was also pointed out that the Naxalbari movement lost its 'vitality' because it failed to mobilize 'the peasant masses' since it lacked a well-defined agrarian programme. The Indian leadership was also criticized for mechanical application of the Chinese model of revolution to contemporary India that was undoubtedly a failure to creatively articulate Marxism-Leninism disregarding the prevalent socio-economic milieu. Peeved with the annihilation line that drew on Charu Majumdar's dictum that 'one who has not smeared his hands red with blood of the class enemy is not fit to be called a communist', Chou Enlai was reported to have asked the Indian Communist leadership to withdraw the campaign for such 'secret assassinations'. And also, the slogan that 'China's chairman is our chairman' displeased the Chinese leadership to a significant extent since it meant that movement was controlled and guided by a foreign power which was certain to alienate 'any sensible human being with self-dignity and pride in one's national identity'.[20] Although this slogan never became popular it appears to have reflected a genuine weakness of the Left's radical movements in India since the formation of the Communist party in 1923 by those charged in the Meerut conspiracy case. Initially, it was the Communist Party of Great Britain that, through its emissaries, almost dictated the Communist Party of India during the nationalist struggle. The most disappointing course of action by the Communist party was undertaken during the Second World War. So long as the former Soviet Union had a pact with Hitler's Germany, the war was 'an imperialist war'. Following Hitler's attack on Moscow, the war became a 'people's war'. As the Soviet Union joined hands with Britain against Hitler, the Indian Communists found it ideologically appropriate not to oppose the British war effort in India. As a result, they did not participate in the Congress-led Quit India movement in 1942 since it would weaken the British government (and thus people's war) that was involved in an historic battle against fascism in the Second World War. The stance that the Indian Communists had adopted in this context was perhaps ideologically tenable though it was 'a betrayal' for the nationalists fighting for independence despite adverse consequences. The Indian Communists later realized that by supporting the colonial government, they alienated the masses. Nonetheless, history was repeated and those involved in Spring Thunder almost two-and-a-half decades after the 1942 open rebellion uncritically accepted the hegemonic role of a foreign communist leadership so long as the Chinese Communist party strongly voiced its annoyance and later disapproval. Thus an analyst, sympathetic to the Marxist ideology, laments that 'the capacity of the communists to independently intervene' in issues of socio-economic relevance to the people remains a critical factor in the gradual decline of the Left in India.[21]

The Naxalbari movement after Charu Majumdar

The history of the post-Charu Majumdar Naxabari movement is characterized by a number of splits brought about by personalized and narrow perceptions about the Maoist revolutionary line and attempts at course correction by some of the major groups. Even Kanu Sanyal, one of the founders of the movement, was not free from this trend. He gave up the path of 'dedicated armed struggle' by 1977 and accepted parliamentary practice as one form of revolutionary activity.

It was during 1974 that one influential group of the CPI (M-L) led by Johar (Subrata Dutt), Nagbhushan Pattnaik and Vinod Mishra launched a major initiative which they termed as 'course correction'. This group renamed itself as the CPI (M-L) Liberation in 1974, and in 1976, during the state of emergency, it adopted a new line that called for the continuation of armed guerilla struggles along with efforts to form a broad anti-Congress democratic front, consisting even of non-communist parties. The group also suggested that pure military armed struggle should be limited and that there should be greater emphasis on mass peasant struggles in an attempt to provide an Indianized version of Marxism-Leninism-Maoism. However, during the next three years the movement suffered further splits with leaders, such as Kondapalli Seetharamaiah (Andhra Pradesh) and N. Prasad (Bihar) dissociating themselves from the activities of the party. This led to Prasad forming the CPI (M-L) (Unity Organization) and Seetharamaiah started the People's War Group (PWG) in 1980. Seetharamaiah's line also sought to restrict 'annihilation of class enemies' but the PWG's emphasis was on building up mass organizations, not on developing a broad democratic front. Since then, the principal division in the Naxalite movement has been between the two lines of thought and action, as advanced by the CPI (M-L) Liberation and the PWG. While Liberation branded PWG a group of 'left adventurists', the PWG castigated the Liberation group as one of the 'revisionists' imitating the CPI (M). On the other hand, the growth of the MCC as a major armed group in the same areas created the scope of multifarious organizational conflicts among the Naxal groups. Liberation took a theoretical stand of correcting the past mistakes of 'completely rejecting parliamentary politics'. On the other hand the PWG and the MCC completely rejected the parliamentary democratic system of governance and vowed to wage 'people's war for people's government'. In the process, as the Liberation group registered its first electoral victory in Bihar in 1989, more Naxalite factions such as the CPI (M-L) New Democracy, the CPI (M-L) S.R. Bhajjee Group and the CPI (M-L) Unity Initiative were formed in that state.

The Naxalbari movement saw different turns and twists in the 1990s. First, the intra-organizational conflict and rivalry among different groups touched several high points resulting in the loss of a considerable number of cadres of rival groups. Second, despite the large-scale inner conflicts there was always an exercise going at various levels attempting for the unity. Third, in 1990 the affected state registered a considerable growth in violent incidents and at the same time a considerable change in policy approach at the government level was also witnessed. If the Naxalite movement is mostly characterized by fragmented groups and innumerable splits, successive governments at the national and state levels were never able to follow a uniform approach to deal with the problem of Naxalism. All these have had a marked impact in the growth of the Naxalite movement.

New threads in continuation with the past

There are three major outfits through which Naxalism operates: the Communist Party of India (M-L) Liberation, the People's War Group (PWG) and the Maoist Communist Centre (MCC). Although these groups draw on more or less same ideological principles, they differ from one another in regard to certain tactical lines, which are as follows:

- The analysis of the first phase (1967–1971) of the Naxalite movement and the line of annihilation that was followed;
- The position that armed struggle is the principal form of struggle and that armed guerilla squad is the primary unit of struggle;
- Because the principal form of struggle is armed struggle, the entire activity of the agrarian struggle should be underground;
- Whether the contradiction between feudalism and Indian masses is the principal form of contradiction in Indian society or whether India has emerged as a capitalist state and hence, the contradiction between capitalism and the general public is the principal contradiction;
- Whether forming a united front with various forces and movements like the dalit movements, farmers' movements, ethnic and regional movements and ecological movements, etc. is advisable.[22]

There is a note of caution, however. Despite having separate nomenclature, these outfits have identical roots since they all were associated with the CPI (M-L) when it was formed in 1969. Several groups later emerged due to either a factional feud within the organization because of ideological differences or due to personality clash that culminated in the division within the party. This resulted in the weakening of the movement that was ideologically innovative, but was not politically as attractive as was expected at the beginning. This is a paradox in India's Communist movement that despite being ideologically creative, never became a pan-Indian political force due to organizational weaknesses and the failure to address them meaningfully. Nonetheless, the Naxalbari movement stands out because of the legacy that it had left. It brought to the fore 'the political urgency of the agrarian revolution in India, of the militant organization of the small and landless peasantry to accomplish this revolution, of the systematic expansion of the sphere of people's power as a preparation for, and not merely as a hypothetical consequences of, the seizure of power … Naxalbari is not simply the story of a few brave lives lost in a futile battle. It represents a political task which must be achieved'.[23]

Communist Party of India (Marxist-Leninist) Liberation

Historically speaking, the origin of the CPI (M-L) Liberation dates back to 1974. However, the post-emergency phase of 1977, when most leaders of the Communist movement were released from the jail, was the time when the activity of Liberation was first noticed. The Party Central Committee (PCC) in a move to unite the splinter groups with their roots in the CPI (M-L) called a meeting during 30 January–2 February 1981. However, the meeting did not derive the expected results. 'From this point onwards whereas the PCC group goes on to become irrelevant and splits up into various factions, the M-L movement begins to polarize between the Marxist-Leninist line of CPI (ML) (Liberation) and the anarchist line of CPI (ML) (People's War).'[24] In 1982 the Indian People's Front (IPF) was launched in New Delhi at a national conference. In the course of time, the IPF became the party's open political platform actively intervening in national politics. At the end of the year the 3rd party congress took place at Giridih, Bihar where the issue of participation in election was clinched. This shift in the outlook of the CPI (M-L) Liberation proved to be vital in designing a later course of activity within the Naxalite movement. As one scholar observes, 'Even though the Liberation group considers itself the true inheritor of the CPI (ML) legacy, its political line has changed dramatically from that of the original CPI (ML).'[25] With this strategic shift in functioning the CPI (M-L) (Liberation) recorded its first electoral victory under banner of the IPF in 1989 and Ara (one Lok Sabha constituency in central Bihar) sends the first 'Naxalite' member to parliament.[26] In a special conference convened in July 1990, the party decided to resume open functioning. This decision was formalized at its 5th congress in December 1992. In 1994, the Indian People's Front was disbanded. The election commission recognized the party in 1995, and since then the CPI (M-L) is contesting successive elections at national and state levels.

The CPI (M-L) Liberation, though functioning over ground within the parliamentary democracy set up, has not completely disbanded the path of armed rebellion.

> The Party does not rule out the possibility that under a set of exceptional national and international circumstances, the balance of social and political forces may even permit a relatively peaceful transfer of central power to revolutionary forces. But in a country where democratic institutions are based on essentially fragile and narrow foundations and where even small victories and partial reforms can only be achieved and maintained on the strength of mass militancy, the party of the proletariat must prepare itself for winning the ultimate decisive victory in an armed revolution. A people's democratic front and a people's army, therefore, remain the two most fundamental weapons of revolution in the arsenal of the Party.[27]

This again points out the dilemmas within the ultra-Left movement, which is very often reflected in the unpredictable character of the Naxalite movement.

The People's War Group (PWG)

The PWG is the most important among all the splinter groups representing the Naxalite movement because today the dominant line within Naxal politics is the PWG line of thought. Though it is popularly known as the PWG or PW its official nomenclature is the Communist Party of India – Marxist-Leninist (People's War). If Naxalism today is being considered as the greatest internal security problem, and if Naxals are claiming to run parallel governments in different parts of the country, its credit mostly goes to the PWG. 'The CPI (ML) (People's War) was formed on the Lenin's birth anniversary on 22 April 1980.'[28] Kondapalli Seetharamaiah, one of the most influential Naxalite leaders from Andhra Pradesh and a member of the erstwhile Central Organizing Committee of the Communist Party of India – Marxist-Leninist, CPI (M-L), is the founding father of the PWG; ironically however, he was later expelled from the group. While elaborating the ideological programme of the party, it was proclaimed that

> the Programme of our Party has declared that India is a vast 'semi-colonial and semi-feudal country', with about 80 per cent of our population residing in our villages. It is ruled by the big-bourgeois big landlord classes, subservient to imperialism. The contradiction between the alliance of imperialism, feudalism and comprador-bureaucrat-capitalism on the one hand and the broad masses of the people on the other is the principal contradiction in our country. Only a successful People's Democratic Revolution i.e. New Democratic Revolution and the establishment of People's Democratic Dictatorship of the workers, peasants, the middle classes and national bourgeoisie under the leadership of the working class can lead to the liberation of our people from all exploitation and the dictatorship of the reactionary ruling classes and pave the way for building Socialism and Communism in our country, the ultimate aim of our Party. People's War based on Armed Agrarian Revolution is the only path for achieving people's democracy i.e. new democracy, in our country.[29]

Rejecting the parliamentary democratic system and branding individual annihilation as individual terrorism, the PWG declares the people's war as the only path to bring about a people's government in the country. It is clear that there was a set of organizational, strategic and tactical conflict going on within the CPI (M-L), which paved the way for the split and creation of a more radical party. Broadly speaking, the party programmes of CPI (M-L) Liberation were mostly focused on the cause of peasants, while the group led by K. Seetharamaih wanted the party to be a platform for peasants, workers, tribal and other weaker sections of society. It was the prime agenda of Liberation to build up a political front focusing on peasant struggles, whereas PWG was more interested in the formation of mass organizations instead of any democratic front. One of the renowned guerrilla leaders of the erstwhile PWG summarizes the essence of conflict between CPI (M-L) Liberation and CPI (M-L) People's War by stating that

In the *Liberation* group, which at one time was one of the strong groups defending Charu Majumdar's revolutionary line, after the martyrdom of Comrade Johar, with the leadership falling into the hands of Vinod Mishra, they began betraying the Indian revolution. As part of a conspiratorial plan, a [sic] once revolutionary party was gradually changed into a revisionist party, like the CPI and CPM. The armed resistance struggles against the state's attacks, taking place under the then leadership of *Liberation*, was ended. The armed struggle to crush the feudal private armies was made a secondary task. In this way, they diverted the entire group away from the basic path outlined by the unified CPI (ML), and particularly of its founder, Com. CM [Charu Majumdar] – that of protracted people's war – into becoming agents of the ruling classes, by surrendering them to the parliamentary path. They converted the Comrade Johar-led *Liberation*, from being a revolutionary movement, into a legalist, reformist and parliamentary movement; and changed the underground organization into an open opportunist and revisionist organization.[30]

The above two official statements of the PWG clearly suggest that the birth of the PWG, which resulted due to another split within the CPI (M-L) Liberation, was mostly designed due to the dynamics of conflict among lots of its cadres. For a considerable period after its birth the PWG's activities were limited to Andhra Pradesh only whereas CPI (M-L) Liberation continued to hold its turf in Bihar. It was during this period that another organization came into existence on 1 January 1982. It was named the Communist Party of India (M-L) Party Unity, which came into existence following the merger between the CPI (M-L) Unity Organizations and the Central Organizing Committee of the CPI (M-L). Hereafter, left-wing extremism in India witnessed some of the worst ever conflicts that forced many of the organizations to take a position and adopt new tactics. Bihar has always remained a strong battleground for Naxal operations and ironically most of the clashes Bihar witnessed were between the CPI (M-L) Party Unity and the CPI (M-L) Liberation in the past, as Table 2.2 illustrates.

When these conflicts were taking tolls on the cadres of both sides, another development was taking place simultaneously. In August 1998, Party Unity merged with CPI (M-L) People's War Group and the group came to be known as People's

Table 2.2 Clashes between the CPI (M-L) Party Unity and the CPI (M-L) Liberation, 1994–1997

Year	Number of clashes	Number of deaths
1994	5	8 (PU 5, L 3)
1995	16	13 (PU 8, L 5)
1996	36	24 (PU 5, L 19)
1997	21	16 (PU 3, L 3)

Source: *The Times of India*, Patna, 7 December 1997.

War. 'The merger of the two parties is the culmination of the unity process which began in March 1993 and continued for over five years during which differences on several political, ideological and organizational questions were resolved through thread-bare discussion.'[31] The statement continues

> The emergence of the united Party – the Communist Party of India (Marxist-Leninist) [People's War] – does not mark the completion of the process of unification of the genuine communist revolutionary forces in India. The newly Unified Party will continue its efforts in right earnest to achieve this unification. We also call upon the other genuine revolutionary elements in the various M-L parties in India who are being led astray by both right and left opportunist leadership, to fight against these deviations and rally under the banner of the United Party. The United Party pledges itself to avenge the death of thousands of martyrs who fell in the course of the ongoing democratic revolution in India paved with blood by these martyrs until their cherished goals are accomplished. This is the era of Revolutions.[32]

By this merger the PWG became another force to reckon with in Bihar and in other areas where PU had a presence. Further developments suggest that with this merger the armed rebellion path of the Naxalite movement became stronger, while on the other hand, with its parliamentary practices Liberation was losing its turf to the PWG. The same Liberation that once was controlling the whole of central Bihar was losing its territory and supporters to the PWG and the MCC. Not only in Bihar, but everywhere Liberation was being systematically wiped-out from the map of Naxalite politics. By participating in electoral methods and by not being able to make an impressive mark the Liberation way of movement became weak and the PWG's armed operation started gaining momentum.

So when the Liberation with its changed modus operandi was being reduced to a small political party, the PWG in the same period managed to register its presence outside Andhra Pradesh and gradually made strongholds in different areas of Bihar, Orissa, Madhya Pradesh, Jharkhand, Chhattisgarh and Maharashtra. Of course, due to this conflict between PU and Liberation both groups lost a considerable number of their cadres, but the merger of PU and the PWG ultimately resulted in the violent consolidation of the movement.

The formation of People's War also resulted in tactical changes in several aspects of the Naxalite movement in general. 'In our agenda for a new democratic revolution, there are two aspects – the agrarian revolution and fight for nationality.'[33] This statement shows the amount of organizational change witnessed by the Naxalite movement in those years. In 1967, it started in the name of agrarian revolution, which gradually took the stance of replacement of the parliamentary form of government, but the question of nationality was never there. This reflects the pattern of conflict between PW and Liberation. By raising the question of nationality PW wanted to make it clear that it wanted a broad revolutionary pattern, and 'land to tillers' was just a programme, not the sole agenda of the revolution.

In between 15–30 November 1995 PW conducted an All India Special Conference in some unknown locality of Dandakaranya. There it adopted two important party documents. The 'Party Programme' as adopted in the conference reads

> India is a semi-feudal, semi-colonial society; here the New Democratic Revolution (NDR) has to be completed victoriously paving way to the Socialist Revolution and to advance towards the ultimate goal of Communism. The Indian people are weighed down by three big mountains: feudalism, imperialism and comprador bureaucrat capital; these are the targets to be overthrown in the present stage of NDR. The four major contradictions in the present-day Indian society are: the contradiction between feudalism and the broad masses; the contradiction between imperialism and the Indian people; the contradiction between capital and labour and the contradiction within the ruling classes. While the first two are fundamental contradictions to be resolved through the NDR, the contradiction between feudalism and the broad masses is the principal contradiction at the present stage. India is a multi-national country – a prison-house of nationalities and all the nationalities have the right to self-determination including secession. When NDR is victoriously completed, India will become a voluntary and genuine federation of all national people's republics.[34]

The second document that was adopted in the conference was 'Strategy and Tactics'. It reads that

> The political strategy to be pursued in the present stage of NDR in India is one of forming a broad united front of all the anti-feudal, anti-imperialist forces – the working class, the peasantry, the petty bourgeoisie and the national bourgeoisie – under the leadership of the working class to overthrow the common enemies – feudalism, imperialism and comprador bureaucratic capital. The military strategy or the path of Indian Revolution is the path of protracted people's war i.e., liberating the countryside first through area wise seizure of power establishing guerilla zones and base areas and then encircling the cities and finally capturing power throughout the country. The unevenness in the economic, social and political development of Indian society calls for different tactics i.e., forms of struggle and organization, to be pursued in different regions of the country, while the political tactic line throughout the country remains the same. In urban areas the political and mass work should be carried out observing utmost precaution and the organizational work should proceed keeping in view the long-range perspective. Caste is a peculiar problem in India; and appropriate forms of organization and struggle should be evolved vigorously to fight out untouchability, caste discrimination and to finally root out the caste system. The tactics of boycott of elections have to be pursued for a long time in the prevailing conditions in India; and participating in parliamentary and assembly elections under any pretext only weakens the class struggle.[35]

These two documents containing different organizational aspects of PW makes a clear-cut demarcation for the issues pertaining to organizational conflict between Liberation and PW. People's War, on the basis of its assessment of the people's level of preparedness for an armed struggle, discarded total annihilation of 'class enemies' as the only form of struggle and stressed on floating mass organizations. It established several front organizations. During the 1980s, the Radical Students' Union and *Rayatu Kuli Sangham* had emerged as organizations with an impressive mass following and most of the PWG's present base and political cadres had developed through that practice. However, during the 1990s, growth of militarization became the characteristic feature of the PWG. The formation of the People's Guerrilla Army (PGA) and special guerrilla squads, Permanent Action Team (PAT) and Special Action Team (SAT), were the distinctive features of PWG activities for quite some time before it merged with the MCC to form the CPI (Maoist).[36]

Maoist Communist Centre (MCC)

The next important group within the broad spectrum of Naxalite movement is the Maoist Communist Centre (MCC). Among a number of organizations it stands apart as it was never was part of the CPI (M-L), which many claim as the mother of all Naxal organizations. 'The MCC, while supporting the Naxalbari struggle, did not join the CPI (ML) because of some tactical differences and on the question of Party formation.'[37] The MCC was formed on 20 October 1969, during the same time when the CPI (M-L) was formed, however, during those days it was known as Dakshin Desh. It was in 1975 that the group renamed itself as the Maoist Communist Centre. In 2003, the MCC merged with the Revolutionary Communist Centre of India-Maoists (RCCI-M) to form the Maoist Communist Centre-India (MCC-I).

Right from its inception, the MCC stood for taking up armed struggle as the main form of struggle and waging a protracted people's war as the central task of the party. This position of the MCC has been repeatedly expressed and emphasized by the Maoists while decoding their strategy. As the *Red Star*, the MCC weekly, firmly declares

> This armed revolutionary war is the war of the armed people themselves; it is 'Protracted People's War' as shown by Mao Tse Tung. The concrete economic and political condition of India leads to the very conclusion that the path shown by the great leader and teacher, Mao Tse Tung, the path of the Chinese Revolution, and to establish a powerful people's army and people's militia and to establish dependable, strong and self-sufficient base areas in the countryside, to constantly consolidate and expand the people's army and the base areas, gradually to encircle the urban areas from the countryside by liberating the countryside, finally to capture the cities and to establish the state system and political authority of the people themselves by decisively destroying the state power of the reactionaries – this very path of the protracted People's War is the only path of liberation of the people of India, the path of victory of the new democratic revolution.[38]

Communist Party of India (Maoist)

The Naxalite movement in India entered into yet another phase of organizational transformation with the merger of two of the principal armed organizations, namely the People's War (PW) and the Maoist Communist Centre of India (MCC-I), which resulted in the formation of the Communist Party of India (Maoist) on 21 September 2004.

> The formation of the unified Communist Party of India (Maoist) is a new milestone in the history of the revolutionary communist movement of India. A unified Maoist party based on Marxism-Leninism-Maoism is a long delayed and highly cherished need of the revolutionary minded and oppressed people of the country, including all our ranks, and also all the Maoist forces of South Asia and internationally. Now, this long-aspired desire and dream has been transformed into a reality.[39]

This statement given by the General Secretary of the CPI (Maoist), Ganapathy, assumes a great deal of importance as it reflects the organizational politics that was going on all these years between these two organizations representing the Naxalite movement.

The exalted aim of the CPI (Maoist) as announced on its formation is to establish a compact revolutionary zone stretching from Nepal to Bihar to Andhra Pradesh and beyond. While continuing their goal of people's democracy the ultimate aim of the CPI (Maoist) is to seize power through protracted armed struggle. According to the press statement issued on the announcement the merger

> The immediate aim and programme of the Maoist party is to carry on and complete the already ongoing and advancing New Democratic Revolution in India as a part of the world proletarian revolution by overthrowing the semi-colonial, semi-feudal system under the neo-colonial form of indirect rule, exploitation and control.[40]

This revolution will remain directed against imperialism, feudalism and comprador bureaucratic capitalism. This revolution will be carried out and completed through armed agrarian revolutionary war, i.e. a protracted people's war with the armed seizure of power remaining as its central and principal task, encircling the cities from the countryside and thereby finally capturing them. Hence, the countryside as well as the PPW (Protracted People's War) will remain as the 'center of gravity' of the party's work, while urban work will be complementary to it. According to the same press release, the CPI-Maoists 'will still seek to unite all genuine Maoist groups that remain outside this unified party'.[41]

It is important to examine the significance of the merger particularly when earlier attempts were not successful. In fact, the merger is largely being seen as a result of the gradual convergence of views of these two groups on areas such as the role of the party, approaches to revolution and adoption of strategies and tactics. In the formative years, Charu Mazumdar and Kanai Chatterjee represented two irreconcilably different lines and approaches to 'revolution'. At the time of the formation of the Communist Party of India (Marxist-Leninist) in 1969, the Dakshin Desh, an earlier form of the the MCC, remained opposed to the process due to sharp differences with the CPI (M-L) over issues such as formation of a communist party, existence of revolutionary mass struggle and preparedness of the people to participate in it. The joint press statement released by the erstwhile General Secretaries of PW and the MCC-I highlighted the essence of merger.

> In the past history there were many splits within the M-L movement. But splits are only one side of the coin; the brighter side was that there were continuous efforts to unify the revolutionaries. The CPI (ML) (PU), though it had its origins in Bengal, it spread and strengthened by unifying several revolutionary groups. The CPI (ML) (PW), though it originated in Andhra Pradesh and Tamil Nadu, it unified with revolutionaries in almost all the states where it was working. The MCC too, had originated in Bengal, unified many revolutionaries groups in it in many States and became the MCCI.[42]

This statement underlines the continuous process of organizational churning within the broad spectrum of the Naxalite movement that resulted in organizational conflict.

Looking back, the need for a joint unified platform was felt by the leadership of both the parties as early as 1981.

> The PW and MCC began unity talks from their very first meeting in 1981. However, the reason for the delay in the process was the lack of continuity of leadership. The arrest of Comrade Kondapally Seet[h]aramaiah (KS), the leader of the PW, and later the internal crisis of the PW and split in the Central Committee (CC) delayed the unity process for several years. In the early eighties, the MCC lost its two top leaders Comrades Amulya Sen (AS) and Kanai Chatterjee (KC), which had some negative impact, resulting in further delay in the unity process.[43]

However, this is not to suggest that the formation of the CPI (Maoist) is the final stage of the Naxalite movement. As one official Maoist document puts it

> Revolutions never proceed in a straight line. The history of all successful revolutions shows this. The path is zig zag, there are ups and downs, there is victory and defeat repeated a number of times . . . before final victory. Of course, there is no final victory until the stage of communism is reached.[44]

The above-mentioned analysis makes one forceful plea that other than anything else the Naxalite movement essentially is a political problem and it needs to be examined from the perspective of organizational politics.

The merger of the CPI (M-L) PW and MCC-I that resulted in the birth of the

CPI (Maoist) also successfully brought the dominant faction of the CPI (M-L) Janashakti to its fold. Amid speculations of merger, both the Janashakti and CPI (Maoist) presented a united front in 2005. A death toll of 892 people that year was largely believed to be a result of the merger. The Naxalite movement, however, continued to conquer new territories in 2006–7. Other than the escalation in violence, the latter part of 2006 also witnessed significant changes in the operational ways of the Naxalite movement.

The honeymoon between the CPI (Maoist) and Janashakti could not last longer than a year and in 2006 it became apparent that both were clearly going different ways to occupy operational areas. During the open session of the CPI (Maoist) held in December 2006, Janashakti was asked to make clear its stand on political aims and programmes; Janashakti, however, chose not to attend the session. Consequently, the CPI (Maoist) withdrew the partner status from Janashakti and decided to provide need-based support only in the case of police actions. The conflict between the CPI (Maoist) and Janashakti became public only recently, when the Orissa Janashakti group led by Anna Reddy killed three forest officials on 31 January 2007. The CPI (Maoist) state leadership immediately distanced itself from the killings. Subsequent police enquiry confirmed the involvement of the Janashakti group in the gruesome act.

Of course, things are at a formative stage today; the setting is ready for a possible realignment of the Maoist forces. In Karnataka, which is largely viewed as the new Naxal target, the CPI (Maoist) recently suffered a major setback as a number of cadres in the state, who disagreed with the Maoist agenda of intensifying the revolution in rural areas first and then spreading it to urban centres, have floated a new party named the Maoist Coordination Committee (MCC). It should be noted that the political cracks in Karnataka have now started to extend to other states.

From the above discussion we can derive the following conclusions. First, the history of Naxalite movement is the history of a continuous process of organizational conflicts, splits, and mergers. This is perhaps indicative of a process of a constant re-generation of the radical outfits drawing on the ultra left wing extremist ideologies.

Second, the ultimate political objective behind all this organizational exercise, as evident in statements of various senior Naxalite leaders, is to build a Leftist alternative and mobilize people on issues such as increased 'imperialist intervention' and 'pro-imperialist policies' pursued by the Union Government in support of 'revolutionary war' based on Chinese leader Mao's theory of organized peasant insurrection. Similarly, the history of the Naxalite movement from its first phase in 1967 demonstrates that even if there has been a continuous evolution in terms of their understanding of the Indian situation, focus of the movement, character, fighting capabilities and financial resources of these groups, they have remained more or less consistent as far as their core ideology is concerned. Barring the Liberation they all reject the parliamentary system of governance and want to bring about a fundamental change in the nature of the Indian state. For this they have adopted the strategy of protracted armed struggle, which entails building up of bases in rural and remote areas and transforming them first into guerrilla zones and liberated zones, beside area-wise seizures and encircling cities and finally seizing political power and achieving nationwide victory.

Concluding observations

Maoism is a contemporary manifestation of 'the ultra left movement' in India although it would not be wrong to characterize the movement as 'a historical continuity' simply because of the broad ideological compatibility with the past movements that drew on Marxism-Leninism and also Maoism. Besides the Naxalbari movement in the late 1960s and early 1970s, the Telangana Liberation struggle (1946–1951) and Tebhaga movement (1946–1949) had also mobilized the marginalized against the so-called 'feudal forces' stalling land reforms and other ameliorating social and economic measures for the majority.

What distinguishes the Tebhaga and Telangana upsurges from past movements was that these were politically inspired and supported by a well-entrenched organization, under the guidance of the undivided Communist Party of India. The Tebhaga movement, as its nomenclature suggests, demanded the reduction of the share of the landlord from one half of the crop to one third. The leadership came from the Kisan Sabha, a peasant front of the Communist Party of India. This Bengal-based movement gradually spread in Dinajpur and Rangpur in north Bengal and 24 Parganas in south Bengal. Despite its temporary success, the movement petered out gradually in the face of organized government-sponsored counter offensive. Yet, the movement forced the ruling authority to introduce 'the *bargadar* act' that legalized demand of the share croppers for 'two-thirds' of the harvested crop. Unlike the Tebhaga movement, which mobilized Bengal peasants in selective districts for enhancing their share of the produce, the Telangana movement was a genuine agrarian liberation struggle to get rid of feudal landlordism and dynastic rule of Nizam in Hyderabad. The movement, however, lost its momentum with the 1947 independence when Nizam's rule came to an end. There were some in the Communist party who wanted to continue the movement against the Indian government, but the majority was in favour of withdrawal. In 1951, the movement was formally withdrawn. In a rather superficial sense, the Telangana movement succeeded because Nizam lost his authority in the changed environment of free India after the 1947 transfer of power. Yet, it would be appropriate to suggest that the movement raised voices against feudal atrocities that were articulated differently in independent India resulting in ameliorating land reform measures.

The Naxalbari movement was an ideological continuity of past movements that sought to organize peasants against feudal exploitation. The name is derived from Naxalbari, a non-discreet place in northern part of West Bengal. Mobilized by those who formed CPI (M-L) in 1969, one of the primary aims of 'the spring thunder' as it is metaphorically characterized, was to bring about radical changes in the prevalent agrarian structure that endorsed 'feudal exploitation' of perhaps very primitive nature. As a 1969 political resolution of the party suggests

The increasing concentration of land in the hands of a few landlords, the expropriation of almost the total surplus produced by the toiling peasantry in the form of rent, the complete landlessness of about 40% of the rural population, the back-breaking usurious exploitation, the ever-growing evictions of the poor peasantry coupled with the brutal social oppression – including lynching of '*harijans*', reminiscent of the medieval ages – and the complete backwardness of the technique of production clearly demonstrate the semi-feudal character of our society.[45]

What is distinctive about Naxalbari is that a majority of peasants are tribals. Exploited by the landlords and their agents, they were employed on contractual basis and in most cases, they did not get even the government-fixed wage for their work in the fields. The movement failed to attain its goal. Nonetheless, it left a far-reaching impact on the entire agrarian scene throughout India. It was like a 'premeditated throw of a pebble bringing forth a series of ripples in the water'.[46] The uprising, though ephemeral in existence, was widely publicized and inspired the rural poor in other parts of the country to launch a militant struggle against feudal exploitation and the failure of the state to evolve an equitable economy. Although the immediate and spontaneous demand of the peasants involved in the Naxalbari movement was the fulfilment of some economic demands it, however, led to a long-range struggle for 'the ultimate seizure of political power' that not only survived but also expanded despite internal factional squabbles and also the organized state counter-offensive.

Notwithstanding obvious similarities, the Maoist movement differs from Spring Thunder of the 1969–1972 period on a variety of counts: first, Maoism seems to have struck an emotional chord with the tribal population unlike the Naxalbari movement that shifted its centre of gravity to the urban and semi-urban areas and drew on the support of the educated middle class youth. It is difficult to clearly identify the class background of the Maoists though there is no doubt that the participants are 'not romantic, middle class babus, as was the case generally during Charu Majumdar's quixotic misadventure of 1969–1972 period especially in West Bengal'.[47] Second, unlike their Naxal counterparts, Maoists are 'better-organized' and also 'well-equipped' with sophisticated fire power, as it was evident in the series of successful attacks on the police and paramilitary armed forces in Bihar, Chhattisgarh and Orissa. There are official reports that Maoists are regularly trained in a military style in areas where the government seems to have lost its control. Finally, Maoists are ideologically better knit than those involved in the Naxalbari movement. One of the major factors that led to the collapse of the Naxalbari movement was internecine feuds not only among the leaders, but also among the grass-roots activists. According to Kanu Sanyal, one of the top Naxal leaders, what led to the downfall of the Naxalbari movement was 'an atmosphere of disrespect and expression of arrogance by the leaders that [resulted in] reducing the Communist revolutionaries in India to groups and sub-groups'.[48] What crippled the Naxalbari movement was the emergence and consolidation of two contradictory trends: on the one hand was 'the urban-based leadership, cloaked in a more sophisticated ideology, claimed superior knowledge and status with regard to the manner in which the movement should be conducted'.[49] Opposed to it was, on the other hand, 'the co-opted indigenous leadership'[50] that followed the principle of democratic consultation at every level of the organization before arriving at a decision. While the first trend is illustrative of 'an elitist leadership' that Charu Majumdar consolidated by evolving a centralized organization with concentration of power at the top, the Kanu Sanyal-led rural wing of the leadership sought to democratize the organization by meaningfully involving the activists at various levels of the leadership. The movement considerably lost its momentum largely due to the division among the leaders that not only weakened the organization, but also caused confusion among the followers. The present-day Maoists seem to have learnt a lesson from the past that was translated into reality when out of four different Maoist outfits emerged the CPI (Maoist) in 2004. Undoubtedly, this merger is a milestone in India's left-wing movements since most of the radical outfits fizzled out in the past due to 'factional fight'. The formation of the CPI (Maoist) is therefore a watershed in so far as the consolidation of those clinging to Maoism is concerned. The gradual but steady expansion of the red corridor since the 2005 merger is also a powerful testimony of the growing importance of Maoism as a political means to get rid of the well-entrenched socio-economic imbalances at the grass roots.

The future of Maoism in India

Maoism is an ideological continuity with the past, and yet this is a contextual response to the peculiar Indian reality that differs radically from one place to another. In the past, ultra-Left movements seem to have uncritically accepted 'the one size fits all' approach by accepting the classical Marxism-Leninism as sacrosanct. Given the socio-economic and cultural diversity of the continental variety, India can never be comprehended in a single axis. By being sensitive to this well-entrenched diversity, Maoism has reinvented Marxism-Leninism in a non-European milieu. Even within India, the issues that Maoists raise differ radically from one state to another. In Andhra Pradesh, Maoism draws, for instance, on anti-feudal sentiments whereas in the tribal belt of Orissa and also Chhattisgarh, rights over forest produce remain the most effective demand for political mobilization. This context-driven articulation of Maoism is certainly a critical factor in its rise as perhaps the most effective ideological voice of the downtrodden notwithstanding the adverse consequences.

It is difficult to predict the future of Maoism though there is no doubt that it has succeeded, so far, in expanding the 'red corridor' by involving mainly the peripheral sections of society in an area stretching almost half of India. This itself is suggestive of the historical limitations of the state-led development programmes that failed to take care of the basic needs of a vast population. The situation seems to have worsened following the acceptance of neoliberal economic reforms in the wake of the serious domestic fiscal crisis in early 1990. The government design for rapid industrialization seems to have received a serious blow because of an organized opposition by those who lost their land for industries. The idea of Special

Economic Zones did not sit well with the people at the grass roots who felt betrayed with the government policy of transferring land owned by many small peasants to a single, privately-owned company. In areas where Maoism was hardly a force, the forcible eviction of peasants from land for Special Economic Zones leads to circumstances in which Maoists are accepted by those fighting for their rights as a natural ally. In other words, the economic reforms, despite being middle-class friendly, seem to have consolidated the class division in India's rural areas by pursuing a path of development that is surely tilted towards foreign capital and its Indian collaborators. Given the appalling socio-economic circumstances in which the vast majority of the Indian population stays alive, it will not be an exaggeration to suggest that Maoism is likely to strike roots since it provides the struggling masses with a powerful voice defending their rights for survival. Maoism is therefore not merely an articulation of ultra-extremist ideology, it is also a well-designed scheme for mobilizing those who remain historically under-privileged for reasons connected with India's interventionist economic strategies under the state-led development planning since independence.

Notes

1 Richard Mahapatra, *Unquiet Forests: A Comprehensive Look at How Forest Laws are Triggering Conflicts in India with a Focus on Naxalite Movement*, Prem Bhatia Memorial Trust, 2004–5, 4.
2 Ajit K. Doval (former director, Intelligence Bureau), 'Code Red Naxals: The Biggest Threat', *Sunday Hindustan Times*, 26 March 2006.
3 Interview with Ganapathy, General Secretary, CPI (Maoist). The text of the interview was released by Azad, spokesperson for the CPI (Maoist) in April 2007.
4 In certain affected areas various Naxal groups have paralyzed the official mechanisms of governance. In these areas they call 'liberated areas' the Naxals are effectively running a parallel system of governance where they impose their dictates through their military units; they even collect tax (ransom) and in those areas they claim that they have established the Janata Sarkar.
5 Javeed Alam, 'Communist Politics in Search of Hegemony' in Partha Chatterjee (ed.), *Wages of Freedom: Fifty Years of Indian Nation-State*, New Delhi: Oxford University Press, 1998, 183.
6 Ibid., 184.
7 For details of these movements, see Sumanta Banerjee, *India's Simmering Revolution:The Naxalite Uprising*, New Delhi: Selection Service Syndicate, 1984, 18–28.
8 'Spring Thunder Over India', editorial in the *Peking People's Daily*, 5 July 1967 – reproduced in Samar Sen, Debabrata Panda and Ashish Lahiri (eds), *Naxalbari and After: A Frontier Anthology*, vol. 2, Calcutta: Kathashilpa, 1978, 188.
9 Kanu Sanyal, 'More About Naxalbari', April 1973, in Samar Sen, Debabrata Panda and Ashish Lahiri (eds), *Naxalbari and After: A Frontier Anthology*, vol. 2, Calcutta: Kathashilpa, 1978, 330.
10 'Spring Thunder Over India', editorial in the *Peking People's Daily*, 5 July 1967 – reproduced in Samar Sen, Debabrata Panda and Ashish Lahiri (eds), *Naxalbari and After: A Frontier Anthology*, vol. 2, Calcutta: Kathashilpa, 1978, 188.
11 Partha N. Mukherji, 'Class and Ethnic Movements in India: In Search of a Pertinent Paradigm for Democracy and Nation Building in the Third World', in Lars Rudebeck (ed.), *When Democracy Makes Sense*, Sweden: Akut, 1992, 19.
12 Interview with Kanu Sanyal on 16 January 1991 – quoted in Arun Prasad Mukherjee,

Maoist Spring Thunder: The Naxalite Movement (1967–1972), Calcutta: K.P. Bagchi, 2007, 3.

13 Kanu Sanyal – quoted in Samar Sen, Debabrata Panda and Ashish Lahiri (eds), *Naxalbari and After: A Frontier Anthology*, vol. 2, Calcutta: Kathashilpa, 1978., 5.

14 Charu Majumdar, 'Why Guerilla War', in Ghatana Prabaha, vol. 2 (1), quoted in Samar Sen, Debabrata Panda and Ashish Lahiri (eds), *Naxalbari and After: A Frontier Anthology*, vol. 2, Calcutta: Kathashilpa, 1978, 6.

15 Charu Majumdar, 'On the Political-Organization Report', 13 September 1970 – reproduced in Samar Sen, Debabrata Panda and Ashish Lahiri (eds), *Naxalbari and After: A Frontier Anthology*, vol. 2, Calcutta: Kathashilpa, 1978, 293–94.

16 Ashim Chatterjee, 'Hold High the Genuine Lessons of Naxalbari', in Samar Sen, Debabrata Panda and Ashish Lahiri (eds), *Naxalbari and After: A Frontier Anthology*, vol. 2, Calcutta: Kathashilpa, 1978, 388–89.

17 Prabhat Jana, 'Naxalbari and After: An Appraisal', 12–19 May 1973, in Samar Sen, Debabrata Panda and Ashish Lahiri (eds), *Naxalbari and After: A Frontier Anthology*, vol. 2, Calcutta: Kathashilpa, 1978, 123.

18 Prabhat Jana, 'Naxalbari and After: An Appraisal', 12–19 May 1973, in Samar Sen, Debabrata Panda and Ashish Lahiri (eds), *Naxalbari and After: A Frontier Anthology*, vol. 2, Calcutta: Kathashilpa, 1978, 124.

19 Ibid., 125.

20 This paragraph is based on the testimonial of Souren Bose, one of the top Naxal leaders who was sent to China during the heyday of the movement to ascertain the support of the Chinese Communist Party and also the government. Bose's statements were recorded while he was in custody on 11, 20 and 24 April 1972. These statements are quoted from Arun Prosad Mukherjee, *Maoist Spring Thunder: The Naxalite Movement (1967–1972)*, Calcutta: K.P. Bagchi, 2007, 232–35.

21 Javeed Alam, 'Debates and Engagements: A Look at Communist Intervention in India', in V.R. Mehta and Thomas Pantham (eds), *Political Ideas in Modern India: Thematic Explorations*, New Dehli: Sage, 2006, 404.

22 Praksh Louis, *People Power: The Naxalite Movement in Central Bihar*, New Delhi: Wordsmiths, 2002, 277.

23 Partha Chatterjee, *The Present History of West Bengal: Essays in Political Criticism*, New Delhi: Oxford University Press, 1997, 92–93.

24 *Thirty Years of Naxalbari*, an undated publication of the CPI (M-L) Liberation.

25 Bela Bhatia, 'Naxalite Movement in Central Bihar', *Economic and Political Weekly*, April 9 2005.

26 *History of Naxalism*, http://hindustantimes.com.

27 A party document of the CPI (M-L) Liberation titled 'The General Programme'.

28 *30 years of Naxalbari*, an undated Maoist literature, Vanguard Publication, 30. Vanguard was the organ of the PWG.

29 'Path of People's War in India – Our Tasks!', a comprehensive PWG party document highlighting its aims, objectives and strategies. The document was adopted by All-India Party Congress in 1992. We obtained this document from one of the principal ideologue of the PWG.

30 Sharvan, the then secretary of the Bihar State Committee of the CPI (M-L) People's War, in an interview given to *People's March*, vol. 2 (3) March 2001.

31 People's War literature titled 'Joint Declaration by Communist Party of India (ML) People's War and CPI (ML) (Party Unity)', August 1998.

32 People's War literature titled 'Joint Declaration by Communist Party of India (ML) People's War and CPI (ML) (Party Unity)', August 1998.

33 Interview with Muppalla Lakshmana Rao *alias* Ganapathy, the then head of the CPI (M-L) People's War, http://www.rediff.com/news/1998/oct/07gana.htm.

34 This report on the special conference was posted on http://www. cpimlpwg/repression. html. The website has been withdrawn. During its existence the site claimed to be the

unofficial website of the PWG. On the basis of interaction with many PW rank and file, we have reason to believe that it was no less than their official website.

35 Drawn on the report of the special conference, posted on http://www. cpimlpwg/repression.html. The website has been withdrawn. During its existence the site claimed to be the unofficial website of the PWG. On the basis of interaction with many PW rank and file, we have reason to believe that it was no less than their official website.

36 In response to a government decision to launch coordinated action against the Naxalites by police forces of the various Indian states affected by Naxal violence, the PWG formed the PGA, its military wing, in December 2000, by reorganizing its guerrilla force. The PGA functions under a single operational command, the Central Military Commission. In the Indian state where the PGA has a presence, there is a State Military Commission and in special guerrilla zones there is a Zonal Military Commission. A Regional Military Commission supervises a group of State Military Commissions or Zonal Military Commission. Each Regional Military Commission reports to the Central Military Commission. All armed cadre of the PWG are organized under the PGA. Reference: 'People's Guerrilla Army', http://www.satp.org/satporgtp/countries/india/terroristoutfits/peoples_guerrilla_arms_left_wing_extremists.htm.

37 *30 years of Naxalbari*, 36.

38 *Red Star*, Special Issue, 20. *Red Star* is the English language organ of the MCC, as quoted by Aloke Banerjee in a pamphlet titled 'Inside MCC Country', dated June 2003. Also quoted in 'MCC India Three Decades Leading Battalions of the Poor', one article published by A World to Win, http://www.awtw.org/back_issues/mcc_india. htm. Though it denies it, many treat this as the unofficial organ of the Revolutionary Internationalist Movement (RIM).

39 Ganapathy, in an interview given on the occasion of the formation of the CPI (Maoist). *People's March*, vol. 5 (11–12), November–December 2004.

40 'Maoist-Influenced Revolutionary Organizations in India', at http://www.massline.info/India/Indian_Groups.htm.

41 'Maoist-Influenced Revolutionary Organizations in India', at http://www.massline.info/India/Indian_Groups.htm.

42 Ganapathy, in an interview given on the occasion of the formation of the CPI (Maoist). *People's March*, vol. 5 (11–12), November–December 2004.

43 Ibid.

44 'State Repression' is the title of the document that was posted at http://www. cpimlpwg/repression.html.

45 Political resolution of the CPI (M-L), 1969.

46 Sumanta Banerjee, *India's Simmering Revolution: The Naxalite Uprising*, New Delhi: Selection Service Syndicate, 1984, 92.

47 Arun Prosad Mukherjee, *Maoist Spring Thunder: The Naxalite Movement (1967–1972)*, Calcutta: K.P. Bagchi, 2007, 30.

48 Kanu Sanyal, 'More About Naxalbari', April 1973, Samar Sen, Debabrata Panda and Ashish Lahiri (eds), *Naxalbari and After: A Frontier Anthology*, vol. 2, Calcutta: Kathashilpa, 1978, 347.

49 Partha N. Mukherji, 'Naxalbari Movement and the Peasant Revolt in North Bengal' in M.S.A. Rao (ed.), *Social Movements in India*, New Delhi: Manohar, 2008 (reprint), 75.

50 Ibid., 76.

3 Maoism

The roadmap for future India[1]

Following the merger in 2004, the CPI (Maoist) brought out an elaborate document articulating its aims and programmes for the future. Seeking to elaborate 'the
Maoist vision for future', the document, prepared by the central committee, was
placed for approval by the party's high command in September 2004. The exercise had the twin purposes of not only reaffirming their ideological commitment to
Marxism-Leninism-Maoism (MLM) in perpetuity but also guiding their rank and
file on strategy and tactics to be followed in waging a people's war. The present
chapter, drawn on a Maoist document on the strategy and tactics prepared by the
Central Committee of the Communist Party of India (Maoist) in 2004, is an elaboration of the Maoist blueprint for future India. Inspired by Marxism-Leninism and
Mao's thought, the Indian Maoists seek to provide an alternative political discourse
by challenging the ideological foundation of the Indian polity that has completely
failed to establish an egalitarian society.

Drawn on Marxism-Leninism-Maoism, the CPI (Maoist) is committed to the
'New Democratic Revolution' in India as a first step towards the establishment
of a socialist state. The task of revolution will remain incomplete unless there is a
complete seizure of power by the proletariat. The centre of gravity of the people's
democratic revolution is obviously the countryside while the struggle in urban
areas will supplement the Maoist endeavour in capturing state power. As a party
committed to Marxism, the entire struggle will be conducted by the party guided by
the Leninist principle of democratic centralism. Like its erstwhile Soviet counterpart, the party also supports 'the struggle of the nationalities for self-determination,
including the right to secession and the fight against social oppression, particularly
untouchability and casteism and will play special attention to mobilizing and organizing women as a mighty force of revolution'.[2]

Conceptual explorations on strategy and tactics

The Maoists put heavy premium on the concepts of strategy and tactics as they form
the core of the overall communist blueprint of attaining their desirable goal of proletariat revolution. Believing in the Stalinist dictum that 'theory should guide the
Programme; Programme should guide the Strategy; and Strategy should guide the
Tactics', the Maoists in India seemed determined to understand and follow Stalin's

ideas on the same. Consequently, they quoted verbatim Stalin's understanding of the ideas of strategy and tactics which runs as follows:

> Strategy is the determination of the direction of the main flow of the proletariat at a given stage of the revolution, the elaborating of the corresponding plan for the disposition of the revolutionary forces (main and secondary reserves), the fight to carry out this plan throughout the given stage of the revolution … Tactics are the determination of the line of conduct of the proletariat in the comparatively short period of the flow or ebb of the movement, of the rise or decline of the revolution, the fight to carry out this line by means of replacing old forms of struggle and organization by new ones, by combining these forms etc. Tactics deal with the forms of struggle and forms of organization of the proletariat with their change and combinations. During a given stage of revolution tactics may change several times, depending on the flow of ebb, the rise or decline of the revolution.[3]

The Indian Maoists, however, do not seem to entirely appreciate the views of Stalin on the ideas of strategy and tactics and would like to qualify that with the views propounded by the Chinese Communist leader Mao on the same. Hence, defining strategy and tactics as well as spelling out their mutual relationship, Mao points out

> Strategy is the study of the laws of a war situation as a whole … the task of the science of strategy is to study those laws for directing a war that govern a war situation as a whole, the task of the science of campaigns and the science of tactics is to study those laws for directing a war that govern a partial situation.[4]

Importantly, suggesting a kind of modification in the Stalinist position on the same, Mao argues that

> the view that strategic theory is determined by tactical successes is wrong because it overlooks the fact that victory or defeat in a war is far and foremost a question of whether the situation as a whole and its various stages is properly taken into account. If there are serious defects or mistakes in taking the situation as a whole and the various stages into account, the war is sure to be lost.[5]

As evident, Mao differed from Stalin on the notions of strategy and tactics. Indian Maoists endorsed the views of the former presumably because of their organic linkage with an agricultural society like China. Given the fact that India still remains a society with clear feudal land-relations, the Maoist formulations are likely to be effective in pursuing the goal of new democracy.

Such a preferential treatment to the views expressed by Mao is reflective of the mindset of the Indian Maoists who found the Chinese precepts, opinions, formulations and methodologies more propitious to the Indian situations, given a choice between the perspectives from the two giant Communist regimes, the Soviet Union and China.

Providing a practical manifestation to the theoretical understanding of the idea of strategy, the Maoists visualized the strategy of their movement in India in terms of political strategy and military strategy. In this context, political strategy aims at identifying and separating the real friends from the real enemies of the proletariat so that the specific targets can be assaulted and overthrown by uniting the motive forces aspiring for a communist revolution in the country. The task of distinguishing the real friends from the real enemies may be accomplished by carrying out 'a general analysis of various classes in the Indian society from the point of view of their respective socio-economic status and their respective political attitudes towards the revolution'. Despite the general analysis in order to find out the real friends and real enemies throughout the country, the Maoists are in favour of adopting different tactics in various parts of the country owing to the variations in the socio-economic and cultural development in different regions of India.

Regarding military strategy, the Maoists agreed on founding such a strategy on the specific characteristics of revolutionary war in the country. Consequently, the military strategy is bound

> to be one of protracted people's war, as enunciated by comrade Mao – of establishing revolutionary base areas first in the countryside where the enemy is relatively weak and then to gradually encircle and capture the cities which are the bastions of the enemy forces'.

Thus, the ideas of strategy and tactics seem to occupy a pivotal position in the overall Maoist movement in the country as they are supposed to provide operational vibrancy to the theoretical notions of proletarian revolution in various parts of India.

Nevertheless, the Indian Maoists unfailingly envision the goal of Indian revolution as an integral part of the world proletarian revolution. Their basic argument rests on the premise that since the whole world has been suffering from the scourges of the class-divided social formations, it is a wanton duty of the Communist parties of the world to liberate the proletariat by ushering in a Communist revolution in all parts of the world. But since the circumstances in various parts of the world are not equally propitious, it would be better to bring about revolution in those countries where the Communist parties have been able to persuade the proletariat for revolution without undermining the point that such a revolution need not be construed to be an isolated act but part of the continuous process of world revolution.

Class structure of Indian society

The Maoists put up enormous efforts to analyse the class structure of Indian society in order to identify the various exploiting classes and the classes having positive value for the Indian revolution. Among the classes branded as the real enemies of the revolution, the landlord class and the comprador bureaucrat bourgeoisie (CBB) class stand out prominently.

Those persons who own considerable tracts of land and instruments of production, do not engage in labour themselves, or do so only to a very small extent and live by exploiting the peasants and the labourers (bonded attached and different degrees of unfairness and other wage-labourers), are called landlords.[6]

The CBB is a class that serves capitalist or imperialist countries and is nurtured by them. In India, the CBB was born and brought up under the patronage of British imperialism drawn from classes of comprador merchants, feudal lords, brokers and big usurers and has been organically linked to feudalism. Thus, the Maoists conclude that in conjunction with imperialism, the CBB and feudalism have emerged as the real enemies of the revolution and need to be suppressed decisively in order to bring about the proletarian revolution in India.

Having identified the forces of exploitation, the Maoists also differentiate the forces that may lie behind the force of revolution in India. Given the mass character of the proletarian class, the Maoists identify as many as eight classes that could be the motive forces of the Indian revolution. These classes are: proletariat, landless and poor peasants, the semi-proletariat, middle peasant, rich peasant, petty bourgeoisie, national bourgeoisie and the lumpen proletariat.

The Maoists argue that the basic motive force in a new democratic revolution is the proletariat. Conceptually, the proletariat is a class that is disposed of all means of production and is compelled to sell its labour power to the capitalist owners of the means of production. Having remained at the backbone of the gigantic nationalist anti-imperialist movement previously, the proletariat class has now been ordained to steer the course of revolution in India. Providing solid and unconditional support to the proletariat class would be the class of landless and poor peasants who have also been at the receiving end at the hands of the exploiting classes. Similarly, the semi-proletariat classes consisting of groups such as poor peasants, craftsmen, carpenters, masons, mechanics and fishermen would also join hands together for the sake of revolution. Another notable group to join the forces of revolution would be the middle peasants who though own some lands and sufficient agricultural tools, are nevertheless exploited by feudalism, imperialism and comprador-bureaucrat capitalism. Thus, the Maoists assert that all those sections of society that are victims of exploitation would be the backbone of the revolutionary fervour in the country.

Interestingly, in the long run, the Maoists also enlist the support of those classes of the society that would otherwise have been the enemies of the revolution. Thus, according to the Maoists, the rich peasants would join the forces of revolution owing to their growing clash of interests with imperialists and the comprador big bourgeoisie. However, due to their inherent class characteristics, the support of this class of people would not be full fledged as some of them might remain neutral while others might join forces with the enemies as well. Likewise, the various components of the petty bourgeoisie, i.e. the intellectuals and students, petty tradesmen, artisans and professionals also join the bandwagon of the revolution owing to their ambivalent position vis-à-vis the other classes in society. Classifying the various components of the petty bourgeoisie into three distinct sections, the Maoists argue that

> the first section consists of the relatively better-off i.e. those whose yearly earnings allow them to have some surplus over and above their consumption needs; the second section consists of those who in the main are economically self-supporting; and third section consists of those whose standards of living are continually declining and who find it difficult to make both end meet.[7]

Of these, the Maoists hold the third section to be solid support base of the revolution in India.

The national bourgeoisie forms another component of the revolutionary forces at work in the country. Consisting of the middle and small bourgeoisie with dual character in the main, the Maoists tread a cautious course when recruiting from this class of people due to their basic tendencies of being reactionary in normal circumstances. However, certain factions of this section can be recruited as they also found themselves being victimized by the forces of exploitation in the country. Finally, the Maoists count on the lumpen proletariat as part of the revolutionary forces due to their deprivation of all opportunities to participate in the social production. Their marginalization in the existing socio-economic structure leads them to develop a kind of hatred towards it. As a result, they become prone to be moulded and made a part of the revolutionary forces at work in India.

Class character of Indian society

Ideologically, the Maoist movement in India is rooted in uprooting the class character of Indian society and replacing it with a classless and stateless social order through proletarian revolution. Therefore, before embarking upon evolving suitable strategy and tactics for revolution, they seek to discern the class character of contemporary Indian society. In their characteristic articulation, they categorize Indian society as semi-colonial and semi-feudal governed by a neocolonial form of indirect rule, exploitation and control. The Maoists offer an interesting explanation as to why they call India as semi-colonial. To them

> After the British colonialists were compelled to give up their direct rule over our country, the power was transferred to their compradors – the big bourgeoisie and big landlords, on condition that the imperialist capital and their interests are protected. Several imperialist powers took the place of British imperialism in oppressing and exploiting our country. It is these imperialist powers that actually control the politics, economy and culture and decide almost all the vital policies of the ruling classes of India under the sign-board of formal independence that is fake in essence. Thus, as no single imperialist power is in a position to exercise its control and rule over the country as a whole, India is not a neo-colony but continues to be a semi-colony under the indirect rule, exploitation and control of various imperialist powers.[8]

Similarly, the Maoist categorization of Indian society as semi-feudal is based on their understanding that

> Unlike in the West, where capitalism developed by overthrowing feudalism, in India, the British colonialism protected feudalism and used it as its social prop. Introduction of capitalist relations by the British imperialist rulers without basically altering the feudal stranglehold over the vast masses of the peasantry had resulted in semi-feudal production relations. The semi-feudal production relations continued even after the end of direct colonial rule. The imperialists used both the comprador bureaucrat capitalism and feudalism as their social props for their neo-colonial control and exploitation.[9]

Elaborating the ancillary components of the semi-feudal character of Indian society, the Maoists point out the perpetuation of the concentration of land in the hands of a minuscule number of landlords and kulaks that not only keeps the number of poor and landless farmers intact but also drives the people to either go for inhumane activities or suffer from miseries. In distress, the people are forced to fall prey to the unscrupulous designs of the money-lenders as well as financial institutions turning them into highly indebted. Such a scenario eventually culminates in the spate of suicides by the farmers in various parts of the country.

Drawing on the analytical characterization of contemporary Indian society as semi-colonial and semi-feudal, the Maoists discern four fundamental contradictions in it:

1   contradiction between imperialism and the Indian people;
2   contradiction between feudalism and the broad masses;
3   contradiction between capital and labour; and
4   internal contradictions among the ruling classes themselves.

The prevalence of these contradictions seemingly compels the Maoists to write off the possibility of a one-shot comprehensive revolution in India. They, therefore, acknowledge that the new democratic revolution has to undergo a number of phases during which one of these major contradictions turns out to be the principal contradiction. Hence, the succeeding phases of revolution and the concomitant principality of the various contradictions remain the highlight of understanding the problems in Indian society and offering plausible solutions to such problems.

Moving over from Indian society to Indian state, the Maoists also offer a class analysis of the basic features of the state in India. They claim that under the garb of the republic and parliamentary democracy, the Indian state is nothing more than a semi-colonial and semi-feudal one under the neocolonial form of indirect rule, exploitation and control. Defining the fundamental characteristics of Indian state, the Maoists assert,

> It is the armed forces, judiciary, prisons, bureaucracy, etc. of the state machinery that execute the actual business of the state and the principal organ of

this state machinery is its armed forces. The present Indian state machinery is the instrument of class repression, class exploitation and class rule of the comprador bureaucratic bourgeoisie and big landlords who subserve the impe-rialists. Thus, the state machinery protects the interests of the imperialists, the CBB and the feudal forces; renders them armed protection; and oppresses the working class, the peasantry and other toiling masses. The Indian state is the joint dictatorship of the big bourgeoisie-led landlord classes who serve imperialism; it ensures democracy for this tiny section of the society which exercises dictatorship over the vast masses of the Indian people.[10]

Thus, the understanding of the true character of Indian society and state motivates the Maoists to identify the three targets of the Indian revolution in terms of imperi-alism, comprador bureaucrat capitalism and feudalism. Taking the three as the 'big mountains that are weighing down the backs of the Indian people', the Maoists see them as mutually reinforcing each other in order to perpetuate the existence of Indian society and state as semi-colonial and semi-feudal formations under the neocolonial form of indirect rule, exploitation and control. It calls upon itself to take these targets head on and smash them right away in order to usher into a new democratic social and political order in the country.

Besides the major contradictions, there are other contradictions that also require immediate attention for liberating the toiling masses from 'the shackles of oppression'. The Maoists have identified four sub-major contradictions which are specific to India's socio-economic circumstances. First, the nationality question that needs to be addressed. The Maoists are opposed to the idea of 'transforming the country as a prison-house of nationalities under the so-called slogan of "unity and integrity" of the country'. Welcoming the struggles for self-determination by the Kashmiri, Naga, Assamese, Manipuri and other nationalities in north-eastern India, the Maoists support the right to secession as perhaps the only honourable solution to such political impasse. Second, in clear terms, the Maoists condemn the caste system and casteism that is manifested in various forms of division. This is 'a specific form of social oppression and exploitation, justified in the name of an archaic interpretation of religion'. Casteism is 'a weapon which is used both by the Indian ruling classes and the imperialists to instigate and divide the poor people and the oppressed [who are subject to] caste oppression in addition to class oppression'. Third, dalits, the lowest rung of the caste hierarchy, are subject to inhumane torture that is justified because of the well-entrenched prejudices endors-ing 'untouchability'. What is striking is the fact that this section of Indian society suffer on a double-count: they are faced with all kinds of deprivation because of their location in the class-divided society where they are most landless, poor peasants and village labourers, and, on top of this, they also suffer because of their social location in the caste hierarchy in which they are considered 'sub-human' given the accident of birth in a particular caste. Fourth, the Maoists also address the question of gender inequality within the broader framework of a class-divided society. Although women constitute half of India's population, they are, as the Maoist document underlines, 'subject to male domination and suppression through patriarchal institutions like family, religion, caste system, property relations and culture in addition to obvious imperialist-feudal exploitation and oppression'. Finally, given the fact that 8 per cent of India's population consists of adivasis or tribes, the Naxalites pay adequate attention to their problems. In fact, a large chunk of Maoist activities and cadres are drawn from the adivasis. In view of the government plan for rapid industrialization, several plans are mooted to take away the forest lands that primarily provide the tribals with their only source of livelihood. They are uprooted from their natural habitat because 'mining, quarrying, other activities supporting various kinds of agro-business and building of big dams'. Not only have they been 'dispossessed and displaced' they have also lost their distinct social system and cultural identities due to the state-sponsored imperial design in the wake of globalization.[11]

Revolution and people's democracy

The Maoists envisage two stages of revolution in India owing to the non-completion of the bourgeoisie democratic revolution in the country. Hence, in the first stage of the revolution to be carried out under the leadership of the proletariat and to be called the new democratic revolution, the process of the bourgeoisie democratic revolution would be completed. The high points of such a revolution would be the elimination of the three main enemies of the Indian people; namely, imperialism, comprador bureaucrat capitalism and feudalism, and creation of a new democratic order in the country. Such a socio-economic order would be marked by the establishment of an independent, self-reliant, democratic society by solving the two fundamental contradictions of Indian society.

The second stage of the Indian revolution would result in the building up of a socialist social order so that the ultimate goal of setting up a Communist society could be realized. The Maoists did not approve of any idea of securing a socialist revolution in the country in one shot.

In the Maoist formulation, the first stage of revolution would inevitably lead to the establishment of what they call people's democracy, which is a stage of transition to a socialist form of governance, as Mao formulated in the following manner

> Although such a revolution in a colonial and semi-colonial country is still fundamentally bourgeois-democratic in its social character during its first stage or first step, and although its objective mission is to clear the path for the development of capitalism, it is no longer a revolution of the old type led by the bourgeoisie with the aim of establishing a capitalist society and a state under bourgeois dictatorship. It belongs to the new type of revolution led by the proletariat with the aim, in the first stage, of establishing a new-democratic society and a state under the joint dictatorship of all the revolutionary classes. The revolution will then be carried forward to the second stage, in which a socialist society will be established.[12]

The forces that constitute 'the basic component of new democratic revolution [consist] of', Mao further continues 'the proletariat, the intelligentsia and other sections of the petty bourgeoisie'. These classes, some already awakened and others in the process of awakening, 'will necessarily become the basic component of the state and government structure of the new democratic republic'. Unlike the bourgeois system in modern states, where the democratic system of governance is monopolized by the bourgeoisie, the new democratic governance provides a democratic system 'which is shared by all common people and not privately owned by the few'.[13] The socialist republic of the Soviet type cannot be replicated in semi-colonial and semi-feudal countries simply because the socio-economic context is different in those countries where colonialism remains a critical force in the shaping of their polity and economy. Hence, new democracy 'suits a certain historical period and is therefore transitional [that] cannot be dispensed with'.[14] So for the Maoists in India, the basic tasks of the people's democracy would be to trounce the semi-colonial, semi-feudal politics, economics and culture and replace it with new democratic politics, economics and culture. Delineating the basic parameters of the people's democratic politics, the Maoists argue that such an order would be a state of the democratic dictatorship of all the anti-imperialist and anti-colonial forces, on the basis of worker-peasant alliance, under the leadership of the proletariat and in its particular embryonic form of the dictatorship of the proletariat. To advance the democratic revolution to victory, it is necessary 'to build a united front comprising the working class, peasantry, petty bourgeoisie and national bourgeoisie under the leadership of the working class based upon worker-peasant alliance'.[15] What is rather disappointing is the rate of success in involving the middle classes in the Maoist endeavour for the new democratic revolution. Ganapathy, while admitting the failure, exhorts his colleagues to draw plans to mobilize the middle class on the basis of their grievances. According to him, this is an opportune moment because the middle class is 'disenchanted with the state that is servile to the global capitalist forces' because they are 'terribly affected by such issues as price rise, insecurity, corruption, unemployment … high cost of education and health care, threats from real estate mafia, among others'.[16] There are reports that the Maoist endeavour paid dividends particularly in their campaign against the imposition of Special Economic Zones in West Bengal and other states.[17] Nonetheless, one can safely argue that middle class does not appear to be as inspired by Maoism as they were during the Naxalbari movement of the 1960s presumably because of the changed socio-economic environment in a globalizing world in which the middle class seems to be 'a pampered lot'.

Further, the nature of the people' democratic economy would be a sort of transition from capitalism to socialism under the people's democratic dictatorship led by the proletariat.

> To overthrow the moribund feudalism and to accomplish the agrarian revolution, to expropriate the imperialist and comprador-bureaucrat capital and transform them into the property of the new democratic state and thus, to open wide the path of the progress and development of the Indian economy and society by establishing the control and authority of the people's democratic state

over the economy of the country – such is the essence of the New Democratic Economy. The development of the people's democratic economy will lay the basis for the socialist economy.[18]

Similarly, the last component of the people's democracy would be to establish a new democratic culture rooted in the anti-imperialist, scientific, democratic and mass culture by uprooting the semi-colonial, semi-feudal culture. Such a culture is assumed to be an inseparable part of the general anti-imperialist, anti-feudal revolutionary people's democratic front. The basic purpose of such a culture would be to enlighten the workers, peasants and the toiling masses on the anti-imperialist and anti-feudal agrarian revolutionary struggle and the protracted people's war.

In ultimate analysis, the Maoists argue that the central task of the revolution would be the seizure of political power through a protracted people's war. What is significant in this regard is the realization on the part of the Maoists that the path of a people's war would be a protracted one and revolutionary forces must be ready for a long-drawn battle with reactionary forces. Drawing on the experiences of the previous socialist revolutions in the countries such as Russia and China, the Maoists urge the revolutionary organizations and volunteers to be mentally and materially prepared for a protracted people's war given the inherent stubbornness of reactionary forces to give up power and the probable support they may receive from the external forces working against the interests of revolutionary forces.

Given their revolutionary aim, the Maoists are opposed to parliamentary democracy that has 'deceived' Indian masses over decades. There is no way that 'the real problems of the people can be addressed by parliament and assemblies, not to speak of solving them', warns Ganapathy, the CPI (Maoist) General Secretary. He further argues

> First, the parliamentary institutions have no real power. They may pass some resolutions that seem to do good for the people but these have to be implemented though the Executive that has the real power ... [And] the man on the street knows how it is the revenue official, policeman and local magistrate who decide his life. However good a legislative act might seem to be, it is money power, muscle power and nepotism that decide every aspect of his life.

Second, parliamentary institutions are meant to defend the status quo, not to change the system. They do, of course, make some cosmetic changes now and then to maintain their credibility among the masses. Most important of all, it is the imperialists, comprador big business houses, big landlords, contractors and mafia who control the parliament. Those who enter the parliament are the representative or mere puppets in the hands of these powerful lobbies. Even a good-intentioned parliamentarian cannot go beyond the rules drawn up by these bigwigs ... Ninety percent of its transactions are just a trash, with no bearing on the real problems of the country'.[19]

Further, clarifying the fundamental characteristics of the revolutionary war to be waged in India, the Maoists list four such features:

1 India is a vast semi-colonial and semi-feudal country with uneven political, economic and social development with favourable terrain for guerilla warfare, that has witnessed a long period of armed struggle by the peasantry and also now witnessing the ongoing agrarian revolutionary guerilla struggle in which the peasantry is playing a heroic role.
2 Our enemy is big and powerful having centralized state machinery and a well-equipped modern army.
3 The Communist party, the guerilla army and the agrarian revolutionary movement in India are still weak.
4 Our country is a prison-house of nationalities where some nationalities are engaged in bitter struggles against the Indian state to achieve their right to self-determination.[20]

These four fundamental characteristics of the revolutionary war in India also double-up to explain the long-held view that, in the first place, a bloody revolution in the mould of the Communist ideology is somewhat improbable. Defending that the armed struggle is most inevitable, Ganapathy confidently argues that the question of armed struggle or non-violent struggle is not

> based on the subjective whims and wishes of any individual or Party. It is independent of ones' will. It is a law borne out by all historical experience. It is a fact of history that nowhere in the world, nowhere in this historical development of the class society, had the reactionary ruling classes given up power without resorting to violent suppression of the mass protests, without violent resistance aimed at clinging on to the power until they are thrown out by force.[21]

In the second place, even if such a Communist revolution is assumed to be a remote possibility, it is a condition upon revolutionary forces to overcome such obstacles in order to wage a protracted people's war for the same. Hence, the Maoists, bent upon bringing about a Communist revolution in the country, visualize the strategic stages of a protracted people's war in order to retain the vehemence of the revolutionary fervour among its cadres throughout the distinct phases of the revolution. Three such stages include:

1 Stage of defensive strategy;
2 Stage of stalemate; and
3 Stage of offensive strategy.[22]

Regarding the parliamentary elections in India, the Maoists stand for the boycott of such elections on the plea that participation in such elections would only sabotage the revolutionary movement. Moreover, since such elections do not promote the development of the subjective forces, they call for the boycott of such elections by forcible methods also. For instance, in the interior districts of Orissa where the Maoists are assumed to have a strong presence, the 2009 parliamentary and assembly elections are did not evoke enthusiastic response from the voters in view of the boycott call given by the Maoists.[23]

Major components of Indian revolution

Charting out the fundamental strategy of the new democratic revolution in India, the Maoists emphasize the centrality of the agrarian revolution, given the fact that she is a predominantly agricultural country. Imbued by the energizing slogans such as 'Land to the Tiller – All Power to the Revolutionary People's Committee', they argue that the agrarian revolution would lay the foundation for conversion of certain areas in the country as guerilla zones. Thus, dwelling on their military strategy, the Maoists evolve the concepts of base areas and other areas. The base areas would be those hilly regions with dense forest cover and sufficient economic resources that would be liberated by the Maoists to set up their bases. Such base areas would act as the lever or fulcrum for coordinating and advancing a people's war in the country and for seizing political power in other parts of the country.

The notion of strategic areas constitutes the nucleus of the military strategy of the Maoist. As explained earlier, strategic areas are the hilly regions with dense forest cover, having sufficient economic resources, a vast population and a vast forest area spreading over a thousand square kilometers. Besides such areas, there would be four more categories of rural areas propitious for being used for waging a people's war:

1   Backward plain and semi-forest areas with some hilly terrain;
2   Relatively advanced areas where capitalist development in agriculture has taken place to some extent;
3   Coastal areas that are adjacent to the mountain ranges and forest belts, i.e. adjacent to the strategic areas;
4   The numerous adjoining rural suburbs of urban centres that have daily organic links with the urban centers.[24]

Given the diversity of geographical locations in the country, the Maoists evolved their future course of action. Such specific strategies include:

1   The first priority is to build the organization at the grassroots by recruiting committed cadres in accordance with the line of a protracted people's war in the concrete conditions of India.
2   We should work with the revolutionary objective of seizure of political power in all areas from the very beginning.
3   The forms of struggle and forms of organization and the main slogans in the different areas should be based on the concrete analysis of the prevalent economic, political, social, cultural and geographical conditions on the one hand, and the level of people's political consciousness and the state of our revolutionary movement, on the other.

4   In all these areas, particularly where there is relatively more capitalist development with greater infrastructure and influence of the market, and where
the influence of the bourgeois and revisionist-reformist ideology and politics
hold the sway and our movement's influence is relatively weak in the present
situation, we have to lay stress on taking up mass issues and politically mobilizing the masses into militant struggles against the state, making the necessary
preparation for building guerilla warfare.

5   The party must give importance to make the necessary preparation from the
very beginning in all these areas for building the guerilla forces along with
the people's militia and strengthening them in the course of guerilla war.

6   In states that do not have strategic areas of significance, plans must be made
from the very beginning to deploy some subjective forces in the strategic areas
in the neighboring states.

7   The party units in all these areas must shoulder the task of sending party cadres,
technicians, doctors and others to the strategic areas and to the people's army,
to give logistical support to them, and to build solidarity movements.[25]

The Maoists assert that the very general line of a protracted people's war points
out that the basic, principal and the immediate task of the present stage of revolution is to arouse and organize the people for agrarian revolutionary guerilla war in
the countryside. Therefore, while developing guerilla zones and the guerilla war,
they need to concentrate their forces in the strategic areas and give importance to
the establishment of liberated areas. Thus, in developing the red resistance, the
preparations for the guerilla zones must be completed first. Subsequently, to turn
a guerilla zone into a base area, the Maoists aspire to have a strong Communist
party, a people's liberation army and a revolutionary united front. In the guerilla
zones and in those areas where their work is going on with the task of forming
liberated areas, they need to organize the people into struggles by rallying them
around the following slogans:

1   Overthrow feudal authority; establish people's political power.

2   Take over the lands of the landlords, the lands of the government, and of other
exploiting institutions and distribute them to the poor and landless peasants!

3   Build armed people's militia!

4   Stop repayment of debts and interests to landlords and moneylenders!

5   Stop paying taxes, cess, and levies to the government!

6   Right over the forest belongs to Adivasis and the toiling people, Stop the
plunder of forest wealth by imperialists, CBB and bid contractors!

7   Develop agriculture and cooperative movement! Increase production and
achieve self-reliance in every sphere![26]

In the course of a people's war, the Maoists reiterate to constantly pay attention to
the following golden yardsticks:

1   Throughout the period of People's War, i.e. from the time of commencement

to the final capture of power – the revolutionary politics that state power must be seized should be in command over the work of preparing, mobilizing and organizing the people for the people's war.

2   The Party should wage the people's war, constantly evaluating their and the enemies' strength and adopting concrete tactics in the concrete conditions corresponding to that strength. By doing so, they will be able to keep the initiative in their hands. The intensification of the people's war while preserving their subjective forces as far as possible and destroying the enemy gradually will be possible only in this way. They should never forget that to lose the initiative in the war means certain defeat.

3   Throughout the course of the people's war, the party must depend on the people: they must never for a moment forget about maintaining organic relations with the people. Com. Mao said: "The revolutionary war is a people's war; we can wage that war by mobilizing the people and relying on the people."[27]

Finally, in their war strategy, the Maoists concede that in their line of a protracted people's war, the liberation of urban areas will be possible only in the last stage of the revolution. They, therefore, seem convinced that the rural areas constitute the immediate target of activities and the urban areas would be targeted in the end.

Three magic weapons

In the Maoists scheme of things, building up of the party, the people's army and the united front constitute the three magic weapons.

Based on the exhortations of Lenin and Mao that party or organization forms the backbone of any revolutionary movement, the formation of an ideologically well-knit party seems to be the top Maoist priority. This is a critical exercise that needs to be undertaken keeping in view the lessons learnt from past revolutions. Accordingly, while building the party, they sought to imbibe certain empirical principles drawn from the experiences in Russia and China. Hence, in building the party, the most crucial question happens to be the correct ideological-political line rooted in the ideology of Marxism-Leninism-Maoism. Next, they go for the underground structure or the clandestine character of the party. Further, they also follow the principle of the unity of will and unity of action within the party, and the unity between the party and the people. Above all, the Maoists take the collective leadership as an important precondition for the vibrancy of the party.

Once the party is constructed, the Maoists graduate to raise the people's army within the constraints of the peculiar problems of India. Consisting predominantly of the peasantry, the people's army in India is to be an armed detachment of the world proletarian army.

Finally, the revolutionary united front would be obtained with an alliance of four classes – peasantry, working class, urban petty bourgeoisie and the national bourgeoisie. In building the front, the guiding principle would be that the proletariat should play the vanguard role. Further, the alliance of the proletariat and the peasantry is to be the foundation of the united front. Later on, the urban petty bourgeoisie and the national bourgeoisie would also become part of the revolutionary united front.

Tactics

Conceptualizing the idea of tactics, the Maoist document notes:

> Tactics are a part of strategy, subordinated to and serving it. Tactics are not concerned with the war as a whole, unlike strategy, but with its individual episodes, with battles and engagements. The function of tactics is primarily to determine – in accordance with the requirements of strategy, and taking into account the experience of the worker's revolutionary struggle in all countries – the forms and methods of fighting most appropriate to the concrete situations of the struggle at each given moment. A most important function of tactics is to determine the ways and means, the forms and methods of fighting that are most appropriate to the concrete situations at the given moment and are most certain to prepare the way for strategic success. Consequently, the operation and results of tactics must be regarded from the point of view of the aims and possibilities of strategy.[28]

In the proper formulation of tactics, the Maoists place greater significance on slogans.

> Formulation of slogans, i.e. concise and clear formulation of the aims of struggle, also forms part of Tactics and the Party leadership has to master the art of placing appropriate tactical slogans subordinate to the principal aim, in accordance with the need and different aims of struggle, basing on the changes in the situation – how a propaganda slogan should be transformed into agitation slogan, the agitation slogan into action slogan, and the action slogan into a party directive i.e. Propaganda-Agitation-Action-Party Directive.[29]

Party building

Being first and foremost weapon of the three magic weapons conceptualized by the Maoists, party building happens to be the primary activity in the direction of the new democratic revolution in the country. The Maoists confine the party-building activity among the revolutionary classes only – the peasantry, working classes, agricultural labourers, students, unemployed youth, dalits, women, adivasis etc. Moreover, the party factions with party members also have to be set up in the executive committees of the mass organizations from the area level to central level in order to establish the working class leadership of the mass organizations.

According to the Maoist formulation, the party is divided into two wings – the professional revolutionaries and the part-time members. Seeking close and lively contacts and interactions between the two, the Maoists argue for the moulding of the party in consonance with the changes in the national and international situation. Importantly, the party organization has to remain underground from the very beginning until the end in order to be able to fight a superior enemy. Interestingly, they call for the coordination of legal and illegal activities of the party in order to have both a public face as well as a striking capability for the party.

Cadres are the backbone of the party, and the party calls for the appropriate ideological and political training of the new recruits. The basic guiding principles for such ideological-political education are:

1   Conduct classes and combine for 10–15 days every year for the education of committees at various levels.
2   Concentrate on the study of economic, social and political developments in the areas and prepare the reports based on such a concrete study.
3   The party press should educate and guide the leading cadres at various levels of the party.
4   The Central Committee should set up a central publishing house for publishing ideological and political literature in English and Hindi. Local language publishing houses should do the same in the local languages.

Aimed at retaining the ideological sharpness of the party and extending it to the cutting edge, the Maoists believe in identifying the non-proletarian trends in the party and the cadres and starting rectification campaigns for the same. Moreover, the party gradually needs to recruit the cadres from the party to form the people's army. The party should also clarify its class line and mass line for better understanding by the cadres. The party also derives methods and styles of leadership from the theory and ideology of MLM.

In conclusion, the party needs to keep the following signposts in consideration throughout its struggle for revolution:

1   With regard to the forms of organizations and struggle, the party has to take decisions based on the level of people's political consciousness and on their organizational strength but always keep the revolutionary objective in mind. It should, under no circumstances, take decisions based on the subjective desires of the leadership.
2   The party should take utmost care to ensure that it does not lose the initiative when the struggle is in transition from one state to another. The party should evaluate beforehand the upcoming stage and make all the necessary preparations. It shall get ready to successfully advance towards the next higher stage. It should impart proper political, ideological, organizational and military training to the cadres at all levels to ensure that the subjective forces do not face any big losses on every occasion the movement takes a turn. This is the most important initiative the leadership has to fulfil.
3   The party should be on the constant alert against alien class tendencies like sectarianism, subjectivism, empiricism etc. that are likely to emerge and

prevail in the party. Similarly, it should be careful about the right and 'left' deviations, which are likely to emerge in the party.

4   The party should ensure that the mass line is implemented in all spheres and in all matters of the movement, from the lower levels to the higher level.[30]

As the above discussion reveals, the party appears to be the nucleus of the new democratic revolution and also the transition to socialism. There is no doubt that Maoism remains the guiding principle. Although the Indian Maoists are appreciative of the fact that specific historical contexts shape the party and the movement while accepting the role of the party in a deterministic fashion, they do not seem to have recognized this. By accepting the centrality of the party in revolution, the Maoists appear to have accepted the Chinese experience uncritically without recognizing the complex historical context in which the party has to grow. The other intriguing point is the uncritical acceptance by the Maoists of the Chinese model, which was the product of peculiar circumstances in which the Soviet-led socialist camp was as powerful as its capitalist counterpart. Following the disintegration of the former Soviet Union in 1989, the world scene has radically changed. India underplaying the socialistic pattern of society and integrating with the global market no longer remains the same. There is hardly a persuasive answer to this in the Maoist literature. Hence, it is not surprising that the available Maoist documents highlight the violent nature of its revolution without attempting a thorough analysis of the revolutionary aims. This is a serious lack because the means of revolution, namely violent armed struggle, does not explain the ends of the revolution. In other words, the Maoists are very clear that a protracted armed struggle is required for the seizure of power; but they do not give enough indication as to how they run the state once the new democratic revolution is accomplished. And that only reinforces its prevailing image, argues an analyst, 'more as a guerrilla formation with considerable military might rather than a political party with clear-cut short and long term objectives'.[31]

Building the people's army

To execute the plan of the new democratic revolution, the Maoists argue for building a people's army. Such an army is unconventional due to two distinguishing features: (a) it's a political army as against the mercenary army of the exploiting classes; and (b) it's an army for a people's war in contrast to a capitalist-imperialist war. In India, the formation of the People's Liberation Guerilla Army (PLGA) took a long time due to certain factors peculiar to the country. Nevertheless, once the PLGA was formed, it would consist of three types of forces:

1   Main forces – these are the platoons, companies central/state special action teams that move anywhere to participate in the war depending on the need of the movement under the instructions of the commissions/commands.
2   Secondary forces – local guerilla squads, special guerilla squads, platoons and district/division level action teams.

3   Base forces – people's militia (self-defence squads at the district, sub-division and village levels).[32]

A careful reading of the constitution of the People's Liberation Guerilla Army reveals (a) its ideological aim, (b) its composition and (c) its leadership.[33] As an organized army, committed to the ideology of people's protracted war, the constitution declares that

> the People's Liberation Army is the main instrument [of the party] and all the people of India in the achievement of the task of overthrow, specifically of imperialism and the state power of the big bourgeoisie, big landlord classes collaborating with it and the establishment in its place a new democratic state under the leadership of the working class. It, will, in every stage of the revolution, strive for the victory of the people and will firmly adhere to the glorious task of preserving the victories won by the people and to the cause of socialism (Article 1).

While delineating the military strategy of the army, Article 2 suggests that to achieve the ultimate seizure of power, the army will

> encircle the cities from the countryside and ultimately capturing state power. Towards the achievement of that aim, the people's army will fight under party's leadership developing its forces to the extent possible, consolidating them, wiping out the enemy forces to the extent possible and building guerrilla zones with the aim of establishment of Liberated Areas (Article 2).

Once the final goal is achieved, the army will continue to function as a protector of people's state power by fighting

> with all its might to defend the People's State Power from enemy onslaughts and to offer support to the People's State Power, in its exercise of its power over the exploiting classes. It will stand by the people, in the implementation of People's Democracy; it stands answerable to the people (Article 4).

The Maoists stand for coordination between the forces through the mechanism of Central Military Commission (CMC). Such coordination would lead to enhancement in the fighting capability of the PLGA and would eventually transform it into PLA. The PLGA should follow the 'Three rules of Discipline' and 'Eight Points of Attention' formulated by Mao. The tactical maneuverability of the army should include both offensive and counter-offensive. Moreover, the army must also formulate its role in the extension services in order to deepen the revolutionary fervour among the masses. Among the forms of revolutionary warfare, the Maoists believe in guerilla warfare, mobile warfare and positional warfare.

United front and work in the basic masses

The formation of a united front of four classes – the working class, the peasantry, the urban petty bourgeoisie and the national bourgeoisie – constitutes an important aspect of the Maoist revolution in the country. The first task is organizing the masses of these classes into revolutionary mass organizations, the people's army, the militia, the revolutionary organizations of the nationalities, anti-imperialist fronts etc. under the leadership of the party. What is most important among these for the purposes of a united front is the mass organization, which can only culminate into mass movement. Energized by the mass struggle, such a struggle may be converted into an armed struggle in due course of time.

The Maoists talk of three forms of mass organizations on the basis of their nature and functions:

1   Underground revolutionary mass organization – to carry out the core armed revolutionary activities of the party;
2   Open and semi-open revolutionary mass organization – to propagate the politics of the new democratic revolution and prepare people for the armed struggle utilizing the legally available opportunities;
3   Mass organizations not directly linked to the party – the organizations sharing the anti-imperialist, anti-capitalist stand of the party but not necessarily part of the party. Such organizations are further sub-divided into three broad categories:

    i   Fractional work – traditional mass organizations of the rural and urban areas set up to fight for their sectional interests and sharing the anti-exploitative stance of the party;
    ii   Party-formed cover organizations – such organizations are set up by party in areas where it is either not permitted or not possible to work openly for the cause of the new democratic revolution;
    iii   Legal democratic organizations – these are the openly and declared formed organizations to carry out the anti-imperialist, anti-feudal programme and policies among the masses.[34]

Tactics for special social sections and nationalities

As explained earlier, the strategy of the Maoists extend to enlist the support of certain sections of the society and nationalities. Important of such social sections include women, dalits, adivasis and religious minorities. Having analysed the nature of oppression and the problems of each of these sections, the Maoists evolve a subtle strategy of integrating these sections within the broad united front for the new democratic revolution in the country. Similarly, they also evolve a distinct strategy to broaden their work amongst the nationalities in various parts of India. They propound the following principles to act as the basis for the unity of the nationalities:

1   To mobilize the peoples of all nationalities in an united front against the common enemies and lead them towards the agrarian revolution and the national and democratic revolution or people's democratic revolution; to fight against national chauvinism encouraged by the reactionaries; to fight against big and advanced nation-boast-fullness and arrogance and narrow sectarian nationalism; to fight against every conspiracy of the imperialists and their agents to create division and disunity among different nationalities;
2   To uproot the national exploitation of the people of 'backward' nationalities and sub-nationalities and to guarantee an equal and all-embracing economic, political and cultural development (including the development of a national language) of all nationalities and sub-nationalities;
3   To fight for the principle, both in words and deeds, that all nationalities are independent, equal and sovereign and to build up a relation of unity and love among the people of all nationalities on the basis of equal rights and the right of self-determination for all nationalities (that is, to be united within a voluntary federation of People's Democratic Republics of India on the basis of equal rights and the right to establish separate state, if so desired).[35]

Political mobilization in urban areas

The Maoists also consider the work among the masses in the urban areas of critical value in the overall interest of the new democratic revolution in the country. In the blueprint that was produced in 2004, the Maoists provide a detailed plan for organizing the masses for revolution in urban India. They are aware that without adequate mass mobilization in cities and towns, the objective of a people's war will remain unfulfilled. As the document entitled 'urban perspective plan' emphasizes,

Work in the urban areas has a special importance in our revolutionary work ... In our revolution ... the liberation of urban areas will be possible only in the last stage of the revolution ... From the beginning we will have to concentrate on the organization of the working class, which being the leadership of our revolution has to directly participate and lead the agrarian revolution and the people's war and on building a revolutionary workers movement. Moreover, on the basis of revolutionary workers movement we will be able to mobilize millions of urban oppressed masses and build struggles against imperialism and feudalism, struggle in support of the agrarian revolution and struggles for democratic rights. We will be able to create the subjective forces and conditions required for building [in the] countryside, a broad anti-imperialist, anti-feudal united front during this course only. The urban movement is one of the main sources which provide cadres and leadership having various types of capabilities essential for the people's war and for the establishment of liberated areas. We should not forget the dialectical relationship between the development of the urban movement and the development of the people's war. In the absence of a strong revolutionary urban movement, the people's war will face difficulties.[36]

There is no ambivalence here. The Maoists are very clear in their minds that without adequately mobilizing the aggrieved masses for a people's war, their ideological mission is likely to face difficulties. The task is difficult because

> the cities and big industrial centres are the strongholds of reaction where the enemy is the most powerful [because] in these places the police, army and other state organs and other forces of counter-revolution are concentrated and are in a dominant position from which they can suppress the people's forces.

Aware that the party organization is terribly weak, the Maoist document thus insists on 'building the party organization by involving the oppressed sections in the cities and towns'. Hence, the party recommends that

> in such a situation, where the enemy is much stronger, we cannot have a short-term approach of direct confrontation to achieve quick results. Rather we should have long term approach. The task of the party is [therefore] to win over the masses, including the vast majority of the workers, and to build up the enormous strength of the working class in preparation for the decisive struggle in the future. [Now, it is not] the time for this final struggle between revolution and counter revolution ... our policy should be one of protecting, preserving, consolidating and expanding the party forces while mobilizing and preparing the broad urban masses.[37]

How to accomplish the goal? There is no ambiguity here. The document clearly identifies the priorities by stipulating three types of activities that the Maoist cadres are expected to undertake for political mobilization in urban areas. They are as follows:

1   'Mobilize and organize the basic masses and build the Party on that basis: this is the main activity of the Party. It is the Party's task to organize the working class, as well as other classes and sections like the semi-proletariat, students, middle class employees, intellectuals etc. It also has the task of dealing with the problems of special social groups like women, dalits and religious minorities and mobilizing them for the revolutionary movement. It is on this basis that the masses are politicized and the advanced sections consolidated into the Party.
2   Build the United Front: This involves the task of unifying the working class, building worker-peasant solidarity and alliance uniting with classes in the cities, building the fronts against globalization, against Hindu fascism, against repression etc. This is a very important aspect of the work of the Party in the city.
3   Military Tasks: while the main military tasks are performed by the PGA [People's Guerrilla Army] and PLA [People's Liberation Army] in the countryside, the urban movement too perform tasks complementary to the rural armed

struggle. These involve the sending of cadre to the countryside, infiltration of enemy ranks, organizing in key industries, sabotage actions in coordination with rural armed struggle, logistical support etc'.[38]

The first task is primary and most critical to achieve the goal of Maoism; the second and third objectives are complementary. The urban perspective plan suggests three types of mass organizations to accomplish the tasks, mentioned above. They are: (a) secret revolutionary mass organizations, (b) semi-open revolutionary mass organization and (c) open legal mass organizations that are linked with the party. What is critical to the party, as these three types symbolize, is the sincere effort to build an organization by mobilizing the masses that are oppressed and also sympathetic to the work that the Maoists have undertaken. With such objectives in view, the Maoists desire to evolve an all-India perspective plan to carry out their works in urban areas. They also wish to have a stronghold in key industries and dislodge parties such as the CPI and the CPI (M) from the trade union activities in these industries. The Maoists plan for key industries would operate at two levels: working from the outside through various forms of propaganda to get a hold in the industries; and sending comrades to clandestinely develop fractional work from within the industry's trade union as per the available opportunities in the long-term basis. At the same time, the Maoists also propose to work in other fronts in order to intrude into the hitherto unchartered domains. Importantly, they do not forget to enlist the military in urban areas in order to strengthen the PLA. The urban areas would also be utilized to hamper the logistical support to the enemies. Gradually, urban areas in the vicinity of liberated areas and guerilla zones would be integrated with such areas in order to facilitate the new democratic revolution in the entire region and build up the party structure in urban areas as well. The contemporary context is most conducive for revolutionary activities, as the Maoists feel. According to them, 'the policies of liberalization, globalization and privatization have hard-hit the urban dwellers. The toiling masses have now-and-then voiced their protests, but have failed to sustain the momentum [presumably because] of the lack of ideological direction and competent political leadership'.[39]

Two important points emerge out the above discussion: first, the party admits that by neglecting urban areas for more than three decades, it has caused immense damage to the party. In the 9th Congress, there was an unanimity that the party had 'failed to grasp the dialectical relationship between the rural and urban movements; instead, the relationship was understood in a rather mechanical way and the party concentrated its activities mostly on building and strengthening its organization in rural areas'. This was therefore a rectifying step for the party, which is required to pay adequate attention to mobilizing masses in urban areas as well. The second point relates to suggested steps to ideologically address the vacuum that was created due to utter negligence of the leadership of political activities in urban areas. Although this neglect was justified in the past since India was basically a semi-feudal socio-economic formation, the review of the Maoist ideological position seems to be the outcome of the emergence of 'a network society' in a globalizing world. It will therefore be suicidal to ignore urban areas that are equally subject to various kinds of inequities because of the obvious impact of an LPG (Liberalization, Privatization and Globalization) regime. Given the growing disenchantment of the urban habitat in most of the metropolitan cities and other towns in contemporary India and the articulation of protests by the aggrieved, there is no doubt that urban India is likely to provide a fertile ground for Maoism to strike roots. So by seeking to meaningfully address the genuine socio-economic concern for those living in urban India along with the 'wretched of the earth', the Maoists seem to have ideologically re-moulded the party and its approach to various constituencies that are critical to the establishment of an alternative order replacing 'the divisive and anti-people' Indian state.

Concluding observations

Maoism is an ideological struggle to establish a regime of new democracy that is a prelude to a socialist revolution. Given the prevalence of semi-colonial and semi-feudal systems of production in India, it is not possible to go for a socialist revolution. Hence, following the Chinese model, Indian Maoists are persuaded to mobilize the masses for the new democratic revolution. This is illustrative of the Maoist documents which are publicly available. Basing most of their ideological and logistical inferences on the theories evolved by MLM (Marxism-Leninism-Maoism) and empirical experiences gained in the course of the revolutionary movements in Russia and China, the Maoists seek to apply the same to the situation in India. The document appears to be a sort of blueprint for managing the operational dynamics of the Maoist movement in the country. Having laid down the basic contours of the strategy and tactics, they call upon their comrades to intensify and expand their people's war bases on such strategies and tactics with final victory supposedly belonging to the people in their so-called 'Just People's War'.

Notes

1 We are grateful to Dr Rajendra Pandey for having prepared a background note for this chapter.
2 The Maoist document, 9, http://satp.org/satporgtp/countries/india/terroristoutfits/ CPI_M.htm.
3 Joseph Stalin, *Problems of Leninism*, 80, 82, 84, quoted in the Maoist Document, 6, http://satp.org/satporgtp/countries/india/terroristoutfits/CPI_M.htm.
4 Maoist document, 7, http://satp.org/satporgtp/countries/india/terroristoutfits/CPI_M. htm.
5 Maoist document, 7, http://satp.org/satporgtp/countries/india/terroristoutfits/CPI_M. htm.
6 Maoist document, 16, http://satp.org/satporgtp/countries/india/terroristoutfits/CPI_M. htm.
7 Maoist document, 23, http://satp.org/satporgtp/countries/india/terroristoutfits/CPI_M. htm.
8 Maoist document, 12, http://satp.org/satporgtp/countries/india/terroristoutfits/CPI_M. htm.
9 Maoist document, 13, http://satp.org/satporgtp/countries/india/terroristoutfits/CPI_M. htm.

10 Maoist document, 15, http://satp.org/satporgtp/countries/india/terroristoutfits/CPI_M. htm.
11 The entire discussion is drawn on the Maoist party programme unless otherwise stated, http://satp.org/satporgtp/countries/india/maoist/documents/papers/party/program. htm.
12 *Selected Works of Mao Tse-tung*, Peking: Foreign Language Press, vol. II, 1975, 359.
13 Mao Tse-tung's speech, delivered on 20 February 1940 entitled 'New-Democratic Constitutional Government', *Selected Works of Mao Tse-tung*, Peking: Foreign Language Press, vol. II, 1975, 409.
14 These excerpts are taken from *Selected Works of Mao Tse-tung*, Peking: Foreign Language Press, vol. II, 1975, 349.
15 Drawn from the Maoist party programme, http://satp.org/satporgtp/countries/india/ maoist/documents/party/program/htm.
16 Quoted from Ganapathy's interview in April 2007, http://satp.org/satporgtp/countries/ india/terroristoutfits/CPI_M.htm.
17 *Ananda Bazar Patrika*, Calcutta, 23 August 2008.
18 Maoist document, 29, http://satp.org/satporgtp/countries/india/terroristoutfits/CPI_M. htm.
19 Ganapathy's interview in April 2007, http://satp.org/satporgtp/countries/india/terrorist outfits/CPI_M.htm.
20 Maoist document, 32, http://satp.org/satporgtp/countries/india/terroristoutfits/CPI_M. htm.
21 Ganapathy's interview in April 2007, http://satp.org/satporgtp/countries/india/ter-roristoutfits/CPI_M.htm.
22 Maoist document, 38, http://satp.org/satporgtp/countries/india/terroristoutfits/CPI_M. htm.
23 *The Hindu*, New Delhi, March 30 2009.
24 Maoist document, 44–45, http://satp.org/satporgtp/countries/india/terroristoutfits/ CPI_M.htm.
25 Maoist document, 45–46, http://satp.org/satporgtp/countries/india/terroristoutfits/ CPI_M.htm.
26 Maoist document, 46–55, http://satp.org/satporgtp/countries/india/terroristoutfits/ CPI_M.htm.
27 Maoist document, 57, http://satp.org/satporgtp/countries/india/terroristoutfits/CPI_M. htm.
28 Maoist document, 66, http://satp.org/satporgtp/countries/india/terroristoutfits/CPI_M. htm.
29 Maoist document, 66, http://satp.org/satporgtp/countries/india/terroristoutfits/CPI_M. htm.
30 Maoist document, 79, http://satp.org/satporgtp/countries/india/terroristoutfits/CPI_M. htm.
31 Tilak D. Gupta, 'Maoism in India: Ideology, Programme and Armed Struggle', *Economic and Political Weekly*, 22 July 2006, 3174.
32 Maoist document, 82, http://satp.org/satporgtp/countries/india/terroristoutfits/CPI_M. htm.
33 For details of the People's Guerilla Army, see Appendix 2.
34 Maoist document, 98–99, http://satp.org/satporgtp/countries/india/terroristoutfits/ CPI_M.htm.
35 Maoist document, 108, http://satp.org/satporgtp/countries/india/terroristoutfits/CPI_M. htm.
36 The Urban Perspective Plan, http://satp.org/satporgtp/countries/india/maoist/documents/ papers/urbanperspective.htm.
37 The Urban Perspective Plan, 17, http://satp.org/satporgtp/countries/india/maoist/ documents/papers/urbanperspective.htm.

38 The Urban Perspective Plan, 18–19, http://satp.org/satporgtp/countries/india/maoist/documents/papers/urbanperspective.htm.
39 The Urban Perspective Plan, 63, http://satp.org/satporgtp/countries/india/maoist/documents/papers/urbanperspective.htm.

4 Growth and consolidation of Maoism in Orissa

Maoism is the latest incarnation of ultra-Left extremism in Orissa. It had its organic roots in the past movements that drew on Marxism-Leninism and Mao's socio-political ideas. Given its geographical spread in the red corridor, it would be incorrect to describe Maoism as a region-specific movement though there are some specific socio-political agenda that are only meaningful to Orissa. In other words, since Maoism has attracted a large number of tribals in Orissa, the Maoist leadership cannot avoid tribal-specific issues to sustain and expand the organization. Unlike its counterparts elsewhere in India, the Orissa Maoists have played significant roles in redefining Maoism by reference to the peculiar socio-political milieu of Orissa and its vicinity. By contextualizing Marxism not only have the Orissa Maoists indigenized the ideology they have also sought to 'universalize' its role as 'a liberating ideology' for 'the wretched of the earth'. In this sense, a critical study of Maoism in Orissa is also a useful theoretical exercise by challenging that Marxism is not merely a derivative discourse since it is being constantly reinterpreted and redesigned contextually. Hence, it is not surprising that a grass-roots response always remains critical to the leadership while seeking to understand the reality that may not conform to the conventional copybook description. Two critical points have therefore emerged: (a) Maoism in Orissa is a historical phenomenon drawing its ideological roots from a variety of ultra-Left extremist movements of the past; and (b) despite being rooted in Orissa, Maoists are inspired primarily by the Maoist variety of Marxism, which was not merely a meaningful analytical device to understand a transitional society, but also articulates a powerful ideological voice for radical socio-economic and political transformation.

In the following pages, we will trace the roots of Maoism in Orissa by looking at its evolution chronologically. The aim of this discussion is two-fold: first, it will acquaint the readers with the circumstances in which the ultra-Left ideology rose as a meaningful voice and second, by elaborating its growing consolidation among the poorest of the poor, this will perhaps reconfirm the success of Maoism, a twentieth century version of Marxism that was articulated in the context of colonialism in China for mobilizing the peripheral sections of society for a political battle despite adverse consequences.

The growth and spread of the Naxal brand of politics in Orissa has been mostly shaped up by the inter-organizational and intra-organizational conflict dynamics within the larger gamut of the Communist movement. The Naxalbari movement of 1967 started with a romantic slogan of 'land to tillers' and subsequent modus operandi of different Naxal groups in Orissa suggest that the slogan still has not lost its vigour. Issues pertaining to the control over land and other natural resources have so far remained a primary cause of conflict, which have considerably helped the growth of the Naxalite movement in remote corners of the state. Similarly, industrialization, mining, displacement and rehabilitation are other dynamics of conflict, which have substantially affected the course of the Naxalite movement in the state. Notwithstanding the targeted Naxal attack on security forces and other symbols of state authority have become an inseparable feature of left-wing extremism in Orissa.

To understand the genesis of the Naxalite movement in Orissa one has to go back to pre-independent India. During colonial days, the undivided Koraput district was under 'Jaipur' Zamindari and the undivided Ganjam was with the Vishkhapattanam district of Madras Presidency.[1] It was during this period that a number of 'Shaukars' (moneylenders) and 'King's men' from neighbouring Andhra Pradesh settled in these areas. They not only settled down but took advantage of the simplicity of local tribals, and became their masters by usurping their lands. The rural people of these areas were subjected to severe oppression and exploitation by Sahukars and King's men. Alluri Sitaram Raju led a massive popular movement during 1930 in the Malkangiri area to protest against injustice to the local rural-tribal people.[2] Later on, people of these areas responded to the call of Mahatma Gandhi and joined the national movement because they understood independence would make them free from the evils of monarchy, oppression and exploitation. After independence, the British were gone – but oppression, exploitation, underdevelopment, starvation, illiteracy and poverty continued unabated, and the struggle did not seem to end.

Phase 1

Consolidation of Left extremism in Orissa

In the post-independence era, Orissa has always remained a prime target of left-wing extremism. For long it was confined to the southern part of the state before engulfing more than half of the geographical territory of the state. The armed peasant insurrection of Telengana during 1947–1951 had a far-reaching impact on the consolidation of Communist forces in Orissa. During this period under the leadership of the Communist Party of India (CPI), Orissa witnessed several people's resistance movements in different parts of the state. The people's movement in Nilagiri and Ranapur, the abolition of bethi (slavery) in Koraput, the movement against moneylenders in Ganjam and Koraput, the protest movement against the forest officers and police nexus – these are but a few low-scale protest programmes that were successfully implemented by the Communist cadres and leaders and were instrumental in creating a space for Communist ideology and movement on the map of Orissa politics.

The discontinuance of armed methods from the Telengana struggle by one group of Communist leadership in 1951 created a nationwide polarization among the Communist leaders. The impact of this polarization was strongly felt among the communist leaders from the Koraput and Gajapati regions of the state. For this particular reason the battery of Communist leaders from these areas, Bhuban Mohan Pattnaik, Nagbhushan Pattnaik, Purna Chandra Gomang, Purushottam Pali and Jaganath Mishra, were in constant touch with their counterparts from Srikakulam. As a result, by 1952 under the leadership of Communist Party, *Adivashi Sanghs* were formed to organize the local tribals. By 1961, mostly under the leadership of Nagbhushan Pattnaik, Communists were able to launch a large-scale programme in the name of 'Food Liberation' in the Gunupur subdivision of the Koraput district.[3]

The Communist movement in Orissa experienced a major setback in 1962, when the Indo-China war was drawing towards a close; a majority of its leaders were arrested and put behind bars under the Defense of India Rules (DRI) Act. The year 1964 is an important landmark in the history of the Indian Communist movement as it was in the same year the CPI suffered a major split resulting in the birth of the Communist Party of India (Marxist). The architect of the Naxalite movement in Orissa, Nagbhushan Pattnaik, and a number of his Communist comrades joined the CPI (M) in Orissa. However, right from the beginning Nagbhushan was not so convinced with the ideology and programmes of the CPI (M). In one of his rare interviews, he said that, 'after the division of CPI, I joined CPI (M), but some how I was not able to believe the party'.[4]

Nagbhushan was arrested in 1964 under the DRI Act and was sent to Tihar Jail and it was during his two years stay in Tihar that he came in contact with P. Sundaraya and reinvented his principles of socialist revolution. After his return to Orissa in 1966, Nagbhushan played a pivotal role in connecting the activists of Koraput and Paralakhemundi with that of Srikakulam. It was during this period that they formed Jaipur Motor Shramik Sangha, J.K. Kagaja Kala Shramik Sangha and Balimela Power Project Shramik Sangha, and then successfully linked the trade union activists to the tribal movement. In 1967, when the seeds of the Naxalite movement were shown in Naxalbari, one important development was taking place within the Communist movement of Orissa. The CPI (M) central leadership, concerned with the revolutionary activities of Nagbhushan and his colleagues, instructed them to immediately suspend all revolutionary programmes and join electoral politics. This marks the turning point in the decades-old Naxal history of Orissa. Not impressed by the party directives Nagbhushan led his colleagues to form the Orissa State Coordination Committee (OSCC) and expressed solidarity with Charu Majumdar's All India Coordination Committee of Communist Revolutionaries (AICCR), which later on came to be known as the Communist Party of India (Marxist-Leninist), or CPI (M-L). The other members of the OSCC were D.B.M. Pattnaik (convener), Jaladhara Nanda, Rabi Das, Kundan Ram, Dinabandhu Samal and Jagannath Tripathy.

After the formal split and the formation of the OSCC, its members got themselves involved in the violent programmes and propagandist activities. With active support from Purushottam Pali, Hashnar, Jagannath Tripathy, Bidyadhar Patra,

Yudhisthira Gouda, Shibram Panda and A.K. Biswas, Nagbhushan was able to take the Chitrakonda movement to a new height. A new conflict dynamic emerged from Naxalite politics in Orissa when on 1 May 1968, under the leadership of Nagbhushan, about 5,000 workers raided Chitrakonda police station and looted all the arms and ammunitions. This was the beginning of the integration of the politics of organized violence with Naxalism in Orissa. To get rid of class enemies, Nagbhushan suggested,

> It's not advisable to kill the exploiter at once. Rather we should kill him slowly as his exploitation is like a slow poison for the society. We should torture the devil to death everyday so that he experiences the pain of death every day. Political power flows from the barrel of gun to eliminate the class structure.[5]

Because of their revolutionary programmes, by 1968 the Communists belonging to CPI (M-L) were able to make their presence felt throughout the state. During this period trade union leader Manmohan Mishra was attached to the Bengal-Bihar-Orissa Border Committee and got involved with the labour politics of the Biramitrapur iron mines in Sundargarh district, Naxalism fast reached western Orissa. As a part of the Naxalbari line in the beginning of 1968 the Revolutionary Student Front was formed in Berhampur by Santosh Mohapatra and Ramesh Sahu. Jaladhar Nanda, Rabi Singh and Rabi Das took leadership of the movement in the coastal region of the state. During this period Dr Gananath Patra left his lecturership in Paralakhemundi College to join the CPI (M-L) rank. In a week-long secret meeting of the Orissa leadership at Kapilapur near Gunupur the participants agreed to adopt the revolutionary path of Naxalbari.

This period, particularly from 1960 to 1968, could be seen as the formative phase of the Naxalite movement in Orissa. It was during this phase the Naxalite movement as a whole carved a place for itself in the political map of the state and this was made possible mostly because of the organizational changes that took place within the Communist movement. This phase witnessed a couple of splits, i.e. the split of the CPI resulting in the birth of the CPI (M) and then the split resulting in the birth of CPI (M-L). Both these splits had an electrifying impact on the Left extremists of Orissa, which was not at all negative. Due to the organizational conflict the extremists successfully managed to prove their viability in the prevailing situation of that time and this enabled them to reach different parts of the state. The abject poverty prevalent in southern Orissa provided the CPI (M-L) a perfect Maoist setting to organize a 'protracted armed struggle' against the system. Lack of political involvement and recurring bureaucratic apathy never really allowed development to take place in these areas and in such geo-political conditions Nagbhushan Pattnaik led his brand of Left extremists to a new height. On 28 February 1969 the then Chief Minister of Orissa, Rajendra Narayan Sighadeo, informed the state assembly that, 'There are 32 guerilla squads operating in the Berhampur region of the state.'[6]

It was in these conditions Charu Majumdar visited Andhra Pradesh in 1969, and this had a far-reaching impact on the Naxalite politics of Orissa as well. In a significant decision on 29 March 1969 the Orissa State Coordination Committee was dissolved as per the instructions of Charu Majumdar. Charu Majumdar also effectively attached different regions of Orissa to the extremist organizations of neighbouring states. Obviously, he was aiming to give a concrete shape to his ideas of formulating a guerrilla zone. As a result, the undivided Koraput and Ganjam districts of southern Orissa were attached to the Srikakulam regional committee. Similarly, the northern Orissa districts of Mayurbhanj and Balasore were attached to the coordination committee of West Bengal. The Sambalpur and Sundargarh districts of western Orissa were linked to the South Bihar committee. 'These committees instigated the tribals to commit various acts of violence. They also held classes, distributed leaflets and organized arms training.'[7] This decision of Charu Majumdar marked the beginning of a new phase, i.e. 'formation of Guerrilla Zones' in the border districts of Orissa. Majumdar was quick to understand the ethnic, linguistic and cultural similarities between the people of Koraput/Ganjam and Andhra Pradesh, Mayurbhanj/Balasore and West Bengal, Sundargarh/Sambalpur and South Bihar. The tribals belonging to Sambalpur, Sundargarh and South Bihar use one common language, 'Sadri', for their day-to-day interaction. Similarly Telugu is the common language among the people in the bordering districts of Andhra Pradesh. It was part of a well-thought out strategy to link these bordering areas to give the concept of 'Guerrilla Zone' a concrete shape. Charu Majumdar's strategy proved right as in the subsequent years the emergence of armed action in the border areas became more violent. Northern Orissa witnessed the first spark of Naxalite violence on 26 February 1971, when the extremists killed a schoolteacher and Gram Rakhshi, a low-level police functionary. Again on 5 June 1971, the Naxalites attacked a police post at Bholla, stabbed a havildar and set fire to a police van.[8]

This decision of Charu Majumdar also gave a new dimension to the organizational politics of the Naxalite movement. It marked the beginning of the dominance of Andhra leadership over the course of the Orissa Naxalite movement. This was not a small development as it resulted in more competition among Orissa leadership of the movement. Of course, the then Orissa leadership never had an adverse reaction over the decision of the dissolution of the OSCC, but, 'several times in the history of Naxalite movement in Orissa the Oriya leaders like Nagbhushan Pattnaik, and Sabyasachi Panda engaged themselves in a tussle with the Andhra leadership over several issues including leadership issue'.[9] On the other hand, because of this tussle, the Orissa leadership paid attention to the party building, which in turn strengthened the Naxalite movement in different parts of the state.

The then government of Orissa took strong exception to the recurring violent activities by the Naxal groups. Between 1969 and 1971 the government of Orissa, actively backed by the union government, followed a concentrated anti-Naxal strategy. In the execution of this strategy the state police force received adequate support from their Andhra counterparts. The 'Chitrakonda Conspiracy Case' came for hearing at the Jaipur court in 1969, where Naxal leaders such as Nagbhushan Pattnaik, Purna Gomango, Purushottam Pali, Yudhisthir Goud, Shivaram Panda, Jagannath Tripathy, D.B.M. Pattnaik and many others were sentenced to five years of imprisonment. The verdict of the Gunupur conspiracy case also came up in 1969, where 71 Naxalites including the leader Manmohan Mishra were sent to jail. Similarly in the 'Paralakhemundi Conspiracy Case', 87 Naxalite cadres including Bidyadhar Patra and Navin Bauri were sentenced to two years' imprisonment. The police arrested Naxal leaders, including Parimal Pal, Tapan Ray, Ashok Chowdhury, Surendra Panigrahi and Ireshu Achari, as a fall out of the 'Chatrapur Conspiracy Case'. Between 1969 and 1972 the state police arrested about 300 Naxal cadres including Sarat Panda, Dandapani Mohanty, Bhagirathi Mishra and Surya Patra. Nagbhushan was arrested on 15 July 1969 from the Visakhapatnam University campus. But in a daring jailbreak episode Nagbhushan along with his 11 comrade associates fled the Visakhapatnam jail on 9 October 1969. Thereafter he took charge of the party organization in the Andhra Orissa border area. Meanwhile, Subbarao Panigrahi was given the charge of party building in Uddan and Paralakhemundi. Subsequently, Nagbhushan was arrested in Kolkata on 14 July 1970, after which Subbarao Panigrahi was also arrested. Because of the severity of police action the movement seemed to have lost its momentum, to a significant extent, during 1972.[10]

The founding father of the Naxalite movement in India, Charu Majumdar, died in 1972. The intra-organizational conflict following Charu Majumdar's death had a far-reaching impact on the course of the Naxalite movement in Orissa. The post-1972 inner group conflict and split within the CPI (M-L) created large-scale confusion and frustration among the CPI (M-L) rank and file in Orissa and consequently many of them rejoined the CPI (M) and some preferred to remain aloof.

By 1975 the first phase of Naxal Movement in Orissa came to an end. As many leaders like Nagbhushan were in Jail and some other Ideologues of Orissa Naxals were killed by the police. The period between 1975 to 1985 may be said to be the 'dumb period' in the history of Naxal Movement in Orissa.[11]

The movement also received several jolts during the state of emergency.

The movement might have been pushed back but it was not finished. During 1981, Nagbhushan Pattnaik was released from jail after he was granted a presidential reprieve from a death sentence. After being released Nagbhushan was instrumental in the formation of the Indian People's Front (IPF). In the same year he was elected to the politburo of the CPI (M-L) Liberation. But things were not the same for Nagbhushan any more. His old colleague and comrade of many programmes, D. Bhuban Mohan Pattnaik, developed serious differences and joined the UCCR (M-L) after leaving the IPF. However, Nagbhushan was still assisted by Bidyadhar Patra, Purna Gomango and K.M.M Rao in reorganizing the party in southern Orissa. The death of Purna Gomango in 1982 created a major vacuum in Koraput.

New polarization among the Communist force was taking place during this period. The formation of People's War (PW) in Andhra Pradesh during 1980 had its impact on the course of the Naxalite movement in Orissa. 'During 1985–86 Sabyasachi Panda came in the contact of Nagbhushan Pattnaik and his association with Nagbhushan marks the beginning of the second phase of Naxal Movement in Orissa.'[12] By the end of 1991, the CPI (M) in Orissa suffered another split and hundreds of its cadres, led by Dandapani Mohanty, Sabyasachi Panda, Budha

Gomango, Hitinga Majhi and Tirupati Gomango, joined the CPI (M-L) Liberation. However, by that time Nagbhushan's tryst with violent revolutionary techniques (annihilation of class enemy) was complete and it was on this issue serious differences began to arise between him and Sabyasachi Panda. This difference further proved to be vital in the context of the growth of the Naxalite movement in Orissa.

Under the new leadership in the CPI (M-L) Liberation, the Naxalite movement again tried to consolidate its position. Led by Dandapani Mohanty, Sabyasachi Panda, and Khitij Biswal, the CPI (M-L) Liberation organized people's movement in different parts of Puri, Kalahandi and Sundargarh. The CPI (M-L) organized Pipalapanka agitation in Sorada, land capture movement in Gunupur region and the bamboo cutters' rights movement in Gajapati, Raygada and Ramanaguda. However, by that time PW was slowly but steadily gaining strength in different parts of Malkangiri and other areas bordering Andhra Pradesh. A group of CPI (M-L) Liberation members under the leadership of Sabyasachi Panda was in constant touch with the Andhra leadership of PW. 'Sabyasachi Panda started levelling baseless allegations against Nagbhushan Pattnaik. Instead of spreading party programme and ideology he wanted to impose PW line of functioning on CPI (ML) Liberation.'[13] Finally, during 1996 Sabyasachi Panda revolted against the party and formed Kui Labanga Sangha and Chashi Mulia Samiti. Soon Daku Majhi, Abraham Gomango, Budha Gomango, Kamal Sabar and Bhalu Chandra Sarangi joined him. 'Due to the opportunist politics of Nagbhushan and Vinod Mishra, Sabyasachi Panda declared that gun fighting and guerrilla war are the only techniques to attain revolutionary goals.'[14] With the death of Nagbhushan Pattnaik on 9 October 1998 a significant era of the Naxalite movement in Orissa came to an end.

The period from 1951 to 1996 can be seen as the formative phase in the history of the Naxalite movement in Orissa. As already suggested, during this phase several splits that took place within the larger Communist movement led to the consolidation of Left extremist forces in Orissa. What started as small-scale revolutionary Communist programmes during 1951 in the limited pockets of southern Orissa really took shape into a violence-struck Maoist movement by the end of 1996.

Phase 2

Emergence of splinter groups and its impact on the Naxalite movement in Orissa

This second phase of the growth of the Naxalite movement in Orissa is characterized by the emergence of different Naxalite splinter groups in the map of red politics in Orissa. By the time Nagbhushan Pattnaik died in 1998 different Naxal groups such as the People's War Group (PWG) and the Maoist Communist Centre (MCC) were already a force to reckon with in different parts of Orissa. Prior to their merger, the PWG was successful enough in establishing a substantial guerrilla network in the districts of Koraput, Malkangiri, Nabarangapur, Rayagada, Gajapati and Ganjam; whereas the MCC was largely visible in Sundargarh, Mayurbhanj and Keonjhar. Other than these two prime groups, the Communist Party of India (Red Flag) and the Communist Party of India (M-L) Liberation do have a nominal presence in the Gajapati and Rayagada districts of southern Orissa.

The People's War Group (PWG)

It was during 1989 that one armed battalion of the PWG under the leadership of K. Punam Chand moved into Motu, MV 79, and Kalimela areas of the then undivided district of Koraput and established their control over Girkanpali, Kunanpali and Anantapali villages.[15] However, the PWG got a real shot in its arms when Sabyasachi Panda and his group came to its fold during 1996. Thereafter, a new pattern of guerrilla warfare emerged in the Naxal brand of politics in Orissa. To carry out its armed operations in Orissa the PWG formed a number of dalams, namely Jhanjhavati Dalam, Nagavali Dalam, Nagalkonda Dalam, Kalimela Dalam, Motu Dalam, Mahila Dalam, Korkonda Dalam, Uddanam Dalam, Vasdhara Dalam and Anantagiri Dalam.[16] Along with dalams the PWG formed several guerilla mandals to strengthen its network and to give a concrete shape to its concept of guerrilla zones and liberated zones. Dandakaranya Guerilla Mandal, North Telengana Guerilla Mandal (Koraput, Rayagada, Gajapati and Vijaynagaram, Srikakulam of Andhra), South Telengana Guerilla Mandal, and North Andhra Guerilla Mandal all proved vital to strengthen the power and strength of the PWG in the Andhra bordering parts of southern Orissa.

Over the years, the PWG has managed to develop a number of front organizations of tribal people, women and cultural artists. Some of them are: the Kui Labanga Sangh, the Lok Shakti Manch, the Nari Shakti Bahini, the Kui Sanskrutika Sangathan, the Chasi Mulia Royat Samiti, the Radical Students Organization, the Rajanaitika Bandi Mukti Committee, the Jana Natya Mandali and the Royat Kuli Sangram Manch.[17] These front organizations of the PWG were entrusted with the responsibility of carrying on propaganda work, pasting posters, distributing leaflets, conducting meetings, organizing cultural programmes etc. The importance of these organizations cannot be undermined, as they were instrumental in establishing close links with the local tribal people. They worked as agencies of recruitment. It was through these front organizations that the PWG reached the masses and used them as a platform to justify its armed operations.

> The expansion of Naxalite activities in Orissa intensified after the PWG formed the Andhra-Orissa Border Special Zonal Committee (AOBSZC) in 2001. The AOBSZC covers the four north coastal districts of Andhra Pradesh– East Godavari, Visakhapatnam, Vijayanagaram and Srikakulam – and five districts of southern Orissa Koraput, Malkangiri, Rayagada, Nabarabgpur and Gajapati.[18]

The modus operandi of the PWG proved to be more militarized than the earlier Naxalites and with its guerrilla attacks and lethal capability in the use of landmines and explosives it proved to be a resilient outfit. The integration of military and cultural activities done by its front organizations gave a new dimension to the organizational aspect of Naxalite politics in Orissa. The decade-long Naxalite movement in Orissa proved to be largely successful through the works of its frontal organizations that worked among various marginalized groups in a non-violent manner; through mass mobilization and cultural events like street plays it sufficiently radicalized the local population to support the activities of the military units. Following these organizational techniques the PWG actually aimed to make the state redundant and come up with 'liberated zones'. This brings the PWG into conflict with structures of the state, such as security forces. Even elected leaders and members of organized political parties were largely targeted. The larger aim behind the attacks on political leaders at the grass roots meant to make democratic political activities impossible and to put pressure on the elected leaders to go slow on a counter-strategy.

The PWG mainly targeted the security personnel and political activists to spread terror in the region. By attacking security personnel the PWG intended to make it loud and clear that a 'protracted armed struggle' was the only way to attain the revolutionary goals, and for the attainment of the same it indulged in killing the poor policemen.

> Going by the class structure an ordinary policeman should be our friends. But where government is working for the imperialist and capitalist class, executing the order of such a government means helping them in their anti poor agenda and the policemen are doing the same mistake. It's true that they are working to earn their livelihood but they cannot be allowed to spread state terror.[19]

By attacking the police force the PWG was working on a multi-prong strategy. First, it wanted to demoralize the police force, as it knew that the only credible presence of government in Naxal-infested areas was the presence of police. By attacking them the PWG was successful enough to create a Robin Hood image for its cadres. It was a well-thought out guerrilla strategy applied by the PWG to lead systematic attacks on the police force as it knew that a demoralized police force would allow them to operate freely among the masses and it would also earn them respect and fear among the masses. Second, by leading attacks on security personnel the PWG was working towards its larger aim of establishing a parallel government and liberated zones in its operational areas. Subsequent developments in Orissa prove that the PWG was largely successful in its game plan. After the 9 August 2001 PWG attack on the Motu and Kalimela police station the then officer in charge of Motu said in an interview, 'If the Naxalites attack us again then we will surrender to them immediately. To save our life we are even ready to lick their foot.'[20] A demoralized police force in Orissa provided more opportunities of growth for the Naxalite movement. And by attacking political leaders, the PWG wanted to spread the message that it aimed to replace the prevailing system of parliamentary democracy and for this purpose it drew inspiration from the 'Annihilation Theory' of Charu Majumdar.

The Maoist Communist Centre (MCC)

For a long time the districts of Orissa bordering Jharkhand, namely Sundargarh, Mayurbhanj and Keonjhar, served as a base area for the erstwhile Maoist Communist Centre. Since the late 1990s several villages belonging to Gorumahisani, Jharpokharia, Bangiriposhi, Bisoi and Chiranga police stations of Mayurbhanj district have remained under the influence of the MCC. Similarly, it's been close to a decade now that the MCC cadres from neighbouring Jharkhand have consolidated their position in the villages under Bisra, K. Bolang, Banki, Podia, Gurundia and Tikayatpali police station of Sundargarh district. Also, the mining-rich pockets of Joda and Badbil in Keonjhar are known to be Naxal prone.

The history of the MCC in Orissa can be traced back to its activities in Mayurbhanj. It was not accidental but was part of a well-thought out strategy.

The border districts of three states – Bengal, Bihar and Orissa – were selected as a prospective area to wage and advance the class struggle to higher stage. To achieve this, revolutionary propaganda and contacting people of this remote backward adivasi district Mayurbhanj of Orissa began. At first one centre, Bangriposhi, was started; and later it was expanded to two areas i.e. Badampahar and Gurumoshani. In the process of our work, Badampahar and Bangriposhi were merged and the area was called the Bangriposhi area.[21]

With its rich forest cover, hilly terrains and dominant tribal (Santhal) population, the underdeveloped region of Mayurbhanj provided a natural environment for the growth of the MCC. By the end of 1997 the state police started taking cognizance of the growing Maoist activity in the state. The MCC organizer in Bangriposhi Ajoy along with fellow member Monica were arrested in Jamtoria village in Simlipal forest on 1 August 1999.[22] The MCC in Mayurbhanj operated in the region through several area party committees.

However, it is not Mayurbhanj but Sundargarh, which is known for a spurt of Maoist-related activities in recent times. Though in recent past the MCC cadres managed to put forth some daring attacks on the security forces, for a long time the police were clueless about the organizational modus operandi of the MCC.

Sundargarh was always in the Maoist map. By 1999 we managed to form the Krantikari Kisan Committee (KKC, the Revolutionary Farmers' Committee), and Jungle Surakhya Committee (JSC, Forest Protection Committee) in the Jharkhand bordering villages of Bisra, Bhalulata, Jharbeda, Kaliaposh, Tulsikani, Makaranda, Sanramloi, Badramloi, Jareikela.[23]

These 'committees' were entrusted to mobilize villagers and to recruit unemployed girls and boys. Each KKC consisted of 30 members and the JSCs have 20 members. By now the Maoist ultras have carved a space for themselves in the social structure of this remote corner of Orissa.

MCC members from Jharkhand are regular visitors of our area. They attend every marriage, festivals in the area; eat and go. They come to the market. They visit different villages in the night. They have their members in every border village.[24]

As of now Naxals are functioning through the Krantikari Kissan Sangh, the Local Regular Guerrilla Squad (LRGS) and the Special Regular Guerrilla Squad (SRGS), above which there are military platoons that effectively take all the important decisions.

The LRGS is at the bottom of the Military Command which consists of 15 armed cadres and, above which there is the SRGS consisting of 15 to 30 armed cadres. At the apex we have the 'military platoons' consisting of 30 armed cadres.[25]

In sharp contrast to their PWG counterparts, the MCC in this part of the state has never operated through organized peasant insurrection. Despite chronic poverty and miserable living conditions, people from this side of the border have never been inclined to join the MCC out of any ideological belongingness. Several allegations of forced recruitment have been levelled against the MCC in recent past.

Due to the sheer negligence of police the area has become Naxal infested. The absence of credible mechanisms of governance has encouraged the growth of Maoist forces in this area. The security forces never really operate in a concentrated manner to eliminate Maoist forces. The area has become so unsafe that we had to send our daughters and sisters away from home to save them from forced recruitment in MCC.[26]

For a long time the Jharkhand cadres of the MCC were using these bordering villages as their hideouts and during this they managed to give shape to their revolutionary designs in these tribal-dominated villages.

The first incidence of violence was noticed on 17 January 2002 when they attacked a forest beat house and murdered the Forest Guard. Again on 18 January they murdered another person near Jaraikela. On 4 April 2003, around 30–40 armed MCC activist entered into Orissa from the Jharkhand side of the Sarnda forest through Chiruguda village. First they visited Sanramloi village in Monko Gram Panchayat of Bisra Block. Forcibly they drove out villagers from their house and arranged a public meeting there. To generate fear among the masses the MCC activists burnt a *Tendu* leaf loaded truck and a forest beat house. During October 2003 some armed MCC activists managed to cross the border and enter into Orissa. They stopped a bus near Bhalulata; forcibly made the passengers get down and took them a place nearby to conduct a public meeting. On 6 June 2004, again some MCC activists crossed into this side of Orissa and visited Sanramloi and Badramloi villages in Bisra

Block. They arranged one public meeting in Badramloi village. The message in the meeting was to hamper the entire road and bridge works in the area. The motive behind was to destroy all means of communication in order to enable guerilla warfare.[27]

This statement of a local police officer from Jaraikela covers the high points of MCC operations in the Sundargarh district.

However, the government of Orissa made the biggest blunder of reducing the MCC activity in Sundargarh and the districts of Orissa bordering Jharkhand as a spill over effect from the neighbouring state. This allowed the Jharkhand-based guerilla leaders to spread their network in forest-covered areas of Sundargarh, Sambalpur, Keonjhar and Mayurbhanj. This development became more visible after the formation of the CPI (Maoist) in 2004. Due to administrative and security negligence, the Maoists have now managed to link the Sarnda forest in Jharkhand-Orissa border and the Redhakhol forest in Sambalpur with a strong guerilla network. The details of this will find place in the subsequent parts of this chapter.

Phase 3

Formation of the Communist Party of India (Maoist) and after

The Naxalite movement in Orissa entered yet another phase with the merger of the People's War Group (PWG) and the Maoist Communist Centre (MCC) and the formation of Communist Party of India (Maoist) on 21 September 2004. The merger proved to be vital in terms of metamorphic growth of violence and inclusion of newer areas in the Maoist map of Orissa. Prior to the merger Naxal activities in Orissa were limited to nine districts, but after the merger the Naxalite movement managed to reach new areas and as of now 14 districts of Orissa are under the influence of the Naxalite movement (see map – Appendix 6). Sambalpur, Jharsuguda, Deogarh, Jajpur and Kandhamal were relatively untouched by the growth of the Naxalite movement; however as the post-merger story goes these areas have now become the worst affected.

Despite their organizational and ideological differences, there were no instances of enmity as far as the Orissa operations of the PWG and the MCC were concerned. 'Ideologically PWG is quite nearer to MCC. Talks are going on for the merger of these two parties and if it materializes then there it will be a huge opportunity for the revolutionary forces in India.'[28] What Sabyasachi Panda spoke in the context of India became true for Orissa as well. By merging into a single outfit the PWG and the MCC managed to link their base areas of southern Orissa and western Orissa and in the process also included new areas to their roadmap. Presently, there are two Zonal Committees of the CPI (Maoist) functioning in Orissa, i.e. Andhra-Orissa Border Special Zonal Committee (AOBSZC) and Jharkhand-Bihar-Orissa Special Zonal Committee (JBOBSZC).[29] There are also media reports that in the first quarter of 2006, the CPI (Maoist) central committee formed a state committee in Orissa with Sabyasachi Panda as its head.[30] However, as far as the ground conditions are concerned both the PWG and the MCC have so far maintained the same organizational structure. Since the area of operation for both the groups was clearly distinct, there is absolutely no confusion as far as the ground operations are concerned. Despite all these committees, the Orissa operations are mostly taken care of by the AOBSZC of the CPI (Maoist).

After the formation of the CPI (Maoist) a lot of changes have been noticed in the modus operandi of the Naxalites in the state. Now they have shown more organizational capability, more accuracy in attack and have become more ruthless. The Naxals in Orissa have been able to make impressive inroads into new areas. This unification phase was a period of relative calm. However, the beginning of 2005 witnessed some major incidents in different parts of Orissa. In February 2005, the Naxals masterminded a major landmine blast in the Badigeta village in the Malkangiri district in which two policemen were seriously injured, in retaliation to the killing of two Naxalites and imprisoning of four cadres by the state police. Similarly in late March, Naxalites killed an alleged police informer at his home near Rayagada. Again on 1 April, the District Congress President of Rayagada, Satyanarayan Doki became the victim of this growing 'red terror' when Naxalites looted and attacked his house with explosives. In another daredevil act Naxalites engineered a landmine blast to destroy the Sheshakhol police outpost in the Rayagada district. These are not only specific incidents of violence but the clear signals of the dangerous Naxal game plan. Naxal threats such as abduction and formation of guerilla squads have cropped up in other districts too. Most recently an incident came to light in which Naxals abducted 18 labourers from Pudamal and Phulkusum villages of Sambalpur in early 2005. According to Sushant Nath, the then superintendent of police of Sambalpur, the Maoists have been desperately trying to create a corridor from Jharkhand's Sarnda forest to the Rairakhol forest in Orissa. Similarly, the then police chief of Sundargarh, Yashowant Jethua, confirmed in February 2005 that Naxals have been able to form local guerilla squads in different areas of Sambalpur and Deogarh.

Particularly, the Sambalpur district of Orissa, which did not feature in the earlier Naxal map, has now become a hotbed for Naxal activities. During the past couple of years Naxals have managed to strike terror in the interior areas of the district by killing civilians. On 27 May 2005, Naxals went on rampage and killed three villagers and injured several others in Burda village, under Jujumura police station. Prior to this, the Maoist activities were only confined to abductions followed by ransom. The incident came as a shock as the Maoists generally target the police, forest officials, contractors and other businessmen. This incident has been considered important with regard to the course of Naxal growth in the underdeveloped and tribal-dominated western Orissa. The timing of the incident speaks volumes about the greater aims and ambitions of Naxals in the region. The incident came barely nine hours after an important meeting of high-level police officers was held at Sambalpur district headquarters to discuss problems related to left-wing extremism in the area. It clearly signals the Naxal game plan of defying the government and creating an environment of terror and suspicion. Earlier in May, the head of Chhamunda village council was abducted and was released only after he signed a bond paper to pay Rs. 4 lakhs to the rebels. With the recent daring jailbreak incident in the Gajapati district of Orissa, the Naxals have sent a loud and clear message that they are ubiquitous and can strike anywhere at will. On 24 March 2006, a 200-member armed contingent of the CPI (Maoist) seized the small town of R. Udayagiri and went on a rampage that left three security personnel dead. The Naxals kidnapped the R. Udayagiri police station officer-in-charge, Ranjan Mallick, and sub-jail superintendent, Rabindra Narayan Sethi, ransacked the tehsil building, an inspection bungalow and damaged a BSNL cellphone tower. The administration was caught unaware of the Naxal game plan. The Gajapati district magistrate, Binod Bihari Mohanty, had to run for his life when the Naxalites approached the inspection bungalow. Not finding him there, the ultras ransacked the bungalow. The Naxals also attacked the sub-treasury and burnt stamp papers worth nearly Rs. 40 lakhs. They looted a huge quantity of arms and ammunition from the police camp. According to government reports, the police killed three Naxals, including one woman. However, the three bodies were taken away by the Naxals as they retreated. This Naxal attack brings back disconcerting memories of the November 2005 Jehanabad Jail raid. Three years ago the Naxals had displayed their capabilities in Orissa in the most dramatic way when they raided the district headquarter town of Koraput and looted arms and ammunitions from the district armoury.

If the September 2004 merger of several Naxal groups signalled a new beginning in terms of the direction of the Maoist movement in India, beginning of 2007 signalled the Naxalite movement entering yet another phase in the cycle of Maoist insurgencies in India. The merger of the CPI (M-L) People's War and the MCC-I, which resulted in the birth of the CPI (Maoist), also successfully brought the dominant faction of the CPI (M-L) Janashakti to its fold. However, the honeymoon between the CPI (Maoist) and Janashakti could not last more than one year and in 2006 it became apparent that both were clearly going in different ways to occupy operational areas. During the open session of the CPI (Maoist) held in December 2006, Janashakti was asked to clear its stand on its political aims and programmes, however, Janashakti chose not to attend the session. Consequently, the CPI (Maoist) withdrew the partner status from Janashakti and decided to provide need-based support only in the case of police actions.[31] The conflict between the CPI (Maoist) and Janashakti became public when the Orissa Janashakti group, led by Anna Reddy, killed three forest officials on 31 January 2007.[32] Immediately, the CPI (Maoist) state leadership distanced itself from the killings and a subsequent police enquiry confirmed the involvement of the Janashakti group in the gruesome act.

The beginning of 2008 saw an increasing use of mobile war technology by the Naxalites in the state. Orissa, with a total death toll of 132 in Naxal-related incidents, remained a hotbed of Maoist activity. The incident on 17 February 2008 would always remain a special entry in the Naxal record book as, on this day, armed cadres of the CPI (Maoist) raided a police training school, the district armoury and the district police station in coordinated attacks at Nayagarh, killing at least 14 police personnel and a civilian before fleeing with a huge cache of arms, including AK 47s and light machine-guns.[33] The Nayagarh attack was certainly an attempt by the Naxals to woo the middle class, and particularly the lower middle classes, which seems to be caught between the rich and the poor. It signalled that the Naxals in the state were attempting to reach beyond the tribal belt and venture out to non-tribal areas with a sizeable middle-class population. On 29 June 2008, the Naxals for the first time showcased their ability in the tricks of marine warfare when they chose to attack a motor launch inside the Balimela reservoir in the Malkangiri district which left 34 security personnel dead. Malkangiri is separated from Andhra by the Sileru river and from Chhattisgarh by the Sabrei river. Besides the Sileru and Sabrei, there is another inter-state river, the Mahendrataneya, between Orissa and Andhra. Operationally, this is the area where Naxals recently have raised a boat wing to facilitate faster movement of their cadres, and weapons.[34] On 23 August, Swami Laxmananda Saraswati, a Vishwa Hindu Parishad leader and four others were killed by Naxal cadres in the Kandhamal district. Eyebrows were raised when Sabyasachi Panda claimed Naxal hand in the assassination.[35] There were many who suspected Panda's claim on the grounds that Naxals have no history of interfering in religious matters. However, generalizations are deceptive in the studies of movements; Naxals may not have interfered in religious issues in the past but that does not prevent them from entering into the area of communal politics. The Kandhamal operation was well in line with deliberations of the last party congress of the CPI (Maoist) wherein fundamentalism was considered the second biggest threat, after globalization.[36] The Kandhamal incident led to two distinct Maoist formulations in Orissa. First, a split of the CPI (Maoist) on religious grounds, which led to the formation of a new outfit called 'Idealize of Democrat Guerrilla Army – Maoist (IDGA-Maoist)'. Second, in a related development the central committee of the CPI (Maoist) expelled Sabyasachi Panda, secretary of the Orissa unit, from the party. These two developments are bound to bring in significant changes in the Maoist strategies in the state. Undeniably, Panda was the pillar of the Naxalite movement in Orissa, and it remains to be seen how the state and Naxal actors will react to the changed ground situation.

The growth of the Naxalite movement in Orissa is undoubtedly an interesting story of 'turns and twists' in ultra-left wing extremism in a rather economically backward constituent state of India. It also shows that Naxalism in Orissa was textured in accordance with Orissa's peculiar socio-economic dynamics; it followed different courses by reinterpreting (or rather adapting) Marxism-Leninism to articulate its opposition to the prevalent state power in different times throughout history. However, one can safely argue that Maoism in Orissa is essentially a result of several conflict dynamics – be it inter-organizational conflict, intra-organizational conflict, natural resource conflict or a conflict involving the internal security of the country. What is striking is the fact that despite being ideologically inspired by an identical thought process, Maoists in Orissa seem to have become faction-ridden except for a temporary period after the formation of the CPI (Maoist) in 2004 following the merger of three major Maoist groups. In this respect, Maoism seems to be a continuity of the past when the Indian Communist movement suffered due to a split over ideological disagreements that invariably resulted in the formation of competing political outfits claiming to be pursuing 'true Marxism-Leninism'.

Concluding observations

As evident, Maoism is the latest incarnation of ultra-Left extremism in India. The movement remained confined to West Bengal, part of Bihar and Andhra Pradesh at the outset. Over the course of time, it has spread its tentacles to more than half of Indian provinces. This is suggestive of a failed state that neglected, for a variety of historical reasons, the peripheral sections of Indian society. The sustained growth of ultra-Left extremism is a powerful comment on the failure of the state-led development paradigm. This is one part of the story. The other part is about the application of a correct strategy by the Maoist leadership to articulate their ideological faith in terms of 'a dream' of fulfilling basic human requirements. By itself, an ideology is hardly a force unless backed by a strong organization. The evolution of Maoism as a strong political force in India is illustrative of the fact that a strong organization sustains an ideological campaign against all odds. What is most striking in contemporary Maoism is the successful efforts by the leadership to unify splintered groups drawing on the Maoist variety of Marxism. By amalgamating three major groups – the CPI (M-L), the MCC and the PWG – the CPI (Maoist) has emerged as perhaps the strongest ever ultra-extremist political outfit in India. It cannot be wished-away so easily given its well-entrenched organization in rural areas in those affected Indian provinces, though one must not gloss over the internal tension due largely to the interpretation of the ideological texts. What is evident in Orissa, especially after the recent Kandhmal incident in which a Hindu religious priest was allegedly murdered by the Maoists, is illustrative here. For those clinging to the orthodox Marxist ideological line of thinking, religion is a debilitating force and has, therefore, no place in 'healthy human existence'. Contrary to the classical Marxist position, there is a powerful voice championing the context-driven interpretation of Marxism-Leninism that, instead of outrightly rejecting the importance of religion in transitional societies, prefers to set in motion a thorough debate on this issue to alert 'the masses' to the adverse consequences of submitting to religion for 'supernatural gain'. The debate shall, for obvious reasons, remain inconclusive since it involves a radical shift in the prevalent mindset in reconceptualizing one's social-political existence in societies that are in transition. This also requires a meaningful adaptation of Maoism to an Indian context that is radically different from its place of origin. Unless this is pursued with utmost seriousness, Maoism in India will result in 'an ideological package' with no meaningful substance and, in this sense, the debate that began over the Kandhmal incident has undoubtedly instilled a new political dynamic in the movement with clear socio-economic aims.

Notes

1 In a measure to check the growing Naxalite influence and to make the administration more accessible the then Chief Minister, Biju Pattnaik, divided the Koraput and Ganjam districts in 1992. Four new districts were created, namely Malkangiri, Nabarangpur, Raygagada and Gajapati.
2 Raghunath Patnaik, 'Naxal Problem', *Samaja (Oriya Daily)*, 1 September 2004.

Raghunath Patnaik is a former minister of the state government who hails from the Naxal-infested Koraput district.

3 The 'food liberation' programme that originally started from Gunupur (now in Rayagada district) soon spread to some pockets of Berhampur, Chhatrapur, Phulbani and Koraput. Under this programme the peasants and tribal were successfully persuaded by the Communist leadership to attack the landlords and Zamindars and forcibly distribute food grains among the villagers.

4 The full text of the interview given by Nagbhushan Pattnaik was first published in the 15 February 1986 issue of *Onlooker* magazine. After that it was reproduced numerous times in various languages.

5 Nagbhushan Pattnaik as quoted by Dandapani Mohanty, Mundimkhola Ru Satya Nagar Samshan, in 'Biplaba Sari Nahin, Biplabi Mari Nahin', (Revolution Not Finished, Revolutionary Not Died), an undated Oriya publication of the CPI (M-L), Andhra Orissa Border Committee.

6 As recorded in 'Andhra-Orissa Simanta Re Naxalbad', an undated Maoist literature published in Oriya by the CPI (M-L).

7 Prakash Singh, *The Naxalite Movement in India*, New Delhi: Rupa, 1995, 61.

8 Ibid., 62.

9 Statement of M.M. Praharaj, IPS, the Director General of Police, Orissa, 27 February 2006, during one of several meetings with Dr Rajat Kujur, one of the authors.

10 Most part of this analysis is based on narratives of the present and former activists of the Naxalite movement in Orissa. In many places we cannot disclose their names as they believe it would create security problems for them. In the process we had also accessed several Maoist documents. To get the other side of the story I have discussed many things with Sri M.M. Praharaj.

11 Anadi Sahu, 'Naxals in Orissa: Then and Now', translated from his original Oriya article published in Shatabdi, 15 September 2001. Mr Sahu is the retired Inspector General of Police, Orissa. During his tenure he had supervised many anti-Naxal campaigns in the state. He is also a former member of Lok Sabha from Orissa.

12 Interview with M.M. Praharaj, 27 February 2006.

13 Dandapani Mohanty, Mundimkhola Ru Satya Nagar Samshan, in 'Biplaba Sari Nahin, Biplabi Mari Nahin', an undated Oriya publication of the CPI (M-L), Andhra Orissa Border Committee.

14 Dandapani Mohanty, in an interview with us on 2 June 2005 at his Berhampur residence. His statement is in sharp contrast with his earlier stand as mentioned in his earlier article Mundimkhola Ru Satya Nagar Samshan. This makes it clear that after the death of Nagbhushan Pattnaik, Sabyasachi Panda has established himself as the undisputed leader of the Naxalite movement in Orissa.

15 'Another Current of Naxalism: People's War', in an undated Maoist document titled 'Andhra Odisha Simanta Re Naxalbad', CPI (M-L).

16 Based on several reports of the Orissa police and personal interviews of several police officers taken during the course of the fieldwork.

17 Dandapani Mohany, convener, Daman Pratirodh Manch, a banned Naxal front organization in Orissa, in an interview given to Dr Rajat Kujur, one of the authors, during the Jana Garjan Samabesh, the first ever Naxal show of strength in the state capital of Bhubaneswar on 14 Sepember 2004. During the convention, Dr Rajat Kujur interviewed 25 people who were members of different frontal organizations of the PWG and the MCC.

18 Sanjay Kumar Jha, 'Naxalite Consolidation in Orissa', *South Asia Intelligence Review*, vol. 2, (3), August 4 2003, South Asia Terrorism Portal, http://www.satp.org.

19 Sabyasachi Panda, the then secretary of the Bansdhara Divisional Committee of the PWG, in a rare interview given to *Sambad* (Oriya Daily), published on 19 September 2004.

20 Indramani Behera, the then OIC of Motu Police Station of the Malkangiri district, in an interview published in the *Shatabdi* (Oriya Monthly), 15 September 2001.

21 Sukanta, 'Arrests in Mayurbhanj District, Orissa', *People's March*, November–December 2001.
22 M.M. Praharaj, 27 February 2006.
23 Ajit Baxla, 20 June 2005.
24 Mahesh Singh, a businessman from the Naxal-hit town of Bisra, in an interaction on 19 June 2005.
25 Ajit Baxla, 20 June 2005.
26 Subdar Badaik, a contractor based in Jaraikela, in a conversation on 22 June 2005.
27 C.S. Rout, Assistant Sub-Inspector of Police, Jaraikela Police Outpost, in an interview given on 22 June 2005.
28 Sabyasachi Panda, Secretary, CPI (Maoist), Orissa State Committee, in a rare interview given to the Oriya daily *Sambad* on 19 September 2004.
29 Dandapani Mohanty, convener, Daman Pratirodh Manch, in an interview conducted as a part of our fieldwork.
30 Nihar Nayak, 'Maoist Consolidation Intensifies in Orissa', article No. 70, http://www.sspconline.org, 16 May 2006.
31 Information obtained from a number of senior Naxal leaders of Orissa who we interviewed.
32 Bomai Narsimhulu alias Anna Reddy hails from the Nalgonda district of Andhra Pradesh and was operating in name of Naresh in Uttar Pradesh and Rasul in Andhra Pradesh. He was deputed to take control of the outfit in Orissa in 2005. Anna was asked by his central leadership to prop up anti-displacement movement in the state. The Janashakti group established their base within about a 5,000 square km area of the bordering forest region of Jajpur, Keonjhar and Dhenkanal. He was arrested by the Orissa police in 2008.
33 Nayagarh is 87 km west of Bhubaneswar, the state capital. This was for the first time the Naxals showcased their ability to strike in the vicinity of the state capital.
34 A Maoist Area Commander belonging to Dandakaranya area met Dr Rajat Kujur, one of the authors, soon after in a place near Malkangiri. However, we cannot disclose his name.
35 At an undisclosed destination, Sabyasachi Panda told reporters from private Oriya channels that the Maoists decided to eliminate Saraswati as he was 'spreading social unrest' in the tribal-dominated district.
36 The Ninth Congress of the CPI (Maoist), held sometime in January–February 2007 at some undisclosed location, is believed to have infused new tricks among Indian Maoists for it was held 36 years after the last congress. This information was obtained from a Maoist leader who we met in Kandhamal in November 2008.

5   Maoism in Orissa
Socio-economic indicators

Contrary to popular belief, Maoism in Orissa is not a recent phenomenon. For a long time Orissa's tryst with the ultra-Left extremist movement was merely a spill-over effect from neighbouring Andhra Pradesh. However, Orissa does have a long history in the Communist movement, peasant mobilizations and labour unrest. Left-wing extremism or the erstwhile Naxalite movement in Orissa is altogether a different experience, quite different from that of West Bengal, Andhra Pradesh or Bihar. The history of Naxalism in Orissa does not have a centre such as Naxalbari (as in West Bengal) or Telangana (as in Andhra Pradesh) to boast about yet Orissa does have a distinct experience in the consolidation of ultra-Left extremism right from the beginning. Led by the maverick Nagbhushan Pattnaik, the echoes of Spring Thunder were felt in different pockets of Orissa as early as 1968. Even his worst critics would agree that if the Naxalite movement got recognition in Orissa it was due to the revolutionary leadership and charismatic personality of Nagbhushan Pattnaik.

However, it is during the past two decades that the Naxalite movement gained momentum and strengthened its position. Prior to their merger, the People's War Group (PWG) was already a significant political force in the districts of Koraput, Malkangiri, Nabarangapur, Rayagada, Gajapati and Ganjam; whereas the Maoist Communist Centre (MCC) was largely visible in Sundargarh, Mayurbhanj and Keonjhar. After the formation of the Communist Party of India (Maoist), the Naxalite movement spread to different parts of Sambalpur, Kandhamal, Deogarh, Jharsuguda, Jajpur and Angul. The ultra-Left ideology seems to have gripped a large part of the state due to the socio-economic deprivation of the people who found 'a powerful voice' in Maoism. The aim of this chapter is thus two-fold: (a) to draw out the socio-economic characteristics of those districts where Maoism is a serious political force and (b) to indicate the importance of mass-scale economic deprivation in bringing people together for a cause.

Socio-economic indicators

In a recent white paper on the law and order situation of the state, the Government of Orissa admitted that the Naxalite movement has spread its tentacles to 14 of 30 Orissa districts. The paper reads, 'Naxalite activities, which were reported from southern and northern districts of the state, have affected law and order situation of the state. Of the 30 districts of the state, Naxalites were active in 14 districts in 2005.'[1] The Naxal 'infested' districts as identified by the state government are Koraput, Malkangiri, Nabarangapur, Rayagada, Gajapati, Ganjam, Sundargarh, Mayurbhanj, Keonjhar, Sambalpur, Kandhamal, Deogarh, Jharsuguda and Jajpur. Today, the Communist Party of India (Maoist) has made a formidable base in the underdeveloped, rural terrains of these districts. However, this development has not taken place within one day or one year or even one decade. No single group can take credit for making Orissa a happening place in the Naxal roadmap. Equally difficult is to identify any particular reason for the growth of the Naxalite movement in Orissa. Several factors – poverty, underdevelopment, lopsided development strategy, failure of systemic governance and use of violence and counter-violence in the name of development seem to have contributed to the growth of the ultra-Left extremist movement in the state, as the Orissa Chief Minster confirms:

> [p]eople in the backward regions lack economic opportunities. They are deprived of fruits of developmental efforts. People in socio-economically depressed regions often carry a deep sense of frustration and discrimination against their better off neighbours. Poor and disaffected people are often easily manipulated by anti-social elements and powerful vested interests. These pockets of poverty breed serious socio-economic problems. There is corroborating evidence that the problems of terrorism, Naxalism, increased incidents of crime, law and order and social strife in many pockets are attributed to social and economic depression of such regions.[2]

That the state-led planned economic development failed to bring about uniform development in Orissa is evident from the available socio-economic indicators showing the extent to which people continue to reel under extreme poverty. There seems to be no respite for those living in rural Orissa because governance is equated with 'corruption', 'nepotism' and 'mis-appropriation of funds' in the name of development. It is therefore not surprising that Orissa, despite being a rich depository of natural resources, remains one of the most backward states in India. In such a context, Maoism has emerged as an alternative mode of articulating one's existence free from 'hunger', 'malnutrition' and 'ill-health'. Maoism is a politically-charged ideological battle against human misery, which is, at the same time, a powerful critique of the state-directed development paradigm. What is most paradoxical is the fact that despite 'liberal' state funding for development projects especially in the 'poverty-stricken' districts of the state, the areas remain severely 'backward' and the target groups barely have access to the benefits due largely to 'mis-governance' and well-entrenched vested interests to appropriate a large part of what comes in the name of development funds.

The Planning Commission of India has identified Orissa as having the highest overall poverty ratio of any major Indian state, with 47.18 per cent of people living below the poverty line, as Table 5.1 illustrates.

The prevalence of chronic poverty in Orissa provided a fertile ground for the

Table 5.1 Poverty levels in Orissa

Year	Rural poverty	Urban poverty	Combined
1973–1974	67.28%	55.62%	66.18%
1977–1978	72.38%	50.92%	70.07%
1983	67.53%	49.15%	65.29%
1987–1988	57.64%	41.63%	55.58%
1993–1994	49.72%	41.64%	48.56%
1999–2000	48.01%	42.83%	47.15%
2005–2006	47.02%	41.03%	47.18%

Source: data from Planning Commission Reports, Government of India, since 1973.

Table 5.2 Poverty levels of social groups in Orissa

Social group	1983	1987–1988	1993–1994	1999–2000	2005–2006
Scheduled tribe	86.22%	82.34%	70.76%	72.08%	74.06%
Scheduled caste	56.16%	45.92%	39.55%	33.48%	35.17%
Total	66.24%	56.75%	48.63%	47.15%	49.13%

Source: data from National Sample Surveys since 1983.

growth and spread of the Naxalite movement. Furthermore, the Naxalite move-ment in Orissa is mostly concentrated in the tribal rural pockets of the state. The ratio of poverty among the tribal rural people is even more acute and this is one reason that has allowed the Naxals to exploit the tribal cause and win them over as a formidable support base. Table 5.2 contains the data, which casts a shadow over all the tall claims of social justice and tribal development made by successive governments in the state.

Table 5.2 shows that for more than 20 years the tribal people of the state have been the worst victims of poverty. Even if the overall poverty ratio of the state is very high at 47.15%, the condition of the tribal population is simply deplor-able. There is no doubt that in post-independent Orissa, the peripheral sections of society, namely the scheduled castes and scheduled tribes, remain alarmingly poverty-stricken presumably because of the failure of the state machinery to address their genuine socio-economic grievances. It is true that the number of people in abject poverty has gone down since 1983 but the proportion of those under severe economic stress is still alarmingly high. One can safely argue that tribals are rather easily drawn to the ultra-Left extremist movement as they see it as perhaps the only avenue to ensure their survival in circumstances where the '*sarkar*' (government) seems to have become 'defunct' simply because of the unholy nexus between the government and those involved in implementing the development packages.

Orissa suffers from an imbalanced model of development. Inequitable growth among different regions and different sections of the community has been a major cause spreading dissatisfaction and contributes to an absolute deprivation among the population. The Maoists so far have been able to capitalize on these regional and societal differences and this perhaps explains why Maoism has become a serious threat in areas in which the marginal sections are demographically preponderant and have little access to the basic amenities of life. Table 5.3 shows the poverty ratio of regions in Orissa.

From this statistical data, the following concluding observations can be made: first, poverty in Orissa is overwhelmingly a rural phenomenon. Second, there are significant regional differences in the incidence of poverty within Orissa. The rural poverty ratio in the southern region is more than two-and-half times that of the coastal region and the ratio in the northern region is more than one-and-half times that of the coastal region. These regional results capture differences in the degree of economic deprivation of different ethnic groups and their spatial concentration. A closer examination of the Maoist consolidation in Orissa reveals that over the years the movement has strengthened its position in the districts of southern and northern Orissa, whereas coastal districts are relatively free from ultra-Left extremism. Ironically, Maoism has evolved as a strong political force mostly in the tribal-dominated part of Orissa that is lacking in the basic amenities for human existence. There is no doubt that the lack of economic development is a propelling factor and thus it is not surprising that Maoism has grown in strength in tribal districts while the coastal districts, which are politically more conscious, remained comparatively free.[3]

Table 5.4 shows a detailed demographic profile of the Naxal-affected districts in Orissa.

Table 5.4 shows that the districts in which Maoism is ideologically well-entrenched have a dominant tribal rural population. Another important feature that emerges is that all the districts have a rich forest cover, which both the Maoists and security personnel agree that it provides a genuine setting for guerrilla warfare.[4]

Table 5.3 Poverty ratio of regions in Orissa (%)

Regions	Scheduled tribe	Scheduled caste	Overall
Coastal	66.33	42.18	31.74
Southern	92.42	88.90	87.05
Northern	61.69	57.22	49.81
Orissa	73.08	52.30	48.01

Note: Northern region: Dhenkanal, Keonjhar, Mayurbhanj, Sambalpur and Sundargarh districts; Southern region: Balangir, Kalahandi, Kandhamal, Koraput, Malkangiri, Rayagada, Nabarangapur and Gajapati districts.

Source: Arjan de Haan and Amaresh Dubey 'Poverty in Orissa: Divergent Trends? With Some Thoughts on Measurement Issues' (2003), as quoted in *Human Development Report*, Government of Orissa, 2004, 21.

Table 5.4 Demographic profile of Maoist-affected districts in Orissa

District	Population	Scheduled tribe	Scheduled caste	Poverty ratio	Number of villages	Forest cover (%)
Deogarh	274,108	92,103 (33.6)	42,117 (15.4)	NA	697	56.12
Gajapati	518,837	263,476 (50.7)	38,928 (2.5)	NA	1460	64.16
Ganjam	3,160,635	90,916 (2.8)	586,798 (18.6)	18.18	2762	36.17
Jajpur	1,624,341	125,989 (7.7)	373,513 (23.0)	NA	1560	24.91
Jharsuguda	509,716	159,757 (31.3)	87,011 (17.1)	NA	353	9.09
Kandhamal	648,201	336,809 (51.9)	109,506 (16.9)	75.42	2336	74.64
Keonjhar	1,561,990	695,141 (44.5)	181,488 (11.6)	61.92	2067	37.35
Koraput	1,180,637	585,830 (49.6)	153,932 (13.0)	78.65	1915	23.80
Malkangiri	504,198	289,538 (57.4)	107,654 (21.4)	NA	878	54.12
Mayurbhanj	2,223,456	1,258,459 (56.6)	170,835 (7.7)	68.42	3718	42.18
Nabarangpur	1,025,766	564,480 (55.0)	144,654 (14.1)	NA	880	46.50
Rayagada	831,109	463,418 (55.7)	115,665 (13.9)	NA	2445	37.07
Sambalpur	935,613	322,770(34.5)	159,453 (17.0)	42.02	1247	54.18
Sundargarh	1,830,673	918,903 (50.2)	157,745 (8.6)	36.48	1688	51.08

Note: figures in the parenthesis show the percentage.

Source: *Human Development Report*, Government of Orissa, 2004, 283–312.

Orissa is a poor region, but the ratio of persons living 'Below Poverty Line' (Table 5.5) presents a dismal picture of the living conditions in those districts where Maoism is not merely an ideological campaign, but seems to have crippled the state machinery by regularly undertaking effective 'combative' mission in a guerrilla style.

These poverty-stricken districts stand out from the point of view of two major human development indicators of health and literacy, as Tables 5.6 and 5.7 confirm.

A society is said to be developed when its members have access to education. This is an important parameter of human development because it is the gateway to knowledge and gainful employment. Orissa provides a dismal picture in those districts where Maoism seems to have emerged as a natural choice for respectable human existence. In comparison with the overall literacy in these districts, the literacy rate among the marginal sections remains terribly low, as Table 5.7 suggests.

It is now plausible to argue Maoism has so far consolidated its position in different parts of the state where there is no presence of credible governance. Also, it is evident that the instance of uneven poverty among different groups and regions has also contributed to its consolidation in Orissa. However, this is not to suggest that 'absolute deprivation' caused by uneven growth is the only cause of

Table 5.5 Families in Maoist-affected Orissa districts living below the poverty line (BPL)

District	Total rural families	Total BPL Families	Percentage of BPL
Deogarh	55,298	43,571	78.79
Gajapati	112,029	68,763	61.38
Ganjam	548,308	301,585	55.00
Jajpur	280,769	169,595	60.40
Jharsuguda	68,164	33,415	49.02
Kandhamal	145,335	113,970	78.42
Keonjhar	286,923	220,820	76.96
Koraput	264,707	221,846	83.81
Malkangiri	108,870	89,138	81.88
Mayurbhanj	482,176	374,867	77.74
Nabarangpur	215,429	158,684	73.66
Rayagada	188,499	135,785	72.03
Sambalpur	150,799	90,141	59.78
Sundargarh	285,141	185,969	65.22

Source: *District-wise Abstract of BPL Survey*, Government of Orissa, 1997.

Table 5.6 Health facilities in Maoist-affected Orissa districts

District	Total population (in lakhs)	No. of doctors per lakh people	No. of beds per lakh people
Deogarh	2.74	12	43
Gajapati	5.18	13	38
Ganjam	27.04	17	49
Jajpur	16.23	07	14
Jharsuguda	5.09	10	21
Kandhamal	6.48	23	63
Keonjhar	15.62	13	32
Koraput	11.78	13	30
Malkangiri	4.80	18	60
Mayurbhanj	22.22	12	36
Nabarangpur	10.18	10	23
Rayagada	8.23	13	27
Sambalpur	9.29	43	123
Sundargarh	18.29	12	33

Note: one lakh = 1,00,000

Source: *Human Development Report*, Government of Orissa, 2004, 283–312.

the growth of Maoism in Orissa. There are other districts, such as Kalahandi and Bolangir, where there are also very high instances of poverty but Maoists have hardly succeeded in spreading their tentacles there. The rise of Maoism is a complex story that cannot be reduced to a mono-causal explanation. Undoubtedly, poverty acts as a catalyst and the underprivileged are drawn to a movement that is ideologically committed to 'human well-being' regardless of class, creed or clan. The available socio-economic indicators also confirm that Maoism has gained momentum because of the historical failure of the state-directed development programmes in addressing the genuine socio-economic grievances of the poor and the marginalized. What is striking is also the success of ultra-Left extremist ideology to consolidate its roots by pursuing violent class struggle in circumstances where stark underdevelopment appears to have articulated a socio-economic chasm in clear terms. Drawn on the specific context of post-colonial India that nurtured the Soviet model of state-led development until the adoption of the 1991 reform packages, Maoism reinforces those ideological principles that seem to have lost their appeal in 'the end of history phase' of global civilization; it is also, at the same time, a powerful endeavour to reinvent Marxism in a transitional society with clear pre-capitalist predilections.

Table 5.7 Literacy rates in Maoist-affected Orissa districts

District	Literacy (%)	Tribal literacy ratio (%)	Caste literacy ratio (%)
Deogarh	44.45	27.47	34.06
Gajapati	29.37	15.86	21.74
Ganjam	46.72	19.98	28.01
Jajpur	58.00	16.04	35.53
Jharsuguda	52.73	34.87	42.16
Kandhamal	37.23	27.49	34.51
Keonjhar	44.73	24.89	63.67
Koraput	24.64	8.34	20.18
Malkangiri	20.04	6.77	33.76
Mayurbhanj	37.88	24.10	37.79
Nabarangpur	18.62	9.66	23.38
Rayagada	26.01	10.39	21.46
Sambalpur	51.52	32.06	41.44
Sundargarh	52.97	37.34	43.86

Source: data from booklets prepared under the National Literacy Mission, Government of Orissa, 2001–2007.

Land relationships and Maoism in Orissa

There has been massive alienation of tribal lands in Orissa. According to the Annual Report 2007–8 of the Ministry of Rural Development, Government of India, a total of 105,491 cases alleging alienation of 104,742 acres of land have been filed in the court in Orissa. An estimated 104,644 cases were disposed of by the court. Out of these, 61,431 cases were disposed of in favour of tribals and 56,854 acres of land was restored to tribals.[5]

'Land to the tiller' continues to be the most powerful slogan of the Naxalite movement and the problem of land alienation has been a major cause of Maoist consolidation in the tribal areas of Orissa. The legal framework of land ownership and land rights have remained paper tigers as they prove to be insufficient and have given the Naxals a ready-made platform to put the state on the defensive. 'Manipulation of land records' is the single largest problem that has contributed a lot for the growth of land alienation among the tribal rural poor. The tribals were never legally recognized as owners of the lands that they cultivated. The second important factor resulting in the problem of land alienation is 'benami transfer', where the original owners of the land are reduced to the level of sharecroppers though the land remains to be in their names. The third most important problem is the 'encroachment' that is divesting the tribals of their lands. This is common in all the Naxal-infested districts of Orissa, where systematic manipulation is being done with the date of settlement of land disputes, ante-dating etc., to claim the tribal lands.

Access to land is intensely important in rural Orissa, where the incidence of poverty is highly correlated with lack of access to land. When Orissa was created in 1936 it inherited three sets of laws from Bihar and Orissa, the Madras presidency and the central province. This presented a kaleidoscopic view of the disparate laws. The Orissa Tenancy Act was in force in northern Orissa; the Madras Estates Land Act was enforced in southern Orissa; the Central Provinces Land Revenue and Tenancy Acts were enforced in the Sambalpur and Khariar areas.[6]

Post-independent Orissa has no dearth of progressive legislations on land, however, their successful implementation has always remained a major concern. Table 5.8 presents the main provisions and impacts of land legislation in Orissa.

Despite the enforcement of protective laws to prevent tribal land alienation, very little has been achieved in this regard. Laws have been enacted, repealed, amended and enforced but all failed miserably to check alienation of thousand of acres of land that has been transferred from tribals to non-tribals through legal and illegal means. The problem of land alienation assumes more significance in the context of the Naxalite movement of the state, as alienation of tribal land is intensely felt in Naxal-infested districts of Koraput, Nawarangpur, Rayagada and Malkanagiri. Poverty, illiteracy, settlement of outsiders in tribal areas, development-induced displacement and the systemic operation of land mafias, which also include government officials, are the main causes of land alienation among the tribal population. It starts with an advance of a consumption loan to a tribal household, which is followed by further loan advance, accumulation of debt, failure to repay the debt and finally mortgage of land against the debt. Mortgage, sale, benami (unnamed) transactions, forcible occupation and encroachment are identified as five major processes of transfer of tribal land to non-tribals.

A review of the legislative framework of Orissa confirms that land reforms policies have been based on the principle of redistributive justice and on arguments regarding efficiency (land to the tiller, fixation of ceilings, prevention of fragmentation, etc.). Since Independence, nearly 3.01 million hectares has been declared as ceiling surplus in the country. Of this nearly 2.31 million hectares has been taken over by the government and 1.76 million hectares distributed[7] among 5 million beneficiaries, half of whom are scheduled castes and scheduled tribes. Besides, 7.26 lakh acres of government wasteland has been provided to the landless in the state.[8] In addition, 5.80 lakh acres of *Bhoodan*[9] land has been distributed to the poor in Orissa. Despite all these efforts, access to land still remains a distant dream for the vast majority of the poor.

Land, corruption and resentment

One of the critical factors contributing to the growth of ultra left wing extremism is undoubtedly the well-entrenched malpractices relating to the land survey and settlement in most of the affected districts. During the field survey, we have come

Table 5.8 Land legislation in Orissa, 1952–1972

Name	Year	Provisions	Impact
Orissa Estate Abolition Act	1952	• Abolition of intermediaries in the state. • Vesting of all Land Rights in the state. • Agricultural land less then 23 acres to remain with the intermediaries for personal cultivation.	• No provision of protection for tenants. • Eviction of tenants as the Zamindars were allowed land less then 33 acres, for personal cultivation. • Abolition of intermediaries could not be completed until 1974.
Orissa Land Reforms Act (amended in 1965, 1973, 1974)	1960	• Permanent, heritable, and transferable rights in land for the tiller. • Ban on leasing of land except under special conditions (in 1972). • Under adverse possession, land in continuous cultivation for 12 years or more by a person other than its owner shall pass to the cultivator. • Rent not to exceed one fourth of the gross produce. • Ceiling on individual holdings at 33 standard acres – later reduced to 20 (in 1965), and to 10 standard acres (in 1972).	• Delay in enactment and actual implementation of the act provided sufficient opportunities for large land owners to escape ceiling restrictions. • By explicitly banning tenancy, the law is unable to address the problem of share cropping. • No provision was made to record concealed tenancies.
Orissa Survey and Settlement Act	1958	• Different laws related to survey, record of rights and settlement amended and consolidation in to one uniform law.	• Establishment of uniform (though defective) system of rights of tenants not recorded during settlement operations.
Orissa Consolidations of Holdings and Prevention of Fragmentation of Land Act	1972	• Fragmentation of land declared illegal. • First choice of transfer to adjacent farmer.	• Little impact on land fragmentation. • Occasional land sales but rarely to adjacent farmers. • Consolidation of land holdings ignored by the farmers in western Orissa because of undulating terrain.

(continued)

Table 5.8 Land legislation in Orissa, 1952–1972 (*continued*)

Name	Year	Provisions	Impact
Orissa Prevention of Land Encroachment Act (amended in 1982)	1972	• Unauthorized occupation of government land prohibited. • Penalties on encroachers to be followed by eviction. • The 1982 amendment for settlement of two (later amended to one) standard acres of 'unobjectionable' land (i.e. government wasteland) with 'eligible' beneficiaries (e.g. landless).	• Penalties too low to act as a disincentive to encroachers. • The 1982 amendment not a 'proactive' right-encroacher cannot 'apply' to be regularized as act of encroachment is regarded as illegal in the first place. • Only Revenue Inspector can initiate regularisation of rights. • Considerable scope for rent-seeking by revenue officials.

Source: compiled from data obtained from the Department of Revenue, Government of Orissa, and field notes.

across innumerable instances where the government mission to follow the rules and regulations in this regard was clearly defeated due to the complicity of the large landowners with the government officials involved in the process. On most occasions, the revenue department (responsible for survey and settlement) seems to maintain 'a stoic silence' even when the local land revenue official (the *Tahasilder*) transfers land 'without verifying the government records'. This appears to be a common pattern especially in tribal districts in violation of the statutory provision that 'tribal land cannot be transferred to the non-tribals without the permission of the concerned revenue officials'. Despite clear government directions, poor tribals are forced to sell their lands to the non-tribals for mere survival which is usually endorsed by the revenue official without being, on most occasions, careful about the statutory requirements in this regard. The tribals lose on two counts, as our field data suggest; (a) they do not get the actual price of the land because these are mostly 'distress sale' and (b) they also suffer since the revenue officials taking advantage of the lack of literacy among the tribals are seen to be tilted towards the buyer while interpreting rules and regulations in regard to purchase and sale of land. It is therefore not surprising that a new class of land-owners (who are mostly non-tribals) has emerged in these areas displacing the tribals who are slowly losing their ancestral property. The level of corruption is allegedly so high that there are extreme cases where the revenue officials are directly involved in distorting records to (a) favour non-tribals and (b) reduce the price of the land by raising 'issues of legal complications' forcing the owners to agree to pay a bribe to the concerned official for sorting out the difficulty. A state civil servant who held an important rank in the revenue department thus admits that the root cause of the rise of the Maoism is certainly 'the growing pauperization of the people in the tribal districts of Orissa' largely due to the failure of the government to stop 'the displacement of the tribals from their habitat'. The image of the state as a supportive partner of the land mafia and large landowners seems to have gained ground in view of many instances of the same nature. The revenue officer, on condition of anonymity, illustrated the point by referring to various cases in which the concerned authority went out of their way to complete a land-deal which was heavily tilted towards the buyer at the cost of the tribal-owner. He recalled one such case where about 6.5 acres of land in the Gengutipali village of Sambalpur district was purchased by Jagmohan Singh of Surguja of Chhatishgarh in 2004. The land belonged to a tribal family having seven members including one old lady (of sixty years of age) named Gangi Munda, who was shown dead and childless by the purchaser during the transaction. Without verifying the facts the Sambalpur *Tahasildar* even transferred the land in favour of Jag Mohan Singh and the statutory revenue document, *the Record of Rights*, was immediately revised to offcially recognise the land-transfer. The complicity of the *Tahasildar* with the buyer was evident when the price of the land was drastically reduced from the market price of Rs. 11000/- (approximately $US 280) per decimal to a mere Rs. 1000/- (approximately $US 25) per decimal.[10]

A recent study carried out in 12 villages (Aminguda, Lendrimaliguda, Machhra, Kellar, Podapadar, Badanereka, Dumarpadar, Kudipadar, Gaudaguda, Khajuriput, Suku and Podagada) under Koraput, Laxmipur and Dasamanthapur blocks by a Bhubaneswar-based forestry research organization, Regional Centre for Development Cooperation (RCDC), in collaboration with the Hyderabad-based National Institute of Rural Development (NIRD), indicates that tribal land alienation has been a continuous process in the district.[11] The total number of households taken up for study was 1,850, of which only 6.7 per cent belonged to the scheduled castes. The scheduled tribes constituted nearly 65 per cent of the total households. Nearly 28.4 per cent of the households belonged to other castes. The total population in the villages was 8,062, of whom 4,097 were male. The sex ratio stood at 967 females for every 1,000 males. The study threw up some alarming findings, such as the ones given below:

1   About 90 per cent of the families covered in the study were below the poverty line.
2   In three of the villages under the study, not even a single household was found to be above the poverty line.
3   Despite abject poverty, only 18 per cent of the households got houses under the *Indira Awaas Yojana*.[12]
4   Among the households chosen for study in the selected villages, 10 per cent were of big farmers. The percentage of small farmers' households was 38 and marginal farmers and landless households constituted 32 and 20 per cent respectively.
5   The study found that of the total households having homestead land, only 15 per cent had *pattas* or title deeds. The rest did not possess title deeds although they were in physical possession of the land.
6   Several residents of seven villages (Kellar, Badanereka, Kudipadar, Gaudaguda, Suku, Podagada and Machhra) who were allotted land in 1976–1977 were yet to get *pattas*. In many villages, the land allotted to the legitimate beneficiaries was found to be either unproductive or uncultivable.

Since independence, several mega industrial and mining projects have come up in areas that were under the occupation of tribal communities. When the British occupied India they could not understand and appreciate the customary rights of the people of India, particularly that of tribal communities. Earlier, customary rights were recognized in India because they concerned not only the tribals but also the village communities. The UN document of 1966 defines customary rights as the rights to use or dispose off the rights over land. In the past most of the tribal settlements comprised members of a single clan who held land and forest resources as their own, in their habitat. Land for others may be used for agriculture but land for tribals is a part of larger socio-economic structure of society, which is handed over from one generation to another as a source of life sustenance. Scheduled tribes, which constitute 22 per cent of Orissa's population are the most marginalized and poorest social group in the state, with over 72 per cent living under the poverty line. Though land and land-based resources are central to the livelihoods of tribal people, they have poor access to land and forests. Most tribal communities in Orissa have a strong cultural and social relationship with land, with many practising communal ownership of land, especially hilly land. During the last two centuries, tribal communities have been affected by land loss through alienation of plain lands to non-tribals and the hilly lands to the state, which has categorized these areas as forest land or revenue wastelands. The loss of private land holdings by tribals has been a cause of concern with a number of laws being passed by both pre-independence state and post-colonial state to check land alienation. These laws suffered from many shortcomings and were unable to check transfer of land from tribals to non-tribals.

Land continues to be the central point in the modus operandi of Naxal groups. To gain legitimacy for its violent actions, the PWG never ignored the issues related to the control of land and it gave a significant dimension to the complex character of the Naxalite movement in Orissa. Particularly the Chashi Mulia Samiti and the Kui Labanga Sangh of Sabyasachi Panda were instrumental in leading the land recapture programme. During 1996 the Chashi Mulia Samiti organized its first land recapture programme at Anugur Panchayat in the Gajapati district to reoccupy 6 acres of land. In 1997 tribals in Raba village of Mohana block in the Gajapati district occupied 50 acres of tribal land, which had been under the control of non-tribals for the past three to four decades. Four cadres of the PWG were arrested in this struggle and several of its cadres were also implicated for having waged a war against the state. Finally the tribals won the battle. About 400 to 500 peasants participated in this land struggle. In 1998, the land movement started in Mandrabaju and Sindhba of Mohana block, Murizing-Tabarda of Naugada block and in many other places in the Gajapati district.[13] However, 'these were all small scale programmes with little mass support and the police force was using heavy force to crush such programmes. The local Zamindars were also applying their force to foil the attempts of the Chashi Mulia Samiti.'[14]

After doing the groundwork for nearly five years the Chashi Mulia Samiti really started its land recapture programme after 2000. By that time Sabyasachi Panda had already established himself as an undisputed guerilla leader.

> During 1995 the Chashi Mulia Samiti started to initiate the land recapture programme. However the programme was not that successful. But in 2000 the organization decided to follow a concentrated and anti-lawful approach to free the sealing lands from the clutches of Zamindars (landlords). Right from 2001 [the organization has] been successfully recapturing the lands that are illegally captured by the exploitive local Zamindars.[15]

In 2001 the Chashi Mulia Samiti relaunched its land recapture programme in the Gudari, Ramnaguda and Kolanara areas of the Rayagada district. It identified five villages, namely Dimiriguda, Luhagumma, Siriguda, Bamunidangar and Bijapur. 'In a secret meeting in a village near Gudari on 2 November 2001, it was decided to initiate land recapture programme immediately.'[16] The Chashi Mulia Samiti also released the names of 64 Zamindars and the amount of land they were holding (see Table 5.9).

Between November and December 2001 30 villages participated in the land

Table 5.9 Zamindar land holdings

Zamindar	Residence	Location of land holding	Land amount (acres)
Lokanath Panigrahi	Naira	Dimiriguda	50
Minaketan Padhi	Gudari	do.	20
Rama Patra	do.	do.	23
Ganapati Padhi	do.	do.	41
Bala Panigrahi	do.	do.	40
Dama Mohanty	do.	do.	17
Arjun Panigrahi	do.	Borda	30
Jairam Panigrahi	do.	do.	30
Binod	do.	do.	12
Ganapati	do.	Gummi	40
Kantia Chinnara	do.	Luhagumma	15
Brundaban Panigrahi	do.	do.	30
Sitaram Panigrahi	do.	do.	30
Dr Ramanath Panigrahi	Berhampur	do.	61
Pratap Sahu	Gudari	Siriguda	100
Debendra Sahu	Naira	Burlendi	70
Istu Kumuti	Gudari	Ramuluguda	16
Madhab Panigrahi	do.	Siriguda	30
Radha Krishna Mahapatra	do.	do.	16
Sarbeswar Rao	do.	do.	36
Budha Patrikara	do.	Asada	16
Oma Samba	Gudari	Bamunidangar	14
Relie Panigrahi	do.	do.	15
Ashok Patra	Gudari	do.	24
Nandi Sahukari	do.	do.	20
Subash Panigrahi	do.	do.	12
Bhubani Padhi	do.	do.	24
Ganesh	do.	do.	9
Dandashi Sundhi	do.	do.	15

Zamindar	Residence	Location of land holding	Land amount (acres)
Gopinath Pattnaik	do.	Many villages	80
Subash Panda	do.	Bamunidangar	9
Barada Rajul	do.	Bellamguda	20
Lokanath Gowda	Toradi	Toradi	100
Pichha Sahukar	Karlaghati	Karlaghati	70
Simanchala	do.	do.	30
Padman	do.	do.	30
Sahadev	Sambarlendi	Sambarlendi	60
Hari	Dandapada	Dandapada	250
Damudara	Dumeli	Dumeli	100
Sadhir Das	Durgi	Durgi	400
Sunil Panda	do.	do.	300
Bania Sarapancha	Dhepaguda	Dhepaguda	150
Birata Gouda	do.	do.	100
Krishna Gouda	do.	do.	40
Brundaban Padhi	Dahani	Dahani	50
Purna Majhi	Birapanga	Birapanga	18
Krishna Rao	Gudari	Adda	30
Kuna Pattnaik	do.	Rengam	30
Radhakrushna Mohapatra	do.	do.	40
Bibasuni Karana	do.	do.	25
Mitu Pattnaik	do.	do.	12
Goura Pattnaik	do.	Balipanga	15
Surya Panda	do.	Bhitarapur	25
Ladi Trinath	do.	do.	40
Ladi Swamy	do.	do.	16
Pralay	do.	Bijapur	15
Sunil	do.	do.	30
Mahapatra	Berhampur	do.	7
Bijay	Bijapur	Bijapur	15

(*continued*)

Table 5.9 Zamindar land holdings (*continued*)

Zamindar	Residence	Location of land holding	Land amount (acres)
Purushottam	Gudari	do.	15
Purna Sahu	do.	do.	20
Maharathi Dom	Guluguda	Guluguda	30
Bhima Senapati	Khamariguda	Khamariguda	20
Prakash Senapati	do.	do.	100

Source: '2001 Andolana Pain Parjyabekhyana Prashtuti (Preparations for 2001 Struggle)', circulated by Chashi Mulia Samiti, Gajapati.

Note: do. = as above.

recapture programme of the Chashi Mulia Samiti. They were Bhitarpur, Gajiguda, Parkupuda, Anuguruti, Sidaguda, Balipanga, Rangam, Silimi, Dimiriguda, Siriguda, Kradang, Luhagumma, Luhamunda, Arjunguda, Sargiguda, Burlendi, Rekpankal, Barda, Adda, Ramnagar, Bijapur, Burkadi, Titimiri, Jigidibata, Jalanidhi, Dhepaguda, Titimiriguda, Brahmanidangar, Muliputu and Laxmanguda. As part of the larger guerilla programme, people in these villages were effectively assisted by the armed cadres of the PWG to snatch grains from the agricultural fields of the above-mentioned Jamindars.[17]

The Chashi Mulia Samiti, despite stiff resistance from the police force continued with its programme of land recapturing throughout 2002 to 2005. However, a new conflict dynamic has emerged from this radical programme. As observed by M.M. Praharaj

> As a result of loss of food grains during 2001 most of the land owners deserted their land by 2002. But the tribal people who were instigated by Sabyasachi Panda group to drive out the landowners were in no position to cultivate the land by themselves. This made the life of the poor tribal more miserable. Because earlier they were getting daily wage when they were working as the agricultural labourer but by snatching the food grains from the agricultural field of the mighty land lords they invited their anger.[18]

In one of its reports the Chashi Mulia Samiti admitted that

> Due to stiff resistance from the land owners as well as from the government forces, the common men were not able to transform the food grain capture programme into a land recapture programme as originally envisaged. That was the reason for which most of the land during 2002 remained uncultivated.[19]

In 2003 the Chashi Mulia Samiti again released a list of 23 Zamindars who surrendered before them and also surrendered their claim over the land (see Table 5.10).

Table 5.10 Surrendered Zamindars

Zamindar	Village	Land surrendered (acres)
Lokanath Panigrahi	Naira	50
Minaketan Padhi	Gudari	17
Rama Patra	do.	23
Ganapati Padhi	do.	41
Bhala Panigrahi	do.	40
Dama Mohanty	do.	17
Arjun Panigrahi	do.	30
Jairam Panigrahi	do.	30
Binod	do.	12
Ramanath Panigrahi	do.	30
Budha Sarpancha	Dhepaguda	100
Surendra dama	do.	150
Babula Bania	do.	30
Bhaskar Padhi	do.	30
Surya Panda	Gudari	25
Krishna Rao	do.	30
Ladi Trinath	do.	40
Ladi Swamy	do.	16
Kuna Pattnaik	do.	15
Radhanath Pattnaik	do.	20
Gopinath Pattnaik	do.	12
Bhaba Pattnaik	Gunupur	6
Goura Pattnaik	Gudari	15

Source: '2003 Re Dakhala Hei Thiba Jami (Land annexed during 2003)', circulated by Chashi Mulia Samiti.

Note: do. = as above.

Land as the dynamic of organizational conflict

The 'Gudari Land Recapture Movement' of the Chashi Mulia Samiti, sponsored by the PWG, also set the tones for a fresh round of confrontation between the CPI (M-L) Liberation and the PWG. The CPI (M-L) Liberation did not want to lose its credentials of fighting for the land rights of the people, but it could not support the programme of the PWG for obvious reasons.

In South Orissa districts of Gajapati and Rayagada bordering Andhra Pradesh, illegal transfer of land from the rural poor, particularly adivasis, has become a growing phenomenon. Also there are many cases of landlords, moneylenders and the mafia illegally controlling ceiling surplus or other government lands and reserve forestlands. In its attempt to revive peasant struggle in this bordering region in the spirit of Srikakulam struggle, our Party has concentrated on developing land struggles of the rural poor and tribal people on these issues and this has been instrumental in our advancement in Orissa. On the other hand, certain anarchist outfits have misutilised the land question as well as other aspirations of the tribal people in the recent times to increase conflicts between tribals and dalits. In order to counter this trend, we decided to organize land struggles along the proletarian class line through mobilizing broad masses of the rural poor.[20]

As per one leaflet released by CPI (M-L) Liberation, the activists of the party mobilized the people to recapture 75 acres of land in the Rayagada district during 2001. In the subsequent years they also organized land recapture movements in Chandarpur, Padampur, Indupur, Khomapodar, Laruguda, Koelkota, Koelpatalu and Gunupur area in the Rayagada district. Tirupati Gomago (one-time close associate of Sabyasachi Panda), Karuvu Naiko, Rushi Dandasi, Bhagirathi Savoura, Syam Naiko, Nando Naiko and Lobbo Dandasi are the main leaders supervising the land recapture programme of the CPI (M-L) Liberation.

'Land Rights' is an important slogan in the whole gamut of Naxalite politics. Even if the movement is manifested through several splinter groups, the slogan of 'land to tillers' has not lost its appeal among the leadership and cadres of different splinter groups in Orissa. Through its front organization, Chashi Mulia Samiti, the PWG has always tried to portray land as a major conflict dynamic; other factions such as the Liberation and New Democracy have also never lost interest in the issues pertaining to land rights. The factions have one common slogan yet they follow different modes to achieve the goal that leads to organizational conflict. It shows how the Naxal organizations have transformed themselves for the pursuance of their goals. Even if the Liberation and the PWG fiercely fight for the issue of land rights, they compete with each other for the fulfilment of the organizational goals. This competition among the Naxal groups has led to intra-organizational conflict between the CPI (M-L) Liberation and the PWG in Orissa. In other words, their conflict over the methods of goal achievement have never really allowed the issue to die and this has led to the strengthening of the Naxal cause and organization in the larger course of the Naxalite movement in Orissa.

The paradox

Orissa is a paradox: on the one hand, it is one of the most well-endowed Indian states in natural resources and on the other hand, it is one of the poorest in terms of basic human development. Orissa figures predominantly in the list of underdeveloped states in India and is a victim of the state-led development strategy that contributed to a sluggish economic growth rate in India.[21] Being a rich state in terms of its mines, minerals and natural resources, Orissa has not made any real progress as far as the development of the state and its people are concerned. It is ironic that a state floating on rich mineral resources remains one of the most economically backward states in India. The reasons are not difficult to find. Besides the general failure of the state-led model of development, the mismatch between India's development strategy and 'the limited capacity of the state to guide social and economic change' seems to be a critical factor.[22] As the evolution of Orissa as a constituent state in independent India shows, the development strategy that the political leadership undertook was drawn on certain meta-considerations ignoring, to a large extent, the inherent economic strength of the region by virtue of being a repository of minerals and other natural resources. This neglect was partly political and partly due to lack of proper planning for utilizing the resources for a balanced growth of the state. As a result, the state remained economically backward, and people suffered miserably despite the euphoria associated with planned economic development since India's independence in 1947. The aim here is not to elaborate the processes that led to a lopsided growth in Orissa, but simply to show the economic richness of the state because of the vast mineral reserve that remains under-utilized. Orissa belongs to that region of India that is a rich repository of mineral resources, as Table 5.11 illustrates.

Despite having such mineral resources, Orissa is infamous for poverty, starvation and underdevelopment. Ironically, the underdeveloped Maoism-affected western and southern belts of Orissa are the storehouses of most of the mines and mineral deposits of the state. Besides a small irrigation project, there were hardly attempts to explore these mineral resources for development. The ongoing development process in these areas has not benefited the rural mass, which is evident from the available data. The state-sponsored development in Orissa remains largely divorced from people's participation in decision-making. The nexus between Maoism and lopsided development has considerably damaged the democratic values and institutions.

More than 42 steel plants are poised to be established in Orissa requiring 1,600 million tonnes of iron ore in the next 25 years. Multinational giants such as BHP Billiton, Vedanta Resources, Rio Tinto, Alcan, Aditya Birla Group, Tata Group and Saudi Arabian companies have started queuing up to exploit the state's resources. The state government has already given lease to 1,000 million tones of bauxite ore to different companies. However, these are misguiding signs of development in Orissa.[23] One cannot take this massive industrialization and mining activity as the scale to judge the case of human development among the people in the remote areas of southern and western Orissa. Exploitation, utterly inadequate health care and lack of educational facilities, malnutrition, inhumane torture, rising unemployment, inordinate delay in disposal of land cases and the unwillingness to undertake land reforms seem to have considerably plagued the development aims and programmes.

Tribal exploitation and suffering have become the destiny of many with the establishment of the Rourkela Steel Plant (RSP). The Steel Authority of India

Table 5.11 Mineral reserves in Orissa and India

Mineral ore	Reserves in Orissa (million tonnes)	Reserves in India (million tonnes)	Orissa's share of India's reserves (%)
Bauxite	1,733.0	2,911.0	59.5
Chromite	183.0	186.0	98.4
China clay	311.0	986.0	31.5
Coal	49,406.0	199,282.0	24.8
Dolomite	889.0	4,967.0	17.9
Fire clay	178.0	696.0	25.6
Graphite	2.2	3.1	71.0
Iron ore	4,200.0	12,745.0	32.9
Manganese ore	119.0	176.0	67.6
Mineral sands	82.0	266.0	30.8
Pyrophyllite	8.6	13.2	65.1
Nickel ore	270.0	294.0	91.8

Source: http://orissagov.nic.in/e-magazine/orissaannualreference/ORA-2004/pdf/mineral_resource_of_orissa.pdf.

(SAIL) had acquired about 35,000 acres for RSP and another 12,000 acres for its reservoir, Mandira dam. As per one Gazette of Orissa notification, more than 33 villages covering 2,503,524 acres of land had been acquired by the Government of Orissa in 1954 to set up the RSP. Another 31 villages spreading over 1,192,398 acres were acquired for the construction of the Mandira dam in 1956–1957. In both the projects, a total of 3,695,922 acres had been acquired for the RSP and Mandira dam resulting in the uprooting of 4,251 families.[24] Both the SAIL and state government have failed miserably to rehabilitate and resettle the evacuees during the last 50 years. This has caused considerable damage to the socio-economic condition of the local tribals.

In recent years, hundreds of sponge iron factories have mushroomed throughout the district of Sundargarh, where the Maoists have a stronghold. Existing environmental laws have been flaunted openly by the industrialists who have no concern for pollution and environment degradation. They have been dumping their waste all over and left most agricultural land of the area infertile. Local people have witnessed and complained about the polluted air and water being emitted from the plant of Rexon Strips in Kumarkela village of Gurundia block. The polluting units are emitting ammonia fumes, strong enough to corrode tin sheets and burn paddy and green vegetables, and have become a major threat to life. Thousands of people who live in the villages of Ramabahar, Jampali, Jhagarpur, Bargaon, Vedvyas, Balanda, Kuarmunda, Kalunga, Rajgangpur, Birkera, Koira, Bonai,

Tensa, Birmitrapur, Bijabahal, Tensa, Bersuan, Bonai, Lahunipada and Gurundia in Sundargarh are suffering from various skin diseases, tuberculosis and other allergies. Similar is the case with people in the Barbil and Joda region of the Keonjhar district.[25] The failure of the government to include the local tribals in the development map was successfully exploited by the erstwhile Maoist Communist Center (MCC) in establishing a strong Naxal support base in the tribal districts of Sundargarh and Keonjhar.

Now let us turn our focus to Malkangiri where Maoism seems to have established an emotional chord with local inhabitants. Poverty, rampant corruption and failed government programmes are some of the common features witnessed in this area. The CPI (Maoist), under the banner of the erstwhile PWG has created a red bastion in remote areas of Malkangiri. In the 1970s the Government of Orissa constructed the Balimela Dam Project at Chitrakonda in Malkangiri. Inhabitants of more than 250 villages were displaced as well as a number of villages of Kudugulugumma block remained cut off from the mainland and from most government supplies.[26] The government performance on the rehabilitation front can be simply termed as disastrous. Thousands of people are still living on tiny islands within the dam area, which the government terms as the 'cut-off area'. One would find hardly any sign of governance in these areas of Janbai, Panasput, Jodamba and Andrapali Panchayats; where there is no school, no hospital and no public distribution system.[27] To visit other parts of the district, the villagers solely depend on motorboat, which runs twice a week. The cut-off areas are not even interconnected by road. Government-sanctioned development projects in these areas are just completed in pen and paper; residents of these areas complain gross financial irregularities because of an unholy nexus between contractors and government officials. It is an irony that inhabitants of these areas have sacrificed everything for the dam but they have not seen the electricity produced by the dam. For the people of Malkangiri the Balimela dam symbolizes shattered dreams. Extreme poverty and lack of basic requirements of life among the people in most areas of Malkangiri have made people move closer to the Naxals.

Another affected southern district of Orissa is Rayagada, which bears the same signature of extreme poverty, rampant corruption and a chaotic but violent social atmosphere. It has a dominant tribal population and 72.03 per cent of them in the district are living below poverty line.[28] To the outside world the area is known for its backwardness and starvation resulting in death. Between 1990 and 2000, more than Rs. 100 crores were spent, but a large part of this amount was appropriated by political leaders, bureaucrats, contractors and traders. The state government, as a part of its development activity, started planting eucalyptus and this only helped the J.K. Paper Mill to get cheap raw material. A metal road was constructed from Tikiri to Kashipur via Maikanch only to welcome Utkal Alumina International. To sum up, all these so-called development projects in no way helped the majority of tribals in the region. This has alienated the rural tribal people, which created a natural support base for Maoism. As such the area is blessed with a huge concentration of bauxite: 1957.3 lakh tonnes in Baphli Mali, 810 lakh tonnes in Sasubahu Mali and 860 lakh tonnes in Siji Mali near Kasipur. Utkal Alumina International (a joint enterprise of Aditya Birla Group and ALCAN, a Canadian company) is spending Rs. 4500 crores on constructing an aluminium plant site at Doraguda near Kasipur. The project threatens displacement of more than 20,000 people, and would adversely affect 82 villages.[29] For the last 12 years, the local communities in Rayagada have been protesting against bauxite mining, condemning the breach of constitutional provisions barring the sale or lease of tribal lands without consent. People dissent the devastation of their ecosystems, the destruction of forests, agricultural lands, mountains, perennial streams and the water retention capacity of mountains, all of which are essential for the sustenance of their lives. So far, the government has not been able to come out with an answer to the people's apprehensions; instead it is using police methods to suppress the people's voice. This lackadaisical government attitude creates conditions in which Maoism succeeds in building a support base among the tribals in this area.

The story is the same in another affected district, Koraput, which has a poverty ratio of 78.65 per cent and a literacy rate of 36.2 per cent. With a tribal population of 585,830,[30] this district has remained a hotbed of ultra-Left extremist activities for decades. The government's insensitivity towards basic problems of poverty-stricken rural and tribal people is the main cause for the metaphoric growth of Maoism in Koraput. It is a sad reality in Koraput that the government-declared programmes never really reached the people for whom they were really meant. In March 2000 the state government declared that the tribal people will have the right to collect minor forest products though this has not been implemented to date.[31] The government strategy on the development has been mostly limited to lip service only, without really understanding the problem typical to the lifestyle of majority of tribal people in Koraput. There is no market for minor forest products in Koraput and tribals do not even have the access to financial institutions to get loans for investments. It is surprising as well as shocking that the government has never thought of developing self-help groups for the forest-dependent communities in Koraput; a district that has no dearth of mineral deposits. But the government's failure to take proper steps to utilize these resources in favour of the local people has really worsened the situation. Taking advantage of this alienation among the masses, the Maoists have shown them the dream of a revolution; a Maoist revolution. In the name of revolution the Maoists are now controlling more than 400 villages in Koraput, where they collect tax (extortion) and have established a sort of parallel administration.

Rehabilitation of people displaced by dams, such as Hirakud in Sambalpur district, built in the 1950s, is not yet complete. Compensation amounting to Rs. 154,146,994 was not paid after years. Finally, when some compensation was paid to some people, it was a saga of gross financial irregularity as complained by many displaced persons.[32] People still have not forgotten this sense of humiliation and this has pushed them to the Maoist-fold in different parts of Sambalpur. According to the recently published Ghadei Committee Report, of nine blocks of the district, three are grossly underdeveloped, three are underdeveloped and three are developing. Hirakud is the world's largest dam, yet only 28 per cent of the area is irrigated by it and the remaining 72 per cent of the area has no sign of it. Apart from some areas of Rengali, Maneswar and Jujumura block, the remaining six blocks are not linked with the canal system. What is most deplorable is that in all these blocks (Kuchinda, Jamankira, Jujumura, Naktideul, Bamra, Maneswar, Rengali, Rairakhol, Dhankauda) there is an acute shortage of drinking water.[33] The electricity requirements of the state are mostly catered by the Hirakud dam, whereas most villages in the district are yet to get a proper electricity connection and supply. The government neglect of the poor and the downtrodden is success-fully exploited by the Maoists in their favour.

The mishandling of the Kalinga Nagar incident in the Jajpur district has now created another red bastion in the state. In an ugly incident of firing on 2 January 2006 during a tribal protest meeting, the police killed at least 12 innocent tribals, which again gave the Maoists an issue to prove their point. For Tata Iron and Steel's Kalinga Nagar project, Orissa Industrial Infrastructure Development Corporation (IDCO) acquired the land for Rs. 35,000 per acre during 1992–1994 and is now selling it at Rs 350,000 to the company. The decision of the government to sell land at a price higher than what they fixed while purchasing land from the local owners led to frustration among the people. For the original owners of the land, this was 'unacceptable' because 'the state government is doing business with us instead of helping us in the development process. It is making huge profits from our land. When we ask for our share they offer us bullets.'[34] In and around Kalinga Nagar, people complained that the industries set up in the region, (Neelachal Ispat Nigam, Jindal Steels, Mesco Steels) only brought misery and humiliation; it has crushed them, the proud tribals, and they hate it. In the past people were independent and poor but lived with self-dignity; now they have been reduced to outsiders in their own homeland, to be daily-wage labourers or beggars. Tribal people have also repeatedly expressed their dissatisfaction in other places, such as Kashipur and Lanjigarh, where the tribals are struggling for daily existence.

The inevitable outcome of a thoughtless and inappropriate development strategy in Orissa is that in all of the resettlement operations, the majority of those ousted have ended up with lower incomes, less land than before, less work opportunities, inferior housing, less access to the resources such as fuel and fodder, and worse nutrition and physical and mental health. It is estimated that about 3 to 5 million people have been displaced since 1950 in Orissa on account of various develop-ment projects of which more than 50 per cent are tribal. The Tenth Five Year Plan (2002–7)[35] makes special mention of different poverty alleviation schemes and programmes; however, their impact on rural poverty in Orissa remains dubious. When it comes to implementation, the government agenda is grossly mismanaged, and it mostly comes with a package of corruption, which raises serious doubts over the government's commitment for human rights and social security. These failed efforts so far have been successfully exploited by ultra-Left groups to win over the local tribals as their formidable support base. Asymmetrical development in Orissa causes different kinds of conflict between the values of democratic gov-ernance and aspirations of the people. Maoism in Orissa has succeeded because it moves around the life of marginalized people in these areas. It has established a link between underdevelopment, regional imbalance, economic disparity and gun culture. In the name of ameliorating the displaced tribals, the movement also endorses the use of excessive violence and counter-violence. This gains an easy acceptance given the failure of the government to adopt adequate steps for implementing the developmental programmes. On the other hand, while the Maoist leadership makes a strong claim for fighting for the rights of the poor, the former has so far remained apathetic in enhancing the quality of life in villages, arguing instead that all reforms have to follow from revolution. To them, development is adversary to revolutionary consciousness. In fact, the Maoists in these areas are vehemently opposed to any type of construction work. It seems that they are afraid that the government will win over the poor ignorant tribals once they allow the development process to start.

Concluding observations

A study of Maoist violence in Orissa reveals that today's explosive situation is largely triggered by a continuous process of mal-development. But violence itself is no means to attain development; rather it is the extreme form of exploitation. To evade mal-development and to replace this atmosphere of chaos and terror what is required is to create appropriate institutions, systems and relations. The need of the hour is to bring an end to the system of exploitation and corruption, which would surely bring down societal tension by ensuring equality of status and opportunity. To deal with the rising tide of ultra-Left extremism, the state is expected to sufficiently increase and properly manage fund allocation in the field of health care, education, nutrition programmes, disease control, irrigation, rural electrification, rural roads and other basic requirements, especially in those affected rural areas. The state must ensure that its institutions do not breed exploitation. It must work on a formula where there is larger democratic participation in the process of decision-making and development.

Notes

1 White paper on the Law and Order Situation of the State, tabled in the State Legislative Assembly of Orissa, 17 March 2006.
2 Speech of Naveen Pattnaik, Chief Minister of Orissa, at the 50th National Development Council Meeting, 12 December 2002, New Delhi.
3 Prakash Singh, *The Naxalite Movement in India*, New Delhi: Rupa, 1995, 62.
4 Interview with the Maoists in the areas and also the security personnel employed by the state to combat 'the Maoist menace'.
5 See http://rural.nic.in/annualrep0708/anualreport0708_eng.pdf.
6 Department of Revenue, Government of Orissa.
7 According to the annual report of the Ministry of Rural Development, March 2003, 157,482 acres of ceiling surplus land has been provided to 140,158 landless families in Orissa, of whom 51,644 are tribals and 48,196 belong to the scheduled caste category.
8 Source: report of the Working Group on Land Relations for Formulation of 11th Five Year Plan, Planning Commission, Government of India, New Delhi, July 2006.
9 Donated land.
10 Drawn on the interview with former additional sub-collector, Sambalpur, Orissa, 23 July, 2009. The sub-collector gave his views on condition of anonymity. Undervaluation of tribal lands by the land mafias with the help of revenue officials in Naxal hit tribal

districts of Orissa seem to have justified the Maoist claim that the state is clearly opposed to the tribals and is favourably disposed towards the privileged. The Maoists have won in the first round in the sense that their appeal to the tribals for a radical socio-economic transformation seems to have caught the imagination of 'the wretched of the earth', notwithstanding the adverse consequences of their opposition to a well-entrenched Indian state. Unlike its past counterpart, Maoism, in its twenty-first century incarnation, can thus be shown to have evolved out of the peculiar handling of the agrarian issues by the state in those areas of Orissa where the tribals constitute a sizeable section, if not a majority, of the population.

11 Interview with Mr Sanjoy Pattnaik, director, Research and Advocacy, Regional Centre for Development Cooperation (RCDC), Bhubaneswar, on 12 December 2008.

12 A specially designed housing project of the Government of India for poverty-stricken people.

13 'Revolutionary Adivasi Movement Spreads to Southern Orissa', *People's March*, November–December 1999; http://www.peoplesmarch.com was an unofficial website of the CPI (Maoist). However, the website was closed by the order of Government of India effective from 15 May 2006. The editor of the site was kind enough to provide me all the content of the website on a CD.

14 Statement of Sri Krishna Chandra Mangaraj, a senior journalist from Rayagada who has been covering the Naxalite movement in the local media for the past two decades, during an interview conducted as a part of our fieldwork on 15 May 2005.

15 An undated Oriya Maoist literature titled 'Chashi Mulia Samiti Ra Jami Andolan', (Land Struggle by Chashi Mulia Samiti).

16 An undated PWG leaflet titled '2001 Ra Andolana Pain Prastuti' (Preparation For the 2001 Struggle), obtained from one senior officer of Rayagada district police. The document was seized from a PWG activist who was arrested during the land recapture programme of the PWG in 2001.

17 Interviews with the local residents of Gudari and other villages.

18 M.M. Praharaj, Director General of Police, Orissa, in an interview on 27 February 2006.

19 'Bansadhara Ra Jami Andolan', (Land Resistance in Bansadhara), an undated booklet published by Chashi Mulia Samiti.

20 Malleshwar Rao, 'Waves of Land Struggle in South Orissa', http://www.cpiml.org/liberation/year_2002/september/activities.htm

21 India's economic growth, 1950–2000

	1950–1964	1965–1979	1980–2000
GDP growth (%)	3.7	2.9	5.8
Industrial growth (%)	7.4	3.8	6.2
Agricultural growth (%)	3.1	2.3	3.0
Gross investment (%)	13.0	18.0	23.0

Source: Atul Kohli, *State-directed Development: Political Power and Industrialization in the Global Periphery*, Cambridge: Cambridge University Press, 2004, 258.

22 Atul Kohli, *State-Directed Development: Political Power and Industrialization in the Global Periphery*, Cambridge: Cambridge University Press, 2004, 258.

23 Jatindra Dash, 'Mining Threatens Orissa's Environment', Indo-Asian News Service, 5 November 2004.

24 Dr K. Nayak, 'Rourkela: A Historical Perspective', http://www.rourkela.com/history.html. As a part of our fieldwork we met the president of the Rourkela Displaced Persons Association.

25 Based on the field interview.

26 Kishore Kumar Das, lecturer in Botany, Balimela College of Science and Technology, in his unpublished article, 'Life on the Other Side of the Reservoir'.
27 Personal interview with the villagers as a part of the fieldwork.
28 'Census Report', 2001.
29 Information obtained from the *Prakrutik Sampad Surakshya Parishad*, Raygada. Personal interview conducted among the cross section of the population in and around Rayagada.
30 'Census Report', 2001.
31 *Sambad* (Oriya daily), 25 December 2005.
32 Amrita Patwardhan, 'Dams and Tribal People in India', http://www.dams.org.
33 Interviews with the residents of the villages.
34 Statement of Debendra Jarika, a local resident of Kalinga Nagar.
35 http://planningcommission.nic.in/plans/planrel/pl49ndc/orissa.htm.

6   The Maoist organization and state response

Maoism is an articulation of left-wing extremism in India. It has evolved following the formation of the Communist Party of India (Marxist-Leninist) in West Bengal in 1969 that led the Naxalbari Movement. Initially confined to West Bengal, the Naxalbari Movement gradually spread across the length and breadth of the country. Despite its failure to seize state power, the movement was a sharp comment on India's state-led development programme, which was hardly adequate to bring about uniform economic development in India. Maoism is thus a continuity of Left radicalism in a meaningful way. Like its past counterpart, Maoism draws on the reinterpretation of Marxism-Leninism by Mao Tse-tung in the context of agricultural China. The aim of this chapter is to acquaint the readers with the organization and organizational network of the ultra-left wing CPI (Maoist). This chapter elaborates the principal theme in two ways: first, it will focus on the overall structure of the party and the provisional government (the Janathana Sarkar) that it has established in the so-called liberated zones in India. The second part of the chapter will concentrate on the Maoist organization in Orissa. Not only has this part dealt with the actual organizational structure of the party, it has also brought out how important leadership is in sustaining and expanding the Maoist ideological influence.

Maoism and 'action'

Maoism sustains its support base and also thrives on 'action'. After the latest brutal attack on the police station in Gadchiroli in Maharashtra on 1 February 2009, in which 15 policemen were killed, it seems the only mantra that sustains Maoism is 'organize and strike back'. In order to remain in the reckoning, the secretary of the CPI (Maoist), Satyanarayana Reddy (alias Kosa), wrote a letter to his cadres to hit back at government-sponsored police forces to fulfil their ideological aim of seizure of power. Persuading his followers, Reddy expressed his anxiety over their failure in 'materializing the revolutionary aim' in the division by saying that

> there has been hardly any output from Gadchiroli division. We have been on the back-foot for quite some time. Why has there been a dearth of recruits

for the People's Liberation Guerilla Army in Gadchiroli? Ambush after ambush failed. I would want companies and platoons from Dandakaranaya Special Zonal Committee (DSZC) to join hands with those in Gadchiroli and strengthen our base. The enemy (government) has been carefully devising strategies. And through their policies of development they have tried to gain favour of people [sic]. We have had some setbacks. We need to gear-up in Gadchiroli. And we need to that fast.[1]

The letter is a testimony of how important leadership is in conducting the Maoist operation in the remote areas. Once the decision is taken by the leadership it is invariably executed by the cadres responsible for 'action'. There are, however, reports that decisions are taken after discussions among the key members of the Zonal Committee that, in principle, takes into account the inputs from the grass-roots activists before arriving at a plan of action. In fact, the ambush on the police camp in Gadchiroli that followed the circulation of the above letter confirms that the attack was both an outcome of police atrocities in the peripheral areas of the district and also illustrative of the Maoist capability of inflicting irreparable damage to the administration. What is most disturbing, however, is the increasing number civilian deaths in such encounters between Naxalites and security forces, as it is evident in Table 6.1.

Since the table is drawn out of 'the official data' the interpretation may not always be authentic without cross-checking with comparable data, available from other sources. One can, however, identify specific trends in so far as Maoist violence is concerned. Civilians suffered most, as the table clearly indicates; the role of the security agency in arresting the Naxalites is quite effective and also the growing number of the Naxalites who surrendered is perhaps indicative of 'the disillusionment' of a large section of Maoists in the district with the path of violence. Nonetheless, one cannot gloss over the fact that Maoism is a force to reckon with in contemporary India with its influence over at least a fifth of India's districts and one in six Indian citizens seems to have been swayed by its ideological appeal.

Table 6.1 The outcome of the Naxalite movement showing human casualty, arrest and surrender of the Naxalites in Gadchiroli, 2003–2008

	2003	*2004*	*2005*	*2006*	*2007*	*2008*
Civilians killed	27	20	26	39	24	15
Policemen killed	6	6	18	3	3	6
Naxalites killed	8	4	3	22	7	11
Naxalites arrested	278	155	300	79	123	112
Naxalites surrendered	95	100	83	65	39	146

Source: data from the intelligence bureau and Rajesh Pradhan, Superintendent of Police, Gadchiroli district – reproduced in the *Hindustan Times*, 8 February 2009.

Shaping the organization

The CPI (Maoist) is, as the foreword to its constitution underlines, 'the consolidated political vanguard of the Indian proletariat'. Inspired by Marxism-Leninism and Maoism, the party strives to 'carry on and complete the new democratic revolution in India as a part of world proletariat revolution' by overthrowing the exploiting classes. The new democratic revolution will be 'carried out and completed through armed agrarian revolutionary war [that will be complemented] by the parallel rise of the Maoist cadres in cities and towns'.[2] After spelling out the fundamental guiding principles in the foreword, the CPI (Maoist) constitution, in as many as 61 provisions, provides a detailed exposition of a constitutional arrangement seeking to replace 'the bourgeoisie order'. Since the Maoists are committed to overthrowing the class-divided state, they are very careful while selecting party members. There are two requirements which are stringently followed in this regard: (a) the uncritical acceptance by the prospective party members of Marxism-Leninism-Maoism, and (b) the public pledge of the new recruits to the effect of 'subordinating their personal interests to the interests of the party and people'. In fact, the whole party 'shall follow the principle that the individual is subordinate to the organization, the minority is subordinate to the majority, the lower level is subordinate to the higher level, and the entire party is subordinate to the Central Committee'.[3] In Chapter 6, the constitution spells out steps to maintain party discipline which is most critical for any revolutionary organization. As Article 26 stipulates, 'without iron discipline, no revolutionary party will be able to give capable leadership to the masses in the war and fulfill the responsibility of revolution'. Although the party is the motivating ideological force, the role of the people's army is nonetheless significant in pursing the goal of a new democratic revolution. Under the strict guidance of the party, the Maoist army will, according to Article 54, engage in 'rousing, mobilizing, organizing and also arming the people in carrying out the task of revolution'.[4]

As shown, the constitution is an ideological document motivating the Maoists to organize themselves for the final assault on the state power. Guided by the Leninist principle of democratic centralism, the Maoists appreciate 'democracy under centralized guidance' and hence the Party Central Committee 'decides when and on what questions debates and discussion should be allowed' to avoid wastage of time and energy.[5] So, democracy has a restrictive meaning presumably because of the adverse circumstances in which the party is functioning. Nonetheless, the debates within the party were allowed for constructive purposes, as the party leadership agreed in the 2007 Ninth Congress. For the Maoists, democracy is an initiative to ensure the involvement of the party cadres in what they undertake as part of the revolutionary masses. The initiative must therefore be

> demonstrated concretely in the ability of the leading bodies, the cadres and the Party rank and file to work creatively, in their readiness to assume responsibility, in the exuberant vigour they show in their work, in their courage and ability to raise questions, voice opinions and criticize defects, and in

the comradely supervision that is maintained over the leading bodies and the leading cadres.[6]

Maoism is not merely a sporadic articulation of mass grievances; it is also a serious ideological endeavour to sustain a movement challenging the prevalent state power that seems to have lost its claim over a vast section of socio-economically excluded rural masses. There is no doubt that the movement has gained momentum to the extent of being 'the biggest threat' to India's democracy. One may be persuaded by the argument that Maoism has flourished due presumably to the failure of the post-colonial state to address the genuine socio-economic grievances of the peripherals. So, Maoism has natural appeal to the downtrodden in perhaps the most backward regions of India which are otherwise rich because of a depository of valuable minerals. The story remains incomplete because the ideological appeal is also meaningfully articulated by a sustained campaign, backed by an adequately organized party. The CPI (Maoist) is organized following the idea of Mao Tse-tung. And it is not surprising therefore that there is an uncanny similarity between the Mao-led Chinese Communist party and its Indian counterpart if one is drawn to the constitutional provisions guiding the party, as the following discussion demonstrates.

Chapter 7 of the constitution of the party deals with 'party's organizational structure' which is well-elaborated in Articles 29, 30 and 31, with 18 clauses.[7] Suggesting the basic principles of organization, Article 29 mentions that 'the party organization shall be formed according to geographical division or spheres of production'. According to Article 30, which is a further elaboration of the party structure, the party congress shall be the highest organ setting the tone and tenor of the party. Structurally, the central committee is the highest executive authority, which is supported by (a) special area committee/special zonal committee/state committee, (b) zonal committee/district/divisional committee, (c) sub-zonal/sub-divisional committee and (d) area committee/local level committees – village/*basti* (slum)/ factory/college committees. The primary unit of the party is a cell, defined as 'the nucleus of the organization', that can be formed area-wise, profession-wise or production-wise. As the nucleus of the organization, the party cell is

a living link between the broad masses of an area and the party. The cell will lead the revolutionary war of broad masses of people with full initiative. It shall make relentless effort to bring the masses of factory, locality and peasant areas close to the political line and aims of the party, by involving militant activists and party followers in the revolutionary war against autocratic semi-colonial, semi-feudal state system. It will stress from the very beginning to educate the masses to function secretly, illegally according to the strategy and tactics of the Protracted People's War. [The cell] is also responsible for educating and training those cadres who are entrusted with the task of ideologically preparing the masses for People's War.[8]

The Maoist party organization[9] that seeks to combine democracy with centralism is also a replica of the Chinese Communist party. The constitutional provisions relating to the CPI (Maoist) draw heavily on the report prepared by Mao Tse-tung for the sixth plenary session of the sixth central committee that was held in October 1938. For instance, in regard to three important areas – the policies governing the cadres, party discipline and party democracy – the Maoist constitution resembles the 1938 report by Mao Tse-tung.[10]

Since the CPI (Maoist) is a party for revolution, the organization is structured to achieve its twin goals of (a) spreading the left-wing ideology and (b) preparing the masses for 'action' against the class enemies. At the helm of the organization remains the central committee, which has two major wings: the political wing and the action wing. The political wing comprises of (i) state committee, (ii) district committee, (iii) zonal committee and (iv) sangham; the action wing is structured around (i) armed zonal committee, (ii) regional committee, (iii) dalam committee and (iv) dalam. As the ideological wing of the party, the political wing is entrusted with the task of spreading Maoism at the grass roots. The armed zonal committee is directly involved in military operation against 'the enemy'. A dalam consisting of at least ten cadres, all armed and trained, is the basic building block of the Naxalite military wing. A member is chosen to join a dalam only after a long apprenticeship as a Sangham member where he/she is monitored by the party to ascertain his/her capability in armed encounter. Sangham members are involved in the distribution of pamphlets and carrying messages. They are also used to collect information on those suspected to be police informers. Arms training is given only to members of a dalam, which also includes two or three female participants. Each dalam has a commander and a deputy commander. Dalams generally approach a target area on foot and make their escape on foot. A dalam looks after about 50 villages. For large-scale operations, several dalams join together; otherwise, they operate independently.

At the primary level, young Sangham members are involved in activities for dissemination of Maoist ideology by distributing pamphlets in earmarked areas. Their role is crucial in identifying 'the police informers' in the villages. Only after they discharge their responsibilities according to the expectation of the dalam committee, they are allowed to be recruited for a dalam. In this sense, Sangham is the preparatory ground for a dalam. Hence, those who are sympathetic to the Maoist cause are generally welcome provided the Zonal Committee of the political wing has no objection. Theoretically, this is a full-proof mechanism, yet given the factional feud among Sangham members, there are occasions when 'the so-called unwanted elements' figure even in dalams, resulting not only in infighting among the members, but also, in extreme cases, in disintegration.

The Naxal superstructure is said to resemble a batch of concentric circles: the innermost being the most powerful leadership, located in the remotest forests, forever on the move. The 'zone', 'area' and 'range' commanders are in the middle: the levels of the classic pyramid management structure. These are reportedly the backbone: the hands-on, day-to-day direct leaders to the cadres, leading assaults and tracking the goings-on in the villages on their watch. The outermost circles comprise 'sympathizers' who do not wear a uniform, freely interface with the 'outside world' on the basis of their identity of the average villager, but are the 'eyes and ears'; the runners for the 'brothers' inside. When police claim that they have killed or arrested Naxals, it is believed that they are mostly these outermost cadres. Of course, the Naxals claim that the police arrest or kill only the innocent people.[11]

Maoist organization in the districts

The districts in which the Naxalites have total control (with almost complete decimation of the civilian authority) are organizationally divided into a 'guerrilla zone' or a 'liberated zone'. It was easier for the ultra-Leftists to carve out liberated zones in those districts that share borders with two or three states. Illustrative here is Gadchiroli, which is one of those few districts in the Vidarbha region of Maharashtra sharing a border with Chhattisgarh, where the Maoists have become a strong ideological force given their role in highlighting 'the popular misery' due to government indifference to the increasing number of farmer suicides in the entire area.[12] Sandwiched between the Naxalite-dominated areas of Rajanandagaon, Kanker, Dantewada and Bijapur in Chhatisgarh and Karimnagar and Khammam in Andhra Pradesh, Gadchiroli is a strategic location in which the security forces do not have easy access because (a) it is a difficult terrain that will remain beyond reach unless the local inhabitants provide logistic help and (b) it remains inaccessible because the Naxalites have strongholds in the adjacent districts that always act as a buffer in case of probable operation by the security forces. As the inputs from the local sources suggest, the district of Gadchiroli is divided into three operational divisions: south Gadchiroli, north Gadchiroli and north Gondia. Each division has under its command more than 20 guerrilla squads and platoons.[13] Though the Naxalites previously operated in dalams of 15 and 20 cadres, they have switched to a military-style hierarchy now of local guerrilla squads, platoons, battalions and divisions.[14] There is no doubt that the Maoists have, over the years, built a well-knit organization in the district to support their ideological goal. According to official sources, this increasing influence is largely attributed to government reluctance to initiate punitive measures against those Naxalites who took shelter in 1980 in Gadchiroli when security forces came down heavily against them in the neighbouring districts in Andhra Pradesh. A police officer who spent almost his entire career in the Naxal-dominated districts of Andhra Pradesh and later Maharashtra admits, 'when the Naxalites entered Maharashtra from Andhra Pradesh, our government chose to see it just "a spillover" and decided not to pay attention [and] we are paying the price now'.[15] As the police report suggests, a large section of the Peoples' War Group (PWG) that was founded by legendary Naxalite leader, Kondapallu Seetharamaiah in Andhra Pradesh 'infiltrates Gadchiroli of Maharashtra after a police crack down on Naxalites in Andhra Pradesh in 1980'.[16] Those who are active in the Maoist movement now are either politically baptized by the PWG or are inspired by its cadres. There is no doubt that the failure of the state to ideologically combat Maoism has resulted in the growing consolidation of ultra left wing extremism in Gadchiroli.

Organization in urban areas

Unlike the past, the Naxalites now pay adequate attention to the urban areas where a stable party organization is necessary to accomplish the final goal of the movement, i.e seizure of political power. As Ganapathy argues, 'unless the urban India is drawn to the struggle for the seizure of power, our revolution will remain incomplete'.[17] In its Urban Perspective Plan, the party provides a detailed discussion of the party structure that has to evolve to complement the revolutionary activities in rural areas. The aim is 'to harass the state machinery not only in the villages, but also in towns and cities to attack "the reactionary demon" from all sides'.[18] The principle governing the party organization in urban areas seeks to combine 'political centralization' with 'organizational decentralization'. Such a peculiar admixture of two principles is explained in the Maoist document stating that 'all PMs [Party Members] and all bodies, particularly at the lower level, should have solid ideological-political foundations, so that they are able to independently find their bearings and take the correct organizational decisions according to the political line of the Party'. This is particularly important in the urban areas because (a) it is difficult to maintain close and constant links between secret higher bodies and those at the lower levels engaged in direct open work given 'the openness' of urban space and (b) with the availability of technological gadgets for communication with the state, delay may cause damage to the works in which the party is engaged to advance the cause of revolution.

Controlled by the party's high command, the urban wing of the party is divided into (a) cell, (b) area party committee, (c) part-timer party committees, (d) party fractions and (e) layers. The cell is the primary committee that is entrusted with the task of both expanding its organization and ideologically indoctrinating the fence-sitters. The cell can be formed on the basis of unit of production: for the workers, this could be a factory, shop, department, shift, production line, industrial estate etc.; for students and middle class employees, this could be college, school, institution, office etc. For effective functioning and operation of the cell, it was advised to unite with other cells if there are less than three units in a particular segment. It was suggested that the tasks of the cell 'include organizing masses, politicizing them, educating the advanced elements and recruiting them into the party, and preparing its members and other activists to go to the countryside to work for the success of the agrarian revolution'. Out of the effective cells, a professional revolutionary cell can be created to provide advanced political training to those cell members who have shown the potential to take bigger responsibility for the party by such activities that the party high command deems fit. The second rung consists in the area party committee: two or more cells operating in a locality or unit of production may form the area committee to undertake and monitor the activities in the segment in which they are located. Accordingly, one can think of 'factory committee', 'college committee', 'basti (slum) committee', among others. The area committee may also consist of part-time members who, despite being sympathetic to the Maoist cause, may not have adequate time to work full-time for the party. Nonetheless, these committees play a critical role in sustaining the organization in urban areas by continuously involving in development-centric activities and raising issues that are critical to urban areas. The Maoists are aware that unless a careful selection process is devised, these committees will provide the reactionary forces with easy access to their activities, which will harm the organization and the goal for which the organization stands. Hence, it was forcefully mentioned that while setting up such committees, the party should take care of 'the reliability' of the members by thoroughly scrutinizing the past of the probable recruits; otherwise, the entire purpose stands defeated resulting in an irreparable damage to the party. Besides the cell and party committees, the party sets up factions in various non-party organizations in order to spread the Maoist messages in a discreet manner. The aim is to (a) unite the splinter groups around a common goal and (b) to ascertain the possibility of working together against a common enemy, ie. the state. This is likely to pay dividends because exposure to a non-party organization in urban areas will enable party cadres to mingle with a large group of people who are otherwise 'neutral' in the sense of not belonging to a particular party. The formation of a faction is contingent on the circumstances; if the members feel that the party committee is adequate to handle the responsibility, there is no need for a faction; but if the party feels otherwise, factions may be constituted as and when it is necessary. In the urban party structure, layers refers to 'the various Party organization like city committee, area committee, factory/slum/college committees, cells as well as the links to the mass organizations of the activists and fractions'. Layers are responsible for maintaining the liaison among the units of the Party at various levels. In this sense, their role is most critical in sustaining the organization through links with various units located at the various levels, and given the adverse circumstances in which the Party functions, layers cannot be bypassed and party functionaries are instructed accordingly.

The Naxalites are aware that without a proper coordination among all the units, both in urban and rural areas, it will be difficult to advance their cause. Furthermore, given the centrality of rural party units in agrarian revolution, the ideological activities of the party in urban areas need to be coordinated and led from the rural areas. This arrangement is justified because of the (a) lack of adequate numbers of party cadres who are capable of discharging the responsibilities and (b) the presence of the various state-sponsored coercive agencies to scuttle the Naxalite efforts. Hence, it was suggested that the urban units should 'unite with those organizations involved in struggles against the ruling classes' irrespective of the ideological compatibility. This includes 'the formation of various tactical united fronts as well as building worker-peasant alliance which is the basis of the strategic united front'. Drawn on the Maoist idea of new democracy, the effort is meaningful and justified and this involves (a) building basic working-class unity, (b) mobilizing peasantry (c) uniting other revolutionary classes like the semi-proletariat and petty-bourgeoisie and (d) national bourgeoisie and ruling organizations with people-friendly agenda. From the strict ideological point of view, the Maoist formula of unity with even the ruling-class organizations may not find favour with orthodox Marxists though its strategic utility can never be underlined. The Maoists appear to be alert to this possibility that this strategic alliance may cause a dent among the committed cadres who may not appreciate such a dilution. Hence, there is a clear direction as to when and how this unity is useful from the point of the Maoist primary ideological goal. Three suggestions are made: first, unity with the ruling-class organization is possible in the industries because the goals that they seek to achieve are the same as the Maoists; furthermore, the unity is justified to avoid split among the workers. So, the identical locations lead to unity notwithstanding the ideological incompatibility among those working for the same cause. Second, the Maoists favour issue-based unity with organizations, not strictly ideologically identical, for sustaining the momentum for people's struggle for genuine socio-economic demands. The aim is to build joint fronts with those organization involving masses for a cause. This is perhaps the most effective strategy when the Maoist organization is not strong in urban areas. By adopting a slightly flexible approach for a long-term gain, the Maoist are favourably inclined to coordinate with other Communist revolutionary camps, the large number of democratic organizations ventilating the mass grievances and various other sporadic non-political formations seeking to champion the cause of the people. The third possible union can be achieved with the coming together of the Naxalites and other organizations that are working in particular geographical areas with compatible socio-political aims. Characterized as the area unity, this form of alliance creates unity among those confronting identical problems in a specific location. Issues vary from sanitation, water and transport to safety and security against hooliganism. In the context of growing mass disenchantment with state-sponsored globalization, area unity seems to have provided activists with different ideological inklings with a broad platform to voice their protest. This will not only give the Maoists an opportunity to assess the potential of other democratic organizations addressing mass grievances, but also an exposure to those issues that may have escaped their attention, presumably due to their rural bias when formulating the ideological agenda.

Two basic points have emerged out of this detailed elaboration of the party structure in urban areas: first, to establish a new democratic regime in India, the Maoists cannot afford to ignore the cities and towns. Unless there are complementary efforts from the urban areas, it will be difficult to achieve the goal. Hence, the organization in urban India is as important as it is in rural India. Second, a sincere endeavour in grasping the urban grievances will also acquaint the Maoists with urban-centric issues, which would have been inconceivable if the focus is confined to rural areas. This is an opportunity for them in three ways: (a) helping the Maoists to create a constituency in urban areas using their ideological appeal and (b) enabling them to assess the striking capacity of the ruling class coercive agents who may not visible in rural areas, but are responsible in framing policies and also suggesting various ways of combating the 'red menace' elsewhere and (c) a strong organization in the urban segment will complement the efforts of the People's Guerrilla Army in the final war against the Indian ruling class, which will not only be isolated, but terribly crippled, due to the breakdown of the network of support.

The provisional government: the Janathana Sarkar[19]

In the liberated zone of Dandakaranya in Chhattisgarh, the Maoists are reported to have formed a provisional government which may not be effective in governance terms, but provides adequate inputs to throw light on the Maoist governmental structure. Located in the area (village) level, the *Janathana Sarkar* (people's government) is the first stage of governance seeking to articulate an alternative form of public administration. Ideologically inspired by Mao's idea of new democracy, the provisional government can be formed in areas with a population of 500 to 3000 people. The constitution provides that the government will be formed by the people's assembly comprising those who are elected on the basis of adult suffrage. The term of the assembly is for three years. So far, the Sarkar in the selected areas have been formed through consensus among the elected representatives to the people's assembly though the constitution allows the central committee to dictate in case of imbroglio due to the failure of the members to arrive at a consensus. Those aged 18 and above are eligible to vote, however the minimum age for contesting the election for the assembly is 20. Elections have so far been held in secret locations given the adverse circumstances in which the Naxalites are functioning. Nonetheless, the classified government documents indicate that those who are sympathetic to Maoism seemed enthusiastic when the election was supposedly held. As the operation is so secretive, no alternative sources are available although interaction with the tribals in the specified areas reveals that in the safe zones, elections are held regularly.

One may not get first-hand information regarding the election, but what is striking is the availability of well-written documents in the public domain on the structure of the government. On the Maoist website, the Janathana Sarkar is reported to have eight departments of finance, defence, agriculture, judiciary, education-culture, health, forest protection and public relations. The Maoist document elaborates the specific functions and responsibilities of these departments. Of these, the forest protection and judiciary departments deserve mention because the functions of other departments correspond with the conventional knowledge of government departments in any political system. Seeking to protect the forest-dependent communities, the forest protection department is entrusted with three important tasks that are enumerated in detail in the document: (a) it will regulate the trading of forest products for profit; it will oppose procuring of herbs, fruit trees and other valuable trees that are helpful for medicinal services in methods that would destroy them; (b) it will strive for developing forests; it will stop illicit timber business; it will arrest those involved in illegal timber business and those who help them; (c) it will challenge the government for its policy of displacement and dispossession of the natural heir to the forests by giving away land to the outsiders for anti-people business ventures. Like the forest department, the people's judiciary is popular in the areas controlled by Janathana Sarkar. Following the class-sensitive principles of justice, the judiciary avoids punitive measures unless they are absolutely necessary. The Naxal courts, known as Jan Adalat, are expected to administer justice keeping in view 'the customary traditions of the area' besides upholding the ideological importance of Marxism-Leninism-Maoism. Two specific methods are generally followed by Jan Adalat: (a) for the class enemies, like landlords, agents of semi-colonial and semi-feudal forces and those supporting anti-people activities, the courts are not hesitant to adopt stern measures after having given them a chance to defend themselves and (b) while settling disputes, these courts need to be sensitive to 'those various forums' which the adivasis have developed over generations. The Jan Adalat is expected to strengthen these people-oriented forums, drawn on the local/customary traditions to fulfil its people-centric role.

Notwithstanding the reported excesses committed by Jan Adalat, there is no doubt that the people's judiciary is one of the most popular organs of the provisional government, just like the forest department. The government courts take years to dispense justice while the kangaroo court of the Maoists resolves disputes pretty quickly, as various media reports confirm.[20] 'When there is a dispute', an eye witness account reveals, 'the Jan Adalat call the parties together and the punishment is given right away'. The villagers seem to like it very much because time is hardly wasted. Besides delivering justice without much delay, the Maoists seem to have gained acceptance because the people's courts are generally anti-landlords except on rare occasions. This has given confidence to the tribals because 'if you go to the police, they will invariably support the landlord'.[21] As the discussion shows, the Janathana Sarkar, however rudimentary in its form, is most significant in the articulation and sustenance of the Maoists-led ultra-extremist movement in India in two ways: first, this has projected the capability of the Maoists to provide an alternative form of governance, based on Marxism-Leninism-Maoism, to translate into reality its commitment to new democracy. Because this is emotionally gratifying, it will undoubtedly help the Maoists gain political mileage. The idea is gaining ground at least in the so-called liberated zone that the government is 'vulnerable' to the left-wing extremists. Second, the formation and continuity of Janathana Sarkar, despite severe state repression, also suggests the extent to which it has organic roots in the area. One of the reasons supporting its growing strength is certainly due to its success in addressing the genuine socio-economic grievances of the people. Besides providing 'instant justice' to the aggrieved tribals, the meaningful role that the provisional government plays in adopting schemes that contribute to the well-being of the people in the area under its purview, as a report of its developmental activities in five villages in Chhattisgarh underlines, seems to have brought the government closer to the people. Accordingly, the government agrees, for instance, to financially endorse collective farming as perhaps the only meaningful device for survival of those who are subject to near famine conditions almost every year. This appears to be a top priority of the provisional government, as the party declares by saying that 'we must take up the development of agriculture and production as the main political task … We have to develop irrigation, develop organic manure for augmenting agricultural production'. The party is also aware that 'this development is not possible merely with local adivasi support'. What is thus required is to invite those who are sympathetic to the Maoist cause to help in 'guiding and training the local people for building ponds, canals and other developmental activities [that cannot be] postponed and has to begin now'.[22] Besides seeking to develop agriculture, the Sarkar appears to have gained enormously in those areas where it is seriously engaged in providing medical aid to those who cannot afford treatment. Medicine committees are constituted by the government to provide care to disease-affected tribals. Although the quality of treatment these committees provide may not, for obvious reasons, approximate to the standard of the non-tribal areas, the effort is both meaningful and symbolically empowering for those who usually surrender to 'the supernatural forces or obnoxious black magic' for healing and cure.

Maoist organizational structure and the saga of a failing state in Orissa

Orissa has always remained a hotbed of Maoist organizational exercise. Historically, both the PWG and the MCC were active in Orissa having influence in different areas. While the MCC had influence over the Sundargarh, Keonjhar, Sambalpur, Mayurbhanj, Deogarh and Jajpur districts, the PWG had a substantial presence in the Malkangiri, Koraput, Rayagada, Gajapati, Ganjam and Nawarangpur districts. Not to ignore, the Communist Party of India (CPI) Red Flag and CPI (M-L) had a minimal presence in the Gajapati and Rayagada districts. By merging into a single outfit, PWG and MCC managed to link their base areas of southern Orissa and western Orissa and in the process made inroads to new areas. Since their merger the Naxalites are better organized under different zonal committees with effective coordination machinery. Presently, there are two zonal committees of CPI (Maoist) in Orissa, i.e. Andhra-Orissa Border Special Zonal Committee (AOBSZC) and Jharkhand-Bihar-Orissa Border Special Zonal Committee (JBOBSZC), which functions in close coordination with the Dandakaranya Special Zonal Committee (DSZC).[23] Since the first quarter of 2006, the CPI (Maoist) central committee formed a state committee in Orissa with Sabyasachi Panda as its head.[24] The Naxalites have now formed a 'common war zone' from the Dandakaranya area to the Nepal border and Orissa is part of this zone.

However, as far as the ground realities are concerned, the area of operation of both PWG and the MCC is clearly distinct, and both groups have so far maintained the same organizational structure. The PWG has been using Devagiri and Mahendragad Hills in the Rayagada district as its training ground, they also maintain training camps at Katinguda and night shelters at Ramguda in the Malkangiri district. As of now 14 dalams (squads) of the PWG are operating in Orissa.[25] It has been observed that in the past few years, particularly the Nagavali, Kondavaridi and Bansadhara squads of the PWG have been holding the Naxal fort in the Gudari, Gunpur, Chandrapur, Bissamcuttack and Rayagada blocks in the Rayagada district. Furthermore, the Jan Adalat (People's Court) held by the Naxalites in southern Orissa has helped them enhance their sway.

All Maoist operations in the Malkangiri district of Orissa are carried out by the Jhanjavati, Nagavali and Korkonda dalams of the PWG which are placed under the control of the PWG's 'East Regional Committee', that has its headquarters at Visakhapatnam in Andhra Pradesh. Similarly, its eastern division in the Srikakulam district of Andhra Pradesh takes care of the Maoist activities in Gajapati and Rayagada districts of Orissa. While the Uddanam dalam is active in the Gajapati district, the Basadhara dalam operates in the Rayagada district. These dalams recruit locals and send them to the various training centres in Andhra Pradesh. They also concentrate on developing their frontal organizations, which basically deal with the public relations-related work of propaganda, including pasting posters, distributing leaflets and conducting meetings.[26]

Prior to its merger with the CPI (Maoist), the MCC had a strong presence in three northern districts of Orissa: Sundargarh, Keonjhar and Mayurbhanj. While the Gorumahisani, Jharpokharia, Bangiriposi, Bisoi and Chirang police stations of the Mayurbhanj district have been affected by Naxalite activity, such activity has also been noticed in the Ghantasila Hills of Jharkhand, close to Mayurbhanj. Further, the Maoists have long consolidated their position in the eight police stations of Sundargarh (Birsa, Bolang, Banki, Podia, Tikayatpalli, Kuarmunda, Biramitrapur and Gurundia). These are the areas in which the MCC, with its well-entrenched organizational network, maintains its hegemony. Supported by Local Regular Guerilla Squads (LRGS) and special Regular Guerilla Squads (SRGS), the MCC cadres seem to have evolved an effective control mechanism that draws on blatent coercion as well.

Recent events in 2009 shows that the Sambalpur police have been able to completely dismantle the three LRG squads that were operating in the Sambalpur and Deogarh border areas. 'With the human approach followed by the Sambalpur Police we have managed to nab all the important Maoist leaders in the area without being escalating violence. However, we don't deny the possibility of regrouping of the Maoist forces.'[27]

The Jan Pratirodh Sangharsh Manch (People's Revolution Association), the Krantikari Sanskrutik Sangh (Revolutionary Cultural Association), the Nari Mukti Sangh (Women's Liberation Association) and the Krantikari Chhatra League (Revolutionary Students League) were the frontal organizations of the MCC, which even after the formation of the CPI (Maoist) operate in the same name taking the responsibility of spreading the message of the revolution.[28] On the other hand, the PWG always preferred to reach out to the common people through its front organizations of tribal people, women and cultural artists. These include the Kui Labanga Sangh (Kui Youth Association), the Lok Shakti Manch (People's Power Association), the Nari Shakti Bahini (Women Power Squad), the Jana Natya Mandali (People's Drama Club), the Kui Sanskrutika Sangathan (Kui Cultural Association), the Chasi Mulia Royat Samiti (Farmers and Labourers Association) and the Radical Student Organization.

The killing of Swami Laxmananda Saraswati, a Vishwa Hindu Parishad (VHP) leader and his associates on 23 August, 2008 in Kandhamal caused dissension among the Maoists in Orissa, especially after Sabyasachi Panda, the Maoist leader of Orissa, claimed responsibility for the assassination. This particular incident totally shook the total set-up of Maoist organizations in Orissa. The killing of a Hindu leader and his associates that triggered attacks on Christians in Orissa have split the CPI (Maoist) on religious lines for the first time, with many Hindu members breaking away to form a rival group. Announcing the expulsion, one press release of CPI (Maoist) claimed that Panda has purchased over 100 acres of land in and around Nayagarh with the help of the party fund. Further, the release said that the party suspended Sabyasachi only after getting conclusive evidence of his corrupt practices. Bearing the signature of one Saket, the press release warned Panda with severe punishment in the People's Court unless he apologizes for his anti party activity and refunds the misappropriated funds to the party.[30] Announcing the expulsion, one press release of CPI (Maoist) claimed that Panda has purchased over 100 acres of land in and around Nayagarh with the help of the party fund. Further, the release said that the party suspended Sabyasachi only after getting conclusive evidence of his corrupt practices. Bearing the signature of one Saket, the press release warned Panda with severe punishment in the People's Court unless he apologizes for his anti party activity and refunds the misappropriated funds to the party.[31]

Profile of a Naxal organization: Andhra Orissa Border Special Zonal Committee[32]

As far as the organizational structure goes, the AOBSZC follows a bureaucratic structure with clearly marked role and function for each of its organs. At the apex of the structure there is the Zonal Committee, which consists of nine members. For all practical purposes this is the all-powerful executive body of the AOBSZC, which is responsible for Naxal operations in the region. As per the functional necessity the whole organizational set-up is split into two wings, namely the Organizational Wing and the Military Wing. The Organizational Wing is broadly divided into the South Bureau and the North Bureau. South Bureau consists of the East Division and the Malkangiri Division. North Bureau is divided into the Srikakulam Division and the Bansdhara Division. Malkangiri and Koraput come under the command of the Malkangiri Division and Rayagada, Gajapati and Nabarangpur are placed under the Bansadhara Division. Each division has a Divisional Committee, which again is followed by an Area Committee. At the bottom of the Organizational Wing stands the Local Guerrilla Squad.

The military powers of the AOBSZC are concentrated with the Zonal Military Commission (ZMC), which has five members including one ex-officio secretary. The ZMC is divided into five commands, namely South Command, North Command, Zonal Technical Committee, Special Action Teams, Special Action Teams and Platoon Party Committee.

We present below the details of different organs of the AOBSZC, which are especially important as far as the scope of this study is concerned.

Organizational wing

This wing of the AOBZSC (member profiles shown in Table 6.2) takes care of all the aspects of organization building from membership to training. It is again subdivided into the South Bureau and the North Bureau.

South Bureau

Modem Balakrishna alias Bhashkar is the secretary of the South Bureau with Komala Seshagiri Rao alias Vinay as In-Charge and Chheda Bhishanam and Gopi Sammi Reddy alias Jogal as members. The South Bureau is again divided into two divisions, i.e. the East Division and the Malkangiri Division.

East Division is headed by its secretary, Marpu Venkat Ramanna alias Jagadeesh alias Lenju. It has two types of members. First, the secretariat members are Bhakuru Venkata Ramana alias Ganesh and Kakuri Pandanna alias Pasanna alias Jogan. Second, there are six ordinary members – Ponnoju Parameswara Rao alias Nandu, Kundumula Venkat Rao alias Rewi, Hari alias Ravi, Jaya (wife of Gautam), Krishna Narendra and Karuna (wife of Devanna). The East Division mostly functions within Andhra Pradesh.

The Malkangiri Division is headed by its secretary, Gopi Sammi Reddy alias Jogal alias Santhosh. The other members of the division are Balaram Narayan Swami alias Damodar (surrendered), Kakarala Sunitha alias Guru Smruthi alias

Table 6.2 AOBSZC members profiles

Name	Age (years)	Caste	Native place	Post held	Weapon
Modem Balakrishna alias Bhaskar	43	Gowda	Hyderabad	Secretary	AK 47
Thentu Venkata Laxmi alias Narasimha Chalam alias Sudhakar	47	Velama	Warangal	Secretariat Member	AK 47
Ramachandra Reddy/ Pratap Reddy alias Chalpath	43	Reddy	Chittore	Secretariat Member	AK 47
Gopi Sami Reddy alias Jogal	49	Reddy	Karim Nagar	Member	SLR
Komali Sheshagiri Rao alias Vinay	38	K.Velama	Warangal	Member	AK 47
Chheda Bhushan alias Kathru	36	Valmiki	Vishakhapatnam	Member	AK 47
Chelluri Narayan Rao alias Suresh	35	Agnikula Kshyatriya	Srikakulam	Member	AK 47
Mahendra alias Mahesh	33		Rayalaseema	Member	AK 47
Sabyasachi Panda alias Sarat	37	Brahmin	Berhampur	Member	AK 47
Gautam	35		Warangal	Member	AK 47

Source: data from the field survey.

Tubri, w/o Sudhakar, Swarna (wife of Vinay) (surrendered) and Kolukula Bala Raju alias Bhagat. There is no secretariat of the Malkangiri Division. Table 6.3 shows the main wings of Malkangiri Divisional Committee.

The Local Guerilla Squads (LGS) are the nucleus of the whole AOBSZC. They act as an implementation wing and also are instrumental in membership drive and recruitment. Table 6.4 shows the detailed profile of various LGS functioning under the Malkangiri Division.

North Bureau

Chalapati is the secretary of the North Bureau with Mahendra as its In-charge. Suresh and Sabyasachi Panda alias Sarat are the other two members of the Bureau Committee. Operationally, the bureau is divided into two divisions, i.e. the Srikakulam Division and the Basdhara Division.

Srikakulam Division is headed by its secretary Chemalla Krishna Murthy alias Daya. Other members of the Divisional Committee are Chandu, Chhokari Krishna Rao alias Shanti, Gedam Lakshmi alias Madhavi and Chhokari Ganga Ram alias Komma.

Sabyasachi Panda, noted guerrilla leader, heads the Basdhara Division. Table 6.5 shows the member profile of the Basdhara Division.

The Basdhara Division has five core committees. Table 6.5 shows the details of the leadership, including their social background, whereas Table 6.6 is a detailed elaboration of the structure of these division committees.

Table 6.7 outlines the LGS in the Basdhara Division.

Table 6.3 CPI (Maoist) Malkangiri Divisional Committee

Name	Profile
Papluar Area Committee	ACS: Swarna (DC cum Secretary); surrendered (a) Papluar LGS; CO: Kuda Nageswar Rao alias Suresh (b) Balimela LGS; CO: Kuladeep Rubdar alias Sudhir
Jana Natya Mandali	All members were arrested
Special Guerilla Squad	DC: Gopi Sammi Reddy alias Jogal
Mahila Team	DC: Kakarala Sunita alias Badri, (wife of Sudhakar)
Kalimela Area Committee	ACS: Bellam Narayan Swamy alias Damodar (DC cum Secretary) (a) Kalimela LGS; CO: Buda Kawagi alias Ajit (b) Potteru LGS; CO: Kurubatti (c) Motu LGS; CO: Rama Kawari alias Ashok

Note:
ACS – Area Committee Secretary
CO – Commanding Officer
DC – Deputy Commander
LGS – Local Guerilla Squad

Source: data from the field survey.

Table 6.4 Local Guerilla Squads (LGS) in the Malkangiri Division

Name	Profile
Papluar LGS	(a) CO: Suresh alias Kuda Nageswar Rao (b) Members: Sabitha, Parabati, Sondi Dulla alias Nabin, Ganelli Chandrama alias Akhila
Balimela LGS	Presently no CO. Directly controlled by Papluar ACS Secretary Swarna Members: Suryam (son of Jogal), Raghu alias Jalandar
Potteru LGS	CO: Kurbatti, Kuldeep Rubdar alias Chanti Members: Ranjith, Chandu, Fulmati (wife of Damodar), Sabita, Kamalakka
Motu LGS	CO: Ashok, Paluri rama Rao (surrendered) Members: Prakash, Urmila, Radha, Sama, Phulbhoto (surrendered), Ratna (surrendered)
Kalimela LGS	CO: Ajith Deputy CO: Meena (surrendered) Members: Jamuna, Ranjit, Sushila, Bhatrati, Sumita, Jyothi, Thara
Malkangiri special Guerilla Squad	DC in-charge: Gopi Sammi Reddy alias Jogal CO: Kululula Bala Raju (weapon, Self Loading Rifle) Members: Navin, Rakesh, Raju, Kudabala Laxmi (weapon, .303)
Malkangiri Divisional Mahila Team	DC in-charge and CO: Kakarala Sunitha (weapon, Sten Gun) Member: Reena (weapon, .303)
Malkangiri Jana Natya Mandali	Members: Ajit and Kumari were arrested by Orissa police

Note:
CO – Commanding Officer
DC – Deputy Commander

Source: data from the field survey.

The Zonal Military Commission (ZMC)

Military operations are an inseparable part of Naxalite politics. The military operations of the AOBSZC are controlled and executed by the Zonal Military Commission (ZMC). The ZMC is headed by its ex-officio secretary, Bhaskar. Another expert on guerrilla war, Komala Sehagiri Rao, is designated as In-charge. Other members of the commission are Chenda Bhushanam alias Naga Raju alias Katru alias Bali Reddy, Chelluri Narayan Rao alias Suranna alias Suresh and Gautam. Its South Command is headed by Chenda Bhushanam, Chelluri Narayan Rao heads the North Command, Goutam heads the Zonal Technical Committee, Mahendra heads the Special Action Teams and the Platoon Party Committee is headed by Besai Kama Raju. It is the primary responsibility of the ZMC to conduct

Table 6.5 CPI (Maoist) Basdhara Division

Name	Age	Caste	Native place	Status	Weapon
Sabyasachi Panda alias Sarath	37	Oriya Brahmin	Berhampur (Ganjam)	DCS	AK 47
Sabita alias Bhanu					
Dunna Keshab Rao alias Anand	36	Palli	Srikakulam	Member (surrendered)	SLR
Madiya Harikrishna alias Tapash	30	Palli	Srikakulam	Member	.303

Source: data from the field survey.

Table 6.6 Basdhara Division Committees

Dippaguda Area Committee	DCM in-charge: Vasanthu ACS: Seendri Lingo alias Rama (wife of Vasanthu). She is also the CO of Dippaguda LGS.
Mandravaja Area Committee	DCM and ACS: Dunna Kehav Rao alias Anand (a) Akash is the CO of Mandravaja LGS (b) Uday is the head of Chandrapur LGS
Special Dalam	In-charge: Anand CO: Mahendra Deputy CO: Kiran
Agricultural team	CO: Suryam alias Santhosh
Mahila Coordination Committee	DCM: Sabitha alias Bhanu

Note:
ACS – Area Committee Secretary
CO – Commanding Officer
DCM – Divisional Committee Member
LGS – Local Guerilla Squad

Source: data from the field survey.

Table 6.7 LGS in the Basdhara Division

Name	Profile
Basdhara Division Special Dalam	CO: Mahendra (weapon, .303) Deputy CO: Kiran (weapon, .303) Members: Surendra (weapon, .303) Vanthala Gaddama alias Jyothi (former CO surrendered) (weapon, SLR)
Mandravaja LGS	CO: Akash (weapon, Thampacha) Members: Pangi Puyu alias Prabhakar, Kondu (weapon, .303)
Chandrapur LGS	CO: Uday (weapons, .303, 9 mm pistol) Member: Samara Khara alias Santhosh (weapon, .303)

Source: data from the field survey.

guerrilla operations, the supply of arms and ammunitions and military trainings. The North Command of ZMC functions within the operational area of the North Bureau, similarly the South Command functions within the operational area of the South Bureau. The Special Action Team takes care of specialized operations with in the geographical limits of the AOBSZC. The Platoon Party Committee basically deals with matters pertaining to promotion, suspension, transfer etc.

The dynamics of conflict resolution in Orissa

Indian society follows a policy of transition to modern society based on a modified version of a capitalist mode of production. Mode of production is modified by welfarist concerns of the deprived sections. The penetration of capitalism with justice means the break up of pre-capitalist production relations, feudal and subsistence economy. This affects the poor and weaker sections. For them, development schemes are framed. These are rural development, banking, employment, anti-poverty and resettlement schemes. There is no doubt that there is much to be desired in implementation of the schemes. Plus, a new class of middlemen, contractor and merchants has emerged and that also steals the show. So a large section of the poor get to face the new mode of production and feel cheated by faulty bureaucratic implementation and dishonest middlemen. The latter may also voice political demands for their own narrow interests in the wake of the struggle for the poor in a democracy with periodic elections and a party system marked by coalitions, factional fights and organizational splits. Good governance at a formal level has to be seen. The situation gets complicated by the existence of local leadership with its own mindsets. The federal polity makes agriculture and law and order a state subject. So most of the agrarian and tribal revolts are caused and handled by the local leadership – both in and out of power. As Shiv Raj Patil, former Home Minister of India, observes

> The widespread socio-economic, political and regional inequities prevalent in the country, coupled with poverty, unemployment and lack of proper infrastructure remain the basic causes for continuance and spatial expansion of naxalism. Recognizing this and for tackling Naxalism from the developmental perspective, the central Government has asked the states to accord high priority in the annual plans to ensure faster integrated development of naxalite-affected districts.[33]

Having said this, Shri Patil was also critical about the fact that in the wake of Naxalism development aid has not been properly spent by the state governments.

Even though the problem of Naxalism was treated as a problem of law and order, it was largely left to the police at the local level to deal with the situation with no clear direction from the upper level. This confusion also had a very bad impact over the morale of the police force. The decades of Naxal history in Orissa also pitiably highlights that Orissa could not give a constructive anti-Naxalism policy, as evident in the policies (Appendix 3) that the Orissa government has, so far, devised.

Concluding observations

Maoism is a powerful ideological movement with organic roots in India's socio-economic reality. The spread of the movement shows that the ideology of Maoism is well-conceived and the tactic is sound. There is no doubt that Maoism has struck an emotional chord with a significant section of India's indigenous population. For those suffering due to abysmal poverty, Maoism is an empowering ideology inspiring them to launch an assault on the state power notwithstanding the adverse consequences. The state appears to have failed in providing the basic facilities for human existence to the forest-dependent tribals. It seems that they are destined to suffer because the state is either invisible or where it exists it is just a mute observer, and appears to be absolutely crippled to meaningfully attack the age-old system of exploitation at the behest of the government-sponsored agents. The ground reality is appalling, as a report in the *Economist* underlines

> [i]n one area [in Chhattisgarh], there is a hand-pump, installed by the local government, but the well is dry. There are no roads, water pipes, electricity or telephone lines. In another village, a teacher does come, but, in the absence of a school, holds classes outdoor. Policemen, health workers and officials are never seen.[34]

The vacuum is filled by the Naxalites, looking after the villagers, within their limited capacity. It is conceivable that the Maoists cannot match the government in providing what is required to ameliorate the conditions of the poor; but their endeavour to extend support to the villagers whenever the need arises has led to a symbiotic bond with the local people. The belief that the Maoists are fighting for the tribals has gained ground, particularly in areas producing tendu leaves, with their success in enhancing production by almost 200 per cent for the collection of non-timber forest produce. Adivasis in the state of penury are persuaded to accept that the Naxalites are their saviours in distress. So, the success of the Naxalites can safely be attributed to the stark poverty in which tribals are forced to survive, if that is possible. The aggrieved tribals gravitate towards Maoists who hold out the promise of fighting their cause. Unless a long-term solution to the endemic poverty is meaningfully pursued by the state, the objective conditions supportive of the left-wing extremism continue to thrive. A long-term solution lies in an honest attempt to address the basic causes of poverty, land alienation, unemployment, corruption, displacement and dispossession of tribals and poor governance. True, these problems cannot be solved overnight. But if the state could at least give an impression that 'their severity is being mitigated every year, that itself would go a long way in building confidence among [the affected] people'.[35]

The story remains incomplete without commenting on the organizational network the Naxalites have evolved over the years. Undoubtedly, the 2004 merger of three well-entrenched Naxalite outfits into the CPI (Maoist) is a significant episode in the evolution of the left-wing extremist movement in India. The Maoists are now an organized lot. What is revealing in contrast with its past incarnation is the consistent effort by the Maoists in building an organization to pursue their goal. Unlike the erstwhile Naxalbari movement of the 1960s, the present campaign is primarily rural-based with influences in specific cities and towns. One of the reasons for the decline of the Naxalbari movement was its inability to sustain its momentum in the villages once it began flourishing in specific metropolitan cities and selective towns. Besides other major factors that were responsible for the degeneration of Naxalism as an ideology, the movement was derailed particularly because of its failure to evolve a mechanism of choosing 'the committed cadres' from among those joining the outfit for advancing personal agenda. So, the organization was unable to remain true to its goal with an unstable foundation due presumably to the lack of incongruity of purposes among its members. The present-day Maoists appear to have learnt a lesson, as its recent modus operandi suggests. Although there is no reason to believe that the Maoist organization is well set and not impregnable, the blueprint that the Maoists have prepared is illustrative of the future roadmap in so far as the organization is concerned. Here too, the present-day Naxalites are clearly different from their past counterparts: while the former was constantly engaged in refining the organization in the prevalent socio-economic circumstances, there were hardly serious efforts by the latter in building a well-entrenched organization to sustain the movement. In other words, the Naxalites of the past drew more on spontaneous outburst of those inspired by radicalism of the Marxist variety; contemporary Maoism seeks to build on 'spontaneity' for creating and sustaining an organization supportive of left-wing extremism in India.

What is evident is that Maoism is not a passing phase. It has acquired a base and also a capability to hit the Indian state where it is weakest. Thriving on the government failure of delivering basic services to those who need them most, the Maoists appear to have created a space for themselves in India's recent political history. The possibility of capturing the state power by the Maoists is certainly remote though they have the power to deter investment and development in some of India's poorest regions, which also happen to be among the richest in some vital resources – notably, coal, iron and other useful mineral resources. So, the movement, backed by effective striking power, has the effect of 'sharpening inequity which many see as the biggest danger facing India in the next few years and which is the Naxalites' recruiting sergeant'.[36]

Notes

1 Excerpts from the letter of Satyanarayana Reddy (Kosa), printed in the *Hindustan Times*, 8 February 2009.
2 The CPI (Maoist) documents, 'Party Constitution', http://www.satp.org/satporgtp/countries/india/terroristoutfits/CPI_M.htm
3 These sentences are literally lifted from Mao's 1938 report on the Chinese Communist Party, presented in sixth plenary session of the Sixth Central Committee. *Selected Works of Mao Tse-tung*, vol. II, Peking: Foreign Language Press, 1975, 204.
4 Quoted from the CPI (Maoist) Constitution, reproduced in Appendix 1.
5 The definition of democratic centralism by Vinod Mishra, a Naxalite ideologue is

quoted by Arun Kumar in 'Violence and Political Culture: Politics of the Ultra Left in Bihar', *Economic and Political Weekly*, 22 November 2003, 4983.

6 Mao Tse-tung, 'The role of the Chinese Communist Party in the National War', speech delivered in October 1938, *Selected Works of Mao Tse-tung*, vol. II, Peking: Foreign Language Press, 1975, 204.

7 The Constitution is reproduced in Appendix 1.

8 Quoted from the Constitution that has been reproduced in the Appendix 1.

9 The following discussion is drawn on a report entitled 'Development and Internal Security in Chhattisgarh: Impact of Naxalite Movement', prepared by Rambhau Mhalgi Prabodhini, Mumbai, 18–20.

10 For details, see *Selected Works of Mao Tse-tung*, vol. II, Peking: Foreign Language Press, 1975, 201–5.

11 The inputs on the Maoist structure of the organization is drawn on *Tehelka*, vol. 6 (13), April 2009, 12.

12 As reports suggest, the number of farmers who have committed suicide in India between 1997 and 2007 now stands at a staggering 182,936. Close to two-thirds of these suicides have occurred in the states of Maharashtra, Karnataka, Andhra Pradesh, Madhya Pradesh and Chhattisgarh. Of these states, the Vidarbha region of Maharashtra, where Maoism seems to have struck an emotional chord with the local population, accounts for the largest number of suicides, the highest are recorded in the district of Gadchiroli. P. Sainath, 'The Largest Wave of Suicides in History', *Counterpunch*, 12 February 2009.

13 As the media report underlines, the north Gondia division under the Maharashtra Stare Committee of the CPI (Maoist) maintains two platoons (located around Korchi) and seven guerrilla squads; the north Gadchiroli division, under the Dandakaranaya Special Zone Council has one platoon and six guerrilla squads and there are two platoons and two guerilla squads in south Gadchiroli. *Hindustan Times*, 8 February 2009.

14 Drawn on the basis of the report by Presley Thomas of the *Hindustan Times*, 8 February 2009.

15 The statement of the police officer (on conditions of anonymity) was quoted in the *Hindustan Times*, 8 February 2009

16 The police report that was reproduced in the *Hindustan Times*, 8 February 2009, confirms this.

17 The statement of Ganapathy is quoted in a Maoist document entitled 'Communist Party of India (Maoist)', http://satp.org/satporgtp/countries/india/terroristoutfits/CPI_M.htm.

18 Interview by the Maoist spokesperson, Azad, April, 2007, http://satp.org/satporgtp/countreies/india/terroristoutfits/CPI_M.htm.

19 The discussion on Janathana Sarkar is drawn on the CPI (Maoist) document entitled 'Policy programme of Janathana Sarkar', http://satp.org/satporgtp/countries/india/maoist/documents/papers/constitution.

20 *The Sunday Times*, New Delhi, 29 February 2009, *Tehelka*, 6 (5), 7 February 2009; *Tehelka*, 6 (13), 4 April 2009.

21 Report by Dan Morrison in *The Christian Science Monitor*, 9 September 2008.

22 The report of the social audit of the Janathana Sarkar in Chhattisgarh, http://satp.org/satporgtp/countries/india/maoist/documents/papers/constitution.

23 Dandapani Mohanty, convener of the banned Daman Pratirodh Manch, in an interview conducted as a part of our fieldwork.

24 Dandapani Mohanty, convener of the banned Daman Pratirodh Manch, in an interview conducted as a part of our fieldwork.

25 Information obtained from a top Maoist leader of the Malkangiri area.

26 Information obtained from a top Maoist leader of the Malkangiri area

27 Sanjay Kumar, I.P.S, Superintendent of Police, Sambalpur.

28 An Area Commander of the MCC who we met at an undisclosed location at Jharkhand – Orissa Border.

29 Dr Rajat Kumar Kujur visited many areas of Kandhamal during the period as a part of fieldwork.
30 A Maoist media released under the signature of Saket.
31 A guerilla leader who also works as a police informer in Rayagada.
32 We have collected this top secret information after a lot of painstaking work. However, we cannot disclose the source.
33 Union Home Minister Shiv Raj Patil in his address at the Annual Conference of DGPs/IGPs on 3 November 2004, New Delhi.
34 'India's Naxalites: A Spectre Haunting India', *The Economist*, 17 August 2006, http://www.economist.com.
35 Prakash Singh, 'Terror Won't Work: Both Government and Naxalites Suffer from Delusions', *The Times of India*, New Delhi, 6 July 2007.
36 'India's Naxalites: A Spectre Haunting India', *The Economist*, 17 August 2006, http://www.economist.com.

7 Maoism

Articulation of an ideology and its future[1]

Maoism in India has thrived on the objective conditions of poverty that has various ramifications. Undoubtedly, high economic and income disparity and exploitation of the impoverished, especially 'the wretched of the earth', contribute to revolutionary and radical politics. India's development strategy since independence was hardly adequate to eradicate the sources of discontent. The situation seems to have been worse with the onset of globalization that has created 'islands of deprivation' all over the country. As the state is being dragged into the new development packages, which are neither adequate nor appropriate for the 'peripherals', Maoism seems to have provided a powerful alternative. The argument, drawn on poverty, is strengthened by linking the past deficits with the disadvantages inherent and perceived in the present initiatives for globalization. The Orissa case (and also Chhattisgarh) is an eye-opener because Maoism has gained enormously due to the 'displacement' of the indigenous population in areas where both state-sponsored industrial magnates and other international business tycoons have taken over land for agro-industries. Here is a difference between the present Maoism and the Naxalbari movement. In case of the latter, it was an organized peasant attack against peculiar 'feudal' land relations, particularly in West Bengal, whereas the Maoists in Orissa and Chhattisgarh draw on 'displacement' of the local people – due to the over-enthusiastic state bringing about rapid development through quick industrialization, irrespective of its social consequences for those who are purportedly the beneficiaries. So, issues that are critical to the Maoist organization vary from one context to another. The aim of this chapter is therefore to focus on major contextual issues and their articulation by the Maoists in specific socio-economic milieu in which they appear to have become politically purposeful and ideologically significant agents of socio-economic changes. This will be done in two ways: first, rather than dwelling on context-specific issues, the chapter deals with those critical issues in which the Maoist movement is being articulated in different parts of India; and second, the chapter also seeks to draw out the impact of ultra-left wing extremism on government policy, both in terms of its response to the Maoist movement and also its preparedness to address the socio-economic issues that the movement has raised.

Major contextual issues

It is true that the land question continues to remain significant in the consolidation of left-wing extremism in India. What triggered the present radical Maoist movement, however, was primarily 'forest rights' of the tribal population and also forcible land acquisition for industrialization and the setting up of Special Economic Zones (SEZ). In a significant way, globalization seems to have disturbed the economic balance in the country. With the adoption of the policy of liberalization of the Indian economy and its interaction with the processes of globalization, the rural market has now been integrated with urban commerce producing 'new structures of power based on land and capital' that will further marginalize the rural poor. By creating SEZ, the state seems to have created investment opportunities in industry and trade for the national and global capital. This process has begun to threaten the marginal farmers and those drawing on land with dispossession and displacement – money cannot compensate for their only source of survival, the land, presumably because they are emotionally linked with land and it will be difficult for them to adopt any other means for livelihood.

Maoism is a contextual response to the socio-economic grievances of the peripheral sections of society who, despite the euphoria over the state-directed Soviet model of planned economic development, remain impoverished. Maoism is Marxism-Leninism in an agricultural context where national and global capital are strongly resisted by drawing upon an ideological discourse that has been creatively articulated to take care of the indigenous socio-economic and political forces besides local traditions. In Orissa, Maoism has struck a chord with the indigenous population. Tribals are opposed to the denial of their rights over forest lands and to 'the complicity of the state' and industrial magnates (both national and global) taking the forests away for agribusiness. Those opposing the corporate-led industrialization are considered 'unlawful' and often accused of 'disloyalty' and 'treason'. What is implemented in the name of development is a model for private profit ignoring the basic requirements of the indigenous population. A report of the People's Union for Democratic Rights into three mining projects in Orissa's Kalahandi and Rayagada districts confirms the extent to which local people get marginalized due to 'the application of such a model of development'. The report underlines

> the total dependence on depressed agriculture ... low irrigation facilities ... worsened by inequitable land relations, token and partial land reforms and extremely low educational and health facilities provided by the state. It is in these conditions that these mining projects are pushed through'.

The local people are shown 'the carrot of vague oral promises of permanent jobs and large salaries' by the company and the local administration. To gag the voice of protest, the government resorts to all kinds of punitive measures, including 'regular flag marches through peaceful tribal villages, beatings, threats, arbitrary warrants and arrests, to firing and killing of protestors'. The regions in which the mining projects are underway 'live under the constant shadow of a draconian state'.[2] This is the main source of tension in the tribal areas. Yet the influence of the Maoists varies due to the fact that 'development failures' may not uniformly impact on various social groups at the grass roots. And, this explains why Maoists are more popular among the adivasis and less among those with clear landed interests. Nonetheless, what is deplorable is the lack of basic facilities for the tribals in those areas in India in which the Naxalites roam around rather freely presumably because of their live engagement with the local people, while combating the Indian state for a better future. In a public appeal, Binayak Sen, the medical practioner who was arrested for his alleged link with the extremists in Chhattisgarh, attributed the rising popularity of the extremism to the failure of the state to provide basic human requirements. He thus argued that the state should immediately undertake 'a specific series of measures directed at relieving the humanitarian situation on the ground'. As an immediate priority, the problems to be addressed would include: (a) food and water, (b) shelter and livelihood, (c) health care and (d) transport and infrastructure.[3] This public appeal reveals the appalling circumstances in which the indigenous population survives in the affected areas. The growing expansion of the Maoist influence can thus be said to be an outcome of a socio-economic reality that is party historical and partly due to the mindless application of neoliberal developmental packages.

The merger signalling a new thrust

If the September 2004 merger of several Naxal groups was a new beginning in relation to the course of the Maoist movement in India, the CPI (Maoist) Ninth Congress in January – February 2007, marked yet another phase in the cycle of Maoist insurgencies in India. The Naxal leadership views this as a grand success since the Maoists were holding a unity congress after a gap of 36 years – their Eighth Congress was held in 1970. The Maoists claim that the congress resolved the disputed political issues in the party through lively, democratic and comradely debate and discussion. This Maoist claim hints at the new developments within the politics of Naxalism. It is also significant for the admission of the existence of 'inter-organizational' and 'intra-organizational' conflict within the political gamut of the CPI (Maoist).

The merger of the CPI (M-L) PW and the MCC-I that resulted in the birth of the CPI (Maoist) also successfully brought the dominant faction of the CPI (M-L) Janashakti to its fold. Amid speculations of merger, both the Janashakti and the CPI (Maoist) presented a united front in 2005. A death toll of 892 persons that year was largely believed to be a result of the merger. The Naxalite movement, however, continued to conquer new territories in 2006 though it witnessed only 749 deaths. In 2005, Naxal violence was reported from 509 police stations across 11 states, while in 2006, 1,427 police stations in 13 states came under the shadow of the red terror. Other than the escalation in violence, the latter part of 2006 also witnessed significant changes in the operational ways of the Naxalite movement.

The honeymoon between the CPI (Maoist) and Janashakti could not last longer than a year and in 2006 it became apparent that both were clearly going different ways to occupy operational areas. During the open session of the CPI (Maoist) held in December 2006, Janashakti was asked to make clear its stand on political aims and programmes; Janashakti, however, chose not to attend the session. Consequently, the CPI (Maoist) withdrew the partner status from Janashakti and decided to provide need-based support only in the case of police actions. The conflict between the CPI (Maoist) and Janashakti became public only recently, when the Orissa Janashakti group led by Anna Reddy killed three forest officials on 31 January 2007. The CPI (Maoist) state leadership immediately distanced itself from the killings. Subsequent police enquiry confirmed the involvement of the Janashakti group in the gruesome act.

Of course, things are at a formative stage today; the setting is ready for a possible realignment of the Maoist forces. In Karnataka, which is largely viewed as the new Naxal target, the CPI (Maoist) recently suffered a major setback as a number of cadres in the state, who disagreed with the Maoist agenda of intensifying the revolution in rural areas first and then spreading it to urban centres, have floated a new party named the Maoist Coordination Committee (MCC). It should be noted that the political cracks in Karnataka have now started to extend to other states. Internationally, in 2006, though CPI (Maoist) and the CPN (Maoist) suffered an estranged relationship, the Naxals were, during the same period, successful enough to establish a link with the powerful Russian armed mafias.

The formation of the CPI (Maoist) was not the final stage of the Naxalite movement; the ultimate aim of the Naxalite movement is the seizure of state power and in the process, the movement need not always take a linear route. With new national and international variables taking shape, the politics of Naxalism is bound to accommodate these changes; hence, it is necessary that the government takes notice of these changes at an early stage. Even though the Naxalite movement has always surprised others with its adaptability, the government responses so far have been mostly predictable. In view of the Maoist claim of a 'deciding phase,' the government must think resourcefully, speculate on the new forms that will emerge and construct new frames of reference that will serve as the foundation for strategy formulation and policy implementation. The success of future counter-Naxal programmes will depend on successful integration of intelligence, law enforcement, information operations, targeted military force and civil affairs.

Revealing the capability to strike

One can recall the 2004 Naxal attack in Koraput, the 2006 Naxal attack in R. Udayagiri or the 2008 Nayagarh Naxal attack; incidents of this genre reveal that Orissa has always offered Naxals a safe haven to test their abilities. On 29 June 2008, the Naxals showcased their ability over water when they attacked a motor launch carrying 66 people across the Balimela reservoir in the Malkangiri district. These included 61 policemen from Andhra Pradesh – mostly greyhound commandos, two from the Orissa police and three others. Thirty eight out of these sixty people were left dead as a result of the Maoist water ambush.

Initial reports from the Naxalite zone reveals that the water ambush was masterminded by Chenda Bhushanam alias Naga Raju alias Katru alias Bali Reddy, Kakuri Pandanna alias Pasanna alias Jogan and Ravi, all established guerilla leaders of the Andhra-Orissa Border Special Zonal Committee (AOBSZC). It is also reported that State Militia Commission, a recently constituted force of the CPI (Maoist), engineered the attack. The professionalism that the Naxals displayed leaves no doubt that they had all the information needed about the movement of this force. The Naxals were waiting for the security personnel to fall in their trap at Alampaka, a small mountain inside the reservoir. They fired from there using LMGs, SLRs, AK 47s and rocket launchers. Earlier in the day, the Naxals captured another passenger boat, which they used after the incident to flee to Janbai from where they managed to reach their safe territory of Papluar and Manyamkonda.

The Naxals in the border area of Orissa, Andhra Pradesh and Chhattisgarh have started using inflatable boats for some time; recently the Malkangiri police seized a motor that was attached to an inflatable boat. The liberated zone claimed by the Naxals is the area where the Malkangiri district of Orissa shares a border with the Bastar area in Chhattisgarh and the Khammam district in Andhra Pradesh. Malkangiri is separated from Andhra by the Sileru river and from Chhattisgarh by the Sabrei river. Along with the Sileru and Sabrei, there is another interstate river, the Mahendrataneya, between Orissa and Andhra. The Naxals have now raised a boat wing to facilitate faster movement of their cadres and weapons. S.K. Nath, Deputy Inspector General of Police of the south-western range of Orissa, has confirmed Naxal activities down these rivers.

Orissa has been witnessing a steady increase in incidents of Naxal violence. In fact, the provisional data up to 1 July 2008 reveals that Orissa has suffered the maximum casualties among the Naxal-affected states. Orissa recorded a total of 99 deaths in this period, which includes 57 security personnel, 28 Naxals and 14 civilians. In this same period, Chhattisgarh recorded 94 deaths, there were 82 deaths in Jharkhand, 44 in Bihar and 38 in Andhra Pradesh. Since 2006, the Government of Orissa has banned the CPI (Maoist) and seven of its frontal organizations. The ban order was accompanied by a comprehensive surrender and rehabilitation package for the Naxals. However, the violence graph after the ban shows that the government has not been able to impose the ban successfully, nor has its surrender and rehabilitation package yielded many results. Unfortunately, the government is taking too long to realize that a ban is no solution; the government needs to effectively coordinate its military offensives with socio-economic measures to make the ban effective.

While the Naxals in Orissa are increasingly becoming stronger, the government claims to be suffering from acute shortages of infrastructure and personnel. Of course, the state has every right to ask for central paramilitary forces and central funding for security measures; it cannot fight the Naxals effectively with 12,000 vacancies in the state police. Orissa has only 92 policemen per one lakh of population, whereas the national average is 142 policemen. With extensive industrial and mining activities, the state government constantly boasts about its financial achievements; hence, finance is not a problem to meet its security needs. Given the extraordinary situation in the Naxal-affected areas, Orissa needs a joint command to direct its anti-Naxal operations. The democratization of the development process and modernization of the military process must proceed together in all anti-Naxal policies and operations in Orissa. Anti-Naxal measures (security and socio-economic) need good delivery mechanisms (political, administrative and police) to win over the people, which alone can end the ongoing Naxal violence.

The Maoist capability

On 8 September 2006, the Andhra Pradesh police recovered 600 unloaded rockets, 275 unassembled rockets, 27 rocket launchers, 70 gelatine sticks and other explosives belonging to the CPI (Maoist) from the Mahabubnagar and Prakasam districts. This largest ever arm haul included two tonnes of spares to make 16 rocket launchers, high tensile springs used to propel explosives, fins that could be attached to shells, 500 live .303 rounds, detonators, wire, an electronic weighing scale and two digital thermometers. The ammunition was shipped from Chennai in May 2006 and reached Vijayawada and Proddatur, where it was re-directed to Achampet and Giddalur.

Since its inception in 2004, the CPI (Maoist) has been working on a terror strategy and has emerged as the most sophisticated armed group in India. As revealed in Naxal literature, the CPI (Maoist) now has around 10,000 cadres who are adept in guerilla warfare, with another 45,000 overground cadres. Over the years it has built up an arsenal of 20,000 modern weapons, which includes INSAS, AK-series rifles and SLRs, mostly looted from security forces. Use of fabricated rocket launchers has added to their fire power. Though the Naxals have not yet gained access to RDX, they have frequently used gelatine sticks and Improvised Explosive Devices (IEDs).

In addition, the Naxals have a huge number of country-made weapons which they procure through a chain of underground arms production units. There are over 1,500 illegal arms manufacturing units in Bihar alone, mostly located in the Nalanda, Nawada, Gaya and Munger districts. Recently, Gorakhpur and Ghazipur in Uttar Pradesh have emerged as Maoist centres for production and distribution of illegal arms. Naxals also have an undetermined number of arms manufacturing units in the dense forests of Sarnda (Jharkhand), Redhakhol (Orissa) and Dandakaranya (Chhattisgarh). A recent study conducted jointly by Oxfam, Amnesty International and the International Action Network on Small Arms estimated that 40 million guns out of the estimated 75 million illegal small arms worldwide are in central India with the Naxals active in Bihar, Chhattisgarh, Jharkhand, Orissa, Madhya Pradesh and Uttar Pradesh. The report reveals that along with the mafias, the Naxals have become buyers of assault weapons such as Kalashnikovs and M-16s.

The People's Liberation Guerrilla Army (PLGA) of the CPI (Maoist) has developed into an efficient guerrilla force trained on the lines of a professional armed force. The CPI (Maoist) has an elaborate command structure; at the apex is their Central Military Commission followed by five regional bureaus. Under each regional bureau there is a Zonal Military Commission, which is responsible for executing armed operations. The people's militia is at the bottom of this structure. The Naxals now run at least 80 training camps all over India and each camp has the infrastructure to train 300 cadres at a time. The Naxals, particularly in Andhra Pradesh, have been using wireless scanners, which can tap into the frequency of police communications. The big question is: who is providing such high-tech equipment and training to the Naxals? Though the government is hesitant to provide information, it is speculated that the United Liberation Front of Asom (ULFA) and some retired Indian army officials are involved in training the Naxals. For a long time it has been known that the ULFA has been a major source for supplying automatic weapons to Maoist cadres.

The recent violent operations of the Naxalites, it seems, leave no space for ideological commitment. Indiscriminate use of violence in the name of revolution cannot be countenanced. The Naxals have repeatedly stated that 'armed struggle' is non-negotiable. This position does not make sense. 'Armed struggle' may be the means to the end, but it cannot be an end in itself. The Naxal brand of politics may highlight the evils of the Indian socio-political framework, but it will not be able to eradicate these evils. On the other hand, the state cannot escape the blame for inflicting more violence and suffering upon its civilian population through counter-violence.

In recent years, many high-level meetings have been held to finalize a strategy to deal with the red terror. A number of decisions were taken in these meetings but the ground realities have not improved, rather they have worsened. In most Naxal-affected states there is absolutely no coordination among the police and administration. The frequent coordination committee meetings convened by the Union Government may provide a broad understanding of the problem, but greater coordination is needed between the police and civil administration at the ground level for effective implementation of government decisions taken at the highest level.

The official assessment of the 'red terror'

In May 2006, the Indian Planning Commission appointed an expert committee headed by D. Bandopadhyay, a retired Indian Administrative Service officer instrumental in dealing with the Naxalites in West Bengal in the 1970s along with Prakash Singh, former Director General of Police of Uttar Pradesh and an expert on Naxal issues, Ajit Doval, former director of the Intelligence Bureau, B.D. Sharma, a retired bureaucrat and activist, Sukhdeo Thorat, University Grants Commission chairman and human rights lawyer K. Balagopal as its members to study development issues and address the causes of 'Discontent, Unrest and Extremism'. The committee submitted its report in June 2008.

The committee has done a commendable job in underscoring the social, political, economic and cultural discrimination faced by the scheduled castes/scheduled tribes across the country as a key factor in drawing large number of discontented people towards the Naxalites. The group compared 20 severely Naxalite-affected districts in five states – Andhra Pradesh, Bihar, Chhattisgarh, Jharkhand and Orissa

– with 20 non-affected districts in the same states to establish a correlation between certain human development indicators and their links to social unrest. On the basis of this, it establishes lack of empowerment of local communities as the main reason for the spread of the Naxalite movement. Choosing its words carefully, the report states that, 'We have two worlds of education, two worlds of health, two worlds of transport and two worlds of housing …'.

The committee has delved deep into the new conflict zones of India, i.e. the mines and mineral-rich areas, steel zones as well as the SEZs. The report holds the faulty system of land acquisition and a non-existent Rehabilitation and Resettlement (R&R) policy largely responsible for the support enjoyed by the Naxalites.

> Even those who know very little about the Naxalite movement know that its central slogan has been 'land to the tiller' and that attempts to put the poor in possession of land have defined much of their activity and the notion of a SEZ, irrespective of whether it is established on multi-cropped land or not, is an assault on livelihood.

The committee makes a forceful plea for a policy and legal framework to enable small and marginal farmers to lease land with secure rights and for the landless poor occupying government land not to be treated as encroachers.

For the first time in the history of the Naxalite movement, a government-appointed committee has put the blame on the state for the growth of the movement. Providing statistics of 125 districts from the Naxal-affected states, the committee found out that the state bureaucracy has pitiably failed in delivering good governance in these areas. The committee has also severely criticized the states for their double standards in making panchayats truly the units of local self-governance. Findings of the report recommend rigorous training for the police force not only on humane tactics of controlling rural violence but also on the constitutional obligation of the state for the protection of fundamental rights. Coming down heavily on the civil war instrument of Salwa Judum, the committee has asked for its immediate suspension.

Making a departure from the usual government position, the committee concludes that the development paradigm pursued since independence has aggravated the prevailing discontent among the marginalized sections of society. The report also points out the administration's failure 'to implement the protective regulations in scheduled areas, which has resulted in land alienation, forced eviction from land, dependence of the tribals on the money lenders – made worse often by violence by the state functionaries'.[4] While the government failed to address the grievances of those who lost their land to the moneylenders, the Naxalites in the forest areas of Chhattisgarh, the Vidarbha region of Maharashtra, Orissa and Jharkhand have led the adivasis 'to occupy forest lands that they should have enjoyed in the normal course of things under the traditional recognized rights, but which were denied by government officials through forest settlement proceedings'.[5] The Naxalites seem to have developed organic roots in these areas presumably because of their success in securing the minimum wage for the tribals and also the abolition of 'the practice of forced labour under which the toiling castes had to provide free labour to the upper castes'. Furthermore, the role of the people's court, as the report underlines, in resolving 'disputes in the interest of the weaker party' seems to have created a space in which Naxalites flourished naturally. In the assessment of the expert committee, Naxalites have gained considerably due to (a) the failure of the state to address the genuine socio-economic grievances of the indigenous population and (b) their success in evolving a parallel and alternative order that has benefited the poor – especially the dalits and adivasis.

The report can be termed as an honest attempt to look into the problem of Naxalism from a wider perspective. Though many find the report 'refreshing' for making a forceful plea to depart from a security-centric view of tackling Naxal violence, there is a danger of misinterpreting security measures in the context of the Naxalite movement. Many believe in a law and order approach to tackle Naxalism while others consider Naxalism as the reflection of the prevalent injustice in the society. Naxalism is a security challenge and only an inclusive growth formula will minimize the legitimate dissent of the people. Naxalism is a case where we can not separate policing and development. A police force with a proper agenda for development can ensure the success of any anti-Naxal policy. Dealing with Naxalism needs a holistic approach with development initiatives as an integral part of its security. Security here must be understood in its broader perspective, which includes human development in its scope, as human security is an inseparable component of any human development formula, and vice versa.

The creation of a compact revolutionary zone

It was in August 2001 that the idea of establishing a Compact Revolutionary Zone (CRZ) from the forest tracts of Adilabad (Andhra Pradesh) to Nepal, traversing the forest areas of Maharashtra, Chhattisgarh, Jharkhand and Bihar, was conceptualized at Siliguri in a high-level meeting of the Maoist leaders from India and Nepal. The primary aim of a CRZ is to facilitate the easy movement of extremists from one area in the proposed zone to another. The concept of a CRZ was essentially seen as a prologue to the further expansion of left-wing extremism in the subcontinent. Looked from this angle, the notion of a CRZ seems to be moving in the right direction, for there has been a remarkable Maoist growth between 2001 and 2007 in both India and Nepal. As of now, while the Communist Party of Nepal-Maoist (CPN-M) had formed the government in Nepal, their Maoist counterparts in India have carved out several guerilla zones in different parts of the country. What was once a utopian concept, the idea and reality of a CRZ in India has indeed made big strides.

While the Maoists were busy executing their mega plan of a CRZ, the economic policy of India marked a dramatic shift with the Government of India announcing the setting up of SEZs in its Export-Import Policy 2000. As per the SEZ Act 2005, SEZs are geographical regions that have different economic laws to the rest of the country to facilitate increased investments and economic activity. The politics engulfing the whole issue of SEZs has definitely acquired a Maoist flavour, as can be clearly ascertained from the happenings of Kalinga Nagar in Orissa, Singur and Nandigram in West Bengal.[6] The recent happenings on the SEZ front shows that the idea of SEZs, which was originally formulated as a development strategy, has now become a rallying cry for left-wing extremism.

During their 2007 Ninth Congress, the top-ranking Maoist leadership from 16 Indian states decided to launch violent attacks on SEZs and projects that displace people. The Annual Report of the Central Military Commission of the CPI (Maoist) outlines the Naxal plan of creating disruptions at several proposed infrastructure and mining projects and steel plants. The potential Naxal targets as mentioned in the report are the bauxite mining project of the Jindals in Visakhapatnam, the Polavaram irrigation project, steel plants proposed in Chhattisgarh by Tata, Essar and Jindal, the centre's proposed railway line on the Rajhara-Raighat-Jagdalpur sector, Posco's steel plants under construction in Orissa, power plants proposed by the Ambanis, a proposed steel plant in Jharkhand by the Mittal Group and the Kosi irrigation project in northern Bihar. In the name of development, the tribals are always betrayed, as the Naxal commander Ramgam argues by saying that when the government began mining

> the iron ore are there, it had promised to employ the locals. Did that happen? No. The iron ore is shipped from Bailadila to Vishakhapatnam from where it is sent to Japan. The locals go far and wide for livelihood. Because of that experience, people elsewhere refuse to part with their land.[7]

The Naxal concept of a CRZ and their brand of politics over the issue of SEZs is something that needs to be taken seriously. The Naxal intentions are clear; they want to use SEZs as the most powerful weapon for the complete realization of CRZ. The link between the Naxal concept of a CRZ and the new development mantra of SEZs is no coincidence. The Naxals have grown stronger in the tribal districts of Chhattisgarh, Orissa, Jharkhand, Karnataka and Maharashtra, which so far has attracted US\$85 billion of promised investments, mostly in steel and iron plants and mining projects. Ironically, all these investments and projects are of no benefit to the locals, and in most of the cases, in the absence of a credible R&R policy the locals are forced to lose their lands, which are crucial for their survival. The Naxals have been quick to realize this and reflect it in their agenda.

After the state was forced to withdraw the SEZ from Nandigram in West Bengal due to popular outburst challenging its imposition, the Union Government was forced to take stock of the issues related to SEZs. Recently, after including a few changes in the SEZ Act, the central government's Empowered Group of Ministers on SEZs approved 83 new proposals in addition to the already notified 63 projects. The head of the government has already declared that SEZs are a reality. SEZ in itself is not a bad idea, but the problem lies with its poor implementation. 'Rehabilitation and Resettlement' holds the key to the successful realization of SEZs in India. The government needs to show that SEZs as a development strategy would result in equitable distribution of its gains.

There is no denying that India is growing but certain sections are being continuously denied a share in this growth. Except for symbolic tokenism, such as the Employment Guarantee Scheme, the fundamentals of delivery are missing from most of the plans and projects. It is this tokenism that has given an opportunity to the Naxals to hijack the issue of SEZs in their favour. Today, the Naxals have realized that the Spring Thunder of 1968 failed to give the desired results owing to wide differences in Indian and Chinese conditions. Accordingly, they have reformulated their premises of Maoism. Unfortunately, the government is taking too long to realize that though its SEZ policy is based on the Chinese model, its success would depend a lot on its application to Indian conditions.

The 2007 Ninth Congress and Maoism

The Ninth Congress of the CPI (Maoist) is an ideological milestone for Maoism in India. Besides evolving specific strategies for combating the state power in India, the congress also prepared a blueprint for the seizure of power. In his address to the participants, Mupalla Lakshmana Rao, popularly known as Ganapathy, the general secretary of the party, exhorted that

> the 9th Unity Congress affirmed the general line of the new democratic re-volution with agrarian revolution as its axis and protracted people's war as the path of the Indian revolution that had first come into the agenda with the Naxalbari upsurge ... It set several new tasks for the party with the main focus on establishment of base areas as the immediate, basic and central task before the entire party. It also resolved to advance the people's war throughout the country ... and wage a broad-based militant mass movement against the neo-liberal policies of globalization, liberalization, privatization pursued by the reactionary ruling classes under the dictates of imperialism.[8]

Two important ideas were articulated. First, the Maoists are favourably disposed towards militant mass movement to usher in a new era of people's power; second, they are also exhorted, to take 'the guerrilla war to a higher level of mobile war in the areas where guerrilla war is in an advanced stage and to expand the areas of armed struggle to as many states as possible'.[9] Ganapathy also pledged

> to mobilize masses against the conspiracies and treacherous policies of the rulers to snatch land from people and hand it over to the MNCs [multinational corporations] and big business houses in the name of development through the creation of hundreds of SEZs [special economic zones].[10]

The militant campaign against government efforts to acquire land for SEZs in Orissa, West Bengal or Andhra Pradesh is largely being seen as part of a wider Maoist agenda to resist government agenda on SEZs, as Ganapathy further argued that 'we shall be in the forefront of every people's movement. The Congress has decided to take up struggles against the SEZs which are nothing but neo-colonial enclaves on Indian territory where no laws of the land can be applied'.[11]

There were only a few violent incidents during the Naxal call of economic blockade in 2008–9, but what is more important is the change in the Naxal game plan that the government completely failed to read as it watched helplessly as the Naxals targeted trains, communication and transportation networks and mining companies. On 26 June 2008, the Naxals tried to blow up a BSNL communication tower in the Malkangiri district of Orissa. For the third time in a month, the Naxals targeted BSNL communication towers in the district, having earlier tried to blow up such installations at Kalimela and MV-79 village. Biramdih railway station in West Bengal's Purulia district was raided by about 50 guerrillas who set fire to the stationmaster's cabin and totally destroyed the signalling system. In Bihar, the Naxals reportedly blasted a railway control room near Mehsi railway station in East Champaran. Andhra Pradesh was relatively calm though the Maoists did set fire to a bus.

Jharkhand, on the other hand, incurred a loss of around Rs.1.5 billion. Rs. 300 million was reportedly lost by the railways due to cancellation of goods and passenger trains. The economic blockade disrupted coal and iron ore production and transport, amounting to a loss of around Rs. 600 million. Similarly, traders from the import and export business were forced to bear a loss of around Rs. 500 million. Another Rs. 45 million was lost as buses and trucks remained off the road. In the Bastar region of Chhattisgarh, two Salwa Judum leaders were reportedly killed, and the guerrillas also managed to halt the transportation of iron ore from Dantewada district's Bailadila hills to Visakhapatnam by damaging railway tracks. Hundreds of trucks were seen standing idle on national highways as transporters decided to keep their vehicles off the road. As the Naxals forcefully made their presence felt, life came to a standstill in the Narayanpur, Bijapur, Bastar, Kanker and Dantewada districts of the Bastar region.

Just a week before the Naxals imposed this economic blockade, the top-ranking police officers of the four Naxal-hit states of Andhra Pradesh, Chhattisgarh, Orissa and Jharkhand met at Visakhapatnam to discuss the changed strategy of the Naxals. However, during the Naxal blockade the police were completely on the back foot. Other than patrolling, there was nothing the police could do and even patrolling could not prevent the Naxals from going ahead with their agenda. Of course, the police may claim that there were no major casualties reported but bloodshed was not on the Naxal agenda. As part of their changed strategy, the Naxals wanted to create maximum impact with minimum damage.

It has been quite some time since the Naxals realized that in the wake of massive force deployment by the government, they could not continue with the traditional methods of guerilla war. They, therefore, decided to adopt 'mobile war' as their new strategy. Ganapathy himself is the chief of 'Mobile Operations' and Ganesh, the secretary of the Andhra Orissa Border Special Zonal Committee (AOBSZC) is his deputy. As part of their changed strategy, the Naxals aim to paralyze normal life by attacking the communication, transportation, railway and other essential establishments. They have also learnt that the economic development strategy of the country has created a sense of alienation among certain sections of society and have eyed such alienated groups. The government must try to win over these sections before it is too late. 'Time bound development with target orientated implementation' would definitely fill the gap, which so far has only provided a breeding ground for the extremists. Similarly, police modernization should not be limited to the procurement of arms and ammunitions only; security agencies must work on their intelligence network, and a 'unified command' for the forces at the ground level would solve much operational confusion among the various agencies. A genuine R&R policy with guaranteed implementation is the need of the hour, however, it is time to end failed initiatives like Salwa Judum.

Maoism and Hindutva politics

In a shocking but rare interview given to a private television news channel in Orissa, the secretary of the CPI (Maoist) Orissa State Committee, Sabyasachi Panda,[12] claimed that it was the CPI (Maoist) who had killed Vishwa Hindu Parishad (VHP) leader Swami Laxmananda Saraswati and four others in Jalespata Ashram in Kandhamal district. In the same interview, the mastermind of many Naxal attacks in Orissa also warned that they would kill around a dozen people who he alleged were responsible for the communal tension in Kandhamal unless they stopped their activities. Sabyasachi Panda deserves to be taken seriously for his close proximity with Ganapathy and other top leaders of central committee and Central Military Commission of the CPI (Maoist).

The one-time close associate of the maverick Nagbhushan Pattnaik, Sabyasachi Panda later on developed serious differences with him and in 1996 revolted against the party to form Kui Labanga Sangha and Chashi Mulia Samiti which later became the frontal organizations of the People's War Group (PWG) in Orissa. Sabyasachi Panda is one of the founder members of the AOBSZC of the CPI (Maoist) and was in charge of the dreaded Basadhara Division for quite a long period. Before assuming the charge of secretary of the Orissa state committee of the CPI (Maoist), Sabyasachi Panda formed the People's Liberation Guerrilla Army (PLGA) in the state.

Since 23 August 2008, the day Swami Laxmananda Saraswati was killed, Orissa's Kandhamal district has witnessed an unprecedented and diabolic attack on Christians. With 4,000 houses burned, 300 villages set on fire, 60,000 refugees and over 30 people dead, even today the ground reality in Kandhamal show no signs of normalcy. In this chaotic situation the interview of Sabyasachi was aired on 5 October; many may ask why has it taken so long for the leader of the CPI (Maoist) in Orissa to speak to the media and take responsibility? Some may also wonder what the Naxals would gain by killing an old Hindu priest. Yet others may also suspect his claim on the grounds that Naxals have no history of interfering in religious matters. As the reports (based on evidence) pour in, it is clear that the root cause of the sordid incident in Kandhamal is the ethnic division between the relatively better-placed Kandhas (Hindus) and Panas (dalit Christians).[13] Maoism is not a significant political force in this district though by condemning the alleged Hindu attack on the dalit Christians they are trying to create a space for themselves. Maoists have sympathy for the Panas not because they are Christians, but because they are subject to social atrocities by being dalits. Interestingly, Maoists have not paid adequate attention to this social texture of the Oriya society presumably because the presence of Christians is very negligible in areas in which they have strong grass-roots support.[14]

Sabyasachi claimed in the interview that 'Naxals had left two letters claiming responsibility for the murders, but the state government suppressed both.' There seems to be some truth in his claim, because within the half an hour of the gruesome murder of Swami Laxmananda, the then Director General of Police of Orissa said to the media that the government suspected Naxal involvement in the incident. A few days after the incident, the Superintendant of Police of Sambalpur, Sanjay Kumar, revealed that Prasanna Pal alias Pabitra and Ranjan Rout alias Robin, who were brought on remand from Jagatsinghpur, had confessed to the Naxals' plan to eliminate Swami Laxmananda Saraswati. The job was taken up by the Basadhara division of the banned ultra-Left outfit headed by Sabyasachi Panda and the decision taken after the communal flare-up at Brahmanigoan, Kumar added. All these facts substantiate Sabyasachi's claim.

The politics of Naxalism understands neither religion nor caste; however, growth of Naxalism in Bihar may mainly be attributed to caste factors. For some years now, the issue of conversion and re-conversion has become a driving force in Orissa politics. Naxals may not have interfered in religious issues in the past but that does not prevent them from entering into the arena of communal politics. Naxalites aim at liberating the country by creating an atmosphere of chaos, terror and suspicion. 'The tribals are not Hindu. They are nature worshippers. There are now five lakh (half a million) Hindus in Kandhamal and this number has grown because of these forces,' Sabyasachi alleged. This statement gives a clear indication of Naxal involvement in Swami Laxmananda's murder. The Naxalite movement in Orissa claims to be strong in tribal pockets, however, over the past few years Swami Laxmananda had become an icon among Hindu tribals in and around Kandhamal. There was obvious pressure on the Naxal leadership to expand its support base in non-traditional Naxal areas and it is for this that the Naxals could have killed Swami Laxmananda to spread their message. There are also reports that a few top-ranking leaders of the CPI (Maoist) from neighbouring states of Andhra Pradesh and Chhattisgarh recently complained that Sabyasachi was going soft in Orissa and had confined himself to only the Gajapati and Rayagada jungles. Sabyasachi might well have attacked the symbol of VHP in Orissa to prove his detractors wrong.

The Naxal brand of politics has changed course many times in the past; today, there does not seem to be any ideology left in their modus operandi. The killing of Swami Laxmananda may be an incident in isolation or it may also be the signal of new formations within Naxal politics. It is for the investigating agencies to find out the truth. At the moment, however, there are reasons to believe that there is no spokesperson for the CPI (Maoist) in Orissa who is more authentic than Sabyasachi Panda.

Maoism and child soldiers

It is an established policy of the banned CPI (Maoist) to recruit children above age of 16. However, the process starts earlier with the recruitment of children in the age group of six to twelve for children's associations called Bal Sangham, where children are trained in Maoist ideology, used as informers and taught to fight with sticks. Depending on their skills and aptitude, children from a Bal Sangam are 'promoted' to other Naxalite departments like Sangams (village-level associations), Chaitanya Natya Manch (CNM, street theatre troupes), Jan Militias (armed informers who travel with the dalams), and dalams (armed squads). In the Sangams, Jan Militias and dalams, Naxalites provide rifle training to children and teach them to use different types of explosives, including landmines. Children in Jan Militias and dalams participate in armed conflicts with security forces. Children in Bal Sangams, Sangams and CNMs do not participate directly in hostilities, but are vulnerable to attacks by security forces during anti-Naxalite combing operations. Children recruited into dalams are not permitted to leave, and may face severe reprisals, including the killing of family members, if they surrender to the police.

There are police reports suggesting that Maoists are targeting the children from poor families, promising them 'a future to live in dignity'. Young girls too join Sangham to escape being 'forced into early marriage and other kinds of exploitation'. The police further confirm that 'these child soldiers perform several tasks ranging from actual combat to the laying of mines and explosives, tracking combing operations and spying, besides serving as couriers for the Maoist groups'.[15] However, the most dangerous and most recent Naxal strategy is of the CPI (Maoist) that has formed a Child Liberation Army (CLA). Recently it was reported that at least 300 children were being trained in the dense forests of Dhanbad and Giridih in Jharkhand in a crash course on the use of small arms. Apart from jungle warfare those children were trained to collect information about the movement of security forces and pass it on to the outlaw group. 'The Maoist rebels use children in their propaganda war against the government and security forces,' claimed S.N. Pradhan, spokesperson of the Jharkhand Police.[16]

Use of child soldiers in contemporary armed conflicts is not a new phenomenon; it is a common phenomenon in Sierra Leone, Uganda, Mozambique, Nepal, Sri Lanka and Myanmar. Since 1996, approximately two million children have died in war, at least six million have been injured or physically disabled and 12 million have been left homeless. However, given the conflict dynamics of the Naxalite movement, if the use of children gets institutionalized in its self-proclaimed war against India, and if state agencies continue to ignore international covenants on not using child soldiers, the situation will worsen, affecting an entire generation.

The 'civilian protest': Salwa Judum

The sustained Naxalite campaign has provoked counter-mobilization of people in the form of Salwa Judum, especially in Chhattisgarh. In the local Gondi dialect, Salwa Judum means 'purification hunt' and 'collective hunting', though the government prefers to translate it as 'peace march'. For the government, this is a spontaneous movement to save the tribals from the evils of Maoism. However, Salwa Judum is, as the evidence from the file suggests

> another card in the game of counter-insurgency, which essentially pits groups of state-sponsored vigilante tribals – those frightened by the Maoists as well as those forced by police and paramilitary to herd into special camps – against the Maoist-indoctrinated and controlled tribals.[17]

Salwa Judum has a three-prong approach: first, the Naxal-hit tribals are marched to state-run relief camps while the women and children are left behind. Second, Salwa Judum activities, accompanied by police and security forces, march into the enemy (Naxalite) stronghold areas to conduct meetings and distribute pamphlets condemning the Naxals for having endangered the existence of the local population. More importantly, they hunt for Sangham members who are then asked to surrender or hand themselves over to the police. Third, the government appoints Special Police Officers (SPO) among Salwa Judum activists, who are entrusted and armed to protect the camps as well as accompany the march. The SPOs are allowed to conduct raids in the Naxalite villages to capture and kill the dreaded Naxalites.

Contrary to popular belief that Salwa Judum is a government-initiated anti-Naxal programme, Konda Madhukarrao, a little-known schoolteacher from Kutru in the Bijapur police district of south Bastar, first initiated a public campaign against atrocities committed by the Naxals.[18] However, it took an organized form under the leadership of Mahendra Karma, the former leader of the opposition in Chhattisgarh and soon the state government decided to provide patronage to the programme. Those who joined the campaign of their own accord are (a) those who suffered due to Maoist atrocities, (b) wealthier adivasis, (c) local tradesman and contractors, (d) local politicians and panchayat members and (e) others with regional independent economic interests and power. As the composition suggests, Salwa Judum is a platform for the 'haves' against the 'have-nots'. On 25 August 2005, the state government announced that it had set up a committee headed by chief secretary A.K. Vijayvargiya to extend support to Salwa Judum in the form of logistics, arms and funding.[19]

What started off as a genuine anti-Naxalite movement has rather exposed the tribals to more violence and made them refugees in their own land. As observed by Ajay Sahni of the Institute of Conflict Management, Salwa Judum has exposed the hapless tribals to repeated rounds of violence by the Maoists, and had displaced, according to various estimates, as many as 40,000 tribals who are now huddled in ill-equipped government relief camps in the worst conceivable conditions.[20] Reports based on independent investigation by several civil society organizations and human rights groups reveal that the Salwa Judum campaign is 'a cover-up' government-sponsored counter-insurgency programme that, instead of providing relief to those living in violence-prone areas, has made the situation further complicated by instigating the tribals to fight among themselves. The following report of 2 December 2005[21] prepared by a group of civil and human rights activists is illustrative here. The report that first blew the lid on Salwa Judum claims:

1   The Salwa Judum is ... an organized, state-managed enterprise that has precedents in the Jan Jagaran Abhiyans that have occurred earlier under the leadership of the current Dantewada MLA, Mahendra Karma. The Collector himself has been part of the of 75% of the Salwa Judum meetings and security forces have been backing the Judum's meeting. The main cadre of Salwa Judum are paid and armed by the state, at a rate that is standard in counter-insurgency operations across the country.

2   The Salwa Judum had led to the forcible displacement of people throughout Bhairamgarh, Geedam and Bijapur areas under police and administrative supervision ... People have left behind their cattle and most of their household goods. The entire area is being cleared of inhabitants even as new roads are being built and more police and paramilitary stations are being set up. The region is being turned into one large cantonment.

3   When Salwa Judum meetings are called, people from neighbouring villages are asked to be present. Heavy security forces accompany the meeting. Villagers that refuse to participate face repeated attacks by the combined forces of Salwa Judum, the district force and the paramilitary Naga battalion which is stationed in the area ... These raids result in looting, arson and killings in many instances. In some villages, the raids continue till the entire village is cleared and people have moved to camps, while in other cases only old people, women and children are left. Many villages are coming to camps to avoid these attacks in the first place.

4   Once in camps, people have no choice but to support the Salwa Judum. Some of them are forced to work as informers against members of their own and neighbouring villages and participate in attacks against them, leading to permanent divisions within the villages. We also come across instances where the Salwa Judum took young people away from the village and their families were unaware of their whereabouts.

5   Salwa Judum members man checkpoints on roads, search people's belongings and control the flow of transport [in those areas, supposedly under the Naxal influence]. They enforce an economic blockade on villages and resist coming to camps. They also try to force civil officials to follow their dictat.

6   FIRs (First Information Reports) registering the looting, burning, beatings/torture by Salwa Judum mobs and the security forces are not recorded. We were told of specific instances where security forces threw dead bodies inside or near villages. The intention seems to be to terrorize people not leaving their villages. These killings are

not reported, and therefore hard to corroborate. Some report suggests that ninety six people from thirty six villages have been killed. However, the only killings that are officially recorded are those by Maoists. In the period since Salwa Judum started, it is true that the killings by Maoists have gone up substantially and the official figure today stands at seventy. Rather than being 'a peace mission', as is claimed, the Salwa Judum has created a situation where violence has escalated.

7   Salwa Judum has strong support among certain sections of local society. This section comprises some non-adivasis immigrant settlers from other parts of India, *sarpanches* (village chief) and traditional leaders whose power has been threatened by the Maoists ... Both the local Congress and the Bharatiya Janata Party are supporting the Salwa Judum together.

8   We have heard from several high-ranking officials that there is an undeclared war on in Bastar, and we fear that the worst is yet to come ... In addition, people are being encouraged to carry arms. Village defence committees are being created, SPOs are being trained and armed, and the entire society is becoming more militaristic.

There are reasons to believe that the Salwa Judum campaign may have begun spontaneously, which the government appropriated to combat the Naxalites. It is therefore not surprising that in course of time the government provided support primarily 'through their security forces, dramatically scaling up these local protest meetings into raids against villages believed to be pro-Naxalite, and permitted the protestors to function as a vigilante group aimed at eliminating the Naxalites'.[22] The growing strength of the Salwa Judum campaign is undoubtedly due to the support of the state government of Chhattisgarh, which claim that the support extended to 'the peace mission' is merely to 'discharging the constitutional obligation of providing security and safety to the tribal population'.[23] The idea of supporting the so-called 'people's campaign' can be traced back to the 2005–6 annual report of the Ministry of Home Affairs, Government of India directing 'the state to encourage the formation Local Resistance Groups/Village Defence Committee/*Nagrik Suraksha Samitis* [Civilian Protection Committees] in the naxalite affected areas'.[24] With paramilitary forces at their back, Salwa Judum activists resort to brutal means to terrorize the villagers. As an eye-witness account reveals 'villages that refused to attend [the Salwa Judum] meetings were automatically assumed to be Naxalite villages, and were burnt, and people were herded into [the relief] camps'.[25] Although these relief camps are meant to provide shelter and protection to those seemingly haunted by the Naxalites, they are actually reduced to be the preparatory ground for the Salwa Judum campaign. Even though the relief camps in Bastar (Chhattisgarh), for instance, are meant to be 'the temporary shelters for the [violence-affected] adivasis, road-side signs call them Salwa Judum camps, further obfuscating the boundary between state and Salwa Judum'. A fact-finding mission to camps in Bastar found that these places 'were guarded by both uniformed officers [of the paramilitary forces] and also armed civilians'.[26] Further exploration reveals that 'these camps are in fact largely occupied by a combination of Salwa Judum activists, security forces and Adivasis and serve a variety of purposes beyond (and often contradictory to) that of a sanctuary'.[27] These camps, as the report further confirms, 'seemingly act as security bases ... from which counter-insurgency operations are conducted by both official members of the security forces as well as Salwa Judum'.[28] These relief camps are nothing but 'internment camps' that 'allows the security forces to remove and monitor the villagers who are the primary support base for the Naxalites' by forcibly detaining the adivasis in the name of fulfilling a humanitarian mission.[29]

As evident, Salwa Judum, instead of meaningfully addressing the genuine socio-economic grievances of the people in the affected areas, is an attempt to forcibly suppress the voice of protest. In explaining the growing strength of movements against Salwa Judum, Rangam, a Naxal commander thus argues that 'with the rich robbing the poor, the poor had begun to organize against their exploitation. This scared the government and it launched this brutal movement (Salwa Judum) so that it could continue to loot'.[30] In the name of a counter-insurgency campaign, Salwa Judum seems to have unleashed 'a reign of terror' to scare the Naxalites away. A pattern appears to have developed in whatever Salwa Judum undertakes to re-establish government authority, as an eye-witness account graphically illustrates:

> Salwa Judum attack and rob villagers. They burn down crops and kill cattle. They forcibly took away young men and women from the villages, made them SPO (Special Police Officer) and told them to fight us. Fearing them, many committed suicide. Salwa Judum men raped village women, murdering several afterward. They cut off their breasts. They slashed the bellies of pregnant women.[31]

The field inputs corroborate that 'this so-called "people's movement" ... of Salwa Judum has resulted in life being disrupted in nearly 644 villages or over fifty percent of the district, some 150,000 displaced, of which 45,958 [are] officially in the relief camp as of February, 2006'.[32] Dubbed as 'a state-sponsored terrorism', this campaign has provoked mass consternation involving different layers of society. When deliberating on a public interest litigation in February 2009, the Supreme Court of India censured the government for arming the common man by saying

> how are [the members of Salwa Judum] getting arms? Once you give them arms, it will be difficult to retrieve them and we are going to get disastrous consequences. If you continue with the arms, we may have to take a drastic position. We do not underestimate the enormity of the problem. But you cannot encourage common men by arming them to fight naxalites.[33]

In the opinion of the apex court, the military solution does not appear to be effective in combating Maoism; the root of which is located elsewhere. Hence, the court insists that the government should 'create employment opportunities in the naxal areas under the National Rural Employment Guarantee Act, provide infrastructure and education facilities in the area'.[34]

Given the war-like situation in Chhattisgarh, all these security-related measures seem to be necessary. Some may term these measures as 'short term'. But government long-term measures would yield results only where the presence of the government is felt in Naxal-affected regions. To make this happen, the government needs to ride on an effective mechanism of scientific planning that would balance the strategic implication with people's aspirations. At the same time, in order to push its military agenda, the government needs to win over the local tribals for which it needs to work on a comprehensive formula of sustainable development. Unfortunately, though everybody is disturbed by the escalation of violence, it seems to have underplayed the fact that 'poverty is the greatest form of human rights violation and violence in the name of development is the greatest form of exploitation'. Other than anything else, Chhattisgarh today needs the basic amenities for human existence, including minimum health care, recognition of forest rights and a credible system of governance involving tribals not only in its articulation, but also in framing and implementing meaningful and people-sensitive developmental plans and programmes. Only such a comprehensive solution will translate the governmental pro-people agenda into a reality.

Salwa Judum is not a unique campaign. As evidence from the past shows, attempts were made to undertake counter-insurgency campaign seeking to combat socio-political movements threatening state power. During the Naxalite movement in the late 1960s, the West Bengal government was reported to have organized 'resistance groups' (*Pratirodh Bahini* in local parlance) in those districts which were hard-hit by the red campaign. The sub-divisional police officers were instructed to mobilize 'the local goons and anti-social elements' in their efforts to counter the Naxalites. There are reports that during 1971 the district officers conducted raids, inflicted tortures and threatened to arrest in the Naxal-affected areas 'to force people to join the police-sponsored anti-Naxal cell in the district'.[35] Despite assuring government support, it was not possible for the police to form resistance groups in most of the areas, barring a few worse-affected areas in the district of Birbhum in western West Bengal. In 2007, a serious effort was made to 'regroup village youths and motivate them to take on the Naxalites'. In villages located in the Jharkhand-West Bengal border, the villagers have reportedly organized themselves against 'the red menace' by forming Nagarik Suraksha Samities (Citizens' Protection Group). Despite the enthusiastic endorsement by the local police, these Samities never became effective presumably because of the lack of support from among the villagers.[36] Similarly, the Shanti Sena (army for peace) that was formed in Orissa in 1998 had same objective as that of resistance groups of countering the Naxalites. The campaign was short-lived because of (a) lack of zeal for vigilante operation from among the local people and (b) gradual withdrawal of government support. Recently, in the Naxal-hit district of Malkangiri, the police have started a low-scale programme of 'community policing' to win over the local tribals and checkmate the Naxals in their heartland. Led by the

Malkangiri Sub-Divisional Police Officer (SDPO), the district police initiated a campaign to reach out to the villagers in remote areas of the district. There are two stages in such mobilization: first, by organizing sports tournaments and cultural events, the policemen initiate interaction with the villagers; the second stage involves the creation of a unit consisting of villagers who are willing to take on the Naxalites by organizing campaign against them. Under the programme of community policing, Special Police Officers are appointed from among the villagers who are both in charge of the units and also maintain a constant liaison with the district Superintendant of Police.[37] The programme is still in the embryonic stage. Nonetheless, unlike Salwa Judum, which is a violent campaign, the Orissa experiment is a testimony of a clear change in the attitude of the police while combating 'the red terror'. Violence is not an effective shield against Maoism that has thrived presumably because of an emotional chord with the local communities. By inculcating a meaningful relationship with the people at the grass roots, the Orissa government, through community policing, has shown the extent to which counter-violence is both counter-productive and thus futile.

Expanding the Maoist domain

In one significant way, the contemporary Maoist movement in India is different from its past incarnation in the form of the Naxalbari upsurge of the late 1960s. In order to show solidarity with ultra-Left movements elsewhere, the Indian Maoists undertook steps to form a unified group of left-wing radical outfits in South Asia. The outcome was the formation of the Coordination Committee of Maoist Parties of South Asia (CCOMPOSA) in 2000. In its second annual conference in 2002, the committee, in order to underscore a sense of solidarity among the south Asian Maoist groups, declared

> People's Wars, waged by the oppressed masses and led by the Maoist Parties of Peru, Nepal, India, Turkey, Bangladesh and armed struggle in other countries provide living testimony to this truth. Not only the oppressed countries of Asia, Africa and Latin America, but also the people of imperialist countries are fighting against globalization and privatization, which has plunged the working class and sections of the people of the imperialist countries into crisis and despair never felt before.[38]

What brought these outfits in different geographical locations is an ideological affinity: these outfits are drawn on Marxism-Leninism-Maoism. Inspired by the theory of a new democratic revolution, the coordination committee seeks to 'build a broad front with the ongoing struggles of the various nationality movements in the subcontinent'.[39] With the creation of such a coordination committee, Maoism seems to have spread its tentacles in most South Asian countries. For the Maoists, the committee plays a critical role in the consolidation of what they call 'a compact revolutionary zone', which is also christened as 'red corridor' by the media and government officials. Whatever the nomenclature, the CCOMPOSA or the red corridor is an articulation of a voice, powerful indeed, that has gained momentum particularly in a vast tract of Indian territory with the growing consolidation of Maoism.

In the last week of August 2007 the CCOMPOSA successfully concluded its fourth conference at an undisclosed location in Nepal. The conference was attended by the Proletarian Party of Purba Bangla-CC, the Communist Party of East Bengal (M-L) Red Flag, the Bangladesher Samyobadi Dal (M-L) (all from Bangladesh), the Communist Party of Bhutan (MLM), the Communist Party of Nepal (Maoist), the Communist Party of India (Maoist), the Communist Party of India (M-L) Naxalbari and the Communist Party of India (MLM). The Communist Party of Ceylon (Maoist), which attended the meeting, is not a signatory to the resolution, thereby indicating that it was invited as an observer to the conference.

At a time when the relevance of the South Asian Association for Regional Cooperation (SAARC) is being widely questioned, the political leadership in South Asia can hardly afford to ignore this Maoist quest for redemption in the region. When SAARC was formed it was looked upon not only as the unified platform of South Asia in world politics, but also as a platform for regional cooperation and development. However, the experience of the past few years shows that many things are still lacking in attaining that goal. When CCOMPOSA was formed it was seen as just another Maoist platform. The last four years, however, show that it has established itself as the principal coordinator of the Maoist movement in different parts of the region. The fourth CCOMPOSA meeting, through its political resolution, vowed to strengthen and expand relations among the Maoist organizations in the region and to assist each other to fight the foes in their respective countries.

During the conference, the member representatives took a close look at the ground reality and declared unanimously that South Asia has become a "burning cauldron" of revolutionary movements. Even though the political leadership in South Asia is often shy to accept this, Maoist movements have become an obvious geopolitical feature of the region. In Nepal, Maoists have carved out a distinct place for them in the political structure of the country. Similarly in India, the merger of two major Maoist parties have given them so much strength that even Prime Minister Dr Manmohan Singh was forced to declare Naxalism as the single largest security challenge before the nation. In Bangladesh, despite divisions in ranks, Maoists have made strenuous efforts to unite and spread revolutionary activity to new areas. In Bhutan 'sprouts' of new Maoist movement have also begun.

In hailing the People's War in Nepal, the conference also provided a suitable platform to restore normalcy in the relationship between the CPI (Maoist) and the CPN (Maoist). Recently, both Maoist outfits were involved in a serious introspection on the applicability of Maoism in both of their countries. During the conference, both parties came out with a joint press statement in which they agreed that all tactical questions being adopted in the respective countries would be the sole concern of the national parties. Also, the political resolution passed at the conference asserted that the coordination committee would 'deepen and extend the links between genuine Maoists of the region and increase the coordination to fight back the enemies in the respective countries'.

These recent developments leave one wondering why and how Maoism has prevailed here in South Asia. Does Maoism as an ideology suit South Asia or do conditions in South Asia allow Maoism to grow, or is it a combination of the two? The study of specific Maoist movements in South Asia reveals that Maoist forces have proved to be effective in mobilizing and exciting people to commit acts of violence, with the expectation that it will bring about positive social, economic and political change. However, the use of violence in the name of development cannot be justified as violence itself is the greatest form of human exploitation.

Effective dealing with Maoist insurrections in South Asia will necessitate the implementation of a policy that brings new ideas, goals and projects to the peasants and the rural poor. In the context of a steady Maoist march in South Asia, SAARC has a crucial role to play. The SAARC member states should initiate and encourage such consultations to develop counter-insurgency measures through joint strategies, action plans and cooperative programmes. Besides, the region shares common problems such as poverty, unemployment and population explosion and successfully tackling Maoism in the region would depend on how these variables are perceived and undertaken. A comparison between SAARC and CCOMPOSA may sound unrealistic today, but the political leadership in the region must not allow the Maoists to hijack the notion of regional cooperation. SAARC nations must ensure that such a situation never arise or else it would give a completely new dimension to the concept of regional cooperation.

Sources of sustenance for Maoism

Unlike their counterpart elsewhere, the Maoists in Orissa seem to have created a corpus fund to sustain and support the movement. There are conflicting reports on the sources of funds. Nonetheless, the CPI (Maoist) in Orissa has, at its disposal, sources of income which are not likely to dry up in near future. This is a common knowledge that Naxalites raise fund through extortion from farmers, teachers, contractors and businessmen. For instance, as soon as a contractor receives a tender for the construction of an overhead bridge, he is charged ten per cent of the total project money, as admitted by a civil contractor.[40] Other sources of mobilization of funds include 'the operation of illegal mines, sale of tendu leafs' and illegal sale of various forest products and narcotics'. According the available inputs,[41] Naxalites are involved in 'opium cultivation' at Chitrakonda in the district of Malkangiri. A rough estimate shows that as much as Rs. 60 million worth of opium is produced in this district and the cultivation is controlled by Naxal cadres in association with local people. A police report confirms that 'every year over 10,000 quintals of ganja (marijuana) are produced in the hilly terrain of Orissa-Andhra Pradesh under the Kalimela and Chitrakonda police stations in the district. Despite earnest efforts, the police fail to control the production and marketing of ganja because of the complicity of the local tribals. Furthermore, ganja, packed in small quantities, is smuggled out to the neighbouring states of Chhattisgarh, Andhra Pradesh, Bihar and Madhya Pradesh by the tribals who are well-acquainted with the routes in the difficult hill terrain. Neither the police nor the excise department officials are able to track the carriers simply because (a) they are not familiar with area and (b) they are not adequately equipped to counter-attack in case they are attacked by the Naxalites.

There is another important source of funds for the Naxalites. The district of Malkangiri, in particular, produces tendu leaves which are required to make bidi, a country-made cigarette. Bidi has a huge market simply because it is very cheap compared to cigarettes. The forest department divides the district into 50 units and a tender is invited from among the traders. Once a particular unit is auctioned, the businessman is allowed to take as many bags of tendu leaves as is prescribed for that unit. The picking session lasts only 15 to 20 days in a year; the plants do not require special care for the rest of the year but keep on producing leaves with commercial value presumably because of the conducive ecology of the district.

Before the Naxalites intervened, the tribals were never given the minimum wage of Rs. 90 per day, as fixed by the government. Those who worked for the businessmen remained at the mercy of the contractors and because of the nexus between government officers and contractors, the minimum wage formula was never implemented. In their effort to ameliorate the conditions of the tribals, the Naxals fixed the minimum wage at Rs. 145 per bundle of tendu leaves. As a result, the income of those hired for plucking leaves, substantially increases. This step has a long-term effect: not only did the Naxalite succeed in changing an unjust and exploitative system in regard to minimum daily wage for those picking tendu leaves, it has resulted in creating a strong support base for the Naxalites. There are reports that 'people who are living in Naxal-free areas, are also inviting naxalites to come to their villages and establish their hold so that the contractors in their areas can also be forced to pay higher wages'.[42] The gain that the tribals made with the intervention of the Naxalites was not without a premium. One day's wage is charged from the tribals as reward for enhancing their wages. The demand is not unjustified as Ganapathy, the CPI (Maoist) secretary, argued that

> one day's wage is the people's contribution towards the movement and people should give the money voluntarily [because] if we don't support, the tribals would get only Rs. ninety. So their income is enhanced because of our movement and there is nothing wrong in collecting the contribution from their wages in advance [and hence he suggested that the contribution] has to be collected at the tendu-leaf collection centre itself.[43]

Inputs from the field corroborate that the tribals have found this arrangement appropriate for their self-dignity and survival although the tendu-leaf collection is just a seasonal job. The Maoist intervention was therefore welcome from the very beginning. The support that the Maoists extended for ensuring a better wage not only contributed to the expansion of their organization in remote areas, but also sustained their base despite government atrocities. According to a report, published in the *Guardian*, 'the Naxalites finance their operation by levying "taxes" on around twelve percent on contractors and traders'.[44] A system appears to have emerged in which the role of the government is almost absent and the Maoists seem to have evolved an alternative governance following whatever they decide as 'appropriate and fit' for the exploited masses. The Maoists claim that they have 'brought order if not law to the area – banishing corrupt officials, expelling landlords and raising prices at gunpoint for harvests of tendu leaves'.[45] In such circumstances, the system functions rather smoothly and the contractors also abide by the Maoist 'dictates'; otherwise, they lose everything. For the Naxalites, the contractors are a useful sources of funds and they cannot be dispensed with. As Ganapathy remarked, 'we require money and [the contractors] regularly provide them. Our aim is to collect money for the movement and not to scare them away'.[46]

Similar to the areas in which tendu leaves are grown, the Naxalites seem to have evolved a pattern in regard to forest produce elsewhere. In the Simlipal Tiger Reserve Forest in Orissa, the traders are involved in illegal trade of timber and other forest produce only in connivance with the Naxalites. As an eye-witness account reveals, 'the business of timber running into crores (ten million) [goes] unchecked [and] the Naxalites sheltering in forest [derive] their finances from trading in forest produce, including timber, and to a certain extent, wild derivatives, like ivory, rhino horn, tiger skins, among others'.[47] The local villagers are beneficiaries of such deals because the Naxalites usually take care of their bare needs. Hence, there is hardly an opposition to what the Naxalites undertake in the name of protecting the villagers. The traders have found the arrangement acceptable because the government hardly exists in forests and the Naxalites' writ reigns supreme. A situation has emerged in which traders, local villagers and Naxalites seem to be bound together in a mutually-beneficial bond. The red flag thus continues to remain a powerful symbol of protest not merely because of the ideological commitment of the indigenous population but also due to effective Maoist strategies for mobilizing adequate funds for the movement.

The government response to Maoism

The Naxalite movement has acquired devastating capabilities in Orissa with the party reportedly being in possession of firearms. The state does seem to be alert to the problem that usually crops up with significant intensity only during the election; otherwise, it is treated as a problem, confined to specific localities. Today's alarming situation seems to be outcome of the 'no Naxal policy' in the state. It is absolutely a case of failure of governance in Orissa as none of the successive governments have been able to come out with a policy to win over its own people from the Naxals nor did they effectively use force to suppress the rebels. Recognizing Naxalism as a problem is something different and coming up with solutions is something different. It was late Biju Pattnaik, former Chief Minister of Orissa, who once declared in the state assembly that his name be put first in the list of Naxalites and such political gimmicks cannot be a solution to the serious problem of left- wing extremism. It was in the mid-1990s that the Naxals made their presence felt in several pockets of the state. The next incumbent government of Sri J.B. Pattnaik in the state preferred to ignore the Naxalite movement and that apathy became a blessing for the Naxals as it gave them a free hand to reach into every nook and corner of the state.

The present government of Naveen Pattnaik in Orissa also could not get away with the prevailing confusions on policy formulations on Naxalism. It allowed the Naxals to hold a rally in the capital in September 2004 and even had a dialogue with the frontal organizations of the PWG. However, soon after the rally it arrested some of the people who were returning from the rally. Such contradictory signs only proved to be worsening the already chaotic atmosphere in the state. Such illusions (self-proclaimed) are best explained by one of the leading security experts of India and it certainly suits the prevailing atmosphere of Orissa.

> There is a pattern here. Each new incumbent, be it in North Block or in the State Governments, sets about reinventing the wheel with little concern for what history points out. The cycle is almost invariable: 'peaceful' and political resolutions passionately advocated in the early days of incumbency, yield gradually to an eventual return to the use of 'force' as Naxalite depredations mount . . . The interregnums of 'sympathy and understanding' have, however, been the periods of the most rapid consolidation for the Naxalites.[48]

In 19 April 2006, during a meeting of the 'Coordination Committee' of the Naxal-affected states, the Union Government conveyed its anguish over the 'no Naxal' policy in the state.

> The Centre has asked Orissa government to pull up its socks and work out a strategy to deal effectively with Naxalites as otherwise there could be more Naxal violence in the state than neighbouring Chattisgarh. Orissa Chief Secretary Subas Pani along with the Additional Director General of State Intelligence M. M. Praharaj faced a tough time during the coordination committee meeting where central security agencies pointed to several weaknesses in the state's policy in dealing with Naxalism. Orissa could not give a constructive anti-naxalism policy and continued to harp on that no Naxal violence was witnessed in the state during the last year. However, the officials were told that no incident was witnessed only because it was giving a free run to extremists.[49]

In a significant decision on 9 June 2006, the Government of Orissa imposed a ban on the CPI (Maoist) and seven of its frontal organizations under the Criminal Law Amendment Act 1908. The frontal organizations declared unlawful are: Daman Pratirodh Manch, Revolutionary Democratic Front, Chasi Mulia Samiti, Kui Labanga Sangh, Jana Natya Mandali, Krantikari Kisan Samiti and Bal Sangam.[50]

The ban order was accompanied by a comprehensive surrender and rehabilitation package for the Naxals.[51] Following are the main features of the said package:

- Payment of up to Rs. 10,000 on acceptance of surrender;
- Up to Rs. 20,000 on surrender of arms and ammunition. Rs. 15,000 for rocket launchers, light machine guns and other heavy arms. Rs. 10,000 for AK 47s and INSAS rifles. Rs. 5000 for rifles, revolvers, pistols and wireless sets. Rs. 3000 for remote controlled devices and improvised explosive devices;

- Allotment of land and house building grants up to Rs. 25,000;
- Rs. 15,000 assistance for marriage;
- Up to high-school level the government would bear the education-related expenses of the children of surrendered Naxalites;
- It includes bank loans up to Rs. 2 lakh; subsidies up to Rs. 50,000 after repayment of 75 per cent of the loan; payment of interest after two years from the date a loan is availed of;
- Free medical treatment in government hospitals;
- Those surrendering will also get the reward money on their head;
- The state government has also announced that all minor cases against those who surrender will be withdrawn.[52]

Announcing the ban, the state Home Secretary Santosh Kumar said that a District Level Screening Committee with the Collector, the Superintendent of Police and an officer from the Intelligence Department as its members would recommend the package for the surrendered Naxalites.

For quite some time the Government of Orissa was under tremendous pressure to take a tough stand on the growing problem of Naxalism in the state. Whatever the reason, a major policy shift has undoubtedly occurred, which will have far-reaching implications for the complex problem of Naxalism in the state. Although it is too early to predict anything, there are reasons to believe that the CPI (Maoist) will not keep quiet. With a newly formed People's Liberation Guerrilla Army (PLGA) and a state committee, both headed by the undisputed guerilla leader Sabyasachi Panda, the Naxalites will definitely challenge the state government. Barring the Daman Pratirodh Manch, all other banned outfits are operating underground; hence, this ban will not affect their functioning.

Nevertheless, the ban would boost the morale of the police force, which was waging a lonely battle against the red terror in Orissa. The next logical step for the government is to embark on police modernization. In recent years, Naxal attacks have proved that they have become masters of guerrilla warfare. To tackle them the government needs a modern police force. As per the statement of the Chief Minister, an amount of Rs. 216.22 crores has been spent from 2000 to January 2006 to enhance the ability of the state police to deal with the growing problem of Naxalism in the state. Table 7.1 shows the details as furnished by the Chief Minister.

Continuing with the statement, the Chief Minister informed that, 'the shares of the State and the Union Government in the expenditure, respectively are Rs. 97.03 Crore and Rs.119.19 Crore. The Central Assistance of Rs. 150.51 Crore has been received during the said period.'[53]

However, police modernization does not mean procurement of arms; it is linked to crucial elements of recruitment, training, counselling and intelligence. The government's decision to ban the Naxalite movement will yield results only when an effective police force implements the ban. The state government should come out with a package for its police force who are working in the Naxal-hit areas; the neighbouring state of Andhra Pradesh has declared several such incentives for its police personnel.

Table 7.1 Government of Orissa expenditure for police modernization (amount in Indian currency)

Arms and ammunitions	Rs. 31.00 crores
Equipment for police	Rs. 5.72 crores
Mobility	Rs. 45.19 crores
Communications	Rs. 5.11 crores
Training equipment	Rs. 0.20 crores
Traffic control equipment	Rs. 0.26 crores
Central Intelligence Department equipment	Rs.0.45 crores
Security and intelligence equipment	Rs. 5.08 crores
Forensic science laboratory equipment	Rs. 1.33 crores
Fingerprint bureau equipment	Rs. 0.03 crores
Photo bureau equipment	Rs. 0.50 crores
Police telecommunication network	Rs. 1.87 crores
Non-residential buildings	Rs. 71.64 crores
Residential buildings	Rs. 47.84 crores
Total	Rs. 216.22 crores

Note: one crore = 1,00,00,000

Source: statement of Sri Naveen Pattnaik, Chief Minister of Orissa, in the State Legislative Assembly on 6 February 2006.

The most important part of the government announcement is the policy on surrender and rehabilitation. If properly executed this would provide the government with an opportunity to crack the Naxal network and reveal the human face of the government in its war against the red terror. The growth of Naxal violence in Orissa necessitated a tough stand by the government. Now, after imposing the ban the government has made it clear that violence cannot be allowed to impede development. The success of this ban impact depends on the government's ability to integrate its military and developmental approaches into its counter-Naxal programmes and policies.

Naxal growth in Orissa is all about the organizational consolidation by rival Naxal groups on the one hand, and successive state governments falling prey to the Naxal game plan on the other. With state governments at best being apathetic about the Naxal problem, the Naxalite movement in the state touched several points of inter- and intra-organizational conflict, which all contributed to its growth. As per the available statistics, a huge fund is already being made available to the state government to strengthen the capabilities of the state police, however, the security forces are yet to pose a major challenge to Naxal growth in the state.

Police Force is neither technically nor morally strong enough to take on the Maoists. We are not empowered to open fire on the Naxals on our own; we can only open fire on the grounds of private defense. Police Intelligence is a total failure. Therefore most of the arrests made by the Police are false and fabricated. Police force goes for a combing operation just for the namesake. It is just a farce because unless and until they (Naxals) open fire at us we (Police) can't fire. No one understands. They are armed with automatic weapons and if we wait till they fire on us then they can shoot 30 people at one go. This is the reason whenever there is a combing operation; we just go, move around and come back. How many Naxalites have so far been killed in a combing operation? Negligible.[54]

The above statement of one senior police officer gives us the real but dismal picture of the police front in Orissa. It is a reality that policemen consider stints in Naxalite-affected areas as 'punishment postings'. Orissa does not have a rule where every Indian Police Service (IPS) and state cadre officer has to be posted in Naxal-affected districts. This drawback has led to corrupt practices and this is a serious cause of de-motivation among the security personnel who are posted in the guerrilla zone. 'Why should I take extra care and risk my life while the state government is not keen on solving the problem? Instead I will prefer to wait for my three years to be completed and so that I will be transferred to a better place.'[55]

Undoubtedly, forces belonging to the central police organization are better equipped in comparison to the state police force. As per the government statistics, presently 'three CRPF Battalions have been deployed in the bordering districts-two in South Orissa and one in North Orissa. The state government's request for three more companies of CRPF in Orissa is still pending with the Union government.'[56] But the past experience shows that rushing central battalions doesn't give favourable results all the time. Naxals operate in small groups usually over difficult terrain. A paramilitary battalion, rushed into an area they don't know and unable to gather local intelligence, can't track down and fight Naxals. Moreover, when the centre says it is sending a battalion, what it means is that it is sending, on average, around 400 fighting men. The rest of the battalion are support staff.

Given the unusual conflict dynamics of the Naxalite movement, what would put the Naxals on the defensive is not a large-scale deployment of paramilitary forces but an extensive network of police stations. Capable officers should head the police stations in Naxal-infested areas and they should be allowed to develop local intelligence. They must be given considerable operational latitude and they must have complete political backing.

Orissa has been witnessing a steady increase in incidents of Naxal violence. During the last five years at least 330 people have died in 240 separate incidents.[57] Since 2006, the Government of Orissa has banned the CPI (Maoist) and seven of its frontal organizations. The ban order was accompanied by a comprehensive surrender and rehabilitation package for the Naxals. However, the violence graph after the ban shows that the government has not been able to impose the ban successfully, nor has its surrender and rehabilitation package yielded many results.

Unfortunately, the government is taking too long to realize that a ban is no solution; the government needs to effectively coordinate its military offensives with socio-economic measures to make the ban effective. As the Naxals in Orissa are increasingly becoming stronger, the government claims to be suffering from acute shortages of infrastructure and personnel. Of course, the state has every right to ask for central paramilitary forces and central funding for security measures; it cannot fight the Naxals effectively with 12,000 vacancies in the state police. Orissa has only 92 policemen per one hundred thousand population, whereas the national average is 142 policemen.[58] With extensive industrial and mining activities, the state government constantly boasts about its financial achievements; hence finance is not a problem to meet its security needs. Given the extraordinary situation in the Naxal-affected areas, Orissa needs a joint command to direct its anti-Naxal operations. The democratization of the development process and modernization of the military process must proceed together in all anti-Naxal policies and operations in Orissa. Anti-Naxal measures (security and socio-economic) need good delivery mechanisms (political, administrative and police) to win over the people, which alone can end the ongoing Naxal violence.

Concluding observations

This chapter can be concluded by summarizing the discussion in three fundamental points which are as follows: first, Maoism is a constantly expanding ideological influence stretching from the Indian border touching Nepal in the north to Tamil Nadu in the south, which is euphemistically described in the official parlance as 'red corridor' and in the Maoist articulation as 'the compact revolutionary zone'. This is 'a biggest internal security threat' to the government, and for those drawn to the extremists, the Maoist movement has given them a voice and a chance to survive with basic human dignity. In fact, the movement survives and gains strength just because of its strong support at the grass roots. The state seems to have 'disappeared' and 'a parallel authority seeking to establish people's power' has emerged in the compact revolutionary zone.[59]

Second, the Maoist movement is a sharp comment on India's development trajectory. This is an outcome of 'distorted development programmes' that were appropriated by the well-off sections of Indian society in the name of equitable share of the fruits of development. Even the Prime Minister of India, in his address to the Chief Ministers of the Naxalite-affected states admitted that 'exploitation, artificially depressed wages, iniquitous socio-political circumstances, inadequate employment opportunities, lack of access to resources, underdeveloped agriculture, geographical isolation, lack of land reforms – all contribute significantly to the growth of the Naxalite movement'.[60] In other words, the hilly and forest belt and the plains that are marked by distressing socio-economic conditions 'favour [the Naxalites] with a secure and popular base'.[61] Echoing the concern of the highest political authority in India, a human rights activist from the Dantawada district of Chhattisgarh confirms by saying that 'decades of exploitation, lack of development, poverty and Forest Acts usurping rights to tribals over "*jal, jangle and*

jameen" [water, forest and land] have made the locals suspicious of any government move'.[62] He further adds that the gradual decline of government authority
had made situation worse. 'There is no administration [and] only a police force
which is still not people-friendly', he laments. 'After Salwa Judum, the situation
has worsened. On the one hand is the terror of Naxals and on the other the terror of
Salwa Judum. Tribals are leaving villages and sleeping in forests. Salwa Judum',
he emphatically suggested, 'cannot be the answer to Naxalism'.[63] In many areas,
including those vacated because of the government-sponsored Salwa Judum campaign, 'the edifice of the state structure' appears to have crumbled down. There
is therefore no 'recognized authority' except perhaps the one that the Maoists
have evolved to translate people's power into a reality. So there is no military
solution to the Naxal crisis. The best way to tackle 'the red terror' is by evolving
meaningful and implementable development packages for these areas that remain
peripheral despite the much-hyped India's remarkable economic growth in the
globalizing world. As is well-known, there has been no dearth of programmes for
the peripherals; but these programmes hardly reach those who need them most.
Even the application of force by the paramilitary forces can never be adequate to
combat 'the red menace', the army brigadier helping the Chhattisgarh government to train policemen in anti-terror encounter insists, 'unless it is supported by
the local people'. Hence, he recommends that 'the paramilitary forces need to be
constantly on foot visiting the villages with people-friendly operations because
people can be the sources of information in the villages'. Unless the tribals 'are
won-over and supplement the activities of the forces by sharing information and
other inputs, the military strategy, however advanced it may be, will hardly be
effective'.[64]

Third, Maoism is a creative experiment of people's power. This is a device
through which 'the initiative and energy of the masses ... are released and come
into full play'. This is translated in

> the active participation of masses in administering their own lives, collectively
> developing their villages through construction of schools, tanks, hospitals etc.
> and increasing production, resolving the local disputes by themselves without
> ever the need to go to the bourgeois-feudal courts, in short, shaping their own
> destiny.[65]

The Maoist parallel government, christened Janathana Sarkar, argues a Naxal
cadre, is 'in an embryonic stage' paving the way for the emergence of a full-fledged
government with the seizure of power. The government has eight departments: education and culture, finance, law, defence, agriculture, forest conservation, health
and sanitation and public relations. The conspicuous absence of a land-reform
department is attributed to the fact that the equitable distribution of land among
the tribals has completely ruled out land-related disputes and hence the department has become redundant. Of all the departments, the law department seems
to be most effective and well-respected for its success in resolving, particularly
'family disputes'. In fact, the Maoists claim that during the period of last three

years (2006 to 2009), the Jan-Adalat (people's court) 'has settled about two hundred disputes between brothers, husband-wives, neighbours'. With the growing popularity of the people's court, the local police station seems to have become defunct.[66] Whatever be the rate of success, these parallel institutions continue to symbolize efforts drawn on an alternative ideological discourse in which the role of 'the people' remains most critical. This is what makes the Maoist endeavour interesting to study and comprehend.

It is true that Maoism is a meaningful statement on the articulation of governance at the grass roots. It is also true that Maoism is dismissed as 'another terrorist campaign' seeking to achieve 'not the social and economic advancement of the adivasis but the capture of power in Delhi through a process of armed struggle [in which] the tribals are a mere stepping stone or ... merely cannon fodder'.[67] Nonetheless, there is no denying the fact that the Maoists, by being integrated with the local population in the remote terrain of India, have gradually become part of the community due partly to their involvement in the 'day-to-day struggle' for existence and partly due to their success in getting what is due to the tribals for collecting tendu leaves for the contractors. This is not a mean achievement and it is the image of the Maoists as a saviour of the dispossessed that has helped them build a base in these areas. What is strikingly missing in the entire Maoist endeavour is the absence of a blueprint for future. Their hostility to the construction of roads, schools or hospitals in the forest areas or the hilly terrain in Orissa-Andhra Pradesh and Chhattisgarh border provides credibility to the campaign that the Naxalites are opposed to development. The Maoists admit that roads, schools and hospitals are necessary for development, but they are not persuaded because roads will be used to transport police and paramilitary forces, schools and hospital buildings will provide them accommodation. Hence, they are determined to scuttle such government endeavours. This results in circumstances in which the primary sufferers happen to be the tribals who reel under underdevelopment due mainly to a Maoist-sponsored ideological battle justifying the resistance to development to sustain a campaign that is surely limited in scope and goal. This is perhaps most ironic in Maoism though the decision is politically comprehensible. In the absence of a clear roadmap for future, it is difficult to appreciate the Maoist arguments challenging the governmental development strategy that, despite being politically-governed, would have radically altered the prevalent socio-economic texture of the remote areas. Here is a major contradiction, which the Maoists cannot avoid addressing except to the detriment of their popularity as an organically evolved ideological group seeking to accomplish a new democratic revolution in India.

Notes

1 Some of the ideas in this chapter appeared in some of our earlier writings. We gratefully acknowledge the support that we received from various journals and the public forum in which we presented our views.
2 The report, prepared by the people's Union of Democratic Rights is reproduced from Gautam Navlakha, 'Savage War for Development', *Economic and Political Weekly*, 19 April 2008, 17.

3 Binayak Sen's public appeal was reproduced in *Economic and Political Weekly*, 25 October 2008, 4,114, first printed in *The Hindu*, 21 October 2008.

4 Sumanta Banerjee, 'On the Naxalite Movement: A Report with a Difference', *Economic and Political Weekly*, 24 May 2008, 11.

5 Sumanta Banerjee, 'On the Naxalite Movement: A Report with a Difference', *Economic and Political Weekly*, 24 May 2008, 11.

6 For the Kalinganagar incident, see Ish Mishra, 'Heat and Dust of Highway at Kalinganagar', *Economic and Political Weekly*, 10 March 2007, 822–25; for Singur, see Ranjit Sau, 'A Ballad of Singur: Progress With Human Dignity', *Economic and Political Weekly*, 25 October 2008, 10–13; for the Nandigram episode, see Bidyut Chakrabarty, 'Indian Marxists Throws Down the Gauntlet in Nandigram: Development at All Costs', *OpinionAsia*, 8 December 2007; there are, however, strong views supporting the decision of the Left front government in West Bengal for imposing SEZ in Nandigram: Malini Bhattacharya, 'Nandigram and the Question of Development' and Prabhat Patnaik, 'In the Aftermath of Nandigram', by a CPI (M) supporter, 'Reflections in the Aftermath of Nandigram', *Economic and Political Weekly*, 26 May 2007.

7 The entire interview with Rangam was published in *Tehelka*, New Delhi, vol. 6 (13), April 2009.

8 Quoted in Sudeep Chakravarti, *Red Sun: Travels in Naxalite Country*, Penguin, New Delhi, 2008, 293.

9 *The Times of India*, New Delhi, 15 May 2008.

10 *The Times of India*, New Delhi, 15 May 2007.

11 Ibid.

12 The 39-year-old bespectacled Sabyasachi Panda who hailed from Mayurjholia village in the Nayagarh district is the son of Ramesh Chandra. Panda's father, who belonged to the CPI (Marxist), had served three terms as a member of the Orissa Legislative Assembly, and in 1997 he joined the ruling BJD (Biju Janata Dal). Panda is also known as Sarat and Badal in the police records. He is the secretary of the Bansadhara division of the CPI (Maoist) Andhra Pradesh-Orissa Border Special Zonal Committee and is perhaps the most charismatic leader, who is fluent in Oriya, Telegu and Hindi, with a large following in the Orissa-Andhra Pradesh border area; *The Times of India*, New Delhi, 20 February 2008.

13 The Kandhamal incident is attributed to 'deep-rooted' social and ethnic antagonism among the local communities, which were engineered by 'the Hindutva brigade'. This argument is pursued by Harish S. Wankhede in 'The Political Context of Religious Conversion in Orissa', *Economic and Political Weekly*, 11 April 2009, 36–38.

14 This discussion is drawn on Pralay Kanungo, 'Hindutva's Fury Against Christians in Orissa', *Economic and Political Weekly*, 13 October 2008, 16–19.

15 This report is reproduced in *Hindustan Times*, 30 April 2008. The police got ample proof, the report confirms, 'of child soldiers being recruited by Maoists when two juvenile Naxalites surrendered to Dhenkanal Superintendent of Police, Sanjay K Kaushal on 9 April, 2008'. The surrendered children, Bijaye Hembram (14 years) and Babuli Darel (12 years) admitted that they got firearm training in a reserve forest for 15 days. Both of them had joined the Maoists in June 2006. They also admitted having witnessed 'the killing of three forest officials by their cadres in Kankadahada forests of Dhenkanal district of Orissa in February, 2007'.

16 Interview with S.N. Pradhan of Jharkhand police, 18 December 2008.

17 Sudeep Chakravarti, *Red Sun: Travels in Naxalite Country*, New Delhi: Penguin, 2008, 17.

18 Information obtained from a senior police officer (intelligence), Chhattisgarh, on condition of anonymity. The officer was interviewed by Dr Rajat Kujur on 18 August 2008.

19 South Asia Intelligence Review, weekly assessment and briefing, vol. 4 (7), 29 August 2005, http://www.satp.org/satporgtp/sair/Archive/4_7.htm#assessment2.

20 Ajay Sahni, 'Look Who Is Waving Red Flag Now?', *The Indian Express*, New Delhi, 2 March 2006.
21 'Fact-Finding Report on the Salwa Judum, Dantewara District', All-India team, People's Union for Civil Liberties (PUCL), Chhattisgarh and PUCL, Jharkhand, People's Union for Democratic Rights (PUDR), Delhi, Association for Democratic Rights (APDR), West Bengal and Indian Association for the Protection of Democratic Rights (IAPL), November 2005. The report was released to the press on 2 December 2005, http://www.pucl.org/Topics/Human-rights/2005/salwa-judum-report.htm.
22 'Being Neutral Is Our Biggest Crime', Human Rights Watch, http://www.hrw.org/en/node/62132/section/6.
23 Nandini Sundar and others versus the state of Chhattisgarh, Writ Petition (civil) no. 250 of 2007: counter affidavit on behalf of the respondents, 22 Janaury 2008, 308–9 and 312–13, http://www.hrw.org/en/node/62132/section/6.
24 The Ministry of Home Affairs, Government of India, Annual Report, 2005–2006, http://www.mha.nic.in. Given the clear direction from the Government of India, it may not be a mere coincidence that the Salwa Judum campaign took off in Chhattisgarh in 2005.
25 Nandini Sundar, *Subalterns and Sovereigns: An Anthropological History of Bastar (1854–2006)*, Oxford University Press, New Delhi, 2008, 279.
26 A report on the functioning of these relief camps was published with the title 'Salwa Judum and society in Bastar', in a web-journal of the Forum for Fact-Finding Documentation and Advocacy, http://ffdaindia.in/Members/subash/salwa-judum-and-society-in-bastar.
27 Ibid.
28 Ibid.
29 Ibid.
30 Interview with Rangam, the Naxal Commander involved in anti-Salwa Judum campaign in Chhattisgarh, *Tehelka*, vol. 6 (13), April 2009.
31 Quoted from a report prepared by Ajit Sahi, published in *Tehalka*, vol. 6 (13), 2009, 12–13.
32 Nandini Sundar, *Subalterns and Sovereigns: An Anthropological History of Bastar (1854–2006)*, Oxford University Press, New Delhi, 2008, 287.
33 The Supreme Court Order was excerpted in *The Hindu*, 6 February 2009.
34 Ibid.
35 Prabir Basu, 'Lessons of Birbhum', in Samar Sen, Debabrata Panda and Ashish Lahiri (eds*), Naxalbari and After: A Frontier Anthology*, Kathashilpa, Calcutta, vol. 1, 1978, 128–29.
36 *Hindustan Times*, New Delhi, 9 September 2007.
37 Drawn on the telephone conversation with Mr Himanshu Lal, the Malkangiri SDPO, and Dr Rajat Kujur in August 2008.
38 Sudeep Chakravarti, *Red Sun: Travels in Naxalite Country*, New Delhi: Penguin, 2008, 93–94.
39 Ibid., 94.
40 The statement of Ashok Mahallick is quoted in Nihar Nayak, 'Maoists in Orissa Growing Tentacles and a Dormant State', South Asia Intelligence Review, vol. 17, http://www.satp.org/satporgtp/publication/faultlines/volume17/nihar.htm.
41 In elaborating the sources of income for the Naxalites, we have drawn on Nihar Nayak, 'Maoists in Orissa Growing Tentacles and a Dormant State', South Asia Intelligence Review, vol. 17, http://www.satp.org/satporgtp/publication/faultlines/volume17/nihar.htm.
42 Vineet Agarwal, *Romance of a Naxalite*, New Delhi: National Paperbacks, 2006, 33.
43 The statement of Ganapathy is quoted in Vineet Agarwal, *Romance of a Naxalite*, New Delhi: National Paperbacks, 2006, 55.
44 Randeep Ramesh, 'Inside India's Hidden War: Mineral Rights are Behind Clashes Between Leftwing Guerrillas and State-Backed Militias', *The Guardian*, 9 May 2006, http://www.guardian.co.uk/world/2006/may/09/india.randeepramesh.

45 Ibid.
46 The statement of Ganapathy is quoted in Vineet Agarwal, *Romance of a Naxalite*, New Delhi: National Paperbacks, 2006, 55.
47 Prerni Singh Bindra, 'Enemies Within', *Tehelka*, vol. 6 (16), 25 April 2009, 59.
48 Ajay Sahni, 'Bad Medicine For the Red Epidemic', South Asia Intelligence Review, vol. 3 (4), 4 October 4 2004, www.satp.org.
49 As reported by Press Trust of India (PTI) on 2 April 2006.
50 *Sambad* (Oriya daily), 10 June 2006.
51 For details of the rehabilitation package, see Appendix 3.
52 *Sambad* (Oriya daily), 10 June 2006.
53 Statement of Sri Naveen Pattnaik, Chief Minister of Orissa, in the State Legislative Assembly, 6 February 2006, in response to the State Assembly question no. 9.
54 Statement of Mr Patnaik, an Assistant Commandant of Orissa Special Armed Police. However, as desired by him, we cannot disclose his full name and designation.
55 An Oriya I.P.S officer who is posted in a Naxal-infested told this to Dr Rajat Kujur, one of the authors.
56 Statement of Shri Naveen Pattnaik on 'Maoist Movement in the Border Districts', State Assembly question no. 1, State Assembly, 6 February 2006.
57 Based on media reports to the first quarter of 2009.
58 Ibid.
59 Interview by Misir Besra, the incarcerated Naxal leader to the press, *Hindustan Times*, 16 March 2008.
60 The address of the prime minister was reproduced in *The Times of India*, New delhi, 14 April 2006.
61 Sumanta Banerjee, 'Beyond Naxalbari', *Economic and Political Weekly*, 22 July 2006, 3159.
62 Press interview by Manish Kunjam, a former member of Chhattisgarh Legislative Assembly, published in *The Times of India*, New Delhi, 18 March 2007.
63 Ibid.
64 A new report entitled 'Dantewada Police Camp Didn't Even Have Fence: Cops Were Operating from a Girls' Hostel', *Sunday Times of India*, New Delhi, 18 March 2007.
65 Press interview of Ganapathy, secretary of the CPI (Maoist), April 2007, the text is reproduced in *The Times of India*, New Delhi, 15 May 2007.
66 The entire description of people's government in Bastar (Chhattisgarh) is drawn on the news report entitled 'Area Liberated … No Salwa Judum Here', *The Times of India*, 20 February 2009.
67 Ramchandra Guha, 'Adivasis, Naxalites and Democracy' in Rajesh M. Basrur (ed.), *Challenges to Democracy in India*, New Delhi: Oxford University Press, 2009, 179.

Conclusion

I

Maoism is not an academic expression. This is an ideological movement seeking to replace the semi-feudal and semi-colonial state that has flourished in India since independence. Maoism in India is both a continuity and a break with the past: continuity because it has elements of those Marxist-Leninist movements of the past that sought to mobilize peasants and workers; it is also a break with the past simply because of the fact that Maoism, instead of being dogmatic, is a 'creatively interpreted' Marxism-Leninism and Mao Tse-tung's idea of new democracy in the context of a typical agrarian society. Furthermore, there is one unique feature: unlike their counterparts in the past, instead of rejecting the indigenous ideological traditions, Maoists seem to have provided adequate space for these traditions while mobilizing masses for 'a political cause'. It is not therefore surprising that Gandhi is also appreciated for his concerted effort to eradicate 'social evils', justified in the name of religion and long-drawn traditions. This suggests that 'Indian Maoism' cannot be comprehended in 'the derivative discourse' format. Nepalese Maoism may have ideological affinity with its Indian counterpart though the movement got crystallized largely against a feudal monarchy that was, for obvious reasons, clearly opposed to the ideas of people's empowerment. In two major ways, the Indian example is different: the socio-economic indicators (reflective of 'distorted' state-led planned development) and the deepening of democracy since independence was inaugurated in 1947. The historical legacy of the freedom struggle in which several ideological streams coalesced with Gandhian 'non-violence' remains critically important in the articulation of democracy involving different layers of Indian society. Maoism is a contextual response to the socio-economic grievances of the peripheral sections of society that, despite the euphoria over the state-directed Soviet model of planned economic development, remain impoverished. In the changed socio-economic environment following the acceptance of neoliberal economic reforms by the Indian state, Maoism is Marxism-Leninism in an agricultural context where national and global capital are strongly resisted by drawing upon an ideological discourse that has been creatively articulated by taking into account the indigenous socio-economic and political forces besides local traditions. In this sense, Maoism is undoubtedly a creative articulation of left-wing ideology by providing a contextual interpretation of Marxism-Leninism-Maoism when even a sympathizer of Marxism laments, 'the capacity of the communists to independently intervene is on the wane'.[1]

Maoism is an ideological movement challenging the so-called democratic state in India that miserably failed to address the genuine socio-economic grievances of the poor. It has thus been argued that

> despite a relatively progressive Constitution what came into practice was a pot-pourri of democratic symbolism with highly reactionary and repressive system of patronage and power sharing. For all practical purposes, the poor and the dalits were driven out to the margin of the everyday existence of the nation.[2]

As a nation, India is thus genuinely fractured: while the elites have access to all comforts of life, the poor, the dispossessed and the marginalized continue to remain mere statistical details in the annual census reports. What is striking is the pace in which the Maoists have been growing. No longer confined to dense forests of Orissa, Bihar, Jharkhand or Andhra Pradesh, Maoist cadres are reported to have expanded their domain of influence in other states as well. A government report suggests that as many as 170 districts, located in 15 Indian states have already been affected by 'the red terror'.[3] Maoism continues to attract millions of the impoverished and oppressed masses presumably because not only is it ideologically empowering, it is also meaningful conceptually in projecting an exploitation-free human society. The conditions of the poor are getting precarious day by day with the massive transfer of forest and agricultural land for developing industry, mining, infrastructure and agribusiness. Those dependent on the land find agriculture less and less remunerative. Tribals are dispossessed of sources of livelihood by their shrinking access to forest resources and large-scale displacement due to mega-mining projects. As the novelist Amitav Ghosh comments

> [i]n effect, over many decades, there has been a kind of 'ethnic cleansing' of India's forests: indigenous groups have been evicted or marginalized and hotel chains and urban tourists have moved in. In other words, the costs of protecting Nature have been the thrust of some of the poorest people in the country, while the rewards have been reaped by certain segments of the urban middle class. Is it reasonable to expect that the disinherited groups will not find ways of resisting, whether it be through arms or [otherwise].[4]

The ideological appeal of the Naxalites has thus, comments an analyst, 'a material basis in the Indian environment and that explains their expanding social base'.[5] The increasing presence of Naxalites in large areas speaks of their success in building a base for Maoism. The growing popularity of ultra-Left forces in Indian villages is largely due to their involvement in various kinds of developmental works in those areas. With their sustained work for the villagers, they become part of the community sharing their joys and sorrows. The aim is to create a sense of belonging to the community that is the only insurance against government neglect and indifference. This was articulated very clearly by Ganapathy, the CPI (Maoist) General

Secretary, when the only available bicycle was not given for shifting a person with fever to the nearby health centre. Condemning the owner of the bicycle, Ganapathy did not conceal his anger when he said that the refusal of the owner of the bicycle for taking the ailed villager to the health centre was 'inhuman' and could never be justified.[6] This is a lone incident that suggests the Maoists are seeking to create a sense of collectivity among the villagers. In explaining 'the natural inclination' of the villagers for Maoism, an eye-witness account suggests that the attraction to Maoism is less ideological and more due to the involvement of Naxalite cadres in those activities contributing to the well-being of the villagers. This is a part of a well-planned strategy, as the following report suggests

> Instead of carrying out a recruitment drive, the Maoist leaders wander through the remotest villages, talking to people. In areas where the government has hardly any presence, the Maoists help the villagers in constructing irrigation canals. They also educate the villagers against the problem faced by them. This makes an impact. And, through this process, they become a part of the village. Once inside a village, the extremists offer instant justice for internal problems like theft, cheating, vandalism and land disputes in the area, drawing villagers closer to them. It is at this stage that the villagers develop a trust in them and are ready to protect the Maoists from the police.[7]

It is therefore not surprising when a police report confirmed that the Maoists take 'advantage of the jungles, inaccessible hamlets, poor roads and the tribal population where the government is all but absent'.[8] Besides the logistic difficulties, government apathy towards the indigenous population seems to have created a natural space for the Maoists presumably because of their sincere effort in improving the conditions for the poor by their deeds. The Maoists have gained a mass base among the adivasis 'by taking up cudgels on their behalf against corrupt government functionaries, exploitative traders and money-lenders'.[9] Through their ideological campaign, the Naxalites have also given the villagers in remote areas a sense of identity and a dignified existence. It is thus argued that the historical failure of the Indian state forced the tribal population to join the Maoists since they have gained 'least and lost most from 60 years of political independence'.[10] In remote upland areas, the tribals hardly have access to facilities that are so basic to human existence, like minimum medical care or primary education. Most of the villages are not accessible throughout the year because there are hardly any roads. Undoubtedly, the living conditions are appallingly poor. The government officials appointed for these areas are not available when needed. 'In the absence of any government support and the apathetic attitude of [the government departments] towards the [local] communities', a forest official laments, 'the Naxalites have found fertile ground to proliferate'.[11] Their increasing presence in inaccessible terrain is partly due to their commitment to the downtrodden and partly due to the failure of the government to reach out to the tribals in remote areas. Whatever the reason, the fact remains that Maoism has become a formidable ideological force in those districts, which remain neglected for a variety of historical and contextual factors.

The Naxalites no longer remain outsiders; they are organically linked with the people by their involvement in developmental projects and in such activities that help the villagers combat superstitions and blind faith in 'black magic and witch craft'. On one occasion, Ganapathy was reported to have blamed the villagers for their appreciation for black magic when an infant was brutally sacrificed or a widow was publicly lynched to propitiate God. As he stated

> there are no gods, you are your own god and even if there is one, he shall not be pleased to accept an infant as a gift because that infant would have been his latest and finest creation. Moreover, sacrifice means departing with something of your own. Only your life is your own, not the infant's.[12]

On the lynching of the widow, Ganapathy further added that 'my foolish friends, there are no witches, children die due to malnutrition and due to mosquito bites'.[13] As part of the awareness campaign, the Naxalites insist that hospitals should be built and modern medicine should be made available to the indigenous people. The purpose is two-fold: (a) to provide proper medical care and (b) to convince people that medicine is always preferable to witchcraft to cure ailments. In his address to the villagers in an undisclosed location, Ganapathy exhorted the villagers that

> the medicines should not be avoided when there is ailment. The medicines, which the doctors give you, should not be stored, but should be consumed. These are precautionary dose; you should consume them even if there is no fever. If there is fever, wait for a day or two, then rush to the primary health centre.[14]

On the question as to whether villages should have hospital and schools, there is near unanimity among the Maoist leaders except for a group of cadres who are not comfortable with the building of school blocks in Naxalite areas because 'the government builds a school block and uses it for the police. So the people do not want schools'.[15] As for the building of roads for better connectivity, the Maoists do not seem to appreciate this either, because 'roads are built for the police to [gain] access to our villages and tyrannize us'.[16] There is no doubt that roads will ensure easy movement for the police and paramilitary forces and a significant section of Maoist cadres are vehemently opposed to this idea though there are voices within the group in its favour because roads are synonymous with development. Hence, they argue that

> Naxalites do not want development. They, for instance, are opposed to con-struction of metalled roads [which] are synonymous to development ... But as the network of metalled roads is increasing, the police accessibility is also improving. So, now the COC [Central Organization Committee] wants us to lay ambush on the metalled roads to discourage the government from building metalled roads. Is this not a contradiction? [This is a] clear case of confused state of leadership.[17]

The cadres at the grass roots are also bewildered at the decision of the Naxalites to utilize government facilities when the aim is the seizure of power. As a Maoist was constrained to admit

> we exhort the villagers to pick up arms and overthrow the tyrant government but how the government is tyrant that we are not able to explain. The naxalites tell the tribals to use these government facilities and at the same time exhort them to boycott the government and elections. Either Naxals should say that they are [a] pressure group forcing the government to spend money for development in sparsely populated tribal areas. Or [b] they should say they are revolutionaries trying to overthrow the democratic system of government.[18]

Ideally speaking, the differences of opinion should not lead to split within the party. But as the past shows, Naxalites became divided on both ideological and leadership issues. What is striking in regard to the CPI (Maoist) is the success of a group of ultra-Left extremists in bringing together various splinter groups under one platform. Differences were sorted out, claimed Ganapathy, at the 2007 Ninth Congress through 'politico-ideological debates' among the participants. Such debates are 'the sources of strength of the party' underlining

> the democratic credentials of the party which allows freedom of expression for all kinds of opinions and viewpoints, and its ability to digest various opinions if they are expressed in a constructive way to enrich the Party line and not with a malafide intention to wreck the Party.[19]

Serious differences over major contradictions in the globalizing world were resolved through 'sharp debates' among those appreciative of the Leninist principle of democratic centralism.

Following the merger of the three major outfits, the Maoist Communist Centre, the Communist Party of India (Marxist-Leninist) and the People's War Group (PWG), a new outfit, known as the Communist Party of India (Maoist) was formed. According to an official report, the CPI (Maoist) is active in 15 Indian states, including Andhra Pradesh, Chhattisgarh, Jharkhand, Bihar, Orissa, Uttar Pradesh, Madhya Pradesh, Maharashtra, West Bengal, Karnataka, Tamil Nadu, Uttaranchal and Kerala. The merger makes the Maoist group a pan-Indian entity with its tentacles in what they call 'the compact revolutionary zone', which extends from Nepal through Bihar in the north to the Dandakaranya region (forest areas of central India) and Andhra Pradesh. Maoism is thus not a mere descriptive category but an organized revolutionary movement for the seizure of political power in India.

II

The story of Maoism remains incomplete unless one draws attention to its relative decline in recent years. It is true that Salwa Judum would not have become strong without government support; it is also true that a large number of people are also voluntarily joining the Salwa Judum campaign to avoid Naxal atrocities. As E.A.S. Sarma, former secretary of the Government of India who was part of the 2005 fact-finding team on Salwa Judum to Chhattisgarh, noted that the trouble began for the Maoists

> when they started dismantling the traditional political structures of the adivasis and began tinkering with landownership. Those that did not belong to their '*sanghams*' in the villages were considered anti-Maoist and dealt with firmly, sometimes brutally. The headman of the villages and others intimidated by the Maoists, along with the non-tribals, started grouping together and working out ways to sabotage the Maoists' effort.[20]

Hence, it would be wrong to characterize the Salwa Judum campaign as a solely government-sponsored design. Whatever the nature of the campaign, be it Salwa Judum or Maoist revolutionary violence, the outcome is disastrous for those surviving in uncertainty. Salwa Judum supporters have unleashed a reign of terror and the Naxalites have retaliated by killing those allegedly working for the state. Families and villages are divided, 'some living with or in fear of the Maoists, others in fear of or in roadside camps, controlled by Salwa Judum'. Tribals continue to be harassed on the one side by the state and on the other by the insurgents. There is no respite, as an adivasi from the Bastar district of Chhattisgarh expressed his anguish by saying that '*Humme dono taraf se dabav hain, aur hum beech me pis gaye hain* [pressed from both side, we are crushed in the middle]'.[21] Indiscriminate violence has not only made the conditions of the local people most precarious, but has also led to the situation in which development projects in these areas come to a standstill. The state may not be enthusiastic in undertaking programmes for development given the circumstances; Naxalites also oppose various forms of development, which if implemented, are likely to reduce their importance. They have their own arguments: for instance, if roads are constructed this will speed up the transfer of police and paramilitary forces for controlling the insurgents and hospital and school buildings will be used to house them. The argument may have viability among the Naxalites though it is hardly meaningful to those reeling under massive poverty. The areas in which Naxalites have gained preeminence are among the poorest in India and there is no dearth of essential demands for schools, electricity, water, health centres etc. However, these issues hardly get attention presumably because both the state and the Naxalites are engaged in activities, including violent attacks, to prove their point. In the crossfire of purposes, the obvious victims happen to be the tribals, who remain 'deprived' on all counts for no specific fault of their own. They become 'targets' either way: targets for the state given their alleged complicity with the Naxalites; targets of the Naxalites for their alleged support to the state.

The debates over the appropriateness of violence will remain inconclusive given the contradictory politico-ideological aims that the state and the Naxalites strive to fulfil. The Maoist movement suffers on another count: as a movement that aims to be transformative, it has not always been able 'to ensure equality in all respects to its "weaker" constituents: dalits and women. It is more or less a well-established fact that dalits, despite their critical role in "encounter", are not adequately represented in the upper echelons of the Maoist organization'. It has also been observed that those who get killed are mostly dalits or persons belonging to the lower strata simply because they are the ones who are pushed in encounters leaving behind the upper caste Maoists. A similar criticism is made regarding the position of women within the movement and concerted attempts are made by the leadership to recruit as many women as possible for the organization. A media report suggests that in villages located in the Orissa-West Bengal-Jharkhand border the 'Naxalites have launched a serious recruitment drive with special emphasis on girls and women'.[22] Women who are 'strange mix of girly behaviour and warrior grit'[23] are not reportedly discriminated and they are also welcome in dalams, the action squad, as much as their male counterparts. Nonetheless, like the dalits, they are hardly well-represented in the leadership. The reason is to be located in the hegemonic influence of 'patriarchy which permeates the functioning and ethos of the movement'. The violent nature of the movement has, it has further been pointed out, 'contributed to this, since patriarchy and violence have much in common and tend to reinforce each other'.[24] Interestingly, one notices a pattern in this regard if one follows the trajectory of the Naxalite movement since it was conceptualized in the late 1960s. The role of women as fellow revolutionaries in the ultra-left wing movement in the past was structured around patriarchy. A female participant in the Naxalbari movement in its earlier manifestation reminisced that 'never in the party has a woman received the same status and respect as a man and women were never welcome in the highest decision making. If women had an equal say in the decision making', she further exhorts, '[p]erhaps the history of the Naxalbari movement would have been written differently then'.[25] This was not an exception. Patriarchy seemed to have governed the Naxalite organization. In the southern Indian province of Kerala, a female cadre, Ajitha, had a similar kind of experience when she, inspired by left-wing extremism, joined the Naxalbari movement. Although she was equally adept at handling firearms like her male colleagues, the leadership did not have as much confidence in her as it had in the male members. She lamented that

> even while in the movement, I used to get upset by the denial of opportunities on the basis of gender. There were occasions when the attitude towards women in the revolutionary movement was condemnable. At one level the 'men-comrades' had a protective attitude towards 'women comrades' and at another level instead of being regarded as comrades, women were never involved in the decision making process and were looked at as sex objects.[26]

This was a perennial problem experienced by women revolutionaries, whether in West Bengal, Kerala or elsewhere. Reflective of a well-entrenched male bias, the attitude of the 'men-comrades' towards their women counterparts was neither meaningfully challenged nor was subject to scrutiny even in the party congress. In this sense, the Naxalites, despite their venom against feudalism, did not seem to have effectively challenged the deeply ingrained social values, which they internalized presumably because of their upbringing in a gender-biased social milieu.

III

How will a democratic state combat the red terror? It can do so by (a) initiating and meaningfully implementing various developmental programmes in the affected areas and by (b) effectively employing the coercive forces to unleash a reign of terror. Unfortunately, the state has so far failed on both counts. With regard to the first, despite good intentions, the fruits of development do not reach the rural masses due largely to the complicity of government officials with the local mafia. The inevitable outcome is that one-third of India's population live in sub-human poverty. It is therefore not surprising that the poorest of the poor, the dalits and adivasis provide 'the main support to [the ultra-left wing extremist] movement suggesting a combination of economic and socially oppressive factors as a major cause'.[27] These areas remain peripheral as most of India has taken off with growth. Partly due to government negligence and Naxalite opposition to development, a sizeable section of India's population languishes. Whether it is a green revolution, a white revolution or IT (Information Technology), the wretched of the earth find their life as miserable as before. The situation is worse in the BIMARU (Bihar, Madhya Pradesh, Rajasthan and Uttar Pradesh) states where the dividends of development hardly percolate down to the village that has automatically fuelled 'the politics of revenge' over development. The reasons are not difficult to seek. These are the states with a terribly high level of landlessness. How do you get out of this impasse? The government does not seem to be forthcoming. A peculiar situation has emerged in which 'the policies that would address [the] challenges in inequality and emancipate our farmers, our illiterate and our rural poor are precisely the ones that are now politically volatile and locked in debate or in committee'.[28]

Along with a policy paralysis, the government policy supporting economic liberalization seems to have consolidated the demarcation between the rich and poor and between the urban and rural society. Zealous reliance on the market mechanism as the main driving force of efficient resource allocation and growth accentuated a crisis in agriculture, an industry on which 60 per cent of India's population, nearly 600 million people, depend. There has been a rural employment crash. It has driven thousands of people from villages towards towns and cities in search of jobs. It has pushed millions deeper in debt, and according to a conservative government estimate, more than 100,000 farmers have committed suicide in the last decade or so.[29] Close to two-thirds of these suicides have occurred in the states of Maharashtra, Karnataka, Andhra Pradesh, Madhya Pradesh and Chhattisgarh, which are also Naxalite strongholds. In explaining the phenomenon, P. Sainath, a journalist who has launched a campaign to sensitize the concerned citizens on this issue, argues that

> as costs rose, credit dried up. Debt went out of control. Subsidies destroyed some prices. Starving agriculture of investment (worth billions of dollars each

year) smashed the countryside. India even cut most of the few, pathetic life supports she had for her farmers. The mess was complete. From the late 1990s, the suicides began to occur at what then seemed a brisk rate.[30]

Most of the victims of the suicide epidemic are men, mostly in the 30 to 50 age group, married and educated, with many social responsibilities, especially in the form of unmarried daughters or sisters. There are two things that seem to be common among the suicide victims, as a fact-finding team observes: (a) a feeling of hopelessness in being unable to resolve the dilemmas of personal life and to raise funds for discharging responsibilities and repaying loans and (b) the absence of any person, group or institution to turn to in order to seek reliable advice for agricultural operations, for obtaining funds or for handling personal problems.[31] What triggered-off suicide on a mass scale was the failure of the farmers to repay loans. The fact-finding team also found out that 'of the 48% odd farmers who had committed suicide had availed of informal loans, about 39% loans were from moneylenders, another 38% loans were from relatives and 18% were taken from both moneylenders and relatives'.[32] The overwhelming importance of the conventional sources of informal loans also suggests the absence or reluctance of the public financial institutions to provide loans to the producers. Chased by the moneylenders and the inability to take care of the responsibilities, the farmers have no better option but to kill themselves.

Tribal India is now a tinder box, created by the crystallization of peculiar socio-economic and political processes resulting in a permanent fissure between the 'haves' and 'have-nots'. The state appears to be inclined to gag the voice of protest through coercion. Instead of making the tribals partners in economic development, the military solution further marginalizes the tribals. It has been emphasized at the highest level of decision-making that strong coercive forces are required to completely decimate 'the red menace'. The government response is the formation of the greyhounds, a specially trained commando wing of the Andhra Pradesh police, notorious for its ruthless killing of Maoists and their sympathizers, mostly in fake encounters. In Orissa, the government seems to have refined its coercive apparatus by forming the India Reserve (IR) battalion and the Orissa State Armed Police (OSAP) battalion to deal exclusively with Naxalite and extremist forces. Furthermore, the police department has launched a public contact campaign in the districts of Rayagada and Malkangiri in Orissa to counter the anti-government propaganda carried out by the Maoists. As a strategy, it was welcome by the police though this has not yet yielded impressive results presumably because of the inability of the state government to equip the police forces adequately to combat the Naxalites, who are trained and have modern firearms at their disposal, as a police officer has admitted on condition of anonymity.[33] What is also alarming is the government outsourcing of the responsibility for maintenance of law and order in the Naxal-affected districts by forming Salwa Judum (in Chhattisgarh) in the form of a vigilante army and parallel defence administration. Ironically, by arming the civilians, the state government has created a Frankenstein that is simply not controllable. The gun-trotting youth, the Special Police Officer, in Salwa Judum parlance, are freely moving in the countryside, forcing those without guns to fall in line. The circumstances that have emerged are disastrous, as a commentator argues

> the machismo of revolution is being answered by the machismo of counter-revolution. Call them Sangham organizer or special police officer, the young men [in the affected districts] have been seduced by their new-found – and essentially unearned – authority ... There is thus a double tragedy at work in tribal India. The first tragedy is that the state has treated its Adivasi citizens with contempt and condescension. The second tragedy is that their presumed protectors, the Naxalites, offer no long-term solution either.[34]

There are two important points that need to be addressed before concluding this book: first, Maoism is a sharp comment on India's democracy, which is not merely seasonal, but remains a constantly creative driving force for the peripherals to articulate their demands for justice, equity and self-dignity. In this sense, democracy in India seems to have unleashed a unique process of inclusive politics. As Nilekani comments, 'the move to bottom-up democracy has brought with a far more topsy-turvy politics than we have been used to'. But the clamour has, he further argues, 'come with more access than ever before, and carries with it an immense potential for change, new answers and better polity ... [D]emocracy in India has [thus] shifted from being "essentially foreign" to being, simply, essential'.[35] There are various politico-ideological forces, including Maoism, that are crystallized because of the changing boundary of democracy and democratic politics. This is a very interesting juncture in India's post-colonial history. The Indian state is subject to twin pressures that are contradictory in nature: on the one hand, the forces of globalization seeking to integrate the Indian economy with its global counterpart, which is, on the other hand, being fiercely resisted by various kinds of violent and non-violent movements at the grass roots. In such a paradoxical situation, the state, though 'omnipresent', is 'feeble', though 'centralized' and 'interventionist', is 'powerless'.[36] Political institutions are 'in disarray' and the state is constrained by legitimacy deficit. This is therefore an era of possibilities relocating the locus of Indian polity that is no longer confined to the glittery urban world, but has shifted to the periphery where political ideology is being articulated through a process of contestation, accommodation and negotiation. Democracy not only sustains but also refines this mechanism, which is politically meaningful, ideologically innovative and emotionally gratifying. This is what explains 'the continuing survival in India of democracy, ramshackle and battered but still full of life and resilience'.[37] Maoism is one of those offshoots drawing its sustenance from what is euphemistically described as the 'deepening of democracy' giving voice to the voiceless.

The second equally critical point relates to the Maoist role in keeping alive the agrarian demands of the rural poor. As India is characterized as a society with a semi-feudal mode of production, agrarian agenda remains at the top of the Maoist political manifesto. In this sense, the erstwhile Naxalite movement of the 1960s and its contemporary manifestation have identical socio-economic objectives, i.e.

meaningful land reforms hold the key for equity in rural India where the majority survives on agriculture or agriculture-related works. Even after six decades of national independence, India continues to remain 'semi-feudal' probably in its ugliest form. The semi-feudal production system results in

> land concentration in the hands of a few landlords and kulaks on the one hand and poor and landless of the rural population on the other continue to suffer due to usurious and mercantile exploitation of the landed gentry in collaboration of the agents of neo-liberal forces. Due to dearth of jobs, [the landless peasants] are obliged to do inhuman labour like bonded servants of the landlord and plantation owners. Due to want of jobs, most of them are compelled to live most wretched life, millions of people die or terribly suffer due to starvation or semi-starvation.[38]

While the continuity of feudalism results in the severe suffering of those depending on land for survival it also hinders the growth of the agrarian economy. Feudalism is, in other words, a major obstacle to India's economic and social progress. Hence, for the Maoists, the major contradiction that the movement needs to address is between feudalism and the impoverished masses. So, Maoism is not merely an ideological warfare against the Indian state, it is also socio-political movement with a reasonably clear economic agenda that has created and strengthened a voice in rural India. This is a serious challenge to the neoliberal attempt against displacement and dispossession of the tribals and those associated with land for sustenance. It is true that the Maoist agrarian policy is still very nebulous and yet the very demand for land reforms as the most critical for equity and self-dignity for the rural masses has provoked various grass-roots transformative movements. Similarly, the campaign by the Maoists against the imposition of Special Economic Zones (SEZ) in various parts of India for rapid industrialization seems to have made people aware of the adverse consequences of such a scheme seeking to translate the neoliberal development agenda into reality. The outcome of the campaign in which ideological forces other than Maoists also participate is not uniform. Nevertheless, the fact that it was challenged squarely in some Indian states is adequate proof of how effective the Maoist campaign was in defending the socio-economic and political demands of 'the wretched of the earth'. In the overall assessment, Maoism is both a campaign for agrarian reforms and a powerful challenge to the neoliberal economic agenda of dispossessing the rural masses for either agribusiness or for rapid industrialization.

There is one last point. The Naxalites in the past confronted the landlords, who more or less remained isolated except for the support they had from state-sponsored coercive agents. The situation in the twenty-first century has radically changed. The feudal forces, aligned with those appreciative of the neoliberal development agenda, pose a much bigger threat due to the support that they receive from the state and global forces. Similarly, the support base of left-wing extremist groups has also been extended. The carefully prepared neoliberal design to exploit the forest resources results in massive displacement of the forest-dependent tribal community. Bereft of any alternative sources of income, the tribals are only left with a feeling of anguish and disappointment over the policy of the state that is identified with exploitation and dispossession. The Maoist violent campaign for protecting their rights and human dignity has brought the displaced and marginalized to the Maoist fold. In other words, a symbiotic bond between the tribals and the Maoists seems to have evolved to address the genuine socio-economic grievances of those pushed out of their natural habitat because of an anti-people industrial agenda. Maoism is therefore an ideology of hope for those at the lower rung of rural society. It is articulated differently in different circumstances: in Hindi heartland or BIMARU states Maoism is an attack against caste atrocities and class exploitation while in the forests of Andhra Pradesh, Jharkhand or Orissa, left-wing extremism seeks 'to combine class demands with that of self identity and autonomy for the marginalized minority nationalities'.[39] This is what makes Maoism an interesting area of study that is ideologically innovative and politically meaningful not only for the wretched of the earth, but also for articulating a people-centric alternative political discourse.

Notes

1   Javeed Alam, 'Debates and Engagements: A Look at Communist Intervention in India' in V.R. Mehta and Thomas Pantham (eds), *Political Ideas in Modern India: Thematic Explorations*, New Dehli: Sage, 2006, 404.
2   Arun Kumar, 'Violence and Political Culture: Politics of the Ultra Left in Bihar', *Economic and Political Weekly*, 22 November 2003, 4979.
3   Figures are quoted in *The Times of India*, New Delhi, 30 June 2008.
4   Amitav Ghosh, *Two New Essays: Confessions of a Xenophile & Wild Fictions*, Outlook, New Delhi, 2008, 64.
5   Manoranjan Mohanty, 'Changes of Revolutionary Violence: The Naxalite Movement in Perspective', *Economic and Political Weekly*, 22 July, 2006, 3163.
6   The address by Ganapath is quoted in Vineet Agarwal, *Romance of a Naxalite*, New Delhi: National Paperbacks, 2008, 67.
7   A report prepared by a journalist after having travelled the difficult terrain of the Orissa-Andhra Pradesh border. This report was published in *The Times of India*, New Delhi, 30 June 2008.
8   The police report was quoted in a news item, published in *The Times of India*, New Delhi, 30 June 2008.
9   The report of the fact-finding team to Chhattisgarh in 2006 was quoted in Sagar, 'The spring and Its Thunder, *Economic and Political Weekly*, 22 July 2006, 3177.
10   Ramchandra Guha, 'Advasis, Naxalites and Democracy' in Rajesh M. Basrur, *Challenges to Democracy in India*, New Delhi: Oxford University Press, 2009, 179.
11   The statement of a senior forest official was quoted in Ramchandra Guha, 'Advasis, Naxalites and Democracy' in Rajesh M. Basrur, *Challenges to Democracy in India*, New Delhi: Oxford University Press, 2009, 179.
12   The address by Ganapathy is quoted in Vineet Agarwal, *Romance of a Naxalite*, New Delhi: National Paperbacks, 2008, 66.
13   Ibid., 67.
14   Ibid, 67.
15   Interview by Naxal commander, Rangam of Bijapur, *Tehelka*, vol. 6 (13), April 2009.
16   Interview by Kunjam, the Naxal Commander in Dantewada in Chhattisgarh, date not known, from *Tehelka*, vol. 6 (13), April 2009.

17 The anonymous interview is quoted in Vineet Agarwal, *Romance of a Naxalite*, New Delhi: National Paperbacks, 2006, 94–95.

18 Ibid., 94.

19 Text of the interview of Muppala Lakshman Rao alias Ganapathy, General Secretary, CPI (Maoist), available in April 2007, http://satp.org/satporgtp/countries/india/terroristoutfits/CPI_M.htm.

20 The note of E.A.S. Sarma is quoted in Sagar, 'The Spring and Its Thunder', *Economic and Political Weekly*, 22 July 2006, 3177.

21 Quoted from Ramchandra Guha, 'Adivasis, Naxalites and Democracy' in Rajesh M. Basrur, *Challenges to Democracy in India*, New Delhi: Oxford University Press, 2009, 186.

22 'Maoists on "Women Hiring" Spree', *Hindustan Times*, New Delhi, 9 September 2007.

23 *Sunday Times of India*, 27 February 2009.

24 The dalit and gender critique of Maoism is drawn on Bela Bhatia, 'An Armed Resistance', *Economic and Political Weekly*, 22 July 2006, 3180.

25 Krishna Bandyopadhyay, 'Naxalbari Politics: A Feminist Narrative', *Economic and Political Weekly*, 5 April 2008, 59.

26 *Kerala's Naxalbari: Ajitha: Memoirs of a Young Revolutionary*, (translated version of a memoir, originally written in Malayalam), New Delhi: Srishti, 2008, 284–85.

27 Amit Bhaduri, 'A Failed World View', *Economic and Political Weekly*, 31 January 2009, 37.

28 Nandan Nilekani, *Imagining India: Idea for the New Century*, New Delhi: Penguin, 2008, 483.

29 Unless otherwise stated, this discussion is drawn on Amit Bhaduri, *Development with Dignity: A Case for Full Employment*, New Delhi: National Book Trust, 2006.

30 P. Sainath, 'The Largest Waves of Suicides in History', *Counterpunch*, 12 February 2009.

31 This discussion is drawn on Meeta and Rajivlochan, 'Farmers Suicide: Facts and Possible Policy Intervention', Yashwantrao Chavan Academy of Development, Pune, 2006.

32 Ibid.,96

33 This statement is made by a senior police officer during an interview that Dr Rajat Kujur conducted in December 2008 in the district of Malkangiri.

34 Ramchandra Guha 'Adivasis, Naxalites and Democracy' in Rajesh M. Basrur, *Challenges to Democracy in India*, New Delhi: Oxford University Press, 2009, 183.

35 Nandan Nilekani, *Imagining India: Ideas for the New Century*, New Delhi: Penguin, 2008, 175.

36 Atul Kohli, *Democracy and Discontent: India's Growing Crisis of Governability*, Cambridge: Cambridge University Press, 1991, 8.

37 Pranab Bardhan, 'Dominant Proprietary Classes and India's Democracy' in Atul Kohli (ed.), *India's Democracy: An Analysis of State-Society Relations*, New Delhi: Orient Longman, 1991, 214.

38 The Maoist document, http://satp.org/satporgtp/countries/india/terroristoutfits/CPI_M.htm.

39 Tilak D. Gupta, 'Maoism in India: Ideology, Programme and Armed Struggle', *Economic and Political Weekly*, 22 July 2006, 3173.

Appendix 1

Left-wing extremist (Naxalite) affected areas in India

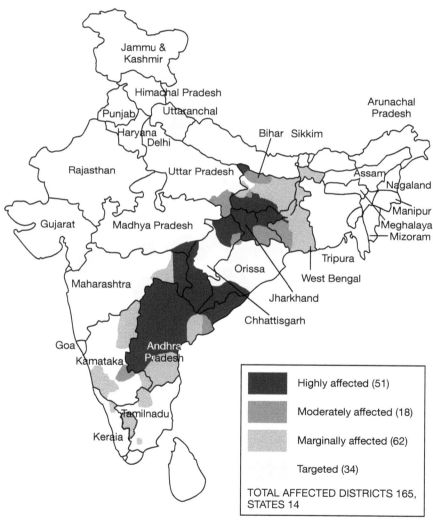

Jammu &
Kashmir

Himachal Pradesh

Punjab   Uttaranchal

Haryana
Delhi

Arunachal
Pradesh

Rajasthan   Uttar Pradesh   Bihar Sikkim

Assam

Nagaland

Manipur

Gujarat   Madhya Pradesh   Meghalaya

Mizoram

Tripura

Orissa

Maharashtra   West Bengal

Jharkhand

Chhattisgarh

Goa   Andhra
Pradesh

Karnataka

Tamilnadu

Kerala

	Highly affected (51)
	Moderately affected (18)
	Marginally affected (62)
	Targeted (34)

TOTAL AFFECTED DISTRICTS 165,
STATES 14

As on 2009 (drawn on inputs from various official and non-official sources)

Appendix 2

Party Constitution of the Communist Party of India (Maoist)

From http:/satp.org/satporgtp/countries/India/terroristoutfits/CPI_M.htm

Party Constitution of the Communist Party of India (Maoist)

The Joint CC meeting deeply studied these five draft documents, freely exchanged the rich experiences acquired through the revolutionary practice during the past three decades and more, and arrived at a common understanding on several vexed questions confronting the Indian revolution in the backdrop of the international developments.

The present document – **Party Constitution** – is the synthesis of all the positive points in the documents of the two erstwhile parties, as well as their experiences in the course of waging the people's war, fighting against revisionism, and right and left opportunist trends in the Indian and international communist movement, and building a stable and consistent revolutionary movement in various parts of our country.

We are placing the present document before the entire rank and file of our new Unified Party for immediate guidance and implementation. At the same time, it should be borne in mind that this is a draft for the forthcoming Congress of the Unified Party. Hence, it has to be enriched further by the participation of all the Party members and suggesting amendments where necessary. Thus it should become an effective weapon in the hands of the Party for solving the fundamental problems of the Indian revolution and to advance it towards victory.

The Communist Party of India (Maoist)
21 September, 2009

Chapter-1: General Programme

The Communist Party of India (Maoist) is the consolidated political vanguard of the Indian proletariat. Marxism-Leninism-Maoism is the ideological basis guiding its thinking in all the spheres of its activities. Immediate aim or program of the Communist Party is to carry on and complete the new democratic revolution in India as a part of the world proletarian revolution by overthrowing the semi-colonial, semi-feudal system under neo- colonial form of indirect rule, exploitation and control and the three targets of our revolution—imperialism, feudalism and comprador big bourgeoisie. The ultimate aim or maximum programme of the party is the establishment of communist society. This New Democratic Revolution will be carried out and completed through armed agrarian revolutionary war i.e. the Protracted People's War with area wise seizure of power remaining as its central task. Encircling the cities from the countryside and thereby finally capturing them will carry out the Protracted People's War. Hence the countryside as well as the Protracted People's War will remain as the center of gravity of the party's work from the very beginning. During the whole process of this revolution the party, army and the united front will play the role of three magic weapons. In their inter-relationship the party will play the primary role, where as the army and the united front will be two important weapons in the hands of the party. Because the armed struggle will remain the highest and main form of struggle and army as the highest form of organization of this revolution, hence armed struggle will play a decisive role. Whereas the united front will be built in the course of advancing armed strug-gle and for armed struggle. Mass organizations and mass struggles are necessary and indispensable but their purpose is to serve the war. The immediate and most urgent task of the party is to establish full-fledged people's liberation army (PLA) and base areas by developing and transforming the guerilla zones and guerrilla bases. Just after completing the NDR the party will advance towards establishing socialism without any delay or interception. Because the NDR will already lay the basis for socialism and hence there will be no pause. Thereafter, the party will continue to advance towards realizing communism by continuing the revolution under the dictatorship of the proletariat.

Socialist society covers a considerable long historical period. Throughout this historical period, there will be classes, class contradictions and class struggle. The struggle between socialist road and capitalist road will also continue to exist. Only depending on and carrying forward the theory of continuing the revolution under the dictatorship of the proletariat can correctly resolve all these contradictions. In this context the GPCR (Great Proletarian Cultural Revolution) initiated and led by Mao Tse-tung was a great political revolution carried out under the conditions of socialism by the proletariat against the bourgeoisie and all other exploiting classes to consolidate the dictatorship of the proletariat and there by fighting against the danger of capitalist restoration. Party will also continue to hold high the proletarian internationalism and will continue to firmly contribute more forcefully in uniting the genuine M-LM forces at the international level. While uniting the M-L-M forces, it will also establish unity with oppressed people and nations of the whole world and continue its fight together with them in advancing towards completing the world proletarian revolution against imperialism and all reaction, thereby pav-ing the way towards realizing communism on a world scale.

During the whole course the comrades throughout the party must cherish the revolutionary spirit of daring to go against the tide, must adhere to the principles of practicing Marxism and not revisionism, working for unity and not for splits, and being open and aboveboard and not engaging in intrigue and conspiracy, must be good at correctly distinguishing contradictions among the people from those between ourselves and the enemy and thereby correctly handling those, fighting left and right opportunism and non proletariat trend must develop the style of integrating theory with practice, maintaining close ties with the masses and practicing criticism and self-criticism.

The future is certainly bright, though the road is tortuous. All the members of our party will wholeheartedly dedicate their lives in the lofty struggle for communism on a world scale must be resolute, fear no sacrifice and surmount every difficulty to win victory!

Chapter-2: The Party, Flags and Objectives

Article – 1: Name of the Party: The Communist Party of India (Maoist)

Article – 2: Flag: Party Flag is red in color with hammer and sickle printed in the middle in white colour. The hammer of the sickle will remain towards the side of the pole. The ratio of length and breadth of the flag is 3:2

Article – 3: (a) The Communist Party of India (Maoist) is the consolidated vanguard of the Indian proletariat. It takes Marxism- Leninism-Maoism as its guiding ideology.

(b) The party will remain underground throughout the period of New Democratic Revolution.

Article – 4: Aims and Objectives: The immediate aim of the party is to accomplish the New Democratic Revolution in India by overthrowing imperialism, feudalism and comprador bureaucratic capitalism only through the Protracted People's War and establishes the people's democratic dictatorship under the leadership of the proletariat. It will further fight for the establishment of socialism. The ultimate aim of the party is to bring about communism by continuing the revolution under the leadership of the proletariat and thus abolishing the system of exploitation of man by man from the face of earth.

The Communist Party of India (Maoist) dedicates itself at the service of the people and revolution, cherishes high affection and respect for the people, relies upon the people and will sincere in learning from them. The party stands vigilant against all reactionary conspiracies and revisionist maneuvers.

Article – 5: The party will continue to hold high the banner of proletarian internationalism and will put its due share in achieving the unity of the Marxist-Leninist-Maoist forces at international level.

Chapter 3: Membership

Article – 6: Any resident of India, who has reached the age of 16 years, who belongs to [the family of] workers, peasants and toiling classes.

Article – 7: Generally party members are admitted as individuals, through a primary party unit. The very application for membership must be recommended by two party members; they must have thorough knowledge about him/her and provide those necessary information's to the party. And the applicant for party membership should submit an application.

Article – 8: Concerned primary unit will investigate the applicant and it will be done secretly with in party as well as among masses. Essentially the application must be recommended by concerned party cell/unit and letter on approved by next higher party committee. The applicant will be admitted into the party as a candidate member. After candidate membership is given, he/she should be observed for a minimum period of six months- for applicants from working class, landless-poor peasants and agricultural laborers; one year for middle peasants, petty bourgeoisie and urban middle class; and two years for those coming from other classes and other parties. From AC to all other higher party committees will also have the right to give new membership, while following the same methods.

Article – 9: Generally party members will be admitted from activist groups organized for party activity working under the guidance of party unit. They must be involved in party activities as decided by the concerned party unit at least for six months before admitting them as candidate member.

Article – 10: By the end of the candidature period, the concerned party unit after reviewing can give full membership or his/her candidature can be extended for another six months, by explaining the reasons. This decision should be reported to the next higher committee. Higher committees may change or modify the decision taken by the lower committee. Zonal/Dist. Committee must approve the new membership. SAC/State Committee will finally approve.

Article – 11: An Indian residing in a foreign country that has all the necessary qualifications for party membership may be given membership; a foreigner residing in India permanently can also be given membership.

If a member of other Marxist-Leninist groups wants to join our party, he/she may be admitted with the approval of the next higher committee. If his/her status is that of primary member in the original party, he/she shall be admitted as full fledged member with the approval of the district/sub-zonal committee. If he/she is an AC member in the original party, he/she shall be admitted within the approval of the state/regional committee. If he/she was of the rank of district or regional level in the original party, he/she shall be admitted by the central committee if he/she was of the rank above regional committee.

If an ordinary member of a bourgeois or revisionist party wants to leave that party and join our party, his/her application shall be recommended by two party members, one of them a being a party member at least for two years. His/Her candidate membership shall have to be accepted by the next higher committee. Similarly, if a member of a bourgeois or revisionist party bearing area level or above responsibilities wants to join our party, his/her application shall have to be recommended by two party members one of them being party members at least for five years. His/her membership shall have to be accepted by the state committee or by the central committees.

Article – 12: Membership fees are Rs.10 per annum. Concerned unit after assessing the economic situation of the party member will fix monthly party levy.

Article – 13: Proven renegades, enemy agents, careerists, individuals of bad character, degenerates and such alien class-elements will not be admitted into the party.

Article – 14: No one from exploiting classes will be admitted in to the party unless he/she hands over his property to the party and should deeply integrate with the masses.

Chapter-4: Rights and Duties of Party Members

The Duties of the Party Members:

Article – 15: He/she shall study and apply Marxism-Leninism-Maoism lively. In the concrete condition of India, he/she must be creative, firm and capable in practice. He/she should try to develop his/her consciousness from the reach experiences of party's ideological, political and organizational line as well as style and method of work.

Article – 16: He/she shall defend ideological and political basis of the party and shall consistently wage ideological and political struggle against various types of non proletarian trends, revisionist policies, trends and style of work; 'left' and right opportunism, economism, parliamentarianism, legalism, reformism, liberalism, sectarianism, empiricism, subjectivism, dogmatism and anarchist concepts and trends.

Article – 17: He/she must study party organs documents and magazines regularly and must take initiative in popularizing party's literature and collecting party fund.

Article – 18: Party members must take part actively and regularly in the day-to-day work of those party units and organizations to which they are attached. They must be following party line, programme, policies, principles, directives and decisions.

Article – 19: Every member must be ready to participate and play a vanguard role in class struggle in the form of armed agrarian revolutionary war i.e. Protracted People's War and other forms of revolutionary mass struggles. They must be prepared to take part in war and give leadership in Protracted People's War for seizure of political power.

Article – 20: He/she must subordinate his/her personal interests to the interests of the party and the people. Party members must fight for the interests of the great masses of the people, must integrate with broad masses, learn from them, rely upon them and strengthen the party relations with the broad masses. He/she must be true servant of the people, sacrifice everything for them and must go to the people for taking the solution of their problems i.e. keep to the principle of 'from the masses to the masses'. He/she must be concerned about the problems of the people, try for their solutions, intimate all those things to the party in time and explain the party line and policies them.

Article – 21: He/She must not practice himself/herself, and should relentlessly fight with a proletarian class outlook against discrimination based on gender, caste, nationality, religion, region and tribe, and ruling class policies of divide and rule.

Article – 22: With the aim of helping each other, he/she must develop the method of collective functioning by comradely criticism and self-criticism. He/she must have attitude to work even with those who raise criticism and hold different views and be able at unite with the great majority, including those who have wrongly opposed them but are sincerely correcting their mistakes.

Article – 23: He/She must accept firmly in theory and practice -party unity, party committee functioning and party discipline. He/She must safeguard the secrecy of the party. He/She must defend the party and hold its cause against the onslaught of the enemy. He/She must safeguard the unity of the party against factionalism. He/She must develop professional attitude towards his/her revolutionary work and must develop his/her level of skills, knowledge and proletarian out look.

Article – 24: The Rights of the Party Members: a) The right to elect and to be elected to party committees at the concerned levels.

b) The right to get Party Magazines, documents, circulars, etc., and the right to freely discuss in the party meetings and party organs about the political and organizational line, policies and decisions of the party and about problems arising in implementing them.

c) In case of any disagreement with the decision of the committee/unit, a member of the concerned committee/unit, must remain loyal to carry out the decision may retain his/her dissenting opinion and demand resettlement of the issue in any subsequent meeting or may even send his/her opinion to higher committees unit the central committee for consideration through his/her respective party unit, when the respective committee fails to solve the problem within six months, he/she has the right to send his/her opinion directly also. It is, however, the discretion of the committee to decide whether to reopen the matter or not.

d) Any member has the right to send criticism against any other party member not in his/her unit to the next higher committee. Any party member has right to send criticism and suggestions.

Decisions taking by any party committee up to Central Committee through the next higher committee.

e) The duties and rights of the candidates members and party members are identical but for one difference. The candidate members have no right to elect or to be elected or to vote.

f) In case of punishment to any unit or party member, detailed explanation and discussion regarding the specific case must be conducted in his/her presence and information regarding decision must be sent to the higher committee in writing.

Chapter-5: Organizational Principles of the Party

Article – 25: a) The organizational principle of the party is democratic centralism. Party structure and internal life is based on this principle. Democratic centralism means centralism based on inner party democracy and inner party democracy under centralized leadership. While discussing open heartedly and being united in party work, such a political atmosphere has to be created where both centralism and democracy, discipline and freedom, unity of will and personal ease of mind and liveliness -all these will be present. Only in such an atmosphere the principle of democratic centralism can be implemented successfully.

b) Most important principle of democratic centralism for organizational structure, the leading committees at all levels shall be compulsorily elected on the basis of democratic discussion. Conferences, plenums and elected committee at all levels shall have approval from higher-level committees.

Essentially the whole party shall follow the principle that individual is subordinate to the organization the minority is subordinate to the majority, the lower level is subordinate to the higher level, and the entire party is subordinate to the Central Committee.

c) Leading committees of the party shall present the organizational report in Congress/Conference or Plenum. These committees will listen to the opinions of people both inside and outside the party and will be answerable to them. Party members shall have the right to criticize and send their opinions/resolutions to the higher committee; even if any party member has a different point of view then he/she can send his views to the higher committee and even up to the central committee.

d) Every member of the leading committee must bear the responsibility to give party leadership to a specified area and a front. They will take direct experience from it and knowledge acquired from this experience can help in guiding other committees, except special responsibility given by higher committees. The central committee can give any member/members of all the leading committees including central committee.

e) The leading committees must regularly send reports to their lower committees and must intimate their decisions promptly. All lower bodies shall likewise be responsible to make regular reports to higher committees about their respective activities.

f) Except those, who are given some special tasks, every party member shall be a member of any one of the party units.

g) Before decisions are taken every party member may freely and fully discuss in the concerned party units. He/She may express his/her opinions on party policies and various problems and some times may abstain form expressing final opinion explaining the reason for it. But, after taking a decision, everybody must strictly abide by them. However, if a member still holds different opinion, he/she has the right to reserve it. It is not permissible to raise discussion on those issues immediately after they were discussed and decisions taken in Congress/conference.

Any member may raise discussion on new issues in the concerned committees. If he/she feels that the issues are concerned with the whole party then he/she may send his/her opinion up to the Central Committee through his/her committees' or/ and in special circumstances, directly. If one third of the Central Committee members opine so and also want to call plenum for its solution then it will be circulated at least up to the State Committees. In case the majority of the State Committees agree with this demand then the Central Committee will call the plenum. In such special circumstances also, the Central Committee will ensure that the democratic method of resolving issues is followed.

h) Keeping in mind the difference between the tactics and method, every unit has the freedom to take initiative in developing new methods of implementation of the party general line and tasks given by higher committees.

i) If a member is arrested, he/she shall be relieved of all responsibilities and the membership will be placed under observation. Depending on his/her behavior during the period of detention by enemy or in the jail or after coming out his/her membership shall be continued/cancelled. If continued he/she shall be admitted into the party committee, which he/she belonged to prior to his/her arrest unless the party decides otherwise.

j) The method of criticism and self-criticism shall be practiced in the party committee at all levels. There must be relentless struggle against bureaucratic, individualistic, liberal, ultra-democratic, Multi-centered factionalist tendencies and trends in the functioning of the committees. The committees should function on the basis of collective leadership and individual responsibility.

k) Comradely relations and mutual co-operation shall be extended in rectifying the mistakes of others. A party member's work has to be reviewed on the basis of his/her overall practice in party life and not on the basis of minor mistakes some trifle matters.

l) It is only the Central Committee that shall have the right to take decision on domestic and international issues. Decisions on various level regarding local issues and problems shall be taken by the respective committees, which will be in accordance with the decisions taken by higher committees.

m) When a party member is transferred to another region, she/he shall be recognized as party member of the same level responsibility in that region. While transferring a member from one region to another all details about he/she shall be sent to the concerned unit in writing.

Chapter-6: Party Discipline

Article – 26: Party Discipline is must to defend unity of the party, to increase the fighting capacity and to implement the policy of democratic centralism. Without iron discipline no revolutionary party will be able to give capable leadership to the masses in the war and to fulfill the responsibility of revolution on. Party discipline is same for all the party members including the leadership.

Article – 27: a) To reject the aims and objective of the party, party programme or organizational structure or to violate them will be tantamount to indiscipline and the member or unit involved in such activities, will be liable to disciplinary action.

b) When party members violate party discipline, the concerned party unit shall take appropriate disciplinary measures warning, serious warning, suspending from party posts, removal from post, suspending or canceling the party membership, expelling from the party etc., subject to the approval of the higher committee. Cancellation and expulsion of party membership shall come into force only after the next higher committees approve them. Time limit shall be specified while suspending a party membership, which should not be more than one year. The next higher committee shall ratify suspension.

c) When any Party unit violates the discipline, the higher committees shall take disciplinary measures such as reprimanding the unit to partially reconstituting the unit. For dissolving the unit, approval of the next higher committee is necessary.

d) When a Central Committee member seriously violates party discipline (acts as enemy agent or indulges in open anti-party activities) the Central Committee shall have the right to remove him/her from his/her rank or to expel him/her from the party. But, such a measure will come into force only when two-thirds of Central Committee members give their approval.

e) The party unit or the party member whom disciplinary measure is taken shall be submitted a charge sheet beforehand. If the unit or the member thinks that such a disciplinary measure was unjustified, then the unit or the member may raise objection, may request for reviewing the decision or may appeal to the higher committee. Such appeals shall be sent to the higher committees by the concerned lower committees without any delay. Every member shall have the right to defend himself/herself in person in his/her committee/unit or to submit his/her written explanation to the higher committee, which takes disciplinary action against him/her.

Article – 28: a) Punishment should be given only if all other options of discussion and convincing to rectify a member or a party unit fails. Even after giving punishment efforts must be made to rectify. Policy of saving the patient and curing disease should be followed. In special circumstances to defend party security and respect, punishment should be given as soon as possible.

b) The lower committee cannot take any disciplinary action on any member of the higher committee. However, in case of dual membership they may send their allegations and suggestions about the members of the higher committees in writing to the concerned committees.

c) In case of gross breach of Party discipline which may cause serious harm to the party, if he/she be allowed to continue his/her membership or post in the party, a member can be summarily suspended from party membership, removed from his/her party post by his/her committee or by higher committees pending framing charge sheet and getting his/her explanation. At the time of taking such disciplinary steps, the concerned committee should specify the period by which a final decision will be taking in the matter.

d) If any party member or candidate member (or a member at any level) does not participate in party activities or does not implement party decisions for six months without showing proper reason does not renew membership and does not pay membership fee and levy he/her shall be deemed to have voluntarily withdrawn from the party and his/her membership shall either be suspended or cancelled. Those members, who are corrupted in economic matters, degenerate politically, becomes characterless or betray the party-secrecy shall be liable to punishment.

e) The harshest measures among all the disciplinary measures taken by the party are expulsion and cancellation from the party. Hence while taking such decision; concerned party unit shall observe utmost care. Such measures will be taken when all the efforts in rectifying the concerned-member failed. The party members appeal must be carefully examined by the concerned higher committee and the circumstances, under which he/she committed the mistakes, must be thoroughly reviewed.

f) If persons whose party membership has been cancelled or have resigned express their willingness again to join the party, the concerned committees, should take a decision after thorough investigation. Membership should give only after testing through practice for a minimum period of six months. Only the state or Central Committee may take members once expelled from the party barring betrayals. Lower committees, may however, forward recommendations in this regard.

Chapter-7: Party's Organizational Structure

Article – 29: a) The party organization shall be formed according to geographical divisions or spheres of production.

b) Party is constituted with two types of membership professionals and part-timers.

Article – 30: The party structure at the various levels shall be as follows:

a) The highest body of the party shall be the Central Committee. Below the Central Committee there will be Special Area Committee/Special Zonal Committee/State Committee; Regional Committee; Zonal Committee/District/Divisional Committee; Sub-Zonal/Sub-Divisional Committee; Area Committee; local level committees such as village/Basti/Factory/College party committee. The primary unit of the party will be cell. The Town and city committee will be formed and the concerned higher committee will decide the status of the committee.

b) All committees will elect their secretaries. All committees may form secretariats according to the needs of the movement and the size of the committee. The secretaries of all committees and the secretariats are of the same level and will have same rights as the committee of which they are part. However they, secretaries and secretariats, will have special duties and responsibilities.

c) All the leading committees from Area Committee onward will be constituted only with professional revolutionaries.

d) The party congress is the supreme authority of the entire party. The Central Committee elected by the congress is the highest authority in between two congresses.

e) Special Area Committee/Special Zonal Committee/State Committee elected by the SAC/SZC/SC conference is the highest authority at the SAC/SZC/State level.

f) Regional committee elected by the regional conference is the highest authority at the region level. Regional committee can be formed by dividing the states or with parts of different states according to the requirements of the movement.

g) Similarly, Zonal/District/Divisional and Sub-Zonal/Sub-Divisional Committees will be elected at their respective level conferences. Area Committees are elected at the Area level conference.

h) Town/City Committee elected at the respective level conference.

i) Party cell – it consists of three to five members in a village, or in two or three villages combined, or a factory, or educational institution, or a locality, or two or three localities combined. In mass organisations units, cells will be formed.

j) In the period between two conferences or congresses, the committees elected at the respective levels are the highest bodies.

k) All committees elect their respective secretaries.

l) Various sub-committees and commissions under the leadership at different levels may be formed to efficiently carry out the party's work in various spheres.

Basic Unit:

Article – 31: a) Party cell will be basic unit of the party. Party cell can be formed area wise or profession wise. Party cells are nucleus for day-to-day activities. The members in cells will be minimum 3 and maximum 5. Cell members will fulfill their responsibilities and duties as full fledged party members and they will avail all the rights of party membership (except candidates members). The cell will elect its secretary.

b) Candidate members will also work according to the decisions of the party cell. They shall participate in the discussions and follow the party directives but they will not have voting rights at the time of decision-making.

c) While forming party cells area wise, efforts will be made to form party cells in factories and in mass organizations.

d) If there are two or more cells in an area, a committee below that of AC can be formed.

e) Party cell is a living link between broad masses of an area and the party. The cell will lead the revolutionary war of broad masses of people with full initiative. It shall make relentless efforts to bring the masses of factory, locality and peasant areas close to the political line and aims of the party. By involving militant activists and party followers in the revolutionary war against autocratic semi-colonial, semi-feudal state system, it will stress from the very beginning to educate the masses to function secretly, illegally and according to the strategy and tactics of the Protracted People's war. By selecting 3-5 party activists and organizing them in a group educating them in party politics and organizing them as members are important responsibilities of party cells.

Chapter-8: Party Congress

Article – 32: Holding the all India party congress shall be decided by the central committee. The party congress shall be held once in five years. Under special circumstances it may either be postponed or preponed decision has to be taken by majority of the CC.

Article – 33: The party congress elects a presidium to conduct the congress and discharges the following tasks:

a) It undertakes the political and organizational review of the party since the preceding congress.

b) It adopts the party programme, party constitution and the strategy and tactics financial policy and formulates other policy matters.

c) Appraises the domestic and international situation and lays down the tasks.

d) Decides the number of central committee members and elects the central committee and alternate CC members.

e) It ratifies the financial statements.

Article – 34: (a) The central committee elects general secretary of the party. It also elects a politburo depending on the requirements of the movement, and will take political, organizational and military decisions according to the party-line and the decisions of the central committee in between the period of one central committee meeting to the next and will get its decisions ratified in the subsequent central committee meeting. It will also setup regional bureaus, CMC, and other sub-committees & departments. The general secretary also acts as the in charge of the Polit Bureau.

(b) To run its party organs, the central committee appoints editorial boards for each organ. The General Secretary will be the chief editor of the theoretical-ideological organ of the central committee.

Article – 35: The central committee may convene central plenums to deal with special problems in the period between congress. These plenums can discuss and take decisions on problems relating to party line and policies in that period. Similarly election of new members into the central committee or removal of Central Committee members can also be taken up by the central plenums.

When ever it is necessary, the central committee can co-opt members not exceeding one-fourth of its existing strength if 2/3 of its members agree.

Article – 36: Special Area, state/regional, special zonal, zonal and/sub-zonal/district/divisional plenums shall be held once in every three years.

Under special circumstances they may be held earlier or postponed. However area conferences/plenums should be held once every two years. These conferences take decisions after holding discussions on problems relating to their respective levels, send their opinions on the party line ... to higher committees and elect the respective committees along with alternate members, if necessary.

Article – 37: In the period between above level conferences, if necessary, plenums may be convened, with the approval of the next higher committee. Decisions may be taken after discussion on problems in the areas under the jurisdiction of the various committees in their respective plenum of the respective committee members may either be elected or removed. If plenums of any committee cannot be held due to special circumstances, the concerned committees may co-opt one-fourth of their respective strengths with the approval of the next higher committee.

Article – 38: a) The number of delegates to the various conferences including the congress shall be decided by the respective committees according to membership strength as per the decisions of different levels of committees and party congress.

b) The respective committees are empowered to specially invite up to ten percent of the strength of delegates attending the congress, and other different level conference. Observes and non-voting delegates may also be invited to the conference of the respective committees.

Article – 39: The Central Committee shall release relevant draft documents to be discussed in the party congress to all party members giving sufficient time as decided by the CC, before the process of the congress starts. All amendments to drafts submitted by the lower level conferences and by members should be sent to the Central Committee, which will place them before the party congress.

Delegates to the party congress shall enjoy the right to move amendments to the draft documents. After going through the draft documents, if any committee delegate/delegates want to move alternative document, he/she/they must immediately inform the Central Committee, and the central committee will decide about the time to be given to the concern delegate/delegates committee for drafting the document. The concerned committee delegate/delegates have to draft the document within a scheduled time as decided by CC, and thus submit it to the Central Committee. The Central Committee deserves the right to circulate it with its own comment.

Article – 40: The out going central committee shall propose to the congress a panel of members of the new central committee to be formed.

Any delegate shall have the right to object to any name in the panel, or can even propose a new panel, with the prior approval of the member whose name is proposed. If there are no [alternative panels] the Central Committee shall be taken by a show of hands, in case of alternate proposal all committees including the Central Committee shall be elected by secret ballot.

Article – 41: The number of delegates to the plenums at various levels along with the basis for the selection of delegates shall be decided by the respective committees.

Chapter-9: Rights and Duties of Central Committee

Article – 42: The Central Committee will be elected by the party congress. In between the two party congresses the Central Committee is the highest leading body of the party. The Central Committee represents the whole party and can take crucial decisions with full authority on behalf of the party. The Central Committee shall meet at least once in a year.

Article – 43: a) Central Committee may form Politburo [sic], Central Military Commission, regional bureaus and various sub-committees for smooth functioning of the party. The PB is of the same level and enjoys the same rights as the CC. However, it has special duties and responsibilities which it will fulfill on behalf of the CC in between two CC meetings.

Article – 44: The Central Committee can take step and remove any Central Committee member for gross breach of discipline, serious anti party activities and heinous factional activities. The punished member has the right to appeal before the congress. Till the matter is not decided or settled, Central Committee's decision will remain standing. If 2/3 of the Central Committee members agree, they can take decision to oust any member of the Central Committee

Article – 45: The Central Committee can co-opt any member in the Central Committee if any post remains vacant or for the need of the movement. Whenever it is necessary the Central Committee can co-opt members not exceeding one fourth of its existing strength, if 2/3 of its members agree. But it is to be ratified in the next congress. Co-option should be made from among alternative members, if there are no alternate members, then CC can co-opt from others.

Article – 46: The CCS will decide the date and time of the Central Committee meeting and will provide the agenda of the meeting beforehand. If 1/3 members of the Central Committee demand a meeting of the Central Committee the secretary will have to call the meeting.

Article – 47: The Central Committee or Politburo holds the right to send its any member or members to check-up the work of any unit or any area. The Central Committee has the right to disband any committee and thereby form any organizing committee at any level.

Article – 48: If necessary the Central Committee can convene special conferences and plenums in between two congresses. The Central Committee will decide the other members of the different committees who will attend this plenum other than the CCMs.

Chapter-10: Internal Debates in the Party

Article – 49: It is very essential to go through deep discussions to unify the whole party ideologically, politically and organizationally and to improve our methods. This is also democratic right of party members. At different levels of party, we should strive to resolve the questions related with the tactics by openhearted and unbridled debates in respective committees. When needed, help and advice of higher committees shall be taken. In the name of democratic rights of party members, endless debates on a particular issue will only harm the party functioning. So, any type of controversial debate or discussion can be permissible only after the consent of the 2/3 members of the concerned committees.

Article – 50: In case any member or committee has different views about the basic a line of the party and it demands its circulation in the party, central committee has the right to take final decisions whether to accept or reject this demand.

Article – 51: If any central committee member has different views, in regard with all India or International questions and he/she demands to take this idea in the party, in that case the above said views will be sent to state/regional committees or to any level according to the 1/3rd members of the central committee. But state/regional committee member cannot send his/her different views to the lower level committees without the permission from the central committee.

Article – 52: If any lower level committee or committee member has different views on the political and organizational line of the central committee, then they can send their views to the central committee according to the party committee functioning. If needed central committee can send these views along with its opinion in the whole party.

Article – 53: All the democratic debates in the party under the control of central committee or under its direction shall be sent to special area, state/regional and zonal committees or to all the levels of party.

Chapter-11: Party Functioning in the Peoples' Army

Article – 54: The people's army is the chief instrument of the party. Hence the party will use this instrument in rousing, mobilizing, organizing and arming the people in carrying out the task of the revolution.

It will participate in social production also. Only through the Protracted People's War, with people's army as the highest weapon the Party will carry out the task of seizure of political power by overthrowing the present reactionary state power represents the interests of imperialism, feudalism and comprador big bourgeois and thereby establishing a new democratic state. It will protect the country, defend the victory of NDR, with the goal of socialism. Party will educate the army with the weapon of MLM.

Article – 55: The Party will exercise full control over the army from the very beginning. Because the party decides the overall political strategy and tactics of revolution hence it also decides the functioning and forms of party organizations in the army by keeping the level of development of the Protracted People's War before it. Central Military Commission constituted by the Central Committee will conduct the military affairs according to the military line of the party as well as the policies, directives and decisions of the Central Committee. In this light the Military Commissions and Commands will be constituted at various levels to conduct the military operations. Being the leader and organizer of the People's Army the party ranks at various levels will play a leading and front-ranking role in all the affairs of the army.

Article – 56: This People's Army will be constituted of three forces that is the main force, the secondary force and the base force.

Article – 57: In our guerrilla army all the formations from platoon, company and above level will have party committees. The party branch will be constituted with party members. Various squads will have party cells and party branches. Where needed, a party committee will be constituted at that level. Party members and ranks will also remain in the militia and play the leading and front-ranking role there.

Article – 58: All members of military formations will function under the leadership of the respective party committees. The decisions of these party committees will be carried out and implemented by the respective military formations. Party members in PLGA will be invited to the party conference/plenums according to their respective level. In general, the party committees in the military formations at and above platoon level will be elected in conferences held at that level.

Chapter-12: Party Fractions

Article – 59: The party fractions shall be formed in the executive committees of mass organizations. Party fractions will guide the executive committees of the mass organizations adopting suitable method in accordance with the correct concrete situation. Fraction committees will function secretly. The opinions of party committee/member guiding the fraction shall be considered as final opinion. If fraction committee members have any difference of opinion, they will send their opinions in writing to the concerned party committee/higher committee. The concerned party committees shall guide fraction committees of different mass organizations at their own level.

Chapter-13: Party Funds

Article – 60: The party funds shall be obtained through the membership fees, levies, donations, taxes and penalties.

Article – 61: The levy to be paid by party members shall be decided and collected in their respective state committees.

Appendix 3

Programme and Constitution of the People's Guerrilla Army

From http:/satp.org/satporgtp/countries/India/terroristoutfits/CPI_M.htm

The People's Guerrilla Army

Programme & Constitution

Article 1: The People's Liberation Army is the main instrument in the hands of the CPI (ML) and all the people of India in the achievement of the task of overthrow, specifically of imperialism and the state power of the big bourgeoisie, big landlord classes collaborating with it and the establishment in its place a new democratic state under the leadership of the working class. It will, in every stage of the revolution, strive for the victory of the people and will firmly adhere to the glorious task of preserving the victories won by the people and to the cause ofwsocialism.

Article 2: The line of protracted people's war is our military strategy. That means, encircling the cities from the countryside and ultimately capturing state power. Towards the achievement of that aim, the people's army will fight under party's leadership developing its forces to the extent possible, consolidating them, wiping out the enemy forces to the extent possible and building guerrilla zones with the aim of establishment of Liberated Areas.

Article 3: In accordance with the changing war conditions the PGA has to acquire expertise in guerrilla and mobile warfare and the People's Liberation Army has to acquire expertise in positional warfare.

Article 4: The PGA will extends full backing to People's State Power, that gets formed in the guerrilla zones and base areas. It will fight with all its might to depend the People's State Power from enemy onslaughts and to offer support to the People's State Power, in its exercise of its power over the exploiting classes. It will stand by the people, in the implementation of People's Democracy; it stands answerable to the people.

Article 5: The PGA is a political and military force quite different from revolutionary mass organisations. It forms a detachment in the Army of the International Proletariats.

Article 6: The party defines the strategy and tactics of the revolution. As a part of it, the CC will formulate in accordance with circumstances, the concrete forms of organization and forms of war that are to be followed during the various stages of the people's war. The Central Military Commission will guide the military affairs in accordance with them. The military (operational) command will give direct leadership to field operations

The people.s army always keeps M-L-M politics in command. The party will have full control over the army. M-L-M ensures that this does not get reversed. The party is the leader who stands at the forefront of the people's army.

Article 7: The peoples army at present exists in the form of PGA. This has to be developed as the People's Liberation Army and expanded. The people's guerrilla army is an armed organization formed for the achievement of political aims of the revolution. While, on the one hand, waging war to destroy enemy's military might, it has to take up other political tasks like, conduction of propaganda among the people, organizing the people, arming of the people, helping the people in the establishment of revolutionary power, formation of Party Organisations etc.

Article 8: The survival and growth of the PGA depends on, going deeply among the people and gaining their love and affection. The PGA firmly opposes the pure military outlook which is divorced from the masses and adventurism. It will function adhering to the mass line.

Article 9: At present PGA will be in the following forms. Military formations at platoon and higher levels that will move to any place and participate in war, according to the demands of war and on the orders of commission/command command, and the action teams will constitute the main forces, the special guerrilla squads, local guerrilla squads and action teams which will be under the jurisdiction of various divisions/districts will constitute the secondary forces and the people's militia will constitute the basic forces. As the people's guerrilla army expands, changes will occur in its forms.

Article 10: In the PGA, all the formations from platoon and above, will have party committees. The party branch will be formed with party members. Various squads will have a party cell or a party branch. A committee at that level can be formed where needed. Party members too will be there in the militia along with ordinary young men and women.

Article 11: All kinds of forces in the PGA will function under the leadership of respective party committees. They must implement the decisions of those party committees.

Article 12: Party members in PGA can be invited according to their level to party conferences/plenums at respective levels. In general, the party committees of military formation at platoon and higher levels will be elected in conferences.

Article 13: Democratic relations only will prevail in the PGA. The PGA will give honourable treatment to the surrendered enemy soldiers. It will strictly adhere to the three rules of discipline formulated by comrade Mao; it will sincerely try to implement the 8 points of attention.

Article 14: The PGA participation in labour and will cherish labour.

Article 15: The PGA will participate in the propaganda and agitations programmes as directed by Party Committees. It will organize the people. The PGA will extensively employ people's art forms in its propaganda. It will try to enhance the consciousness of the people.

Article 16: Any male or female, who has reached the age of 16 will be eligible to join the PGA. They should have the determination to fight with the enemy with hatred. They should be of good health. They must posses the minimum of consciousness of participating in the service of the people with commitment and dedications. They must hate the enemy and cherish the people.

Appendix 4

The resettlement and rehabilitation policy of the Government of Orissa

As stated earlier the Naxal Movement in Orissa is concentrated in the mines and mineral rich areas of the state. It is because of this factor several industrial, mining as well as irrigation projects have come up in those areas resulting in large scale displacement which was ineptly handled by the administration and which gave a powerful weapon in the hands of the Naxals to manipulate the situation in their favor. Till recently the policy of Resettlement and Rehabilitation (R&R) has been more than half blind to the plight of the poor and marginalized tribals who have been the worst victim of such developmental activities. However during 2006 the Government of Orissa constituted a group of Ministers to finalize a comprehensive R&R Policy for the state; following are its high points.

(A) Definition:

'**Family**' has been expanded for the purpose of rehabilitation assistance and now includes:

- A major son irrespective of his marital status.
- Unmarried daughter or sister more than 30 years of age.
- Physically and mentally challenged person irrespective of age and sex; (duly certified by the authorized Medical board). For this purpose, the blind, the deaf, the orthopaedically handicapped/mentally challenged person suffering from more than 40% permanent disability will only be considered as separate family.
- Minor orphan who has lost both his/her parents.
- A widow or a woman divorcee.

'**Cut off date**' which was vague earlier is now specified as the date of notification under LA Act. 1894.

- Verification 1st January every year.
- There has no clear definition of 'periphery' in the earlier draft policy and now district boundary has been identified as periphery.

(B) Comprehensive Survey and Baseline Development

In addition to the prevailing practice of socio economic survey in earlier policies, the new policy proposes a comprehensive socio-cultural resource mapping and in (restructural survey and those shall be conducted by an independent agency to be identified by the Government to ensure proper benchmarking.

Assessment of Land Requirement: A realistic assessment of the land by the project will be made by a committee headed by RDC. This is a new feature of this policy that will prevent land arbitrage.

Several new features added in this policy are as follows:

- Comprehensive communication plan for awareness creation.
- Consultation with gram sabha/panchayat for planning.
- Normal development plans implemented by different agencies should be dovetailed with resettlement and rehabilitation package in resettlement habitats and made available to the displaced community on a priority basis.

(C) Land Acquisition

Options for direct negotiations for purchase and consent award before acquisition under provisions of the relevant Act. A comprehensive action plan before acquisition specified as below:

- Site for the resettlement habitat shall be selected by the RPDAC in consultation with the displaced families.
- No physical displacement shall be made before the completion of resettlement work as approved by RPDAC.
- Gram sabha/Panchayat shall be consulted.
- Where there is multiple displacement additional compensation amounting to 50% of the normal compensation payable, in form 1 of ex-gratia.
- Provisions relating to rehabilitation will be given effect from the date of actual vacation of the land.
- Project Authority shall abide by the provisions laid down in this policy and the decisions taken by RPDAC.
- District administration and Project Authorities shall be jointly responsible for ensuring that the benefits of R&R reach the target beneficiaries in a time bound manner.
- Record of Rights of the land and houses allotted to the displaced persons should be handed over to them by the District Administration while resettling Steps will be taken by the Project Authorities for acclimatization of the resettled people in new habitat including development of cordial social relationship between the host and resettle communities.

(D) Project Types

- Industrial Projects;
- Mining Projects; (separated from Industrial Projects)
- Irrigation Projects, National Parks and Sanctuaries; Urban Projects and Linear Projects like roads and railways,
- Power lines; (newly added) and any other projects that can be notified to make it comprehensive.

(E) Rehabilitation Assistance

Industrial Project

- Employment to one member of the original displaced family. (DF)
- Skill Upgradation of the old Displaced Family.
- House Building Assistance of Rs. 150, 000/(Three fold).
- At least 50% of cash assistance as share convertible share.
- One time cash assistance increased to Rs. 5 Lakh, Rs. 3 Lakh, and Rs. 2 Lakh and Rs. 1 Lakh to category 1, 2, 3, 4, and 5 respectively.
- Shops and service units added to restore livelihood of DF.

Mining Project

- Same as above but the employment applicable to the expanded family.

Irrigation, Park etc.

- Homestead land of 0.10 acre or cash Rs. 50,000/.
- Agricultural Land for SC & ST 2.5 acres irrigated, and 5 acres un-irrigated. For others it is 2 acres irrigated and 4 acres un-irrigated.
- In case land is not available than cash compensation of Rs. 1 Lakh per acre for irrigated land and Rs. 50, 000/per acre for un-irrigated land.

Urban and Linear

- Homestead of 1/10th acre (rural) or 1/25th of an acre (urban) or cash equivalent of Rs. 50,000/. Land near growth centre for DF.
- House building assistance Rs.150, 000/.
- Rs.2000/per month, common assistance to all entire category for a year.
- Maintenance Allowance of Rs.10, 000/.
- Temporary shed/Transportation allowance of Rs. 2000/.

(F) Institutional Arrangement

- Compensation Advisory Committee (CAC) at Project level. (Headed by Collector; if more then one district than RDC)
- A state level Committee by Member, Board of Revenue for Dispute Resolution.
- Rehabilitation and Periphery Development Advisory Committee at the District level headed by the Collector.
- State level Resettlement and Rehabilitation Council (SLRRC) headed by the Chief Minister.
- State level Unified Directorate of R&R.

(F) Special Provisions Introduced in this Policy

- While developing the resettlement plans, the socio-cultural norms of indigenous and primitive tribal groups will be respected.
- Each displaced family of indigenous category shall be given preferential.
- As far as practicable, indigenous communities should be resettled in a compact area close to their natural habitat.
- Indigenous displaced families resettled outside the district shall be given 25 Indexation of benefits to compensate for the escalations in replacement cost against the prevailing concept of depreciated value.
- Comprehensive survey, master planning and investment in common infrastructure development.

(G) Flexibility

- For budget provisioning.
- Amendment when needed.
- Grievance redressal.[1]

Scholars prefer to make a cautious opinion about the new development, as writes Manipadma Jena, 'Though Orissa's draft resettlement and rehabilitation policy is an improvement on the national policy; it does not go far enough in ensuring adequate representation of affected women in rehabilitation and other representative committees. The draft, while it has created separate categories for the displaced, with commensurate compensation, still does not specify norms stringent enough to assess land claims put forward by investing companies.[2] On the other hand observes Mr. L.N. Gupta, IAS, Commissioner cum Secretary, Steel and Mines department, Government of Orissa that 'the new policy reflects the democratic response of the government in policy formulation. It comes as recognition of the voices and choices of the affected families and vulnerable groups, indigenous communities, women and physically challenged.'[3] Of course the new R&R policy as mentioned in the above table seems to be quite comprehensive though it is too early to predict its fall out but undoubtedly a well thought out strategy by the Naveen Pattnaik government.

Notes

1 http://orissagov.nic.in/revenue/R&RPOLICIES/Relief%20and%20Rehabilitation/key%20features/key%20features.html
2 Manipadma Jena, Orissa: Draft Resettlement and Rehabilitation Policy, 2006, *Economic and Political Weekly*, February 4, 2006.
3 A presentation by L.N. Gupta, IAS, Commissioner cum Secretary, Steel and Mines department, Government of Orissa, www.assocham.org/events/recent/event_72/Orissa_R_n_R_ASSOCHAM_L_N_Gupta.ppt -

Appendix 5
CPI (Maoist) Central Committee

The highest decision-making body of the CPI (Maoist) is the Politburo [sic], headed by its General Secretary. It comprises 14 members and six alternate members, selected by the Central Committee from among the cadres who have critical roles in pursuing the Maoist goal of the seizure of power.

General Secretary: Muppala Laxman Rao alias Ganapathy
Permanent members:
Mallojula K. Rao
Cherukuri Raja Kumkar
Parashnath Bose
Nambala Keshavarao
Satya Naryan Reddy
Pramod Mishra
Sumanand Singh
Katakam Sudershan
Akhilesh Yadav
Balraj
Azad (spokesperson)

The Revolutionary Democratic Front (RDF), which is now banned by the Union Government of India, is the chief frontal organization of the CPI (Maoist). However, even after its ban, some of its key leaders and units are known to be functioning in various states. The RDF was also instrumental in the formation of the People's Democratic Front of India (PDFI) in July 2006. It members include Medha Patkar (the leader of the Save Narmada Campaign), Nandita Haksar (famous lawyer), S.A.R. Geelani (academic-activist) B.D. Sharma (former bureaucrat and activist), P. Varavara Rao and Darshan Pal (eminently known civil society activist). Some of its constituent organizations are Samyukta Sangram Committee (West Bengal), Indian Federation of Trade Unions, All India Federation of Trade Unions, Chhattisgarh Mukti Morcha, Daman Virodhi Manch (Orissa) and Jharkhand Progressive Students Union, which is an affiliate of the All India Radical Students Federation (AIRSF).

This information was revealed to the authors by one of the top Maoist leaders on conditions of anonymity, who we met in a small village in Andhra Pradesh-Orissa border and had a long interaction in late April 2009.

Appendix 6

Naxal-influenced districts of Orissa

Key
■ Naxal-affected areas

As on 2009 (drawn on inputs from various official and non-offical sources)

Bibliography

This is not a bibliography in the conventional sense. What we propose to do is to draw the readers' attention to the major publications that are statements on ultra-Left extremism or theoretically informed attempts at unravelling Maoism in its various forms in different phases of Indian's recent political history. The book has two distinct parts: besides providing a critical assessment of Maoism in contemporary India, it has also set the phenomenon in a historical context and this is the reason why there is an elaborate analysis of the past Left radical movements that drew on Marxism-Leninism and Maoism. A comment on the available literature is also in order. Our purpose is not to burden the readers with a long list of books, articles or any other written tracts; the aim is to identify those written works in the public domain that are both explanatory and informative. Keeping in mind the primary purpose of the book, we have drawn on the Maoist texts to get a flavour of how the ideology is articulated and how strategies evolve to fulfil the final goal of the seizure of power. Interestingly, with the merger of three ultra-Left radical outfits in 2004 into the CPI (Maoist), the Maoists appear to have pursued a unified goal of action, duly approved by the party high command unlike in the past when several Naxalite outfits were reported to have had different strategic courses of action that were drawn on a specific interpretation of Marxism-Leninism-Maoism.

Since the book focuses on Maoism in its recent incarnation in India we have decided not to include those written texts that may not be exactly relevant to the phenomenon. We do not deny the critical importance of the literature on the erstwhile Naxalbari movement on which a rich corpus of text is available. Literature on Maoism is not as rich as on the Naxalbari movement presumably because the phenomenon is still being articulated as a powerful ideological expression and an alternative discourse. Nonetheless, this selective bibliography will be of help to those seeking to comprehend the ultra-Left extremism in India by providing a comprehensive list of texts available in the public domain. The prolific literature on the Maoist movement in India is a testimony of a growing interest in the Indian variety of ultra-Left extremism, inspired by Marxism-Leninism-Maoism, that seems to have lost credibility as 'a praxis' following the collapse of the former Soviet Union and rather zealous acceptance of the neoliberal economic package in China by its Communist leadership. It is true that there cannot be any conclusive answer to the question of whether radicalism of the Marxist variety has become defunct though one can surmise that the neoliberal capitalist economic policies seem to have created conditions for 'popular upheaval' challenging the capitalist juggernaut. Maoism is an ideological variety that has thrived in India, mostly in poverty-stricken areas, presumably because it has highlighted the genuine socio-economic issues of those who, despite being stakeholders in the system, continue to remain socially, economically and politically 'peripheral'.

Primary sources

Government documents

'Annual Report'. Ministry of Home Affairs, Government of India, (1990–1991 to 2007–2008).
'Census of India'. Government of India,1991.
'Census of India'. Government of India, 2001.
'District-Wise Abstract of BPL Survey, 1997'. Government of Orissa.
'Draft of the Resettlement and Rehabilitation (R&R) Policy 2006'. Prepared by group of Ministers, Government of Orissa.
'Human Development Report'. Government of Orissa, 2004.
'Orissa Consolidation of Holding and Prevention of Fragmentation of Land Act, 1972'. Government of Orissa.
'Orissa Estate Abolition Act, 1952'. Government of Orissa.
'Orissa Land Reform Act, 1960'. Government of Orissa.
'Orissa Prevention of Land Encroachment Act, 1972'. Government of Orissa.
'State Assembly Question. No. 1'. Statement of Mr Naveen Pattnaik on 'Maoist Movement in the Border Districts', in the State Assembly on 6 February 2006.
Speech of Mr Naveen Pattnaik, Chief Minister of Orissa. 50th National Development Council Meeting, 21 December 2002, New Delhi.
'State Government Notification on Naxal Ban in Orissa', June 2006.
Statement of Mr Naveen Pattnaik, Chief Minister of Orissa. State Legislative Assembly, 6 February 2006.
Statement of Mr Naveen Pattnaik, Chief Minister of Orissa, in response to State Assembly Question No. 9. State Legislative Assembly, 6 February 2006.
'White Paper on the Law and Order Situation of the State'. State Legislative Assembly, 17 March 2006.

Unpublished, semi-published and published Naxal literature

'2001 Andolana Pain Parjyabekhyana Prashtuti'. Chashi Mulia Samiti, Gajapati.
'2001 Ra Andolana Pain Prastuti'. People's War Group, n.d.
'2003 Re Dakhala Hei Thiba Jami'. Private leaflet circulated by Chashi Mulia Samiti, n.d.
'30 Years of Naxalbari'. Vanguard Publication, n.d.
'Andhra-Orissa Simanta Re Naxalbad'. Maoist literature published by the CPI (M-L), Oriya, n.d.
'Another Current of Naxalism: People's War'. Maoist document titled 'Andhra Odisha Simanta Re Naxalbad', published by the CPI (M-L), n.d.
'Bansadhara Ra Jami Andolan'. Booklet published by Chashi Mulia Samiti, Orissa, n.d.

'Biplaba Sari Nahin, Biplabi Mari Nahin'. Publication of the CPI (M-L), Andhra Orissa Border Committee, Oriya, n.d.

'Blazing Trail'. Exclusive Naxal CD containing a video presentation of the history of Naxalite movement in India, n.d.

'Breaking the Barriers to Unity'. Party document, Communist Ghadar Party of India, March 1998.

'Chashi Mulia Samiti Ra Jami Andolan'. Chashi Mulia Samiti, Orissa, n.d.

'Daman'. Naxal document published by Chashi Mulia Samiti, Rayagada-Gajapati Divisional Committee, Oriya, n.d.

'Draft Report of Daman Pratirodh Manch on the Janagarjana Samabesha', 14 September 2004.

'Joint Declaration by Communist Party of India (ML) People's War and CPI (ML) (Party Unity)'. PWG, August 1998.

'Open Letter to the Chief Minister of Orissa'. Issued sometime during 2005 by the then spokesperson of the CPI (M-L) People's War, Andhra Orissa Special Zonal Committee.

Party document of the CPI (M-L) People's War, n.d.

'Path of People's War in India – Our Tasks'. PWG, adopted by All-India Party Congress, 1992.

'Jan Pratirodh (Hindi)'. Organ of Akhil Bharatiya Janapratirodh Manch.

People's March.

Radical publications.

'State Repression'. People's War document posted at http://www.cpimlpwg/repression. html (now withdrawn).

'Summing Up the Past Let Us Advance Victoriously Along the Path of Armed Struggle'. The General Programme, CPI (M-L) Liberation, undated.

Secondary sources

Books

Agarwal, Vineet. *Romance of a Naxalite*. New Delhi: National Paperbacks, 2006.

Ahmad, Muzaffar. *Myself and the Communist Party of India, 1920–1929*. Calcutta: National Book Agency, 1970.

Ajitha: *Memoirs of a Young Revolutionary*. Translated from Malayalam, New Delhi: Srishti, 2008.

Alam, Javeed,. *India: Living with Modernity*. New Delhi: Oxford University Press,1999.

Alam, Javeed. *Who Wants Democracy?* New Delhi: Orient Longman, 2004.

Alvares, Claude. *Science, Development and Violence: The Revolt Against Modernity*. New Delhi: Oxford University Press, 1992.

Arendt, Hannah. *Crisis of the Republic*. Harmondsworth: Penguin, 1973.

Aron, Raymond. *History and the Dialectic of Violence*. Oxford: Basil Blackwell, 1975.

Bakunin, Michael. *Statism and Anarchy*, M.S. Shastz (ed. and tr.). Cambridge: Cambridge University Press, 1990.

Banerjee, Sumanta. *India's Simmering Revolution*. New Delhi: Select Book Syndicate, 1984.

Banerjee, Sumanta. *In the Wake of Naxalbari: A History of The Naxalites Movement*. Calcutta: Subarnarekha, 1980.

Basrur, Rajesh M. (ed.). *Challenges to Democracy in India*. New Delhi: Oxford University Press, 2009

Baviskar B.S. and George Mathew (eds). *Inclusion and Exclusion in Local Governance: Field Studies from Rural India*. New Delhi: Sage, 2009.

Bergmann, Theodore. *Agrarian Reform in India*. New Delhi: Agricole Publishing Academy, 1984.

Bhaduri, Amit. *Development with Dignity: A Case for Full Employment*. New Delhi: National Book Trust, 2005.

Brinton, Crane. *The Anatomy of Revolution*. New York: Vintage Books, 1952.

Burton, J. and F. Dukes (eds). *Conflict: Readings in Management and Resolution*. London: Macmillan Press, 1990.

Calman, Leslie J. *Protest in Democratic India: Authority's Response to Challenge*. Boulder and London: Westview Press, 1985.

Campbell, D. and M. Dillon (eds). *The Political Subject of Violence*. Manchester: Manchester University Press, 1993.

Sudeep, Chakravarti. *Red Sun: Travels in Naxalite Country*. New Delhi: Penguin, 2008.

Chakrabarty, Bidyut and Rajendra Kumar Pandey. *Indian Government and Politics*. New Delhi: Sage, 2008.

Chakrabarty, Bidyut. *Indian Politics and Society Since Independence: Events, Processes and Ideology*. London: Routledge, 2008.

Crossley, Nick. *Making Sense of Social Movements*. Buckingham: Open University Press, 2002.

Dagamar, Vasudha. *Role and Image of Law in India: The Tribal Experience*. New Delhi: Sage, 2006.

Damas, Marius. *Approaching Naxalbari*. Calcutta: Radical Impression, 1991.

Dasgupta, Biplab, *The Naxalite Movement*. Calcutta: Allied Publishers, 1974.

De Reuck, Anthony (ed.). *Conflict and Society*. Boston: Little Brown & Co., 1966.

Dellaporta, Donatella. 'Social Movements and Democracy at the Turn of the Millennium', in P. Ibarra (ed.), *Social Movement and Democracy*. New York: Palgrave Macmillan Press, 2003.

Desai, A.R. *Peasant Struggles in India*. Mumbai: Oxford University Press, 1969.

Desai, A.R. (ed.). *Agrarian Struggles in India after Independence*. New Delhi: Oxford University Press, 1986.

Domenach, Jean-Marie, *et al.* (eds.). *Violence and Its Causes: Methodological and Theoretical Aspects of Recent Research on Violence*. Paris: UNESCO, 1981.

Downtown, James. *Rebel Leadership: Commitment and Charisma in the Revolutionary Process*. New York: Free Press, 1973.

Dube, S.C. *India Villages*. London: Oxford University Press, 1955.

Duyker, Edward. *Tribal Guerillas: The Santals of West Bengal and the Naxalite Movement*. New Delhi: Oxford University Press, 1987.

Eyerman, R. and A. Jamison. *Social Movements: A Cognitive Approach*. Cambridge: Polity Press, 1991.

Fanon, Frantz. *The Wretched of the Earth*. Translated by C. Farington. Harmondsworth: Penguin, 1982 (reprint).

Fernande,s Leela. *India's New Middle Class: Democratic Polity in an Era of Economic Reforms*. New Delhi: Oxford University Press, 2006.

Ganguly, Sumit, Larry Diamond and Marc F. Plattner (eds). *The State of India's Democracy*. New Delhi: Oxford University Press, 2009.

Ghosh, Amitav. *Two New Essays: Confessions of a Xenophile & Wild Fictions*. Outlook, 2008.

Ghosh, Sankar. *The Naxalite Movement: A Maoist Experiment*. Calcutta: Firmal K.L. Mukhopadhyay, 1974.

Ghosh, Suniti Kumar (ed.). *The Historic Turning Point, A Liberation Anthology*, Vol. 1–2. Calcutta: Pragana, 1992.

Gibson, Nigel. *Frantz Fanon: The Postcolonial Imagination*. Oxford: Polilty Press, 2003.

Guevara, Che. *Guerrilla Warfare*. Translated by J.P. Morray, New York: Vantage Books, 1961.

Gupta, Ranjit Kumar. *The Crimson Agenda: Maoist Protest and Terror*. New Delhi: Wordsmiths, 2004.

Gurr, Ted R. *Why Men Rebel*. Princeton: Princeton University Press, 1970.

Haralambos, M. *Sociology: Themes and Perspectives*. New Delhi: Oxford University Press, 1999.

Hasan, Zoya. *Politics of Inclusion: Caste, Minorities and Affirmative Action*. New Delhi: Oxford University Press, 2009.

Honderich, Ted. *Violence for Equality: Inquiries in Political Philosophy*, Harmondsworth: Penguin, 1980.

Kishwar, Mudhu Purnima. *Deepening of Democracy: Challenges of Governance and Globalization in India*. New Delhi: Oxford University Press, 2005.

Jawaid, Sohail. *The Naxalite Movement in India: Origin and Failure of Maoist Revolutionary Strategy in West Bengal*. New Delhi: Associate Publishing House, 1979.

Jerome, Skolnick. *The Politics of Protest*, New York: Ballantine Books, 1969.

Johari, J.C. *Naxalite Politics in India*. New Delhi: Institute of Constitutional & Parliamentary Studies/Research Publications, 1972.

Kohli, Atul. *Democracy and Discontent: India's Growing Crisis of Governability*. Cambridge: Cambridge University Press, 1991.

Louis, Prakash. *People Power: The Naxalite Movement in Central Bihar*. New Delhi: Wordsmiths, 2002.

Mehta, Pratap Bhanu. *The Burden of Democracy*, New Delhi: Penguin, 2003.

Mehta V.R. and Thomas Pantham (eds). *Political Ideas in Modern India: Thematic Explorations*, New Delhi: Sage, 2006.

Mohanty, Manoranjan. *Revolutionary Violence: A Study of Maoist Movement in India*. New Delhi: Sterling Publishers, 1977.

Moore, Barrington. *Social Origins of Dictatorship and Democracy: Lord and Peasant in the Making of Modern World*. Harmodsworth: Penguin, 1973.

Nigam, Aditya. *The Insurrection of Little Selves: The Crisis of Secular-Nationalism in India*. New Delhi,:Oxford University Press, 2006.

Nilekani, Nandan. *Imagining India: Ideas for the New Century*. New Delhi: Penguin, 2008.

Overstree, Gene D. and Marshall Windmiller. *Communism in India*. Berkeley and Los Angeles: University of California Press, 1959.

Phillips, Anne. *The Politics of Presence*. Oxford: Clarendon Press, 1995.

Rajgopal, P.R. *Social Change and Violence: The Indian Experience*. New Delhi: Uppal Publishing House, 1987.

Ram, Mohan. *Maoism in India*, New Delhi: Vikas Publications, 1971.

Ram, Mohan. *Indian Communism: Split Within A Split*. New Delhi: Vikas Publications, 1969.

Roy, Asish Kumar. *The Spring Thunder and After: A Survey of Maoist and Ultra-Leftist Movements in India (1962–75)*. Calcutta: Minerva Associates, 1975.

Sen, Sunil. *Agrarian Struggle in Bengal*. Bombay: People's Publishing House, 1972.

Singh, Prakash. *Naxalite Movement*. New Delhi: Rupa & Co, 1995.

Singh, Prakash. *The Naxal Movement in India*. New Delhi: Rupa & Co, 1995.

Sundar, Nandini. *Subaltern and Sovereign: An Anthropological History of Bastar (1854–2006)*. New Delhi: Oxford University Press, 2008.

Tse-tung, Mao. *Selected Works of Mao Tse-tung*, vols I–IV, Foreign Language Press, Peking 1975.

Articles

A group of citizens. 'Open Letters to Government and Maoists'. *Economic and Political Weekly*, 28 July 2006.

Alam, Javeed. 'Nation: Discourse and Intervention by the Communists in India'. In T.V. Sathyamurthy (ed.), *State and Nation in the Context of Social Change*, vol. 1. New Delhi: Oxford University Press, 1994.

Alam, Javeed. 'Debates and Engagements: A look at Communist Intervention in India', In V.R. Mehta and Thomas Pantham (eds), *Political Ideas in Modern India: Thematic Explorations*. New Delhi: Sage, 2006.

Azad. 'Maoists in India', *Economic and Political Weekly*, 14 October 2006

Bajpai, Rochana. 'Redefining Equality: Social Justice in the Mandal Debate, 1990'. In V.R. Mehta and Thomas Pantham (eds), *Political Ideas in Modern India: Thematic Explorations*. New Delhi: Sage, 2006.

Balagopal, K. 'Maoist Movement in Andhra Pradesh'. *Economic and Political Weekly*, 22 July 2006.

Balagopal, K. 'Peasant Struggle and Repression in Pedapally'. *Economic and Political Weekly*, 15 May 1982.

Bandyopadhyay, D. 'A Visit to Two "Flaming Fields" of Bihar'. *Economic and Political Weekly*, 30 December 2006.

Bandyopadhyay, D. 'Land of the Overlords: A Field Trip to Katihar and Purnea'. *Mainstream*, 12 March 2007.

Banerjee, Sumanta. 'Beyond Naxalbari'. *Economic and Political Weekly*, 22 July 2006.

Banerjee, Sumanta. 'Naxalbari: Between Past and Present'. *Economic and Political Weekly*, 1 June 2002.

Banerjee, Sumanta. 'Naxalites: Time For Retrospection'. *Economic and Political Weekly*, 1 November 2003.

Bardhan, Pranab. 'Dominant Propertied Classes and India's Democracy'. In Atul Kohli (ed.), *India's Democracy: An Analysis of Changing State-Society Relations*. New Delhi: Orient Longman, 1991.

Bhaduri, Amit. 'Development or Development of Terrorism'. *Economic and Political Weekly*, 17 February 2007.

Bhatia, Bela. 'On Armed Resistance'. *Economic and Political Weekly*, 22 July 2006.

Bhatia, Bela. 'Naxalite Movement in Central Bihar'. *Economic and Political Weekly*, 9 April 2005.

Dash, Jatindra. 'Mining Threatens Orissa's Environment'. *Indo-Asian News Service*, 5 November 2004.

Fernandes, Walter. 'Rehabilitation Policy for the Displaced'. *Economic and Political Weekly*, 20 March 2004.

Fernandes, Walter. 'Singur and the Displacement Scenario'. *Economic and Political Weekly*, 20 Janaury 2007.

Gallantar, Marc. 'The Aborted Restoration of Indigenous Law'. In N. Jayaraman and Satish Sabrewal (eds) *Social Conflict*. New Delhi: Oxford University Press, 1996.

Ganapathy. 'Open Reply to Independent Citizens'. Initiative on Dantewada, *Economic and Political Weekly*, 6 January 2007.

Gupta, Tilak. 'Maoism in India: Ideology, Programme and Armed Struggle'. *Economic and Political Weekly*, 22 July 2006.

Hebbar, Ritambara. 'Forest Bill of 2005 and Tribal Areas: Case of Jharkhand'. *Economic and Political Weekly*, 2 December 2006.

Jena, Manipadma. 'Orissa: Draft Resettlement and Rehabilitation Policy, 2006'. *Economic and Political Weekly*, 4 February 2006.

Kannabiran, Kalpana, Volga and Vasanth Kannabiran. 'Peace and Irresponsibility'. *Economic and Political Weekly*, 26 March 2005.

Khatua, Sanjay and William Stanley. 'Ecological Debt: A Case Study of Orissa, India: Integrated Rural Development of Weaker Sections in India'. In Athena K. Peralta (ed.), *Ecological Debt: The People of the South Are the Creditors: Cases from Ecuador, Mozambique, Brazil and India*. Geneva: World Council of Churches, 2006.

Kujur, Rajat Kumar. 'Underdevelopment and Naxal Movement'. *Economic and Political Weekly*, vol. XLI (7), 18–24 February 2006.

Kujur, Rajat Kumar. 'Naxalism in India'. *Human Touch*, vol. 2 (6), June 2005.

Kunnath, George J. 'Becoming a Naxalite in Rural Bihar: Class Struggle and its Contradictions'. *The Journal of Peasant Studies*, 33 (1), January 2006.

Mehra, Ajay. 'Naxalism and Militant Peasant Movement in India'. In K.M. de Silva (ed.), *Conflict and Violence in South Asia*, Kandy: Sri Lanka International Centre for Ethnic Studies, 2000.

Mohanty, Biswaranjan. 'Displacement and Rehabilitation of Tribals'. *Economic and Political Weekly*, 26 March 2005.

Mohanty, Monoranjan. 'Challenges of Revolutionary Violence: The Naxalite Movement in Perspective'. *Economic and Political Weekly*, 22 July 2006.

Mohanty, Monoranjan. 'Chinese Revolution and the Indian Communist Movement'. *China Report*, 27 (1), 1991.

Mukherjee, Partha N. 'Naxalbari Movement and the Peasant Revolt'. In M.S.A. Rao (ed.), *Social Movements in India*, vol. 1. New Delhi: Manohar, 1979.

Narayanan, M.K. 'Naxal Movement's Cruel Spring'. *The Asian Age*, 28 February 2000.

Nigam, Aditya. 'Communist Politics Hegemonized'. In Partha Chatterjee (ed.), *Wages of Freedom: Fifty Years of Indian Nation-State*. New Delhi: Oxford University Press, 1998.

Parthasarathy, G. 'Land Reforms and the Changing Agrarian Structure in India'. In Anil Kumar Gupta (ed.), *Agrarian Structure and Peasant Revolt in India*. New Delhi: Criterion Publications, 1986.

Punwani. Jyoti,. 'Chhattisgarh: Traumas of Adivasi Women in Dantewada'. *Economic and Political Weekly*, 27 January 2007.

Ram, Mohan. 'The Communist Movement in India'. In Kathleen Gough and Hari P Sharma (eds), *Imperialism and Revolution in South Asia*. New York: Monthly Review Press, 1973.

Ramana, P.V. 'Naxalism: Trends and Government Response' *Dialogue*, 8 (2), October – December 2006.

Rao, D.V. 'Telangana Armed Struggle and the Path of Indian Revolution' *Proletarian Path*, Calcutta, 1974.

Rao, K. Ranga 'Peasant Movements in Telangana'. In M.S.A. Rao (ed), *Social Movements in India*, vol. 1. New Delhi: Manohar, 1979.

Rodrigues,Valerian. 'The Communist Party of India'. In Peter Ronald deSouza and E. Sridharan (eds.), *India's Political Parties*. New Delhi: Sage, 2006.

Sagar. 'The Spring and Its Thunder'. *Economic and Political Weekly*, 22 July 2006.

Sahu, Anadi. 'Naxals in Orissa: Then and Now'. *Shatabdi* (Oriya monthly), 15 September 2001.

Sanyal, Kanu. 'More About Naxalbari'. *Proletarian Path*, May – August, 1974.

Singh, Birinder Pal. 'Violence: A Dominant Term of Discourse'. *Studies in Humanities and Social Sciences*, vol. II (1), 1995.

Singh, Sekhar. 'Displacement and Rehabilitation: A Comparison of Two Policy Drafts'. *Economic and Political Weekly*, 30 December 2006.

Singh, Prakash. 'Maoism Unmasked'. *Dialogue*, vol. 6 (4), April – June 2005.

Sinha, Santha. 'Andhra Maoist Movement'. In G. Ram Reddy and B.A.V. Sharma (eds), *State Government and Politics: Andhra Pradesh*. New Delhi: Sterling Publications, 1979.

Sundar, Nandini. 'Bastar, Maoism and Salwa Judum'. *Economic and Political Weekly*, 22 July 2006.

Sundaraya, P. 'Telangana People's Struggle and Its Lessons'. Communist Party of India (Marxist), Calcutta, 1972.

Thirumali, I. 'Dora and Gadi: Manifestations of Landlord Domination in Telangana'. *Economic and Political Weekly*, 19 February 1972.

Wankhede, Harish S. 'The Political Context of Religious Conversion in Orissa'. *Economic and Political Weekly*, 11 April 2009.

Yechuri, Sitaram. 'Learning from Experiences and Analysis: Contrasting Approaches of Maoists in Nepal and India'. *Economic and Political Weekly*, 22 July 2006.

Zindabad, Inquilab. 'The Red Sun Is Rising: Revolutionary Struggle in India'. In Kathleen Gough and Hari P. Sharma (eds), *Imperialism and Revolution in South Asia*. New York: Monthly Review Press, 1973.

Newspapers (English)

'Bringing Rebels into the Mainstream'. *The Hindu*, 20 April 2005.
'Center's Knockout Punch for the Naxals'. *The Hindustan Times*, 27 April 2006.
'Code Red: Naxals, the Biggest Threat'. *The Hindustan Times*, 26 March 2006.
'Face Naxals with Uniform Strategy'. *The Indian Express*, 8 September 2005.
'Look Who is Waving the Red Flag Now'. *The Indian Express*, 2 March 2006.
'Lost in the Woods'. *The Hindustan Times*, 7 March 2005.
'Naxal Terror Goes Hi-Tech'. *The Times of India*, 10 April 2006.
'PW Gives Us Justice; We Give Shelter'. *The Times of India*, 07 February 2005.
'Red Star Over India'. *The Indian Express*, 15 April 2006.
'Reddy to Talk'. *The Times of India*, 20 January 2005.
'Tackling the Maoists'. *The Hindu*, 25 December 2004.
'The Rising'. *The Hindustan Times*, 7 April 2006.
'The Terror of the Coming War'. *The Indian Express*, 27 September 2004.
'They Are the Hollow Men'. *The Hindustan Times*, 21 April 2006.

Newspapers (Oriya)

'Aandolana ra Aatankaraaj'. *Sambaad*, 17 July 2005
Interview with Naxal Neta Sabyasachi Panda. *Sambad*, 19 September 2005.

'Laal Corridor'. *Sambad*, 13 February 2005.
'Naxal Samasya'. *Samaj*, 9 September 2004.
'Naxalanka Maha Tandaba'. *Sambad*, 25 March 2006.
'Niaan ra Naa Naxal'. *Sambad*, 19 September 2004.
'Pathachyuta Maobadi'. *Sambad*, 5 June 2005.

Webliography

'Maoist-Influenced Revolutionary Organizations in India'. http://www.massline.info/India/Indian_Groups.htm.
Armed Conflicts Report, India-Maoist Insurgency. http://www.ploughshares.ca/libraries/ACRText/ACR-IndiaAP.html.
Chandran, Suba and Mallika, Joseph. 'India: The Naxalite Movement, Searching for Peace in Central and South Asia'. Global Partnership for the Prevention of Armed Conflict, 2002. http://www.conflictprevention.net/page.php?id = 40&formid = 73&action = show&surveyid = 44#2#2.
Collier, P. 'Doing Well Out of War'. Paper prepared for Conference on Economic Agendas in Civil Wars, London 26–27 April 1999. The World Bank, The Economics of Crime and Violence Project, Washington DC, 10 April, 1999. http://www.worldbank.org/research/conflict/papers/econagenda.htm.
Gupta, Kanchan. 'Naxals, India's Enemy Within'. http://in.rediff.com/news/2004/nov/25kanch.htm.
'History of Naxalism'. http://hindustantimes.com.
Interview with Muppalla Lakshmana Rao alias Ganapathy, the then head of the Communist Party of India (Marxist-Leninist) People's War. http://www.rediff.com/news/1998/oct/07gana.htm.
Jha, Sanjay Kumar. 'Left Wing Terror: The MCC in Bihar and Jharkhand'. South Asia Intelligence Review, vol. 1 (40), April 2003. http://www.satp.org.
———, 'MCC and the Maoists: Expanding Naxal Violence in Bihar'. Article No. 991, Institute of Peace and Conflict Studies, 15 March 2003. http://www.ipcs.org.
———, 'Naxalite Consolidation in Orissa, South Asia Intelligence Review'. Vol. 2, No. 3, South Asia Terrorism Portal, 4 August 2003. http://www.satp.org.
———, 'Naxalite Consolidation in Orissa, South Asia Intelligence Review'. Vol. 2, No. 3, South Asia Terrorism Portal, 4 August 2003. http://www.satp.org.
Kamboj, Anil. 'Naxalism: India's Biggest Security Challenge'. Article No. 1995, Institute of Peace and Conflict Studies, 20 April 2006. http://www.ipcs.org.
Kujur, Rajat Kumar. 'Andhra Pradesh and Naxal Outfits: Again on Collision Course'. Article no. 48, Society For the Study of Peace and Conflict, 25 August 2005. http://www.sspconline.org.
———, 'Andhra Pradesh: The Naxal Citadel'. Article No. 1962, Institute of Peace and Conflict Studies, 14 March 2006. http://www.ipcs.org.
———, 'Human Rights in the Shadow of Red Terror'. Article No. 6712, issue 12, Peace Journalism, 10 October 2005. http://www.peacejournalism.com.
———, 'Left Extremism in India: Naxal Movement in Chhatisgarh and Orissa'. IPCS Special Report No. 25, Institute of Peace and Conflict Studies, June 2006. http://www.ipcs.org.
———, 'Naxal War Zone in Chhatishgarh'. Article no. 50, Society For the Study of Peace and Conflict, 8 September 2005. http://www.sspconline.org.

——, 'Naxal Warning in Maharashtra'. Article No. 1925, Institute of Peace and Conflict Studies, 14 January 2006. http://www.ipcs.org.

——, 'Red Terror over Jharkhand'. Article No. 1881, Institute of Peace and Conflict Studies, 3 November 2005. http://www.ipcs.org.

——, 'Resurgent Naxal Movement in Bihar'. Article No. 1852, Institute of Peace and Conflict Studies, 3 October 2005. http://www.ipcs.org.

——, 'Train Hijacking: The New Face of Red Terror'. Article No. 1967, Institute of Peace and Conflict Studies, 16 March 2006. http://www.ipcs.org.

——, 'Dantewada Jail Break: Strategic Accomplishment of Naxal Designs'. Article 2446, Institute of Peace and Conflict Studies, 20 December 2007. http://www.ipcs.org.

Nayak, Dr K. 'Rourkela: A Historical Perspective'. http://www.rourkela.com/history.htm.

Nayak, Nihar. 'Maoists in Nepal and India: Tactical Alliances and Ideological Differences'. Strategic Analysis, vol. 32 (3), May 2008.

——, 'Managing Naxalism in Tamil Nadu'. Tamil Nadu Police Journal, vol. 2 (1), January – March 2008.

——, 'Maoist Movement in Nepal and Its Tactical Digression: A Study of Strategic Revolutionary Phases and Future Implications'. Strategic Analysis, vol. 31 (6), November 2007.

——, 'Nepal: Withering of Peace'. Peace and Conflict Monitor (University of Peace, Costa Rica), 1 February 2006.

——, 'Maoist Consolidation Intensifies in Orissa', Article No: 70, Society for the Study of Peace and Conflict, 16 May 2006. http://www.sspconline.org.

——, 'Maoists: Contagion in Orissa'. South Asia Intelligence Review, vol. 3 (44), 16 May 2005. http://www.satp.org.

Pant, Wing Commander, N.K. 'Naxalite Violence and Internal Security'. Article No.523, Institute of Peace and Conflict Studies, 13 July 2001. http://www.ipcs.org.

Patwardhan, Amrita. 'Dams and Tribal People in India'. http://www.dams.org.

Ramana, P.V. 'Copy Cat: PWG and the Al-Qaeda Cell Model'. Article No. 939, Institute of Peace and Conflict Studies, 15 December, 2002. http://www.ipcs.org.

——, 'Unified Response Can Defeat PWG Paper Tigers'. Article No. 819, Institute of Peace and Conflict Studies, 5 August 2002. http://www.ipcs.org.

——, 'Left Wing Extremism in India'. Observer Research Foundation. http://www.observerindia.com/analysis/A072.htm.

Rao, Malleshwar. 'Waves of Land Struggle in South Orissa'. http://www.cpiml.org/liberation/year_2002/september/activities.htm.

Sahni, Ajay. 'Bad Medicine For a Red Epidemic'. South Asia Intelligence Review, vol. 3 (12), October 2004. http://www.satp.org.

Websites

www.sspconline.org
www.ipcs.org
www.satp.org
www.orfonline.org
www.tkb.org

Newspapers

Hindustan Times (English)
The Guardian (English)
The Hindu (English)
Navbharat Times (English)
The Telegraph (English)
The Times of India (English)
The New Indian Express (English)
The Pioneer (English)
The Samaja (Oriya daily)
The Sambada (Oriya daily)
The Prajatantra (Oriya daily)
The Samaya (Oriya daily)
The Dharitri (Oriya daily)

Magazines

India Today (English)
Frontline (English)
Human Touch (English)
Outlook (English)
Shatabdi (Oriya)
Tehelka (English)

Index

www.ingramcontent.com/pod-product-compliance
Ingram Content Group UK Ltd.
Pitfield, Milton Keynes, MK11 3LW, UK
UKHW020356010325
455677UK00021B/496